This book offers a conceptually rich reassessment of the usefulness of international sanctions. However, it does more than that and warrants reading by even those students of international relations not primarily dealing with sanctions. Mark Daniel Jaeger's book demonstrates that theory-building in IR is not something that happens in the thin air of abstract arguments only, but can be driven by dealing with substantive issues.

– **Mathias Albert,** *Bielefeld University, Germany*

This is the most convincing theory to date for the analysis of international sanctions and therefore exceedingly important for practically managing some of the most explosive conflicts on the current policy agenda. At the same time, its careful and creative theory building at the intersection of sociological theories of conflict and International Relations theories of securitization ought to inspire further innovative theorizing for other topics. Go read, go theorize – current conflicts call for work like this.

– **Ole Wæver,** *University of Copenhagen, Denmark*

Coerce Sanctions and International Conflicts

Perhaps the most common question raised in the literature on coercive international sanctions is: "Do sanctions work?" Unsurprisingly, the answer to such a sweeping question remains inconclusive. However, even the widely presumed logic of coercive sanctions – that economic impact translates into effective political pressure – is not the primary driver of conflict developments. Furthermore, existing rationalist-economistic approaches neglect one of the most striking differences seen across sanctions conflicts: the occurrence of positive sanctions or their combination with negative sanctions, implicitly taking them as logically indifferent.

Instead of asking whether sanctions work, this book addresses a more basic question: How do coercive international sanctions work, and more substantially, what are the social conditions within sanctions conflicts that are conducive to either cooperation or non-cooperation? Arguing that coercive sanctions and international conflicts are relational, socially constructed facts, the author explores the (de-)escalation of sanctions conflicts from a sociological perspective. Whether sanctions are conducive to either cooperation or non-cooperation depends on the one hand on the meaning they acquire for opponents as inducing decisions upon mutual conflict. On the other hand, negative sanctions, positive sanctions or their combination each contribute differently to the way in which opponents perceive conflict, and to its potential transformation. Thus, it is premature to 'predict' the political effectiveness of sanctions simply based on economic impact.

The book presents analyses of the sanctions conflicts between China and Taiwan and over Iran's nuclear program, illustrating how negative sanctions, positive sanctions and their combination made a distinct contribution to conflict development and prospects for cooperation. It will be of great interest to researchers, postgraduates and academics in the fields of international relations, sanctions, international security and international political sociology.

Mark Daniel Jaeger is a post-doctoral researcher at the Center for Advanced Security Theory, University of Copenhagen.

The New International Relations

Edited by Richard Little
University of Bristol

Iver B. Neumann
Norwegian Institute of International Affairs (NUPI), Norway

Jutta Weldes
University of Bristol

The field of international relations has changed dramatically in recent years. This new series will cover the major issues that have emerged and reflect the latest academic thinking in this particular dynamic area.

Evaluating Progress in International Relations
How do you know?
Edited by Annette Freyberg-Inan, Ewan Harrison and Patrick James

Russia and the Idea of Europe 2nd Edition
A study in identity and International Relations
Iver B. Neumann

Memories of Empire and Entry into International Society
Views from the European periphery
Edited by Filip Ejdus

Great Power Multilateralism and the Prevention of War
Debating a 21st century concert of powers
Edited by Harald Müller and Carsten Rauch

De-Constructing the Dynamics of World-Societal Order
The power of governmentality in Palestine
Jan Busse

Raymond Aron and International Relations
Edited by Olivier Schmitt

Coercive Sanctions and International Conflicts
A Sociological Theory
Mark Daniel Jaeger

A full list of titles is available here: www.routledge.com/New-International-Relations/book-series/NEWIR

Coercive Sanctions and International Conflicts

A Sociological Theory

Mark Daniel Jaeger

Routledge
Taylor & Francis Group
LONDON AND NEW YORK

First published 2018
by Routledge
2 Park Square, Milton Park, Abingdon, Oxon OX14 4RN

and by Routledge
605 Third Avenue, New York, NY 10017

First issued in paperback 2021

Routledge is an imprint of the Taylor & Francis Group, an informa business

Publisher's Note
The publisher has gone to great lengths to ensure the quality of this reprint but points out that some imperfections in the original copies may be apparent.

British Library Cataloguing-in-Publication Data
A catalogue record for this book is available from the British Library

Library of Congress Cataloging-in-Publication Data
A catalog record for this book has been requested

ISBN 13: 978-1-03-209547-9 (pbk)
ISBN 13: 978-1-138-69717-1 (hbk)

Typeset in Times New Roman
by Apex CoVantage, LLC

Dedicated to Marlene and Sophia.

Contents

Figures

Tables

Acknowledgements

First and foremost, I owe a very special thanks to my wife, Sonja, and to my children for their love and steadfast support during the research for, and writing of, this book. I am also greatly indebted to Mathias Albert, Ole Wæver and Andreas Wenger for their critical assessment, insightful commentary and invaluable support along this journey. My gratitude goes to Jörn Richert for countless discussions and reflections on science, theory and the meaning of academia. The book emerged from my doctoral dissertation at ETH Zurich. I am indebted to my colleagues for their thoughts and comments and for the good times we shared, most of all to Myriam Dunn Cavelty, Jonas Hagmann, Ulla Jasper, Wilhelm Mirow and Alrik Thiem. I would like to thank Charles Glaser and Martha Finnemore for their hospitality at the Elliott School of International Affairs and for their advice at a crucial moment during my time as a PhD student. Many thanks also to the three anonymous reviewers of the initial book project who provided crucial input for the book's further development and refinement.

I also owe the success of this project to the exchange with my fellow colleagues working on other theory-laden topics or partaking in a similar work experience: Olaf Corry, Joscha Wullweber, Julia Sattelberger, Andrew Neal, Trine Villumsen Berling and Malte Gephart. Similarly of essence was the invigorating support of Sebastian Meraner and Tim Kilb.

Finally, I would like to express my gratitude to Lorraine Traynor for her patient and unflinching copy-editing through even the most arduous passages of Luhmannian concepts (or rather my reinterpretations thereof). Any remaining semantic barrier is my responsibility entirely.

Foreword

International sanctions are a very significant feature of contemporary international relations and they have been widely used in attempts to discipline states that have been identified as violating fundamental international norms. Between the two world wars, for example, sanctions were applied in 1935 against Italy when it challenged the territorial integrity of Ethiopia. During the era of decolonization sanctions were applied by the United Nations against Rhodesia in 1966 when the white minority government made a unilateral declaration of independence and then in 1986 South Africa's most important trading partners employed sanctions in an attempt to bring an end to the apartheid policy in that country. In the post-Cold War era international sanctions have been used recurrently all over the world in the attempt to enforce international norms and they are widely considered to be one of the most important tools of modern foreign policy. Unsurprisingly, therefore, innumerable attempts have been made to assess the impact and effectiveness of sanctions as a means of achieving the foreign policy objectives of states that have implemented international sanctions. Yet despite the time and effort spent on the subject, international sanctions remain an extremely controversial and poorly understood policy tool.

Part of the problem associated with any attempt to develop a comprehensive understanding of this subject arises from the fact that sanctions come in many different forms. They can be applied unilaterally by a single state or multilaterally by a group of states or, as has often happened over the last century, they can be initiated by an international organization such as the League of Nations or the United Nations. At the same time, as this book makes clear, sanctions can also take a positive or negative form. Most studies, however, focus on negative sanctions that are designed to cause pain in the targeted country in the hope that this will bring about the change in policy desired by those implementing the sanctions. The problem here is that the people suffering the pain may not be the people who are responsible for changing policy in the desired direction. Recognition of this fact has given rise to so-called smart sanctions that are designed specifically to target individual decision-makers or others with power in a country to effect a policy change. Another difficulty with studying international sanctions is that they can take so many different forms. Negative sanctions include diplomatic sanctions, such as closing an embassy, sports sanctions, such as excluding a national team from an international sporting event, or economic sanctions, such as a trade embargo. Although policy makers may appreciate the fact that they can select what seems to be the most appropriate sanction for the task in hand, this plethora of possible sanctions makes it much more difficult for an investigator to assess the overall impact and effectiveness of sanctions.

Despite the persistent use of sanctions there was for a long period a widespread acceptance that sanctions were an ineffective policy tool. The deployment of sanctions against Italy in 1935 by the League of Nations was often used to demonstrate not only that sanctions failed to prevent Italy's takeover of what was then called Abyssinia but that the failure also played an important role in undermining the credibility of the League of Nations. As the result of such failures, the continued use of sanctions as a policy instrument generated what was sometimes referred to as a sanctions paradox and encouraged researchers to look more carefully and systematically at the success rate of sanctions. The consequence of this research was that that the consensus shifted and it became more generally accepted that sanctions were successful some of the time and so attention turned to an examination of the factors that determined whether sanctions succeeded or failed. This issue seemed to be particularly important by the end of the 20th century because the very extensive sanctions regime imposed by the United Nations on Saddam Hussein's government after Iraq invaded Kuwait in 1990 was largely left in place for the rest of the decade in an unsuccessful attempt to get the government to disclose and eliminate any weapons of mass destruction on its territory. The issue was of vital importance because it was recognized that the sanctions were seriously affecting the quality of lives of the Iraqi people.

The large body of research that has been carried out since then, however, has not significantly moved the agenda forward and there is a growing recognition that there is a need to approach the task of understanding sanctions from a new direction. This book makes a substantial and original contribution to this new turn in the literature on sanctions. It develops a framework that extends beyond the focus on disciplining norm violators and embraces much more widely the use of both positive and negative sanctions to exert power in conflict situations. The framework is applied to two particularly complex conflicts – the international conflict precipitated by the development of the Iranian nuclear program and the longstanding conflict between Taiwan and China, a hangover from the Chinese Civil War. What the framework helps to clarify is that sanctions are often interpreted in very different ways but it also makes it possible to see much more clearly the factors that determine whether sanctions will resolve the conflict that exists between the parties implementing the sanctions and the parties within the sanctioned state that have to respond to the sanctions. In line with the new turn in the sanctions literature the book acknowledges that there can be no simple equation that reveals whether or not sanctions will be successful. Sanctions have to be examined on a case-by-case basis taking account of how both the targeting and targeted states frame the issue.

Richard Little
Emeritus Professor
University of Bristol

1 Introduction

Conflicted sanctions

Since the end of the Cold War, coercive international sanctions have been on the rise. Two prominent examples were the sanctions imposed against Iraq and against Serbia in the late 20th century. The economic impact of the sanctions has been devastating in magnitude.[1] When Iraq invaded Kuwait in 1990, the international community responded by introducing the most comprehensive sanctions the world had ever seen (UN Resolution 661; US Iraq Sanctions Act, November 1990). After the subsequent military liberation of Kuwait in 1991 the sanctions remained in place. They aimed mainly at forcing Iraq to reveal and abandon its weapons of mass destruction program, to recognize Kuwait and to pay reparations (UN Resolution 687).

Sanctions against Serbia introduced in early 1998 by the UN and, more strongly, by Western powers (most notably the US and the European Union) aimed to put a stop to the political violence against Kosovo Albanians organized by the Serbian government. Similar to Iraq, sanctions remained in place after military intervention forced Serbian 'police forces' out of Kosovo. Sanctions aimed to pacify the Balkans, enforce the recognition of a politically separate Kosovo and foster democratic reform.

The aim of sanctions against both Iraq and Serbia was to enforce cooperation in conflict. I define coercive international sanctions among states as measures short of military violence which are socially conceived as being instigated by an initiator to induce the cooperation of an addressee with articulated demands in a mutual political conflict. Coercing cooperation means that the addressee is to significantly change its political position as constructed in the mutual conflict, in line with the demands of the initiator(s). Measures include economic and non-economic instruments, such as economic restrictions or incentives; political encroachment or diplomatic recognition; restricting or increasing non-economic exchanges.

Although the two cases of sanctions were similarly aimed at enforcing cooperation, they had vastly different results, even though the economic impact and accompanying circumstances (military intervention) were comparable. Iraq never gave in to any meaningful degree. It proved impossible to achieve consistent and enduring cooperation with weapons inspectors and thus to bring about any significant change in the political position of Saddam Hussein's regime. The success of the sanctions was limited to containing Saddam Hussein militarily (cf. Blix 2004:272).

The aim of the sanctions against Serbia might be considered more ambitious, yet nevertheless they were clearly more successful (Blockmans 2007; see also Portela 2010; de Vries 2002). Political change was profound. After less than two years, democratic elections were held; a few weeks later, Slobodan Milosevic resigned from power and Serbian nationalism no longer posed an immediate threat to peace and stability in the Balkans. Several high-ranking officials allegedly involved in committing war crimes, among them Slobodan Milosevic himself, have been turned over to the UN International Criminal Tribunal.

This is of course a simplified presentation of the two cases that is nevertheless instructive. Their remarkable difference in outcomes raises *three puzzling observations*. First, using existing approaches to economic sanctions, one would not expect a more successful outcome in the case of Serbia, where economic damage was less severe and international cooperation was significantly lower, with China and particularly Russia actively backing its government. By contrast, the Iraq case fulfilled the conventional criteria for successful sanctions much more so than Serbia: It was politically isolated (cf. Preeg 1999), the coercion attempt had full UN backing (cf. Martin 1993) and the country faced even greater damage to its economy (cf. Dashti-Gibson, Davis, and Radcliff 1997; Pape 1997). In addition, other factors that are considered significant are constant across both cases and thus prevent us from accounting for developments. In neither case was there any reason for the 'sender states' and 'target states' of the sanctions to have anything less than high expectations of future conflict, i.e. they both should have been equally concerned about their relative bargaining positions vis-à-vis the sender states in the future (cf. Drezner 1999).

Second, one of the most significant differences across the two conflicts with respect to sanctions policies was the simultaneous use of negative and positive sanctions, a *combined sanctions strategy* in the case of Serbia. Apart from financial restrictions, a ban on petroleum and petroleum products, a visa ban and a flight ban, the United States and the European Union provided positive incentives to support political change in Serbia (e.g. the 'Energy for Democracy' project).[2] By contrast, sanctions against Iraq resorted heavily to a negative sanctions strategy. Is a combined sanctions strategy possibly more promising in promoting cooperation?

Third, the result of the sanctions against Serbia was not just calculated cooperation with increased demands. Official views regarding what the conflict was about had changed substantially. After the Democratic Opposition of Serbia (DOS) won the parliamentary election in December 2000 and Zoran Đinđić became Prime Minister, a notion of a mutual conflict took hold that allowed for negotiation and cooperation (Schimmelfennig, Engert, and Knobel 2006:88–90). The end of the Milosevic government meant that the conflict matter took on a much more humble shape, as an issue of contested ethnic and territorial affiliations that had to be politically negotiated; it was no longer cast as a centuries-long fight against attacking intruders (Uzgel 2001). Sanctions in turn significantly promoted such transformation (Hufbauer, Schott, and Elliott 2007, Case Study 98–2). How does such transformation occur?

Taken together, the existing literature on coercive international sanctions at best provides partial answers to these conundrums and questions. Corresponding to the three puzzling observations outlined above, there are *three issues* that merit further consideration. First, coercive international sanctions do not seem to entirely conform to a logic whereby significant economic impact would translate into substantial political pressure. This calls their meaning into question. Why did Iraq not acquiesce? For Serbia, if anything, sanctions should have coerced the government into cooperation *earlier*, when GDP fell from USD 23bn to 15bn in the 1990s. Why did cooperation only occur after 1999? In 2004, in another instance of tightening sanctions, US President George W. Bush observed about fruitless US efforts against the Islamic Republic of Iran: "We're relying upon others, because we've sanctioned ourselves out of influence with Iran . . . in other words, we don't have much leverage with the Iranians right now".[3] Essentially, it remains a mystery how an agent in an international conflict could sanction itself out of (political) influence on a target state, as President Bush suggested.

Second, existing literature is fairly silent and discordant concerning the different influence that negative sanctions and combined or positive sanctions strategies have on conflict development. Contributions that attempt to account for developments in terms of domestic political factors by disaggregating the target state treat negative and positive economic sanctions as logically indistinct, part of a zero-sum equation between economic gain and loss. Contributions that account for conflict development in terms of relational factors between adversaries at the international level sometimes recognize the difference between trying the stick and offering a carrot, but do not offer any insight into the peculiarities of combined sanctions strategies.

Third, in the case of Serbia, cooperation did in fact occur only *after* conflict transformation. Such transformation effectively re-defined the interests of the target state that were usually taken as fixed, reflecting the utility calculus that typically underlies conceptions of coercive sanctions. It also changed future conflict expectations that had hitherto been assumed constant by game-theoretical approaches such as Drezner's (1999). Sanctions ultimately transformed the conflict in profound ways. However, the existing literature on coercive sanctions does not provide an in-depth notion of conflict transformation. Thus, there is neither a concept of conflict transformation, nor do existing conceptions consider how sanctions would relate to such a process.

Generally, theory-oriented investigations into coercive international sanctions, which seek to account for cooperation or non-cooperation, approach the subject by focusing on a specific level of analysis, either from a top-down perspective aimed at explaining outcomes through interaction between states, or using a bottom-up logic aimed at explaining conflict outcomes by disaggregating the domestic politics of target states. Thus, some approaches have explored in depth the impact of relations between on the one hand the entities that engage in coercive sanctions, and the states they are supposed to 'convince' on the other hand. Usually, they do so in terms of strategic considerations of states as utility-maximizing rational actors, assuming that, in face of coercion, the target is *in a position to choose* to comply. In turn, other investigations attribute causes for the development of sanctions conflicts to domestic processes, particularities and interplay of interests. These investigations have contributed to a growing knowledge of the effects of sanctions. They help to appreciate the complexity of sanctions as coercive instruments in international conflict.

Despite these achievements, researchers still struggle to account for the development of international sanctions conflicts. The contributions from both perspectives shed light on a complex conflict reality of which sanctions are a part, but also reveal their mutual limitations. Both the top-down and bottom-up perspectives enable us to identify significant elements that contribute to the development of sanctions conflicts. What matters is how the adversaries conceive of their mutual conflict, as well as the influence of sanctions on domestic politics. Yet, connections are not made between these insights. Instead, existing conceptualizations draw boundaries around processes in a problematic way, effectively black-boxing either the international or the domestic.

Artificial analytic boundaries encourage us to consider sanctions external to how agents conceive of conflict. Conflict relations between a 'sender' of international sanctions and a 'target' are considered exogenous to interaction itself; actors, their perceptions of conflict and sanctions, and their preferences are taken for granted. The core of the problem with conventional approaches to international sanctions lies in their utilization of economistic models that incorporate a simplistic sender-receiver model of communication. Effectively adopting the senders' perspective, such models are based on the assumption that coercive sanctions and political demands are unambiguously 'transmitted' to a target state and that economic impact is translated smoothly into political pressure.

These conceptual bases neglect the fundamental contingency of meaning in social relations and remain unable to account for the processes involved in the formation of the political views of adversaries in conflict. The reifications involved in such approaches mean that they omit the dialectical interrelation between the development of conflict and the political meaning that sanctions acquire as part of the social practices which contribute to cooperation and non-cooperation in sanctions conflicts. Coercive sanctions are social facts constructed within evolving international conflicts. The present investigation suggests a conceptualization that sheds light on how sanctions acquire meaning within a dynamically developing international conflict and that specifies the influence of particular sanctions strategies (negative, positive, combined) on conflict transformation.

A different perspective

This study presents a sociological theory of international sanctions conflicts. It develops an approach towards understanding cooperation and non-cooperation based on *three premises*. First, both coercive sanctions and international conflicts are socially constructed facts. Conflicts do not exist without agents constructing relations of disagreement between each other, nor do coercive sanctions exist without being constructed as actions concerning the position of an opponent.

Second, sanctions, as part of international conflicts, are relational phenomena. Coercive sanctions are relational to the extent that they aim to influence an opponent's policies. However, their meaning is relational as well: Conflict opponents might each conceive of negative or positive sanctions differently, and they might attach a different meaning to sanctions as actions in a mutual conflict.

Third, conflict relations between opponents and the meaning that sanctions acquire are endogenous to each other. On the one hand, the meaning that sanctions acquire as coercive relational phenomena is related to how opponents perceive the mutual conflict. On the other hand, sanctions as coercive instruments influence further conflict development, how opponents construct on-going mutual conflict.

These premises reflect that sanctions do not 'transmit' meaning unambiguously in international conflict. They reflect a research interest into how sanctions, conflicts and adversaries are socially constructed and the influence this has on the prospects of cooperation. Thus the main analytical question of the study is: W*hat are the social conditions within sanctions conflicts that are conducive to either cooperation or non-cooperation?* The investigation proceeds along three more specific questions: *First, what is the meaning of coercive sanctions as actions concerning the position of an opponent? Second, how are such positions constructed in international conflict? Third, what influence do coercive sanctions have on conflict transformation?*

The sociological theory developed here conceptualizes how sanctions acquire meaning as part of dynamically evolving conflict relations. It takes sanctions and the conflicts of which they are a part as discursively constructed, synthetic facts. Sanctions and conflicts are relationally constructed social phenomena. Thus, what is of scientific interest are the social processes involved in the relational formation of the meaning that sanctions and conflicts acquire.

Whether sanctions are conducive to either cooperation or non-cooperation depends on how *initiators* and *addressees* construct sanctions within conflict communication. In the analytical model put forward by the sociological theory, coercive sanctions are about *decisions* on international conflict. There are two sides to constructing sanctions as decisions on mutual conflict. When agents construct sanctions relationally as a decision, sanctions convey a tension in their meaning. On the one hand, sanctions raise costs or offer benefits linked to a particular political position, reflecting a *utility rationale.* On the other hand, sanctions aim to impose their initiator's decision regarding the conflict on an addressee, reflecting a *power rationale.*

Sanctions do not occur in a relational vacuum but as part of an on-going conflict. Conflicts as relational phenomena emerge when agents socially construct incompatible positions between each other. *Issue conflicts* consist of communicated interest incompatibilities and are susceptible to a utility rationale. In *identity conflicts*, agents question each other's position and legitimacy and securitize the Other as a threat. Sanctions in this case are more likely to suggest a meaning in conflict along a power rationale, with an initiator enforcing a decision upon an addressee.

Table 1.1 Sanctions strategies and conflict transformation

	Issue conflict	*Identity conflict*
Negative sanctions	Promote securitization	De-securitization unlikely
Positive sanctions	Securitization unlikely	Foster de-securitization
Combined sanctions	May lead to securitization	May lead to de-securitization

A *securitized sanctions conflict* implies non-cooperation. Securitization outlines conflict escalation as a decisive qualitative shift. Depending on on-going conflict communication, sanctions are more likely to communicate either a utility or a power rationale. Yet at the same time, sanctions constructed as actions in conflict communication influence what meaning the conflict acquires and may thus promote conflict transformation. A *non-securitized conflict* opens the way for the possibility of cooperation. Particular sanctions strategies may affect conflict transformation differently, depending on the meaning they acquire (see Table 1.1).

Negative sanctions strategies emphasize a power rationale. They are unlikely to transform securitized identity conflicts but may promote the securitization of a conflict, fostering non-cooperation. That way, initiators may indeed sanction themselves out of influence, as President Bush claimed, unable to bolster the basis of a conflict construction that would make it possible for cooperation to occur. *Positive sanctions strategies* emphasize a utility rationale, proposing an offer the addressee may decide to accept.

In a commentary in the *Washington Post* a few days after President Bush's aforementioned remarks on Iran sanctions, Susan Rice called them a "bizarre statement".[4] Rice was not referring to the sheer implausibility that sanctions may not influence a conflict, nor did she suggest that sticks were just not big enough. Instead, Rice criticized a one-sided resort to negative sanctions, without any substantial offer of positive incentives. Conceptually, positive sanctions make it possible to transform a securitized identity conflict, fostering a de-escalated conflict construction in terms of incompatible interests. Positive sanctions are unlikely to promote conflict securitization.

Combined sanctions strategies are initially indifferent to a utility and a power rationale. They may lead to securitization, yet they may also enable de-securitization. In maximizing their interpretive possibilities and discriminatory impact by offering both costs and benefits, combined sanctions strategies may foster domestic contestation on the meaning of a conflict by an addressee.

This theory-generating study conceptually subscribes and contributes to a 'communicative turn' in International Relations (IR) as a scientific discipline. It applies this perspective to its notion of sanctions as well as international conflicts as relational phenomena constructed in communication. In order to conceptualize these relational processes, the sociological approach takes communication as its analytical basis, along with a pragmatist notion of agency. Niklas Luhmann's (1995) notion of communication as consisting of contingent social selection processes allows us to conceive of sanctions and conflicts as relationally constructed social phenomena. A pragmatist notion of agency, inspired by the work of Hans Joas (1993), grants the flexibility to conceive of agency as the joint result of a creative engagement with contingency and the social recognition thereof. The notion assumes that agents creatively engage with contingent meaning in social relations, instead of going on the assumption that actors have fixed interests and preferences with regard to 'objectively given' facts.

For its sociological perspective on coercive sanctions, this study takes up Luhmann's sociology of risk (1993). Luhmann emphasizes the attribution of decision in actions constructed as a 'risk' in a future-oriented engagement with contingency. An external attribution of decision represents the loss of agency with regard to future developments and a 'danger'. The study highlights the tensions reflected in constructing sanctions as relational decisions on future conflict development and contributes to a different perspective on coercive international sanctions.

The study adopts a notion of conflict as socially constructed in communication which was introduced to IR by systems-theoretical scholars (Diez, Stetter, and Albert 2006; Messmer 2007). Conceptually, the investigation focuses, however, on the notion of securitization as a decisive process in conflict transformation. Besides contributing to the literature on coercive sanctions in IR, the study seeks, moreover, to contribute to the further conceptual development of securitization in two particular ways. First, the study proposes a conceptual re-interpretation of securitization that builds on the construction of agency as engagement with contingency. Inspired by the theoretical work of Mustafa Emirbayer and Ann Mische (1998) on a pragmatist notion of agency, the study conceptualizes securitization as agential engagement with contingency in a crisis constructed through securitizing moves. Such conceptual re-orientation parts ways from 'externalist' notions of securitization and proposes instead a more thorough notion of the securitizing act.

Second, the investigation posits securitization as a causal mechanism in sanctions conflicts. In social practice, securitizing agents engage in causal attribution, linking an external cause (a threat) to a specific effect (security). That practical dimension of causality transcends to an analytical dimension: Building upon Stefano Guzzini's (2011) proposition, securitization represents a contingent process, the effects of which are determinate. Securitizing moves may lead to an identity conflict; their success results in non-cooperation in international conflict.

Empirically, the study illustrates the conceptual insights gained from its theoretical examination of coercive international sanctions. Arguably, the aforementioned cases in Serbia and Iraq are only comparable to a somewhat limited extent. These cases serve well to outline the conundrums that beset research on coercive sanctions. However, to thoroughly demonstrate the conceptual relations developed, a constellation that offers more analytical leverage is preferable. The study opts for a most similar systems design to illustrate its conceptual insights. It will analyze the sanctions conflict between the People's Republic of China (PRC, Mainland China) and the Republic of China (ROC, Taiwan) and between the

United States and Iran on the latter's nuclear program. These conflict systems offer a unique opportunity in that they reveal how various sanctions strategies were applied within a limited time span and in relatively similar and stable social environments. This kind of setting allows for a disciplined comparison of three cases per conflict system, each with distinct sanctions strategies.

Furthermore, the conflicts between China and Taiwan and between the US and Iran represent difficult cases for the developed theory's claim on the prospects of conflict transformation. China and Taiwan mutually contested and denied each other's existence for decades. The history between the US and the Islamic Republic is a similarly protracted imbroglio. Moreover, the conflict on Iran's nuclear program involved some of the most ingenious sanctions policies ever imposed as part of a highly sensitive conflict in world politics. These circumstances provide appropriate conditions for studying the relation between particular sanctions strategies and evolving constructions of mutual conflict with strong security implications for the opponents involved. In both disputes, sanctions led to significant conflict deterioration. Yet, in the end, reconciliation occurred. A common vision of One China prevailed. And the conflict on Iran's nuclear program was tamed by one of the most sophisticated diplomatic agreements in history. This book suggests how and why these astonishing developments in sanctions conflicts occurred.

Why does having yet another concept of coercive international sanctions conflicts matter? For all the puzzling limitations that have been noted, the literature does not put the same effort into accounting for non-cooperation as it does when accounting for cooperation. True, many studies meticulously analyze why particular instances of sanctions have not worked. Yet ultimately, these investigations usually identify factors that effectively inhibit a presumed model of economic impact that translates into political pressure, without questioning the soundness of the underlying presumptions in the first place.

In any case, judging when a stick (or a carrot) will be big enough to coerce cooperation is a daunting task. Knowing when the bases for such a mechanism to play out actually exist in the first place, does not make that task any easier; it merely avoids raising false expectations and perhaps some unintended consequences. In many cases, sanctions do indeed have a significant economic impact, impairing the livelihood of many politically innocent individuals. In this context, when there is the possibility that sanctions might contribute to a deterioration of conflict relations, it should be made transparent. International conflicts involving coercive sanctions are often related to disagreements that are serious enough for the conflict parties involved to bear substantial costs – conflicts that have already escalated beyond an easily negotiated agreement. Politically, knowledge regarding what makes cooperation more or less likely also matters because the alternative, a further deterioration of the conflict and war, is also sometimes possible.

Structure of the book

The study proceeds as follows: The first part of the book engages with international sanctions conflicts at a conceptual level. Chapter 2 critically reviews conceptualizations of coercive international sanctions in the existing literature. The review identifies interesting findings but also points to the inherent limitations of existing research. It raises two main points of criticism that reflect the widespread subscription to a simplistic sender–receiver model of communication, calling attention to the limitations of existing conceptual work. First, the review is critical of the notion that economic or other measures as part of sanctions and the political demands attached to them unequivocally 'transmit' to a 'target'; second, the review questions the broadly assumed model whereby the economic impact translates into political pressure along a more or less simple input/output scheme. At individual levels, existing work steadily hints at the significance of the perceptions and shared meanings that transcend the two limitations, but does not account for the social processes or practices involved in their formation. It fails to substantially theorize the non-economic aspects of coercive international sanctions that reside outside of a rationalist–positivist research paradigm that subscribes to methodological individualism.

Chapter 3 develops a sociological theory of coercive international sanctions. Based on a social ontology that posits the analytical primacy of meaning in social scientific inquiry, it instead emphasizes the social processes and practices involved in the formation of social reality. The sociological theory puts its distinct notion of coercive international sanctions in the context of a socially constructed conflict. Sanctions conflicts evolve as a dynamic relational process, wherein the meaning of sanctions and conflicts are in an endogenous relationship. In that dynamic process, the theory delineates securitization processes involved in conflict transformation as having a key influence on the prospects of cooperation and non-cooperation.

The fourth chapter outlines the study's methodological position and the choice of method. The investigation takes an analyticist position (cf. Jackson 2011): All observation is theory-dependent. Scientific models are logical instruments, the utility of which stems from the leverage gained from the distinctions and configurations proposed by the model in understanding an empirical phenomenon. The case studies serve to demonstrate that utility. In terms of the methods used, the interest in the formation of meaning in the unfolding of sanctions conflicts suggests two techniques with particular purposes. First, the study considers the meaning of sanctions conflicts as it develops within a discursive field and applies a framing analysis to garner substantive meaning within political discourse. Second, the study applies process tracing to capture the temporal unfolding of sanctions conflicts in order to draw causal conclusions on the meaning of conflict and the influence of particular sanctions strategies.

The second part of the book presents the empirical analysis. It applies the developed sociological theory to the sanctions conflicts between China and Taiwan (Chapter 5) and between the US and Iran (Chapter 6) in order to illustrate the analytical utility of the proposed configurations of its elements. The conflict between China and Taiwan exhibits persistent identity incompatibilities, dating back to the Chinese Civil War, between the Chinese Communist Party and the Kuomintang. Both conflict adversaries raised mutually exclusive claims on legitimately representing China. In the early 1990s, PRC ambitions to unify China in order to remove the last scars from the humiliating period of foreign intervention were met with the democratization of Taiwan with a growing, but contested sense of self-determination. Thus an identity conflict evolved, but did not disappear. In a deteriorating conflict, ROC President Lee Teng-hui claimed that Cross-Strait relations were 'special state-to-state' relations and that there was thus no need to declare what was already an obvious fact: Taiwanese independence. By contrast, PRC Prime Minister Zhu Rongji warned that if the Taiwanese public were it to embrace a call for independence, they would not be granted the opportunity to regret their move. Particular sanctions strategies contributed to conflict escalation and, later, to conflict transformation. The empirical analysis distinguishes between three separate cases of negative, combined and positive sanctions strategies applied in the conflict. It traces the meaning that sanctions strategies acquire and their influence on evolving conflict relations. Although of limited economic impact, sanctions nonetheless profoundly influenced the meaning of the conflict in Taiwanese politics. In each case study, the meaning of sanctions and conflict differed significantly. Negative sanctions featured strongly in securitizing moves and fueled conflict escalation. Combined sanctions resulted in deeper deadlock and polarized views on the conflict within Taiwan. Positive sanctions, although contested in their meaning, contributed to conflict de-escalation; they contributed to socially constructed conflict relations that make cooperation possible.

Since the events of the Islamic Revolution, relations between Iran and the US are similarly prone to exhibiting identity incompatibilities. While the US had imposed sanctions on the Islamic Republic before, distinct conflict communication emerged regarding its nuclear program. The Islamic Republic insisted that its nuclear program was in line with its commitments under the Treaty on the Non-Proliferation of Nuclear Weapons (NPT). By contrast, in the view of the US, the Islamic Republic, in a familiar pattern of violating international norms, was untransparent about its program, uncooperative with international supervisory bodies and was dodging its international obligations. The empirical analysis again distinguishes between three distinct cases. After a failed first attempt at combined sanctions, the conflict deteriorated towards a deadlock with the imposition of negative sanctions. In the wake of a second, much more consistent utilization of a combined sanctions strategy, the conflict transformed towards one in which the nuclear program was observed in terms of issue incompatibilities, paving the way for resolving the nuclear dispute.

Chapter 7 presents and sums up the empirical observations made in all six cases across the two conflict systems between China and Taiwan and between the US and Iran, as examined in the two preceding chapters. It presents in a nutshell the sanctions strategies observed and their influence on conflict development, highlighting the peculiarities of negative, positive and combined sanctions.

Finally, the conclusion summarizes the findings and indicates the conceptual and practical implications. It provides an overview of the developed sociological theory and illustrates this theory in the empirical analysis of coercive sanctions in the Cross-Strait conflict and the dispute over Iran's nuclear program. It highlights the insights gained from this new perspective and its focus on conflict transformation. However, it also reflects on the limitations of the current study. In terms of the implications of the investigation, conceptually, the sociological theory of international sanctions conflicts holds that different factors are relevant for cooperation and non-cooperation, more so than many existing approaches, which overemphasize basic economic parameters. The study formulates conditions of possibility for cooperation and non-cooperation in international sanctions conflicts in order to enhance practical knowledge on how to avert conflict deterioration.

Notes

1 Iraq's GDP was reduced to a quarter of its pre-war level at its lowest point; it fell from USD 17bn in 1990 through USD 5.9bn in 1991 to USD 4bn in 1994. Serbia's GDP was reduced to half the level it had reached before the Kosovo conflict and roughly to a third the level it had once reached as part of former Yugoslavia in the early 1990s; it fell from USD 17bn in 1998 to USD 8.7bn in 2000, by comparison to the USD 23bn it had reached in 1990 (UNdata, accessed February 2010).

2 European Commission, MEMO /99/60, Brussels, November 23, 1999. (See Hufbauer et al. 2007, Case Study 98–2.)

3 White House Press Conference, December 20, 2004, available at http://georgewbush-whitehouse.archives.gov/news/releases/2004/12/20041220-3.html; accessed October 24, 2013.

4 Susan E. Rice, 'Assistant Secretary of State from 1997 to 2001,' *The Washington Post*, December 30, 2004, p. A27, available at www.washingtonpost.com/wp-dyn/articles/A35655-2004Dec29.html; accessed October 24, 2013. In 2013, Susan Rice became 24th US National Security Advisor.

Bibliography

Blix, Hans. (2004) *Disarming Iraq*. New York: Pantheon.

Blockmans, Steven. (2007) *Tough Love: The European Union's Relations with the Western Balkans*. The Hague: T.M.C. Asser Press.

Dashti-Gibson, Jaleh, Patricia Davis, and Benjamin Radcliff. (1997) On the Determinants of the Success of Economic Sanctions: An Empirical Analysis. *American Journal of Political Science* 41: 608–618.

de Vries, Anthonius W. (2002) European Union Sanctions against the Federal Republic of Yugoslavia from 1998 to 2000: A Special Exercise in Targeting. In *Smart Sanctions: Targeting Economic Statecraft*, edited by David Cortright and George A. Lopez. Lanham: Rowman & Littlefield Publishers.

Diez, Thomas, Stephan Stetter, and Mathias Albert. (2006) The European Union and Border Conflicts: The Transformative Power of Integration. *International Organization* 60: 563–593.

Drezner, Daniel. (1999) *The Sanctions Paradox: Economic Statecraft and International Relations*. Cambridge: Cambridge University Press.

Emirbayer, Mustafa, and Ann Mische. (1998) What Is Agency? *American Journal of Sociology* 103: 962–1023.

Guzzini, Stefano. (2011) Securitization as a Causal Mechanism. *Security Dialogue* 42: 329–341.

Hufbauer, Gary, Jeffrey Schott, and Kimberly Ann Elliott. (2007) *Economic Sanctions Reconsidered*. 3rd ed. Washington, DC: Institute for International Economics.

Jackson, Patrick Thaddeus. (2011) *The Conduct of Inquiry in International Relations: Philosophy of Science and Its Implications for the Study of World Politics*. Abingdon: Routledge.

Joas, Hans. (1993) *Pragmatism and Social Theory*. Chicago: University of Chicago Press.
Luhmann, Niklas. (1993) *Risk: A Sociological Theory*. Berlin: Gruyter.
Luhmann, Niklas. (1995) *Social Systems*. Stanford: Stanford University Press.
Martin, Lisa L. (1993) *Coercive Cooperation: Explaining Multilateral Economic Sanctions*. Princeton, NJ: Princeton University Press.
Messmer, Heinz. (2007) Contradiction, Conflict and Borders. In *Territorial Conflicts in World Society: Modern Systems Theory, International Relations and Conflict Studies*, edited by Stephan Stetter. London: Routledge.
Pape, Robert A. (1997) Why Economic Sanctions Do Not Work. *International Security* 22: 90–136.
Portela, Clara. (2010) *European Union Sanctions and Foreign Policy: When and Why Do They Work?* London: Routledge.
Preeg, Ernest H. (1999) *Feeling Good or Doing Good with Sanctions: Unilateral Economic Sanctions and the US National Interest*. Washington, DC: CSIS Press.
Schimmelfennig, Frank, Stefan Engert, and Heiko Knobel. (2006) *International Socialization in Europe: European Organizations, Political Conditionality, and Democratic Change*. Basingstoke: Palgrave Macmillan.
Uzgel, İlhan. (2001) Finishing the Unfinished Revolution: The Return of Yugoslavia to Europe. *Journal of International Affairs* 6.

Part I

Conceptualizing international sanctions conflicts

2 Sanctions

Disconnected theorizing of a relational phenomenon

The past decades have seen extensive research into the phenomenon of sanctions in International Relations. The early work, from the mid-20th century on, took important first steps in conceptualizing sanctions and in exploring their operational logic. Concomitantly, sanctions have been increasingly applied in international disputes. By any standards, their use greatly expanded from the 1980s onwards, irrespective of the particular type of sanctions. Two of the most comprehensive data sets on sanctions document such growth (see Figure 2.1).[1] Scholarly attention greatly increased as the use of these measures expanded. Today, there is a broad literature on sanctions, covering such areas as their theoretical underpinnings, particular issues such as the different purposes of sanctions and the factors contributing to their use, and optimizing the regulatory premises of their effective application.

This chapter examines existing work on international sanctions. It largely places an emphasis on concept and theory, in line with the theoretical inclinations of the book. This review of the literature on *coercive international sanctions* focuses on contributions dealing with the way in which sanctions affect the political position of the state they are imposed on. This excludes sanctions that are designed mainly to convey a message to domestic audiences of the imposing states, or to wider international audiences.

The most notorious question raised in the literature on coercive international sanctions is: 'Do sanctions work?' Some earlier work that generated considerable attention aimed to provide a straightforward answer to this question (e.g. Hufbauer, Schott, and Elliott 2007; Pape 1997). However, the issue of 'political effectiveness' already implies conceptual challenges. Evaluations that aim for objectivity often include a significant degree of subjectivity. One of the most direct ways of approaching this issue is to judge the political effectiveness of sanctions against the initially-stated demands of their initiators (Pape 1997; Hufbauer et al. 2007). However, such an approach falls short in several ways. First, it fails to reflect on how ambitious these demands were in the first place. Dissecting the notion of 'success', David Baldwin argues that judging 'success' quite generally is an undertaking marred with difficulties. What dimensions ought to be included? Success seems to be a matter of degree (Baldwin 1985). Second, it refrains from

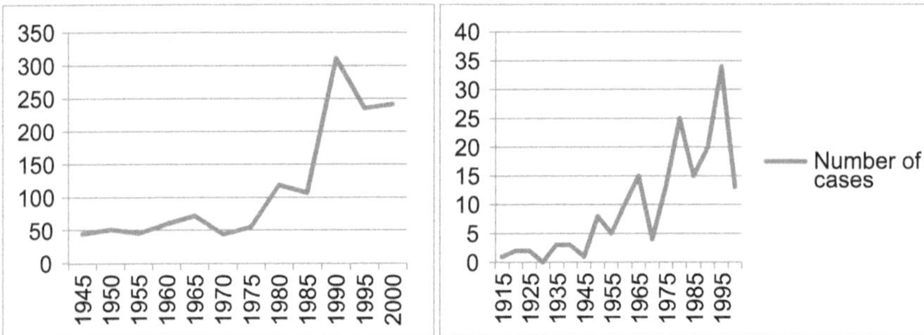

Figure 2.1 Number of sanctions cases, TIES (left, 1945–2004), HSE (right, 1915–2000)

considering the alternatives, and the comparative costs of such possible policy options (Baldwin 2000).

A similarly straightforward approach that seems less subjective is to judge political effectiveness against the *status quo ante*, that is, the situation that existed before the 'target state' started to take the political actions that are being opposed. But as Drezner (1999) notes, a more adequate counterfactual would be the situation that would have prevailed had sanctions not been introduced in the first place. Generally, given the broad variety of contexts in which sanctions are introduced, scholarly debate has more recently begun to address the issue of the political effectiveness of sanctions in a less simplistic way, rephrasing the underlying question as: 'When do sanctions work?' Contributions accordingly seek to theorize coercive international sanctions with the aim of shedding light on this question, or of identifying the factors that might support or hinder their political effectiveness.

In the literature, there are differences regarding the very question of what to include as a case of sanctions in international politics. For example, although they both show a growing use of sanctions, the specific numbers of the two data sets mentioned above are strikingly dissimilar. The 'Threat and Imposition of Sanctions' (TIES; Morgan, Krustev, and Bapat 2013) database includes sanctions applied in trade disputes as well as those applied for political ends, whereas the data set created by Hufbauer, Schott and Elliott (HSE; 2007) is limited to the latter.

As well as differing in the way they define the scope of research on sanctions, contributions differ in a number of other dimensions. First, sanctions come with different instruments such as trade restrictions (or concessions), financial measures such as investment bans (or offers) or even monetary measures such as currency manipulation. Besides such economic instruments, sanctions may also consist of political instruments such as encroachment and refusing (or granting) diplomatic recognition. However, most studies focus overtly on economic instruments. Second, scholars distinguish between comprehensive sanctions and targeted sanctions.

Comprehensive sanctions are aimed indiscriminately at a target state's economy or population so as to generate broad popular pressure on its government. Targeted sanctions, by contrast, are aimed selectively at specific groups deemed particularly politically influential, so as to maximize the political impact. As well as the disastrous contribution of comprehensive sanctions to the suffering of the Iraqi civilian population in the 1990s, researchers point to the fight against terrorism as another reason for the broad switch to targeted sanctions. Third, the research distinguishes between different sanctions strategies. The great majority of investigations are limited to examining negative sanctions policies, with a few contributions also considering positive sanctions. Thus most studies take a one-sided view of the cost/benefit calculus that is presumed to be the logical basis of sanctions. Although a few studies consider positive sanctions, work that systematically examines the combination of both negative and positive sanctions is scant, despite the fact that such combined sanctions strategies can be increasingly observed empirically.

In the broadest sense, research on coercive international sanctions may fall into two different groups. The first group contains contributions which engage conceptually with sanctions. Individual pieces consist of genuine theoretical elaborations or conceptual discussions on the contributions of a number of specific factors. The second group includes either theoretically unaspiring empirical evaluations, or pieces that aim in turn to optimize procedures in the implementation of sanctions policies. In such a categorization, the two groups lie at both ends of a spectrum, where individual contributions can be assigned more or less firmly to one of the groups.

Contributions that substantially engage with sanctions on a theoretical level (first group) can be divided into three sub-categories. By adhering to an observation of different 'levels of analysis', these contributions approach sanctions either from a top-down perspective, locating explanatory factors at the inter-state level, or from a bottom-up perspective which seeks to account for developments in terms of domestic processes. That is, they seek to account for the course of sanctions conflicts primarily by examining them as international disputes or by analyzing their impact on domestic politics. The final category transcends the former two in that the perspective includes both international and domestic factors. All in all, however, explicitly theoretical contributions to the subject of international sanctions are fairly limited in number. Instead, large swathes of the literature regard the basic conceptual issues as settled, assuming a deceptively simple logic for sanctions policies: According to the utilitarian rationale of economic orthodoxy, sanctions aim to manipulate the calculus of the target in making a dis-preferred outcome more attractive than a preferred option.

Many studies refrain from questioning this presumed logic and instead investigate particular factors that possibly impact on or intervene in the operation of the cost/benefit calculus. Furthermore, as part of a technocratic empiricism (second group), research either aims to empirically identify factors which may pertain to processes at the 'sender' and the 'target', or it investigates regulatory procedures in order to maximize the economic effectiveness of sanctions. Such factors may be related to circumstances affecting the economic robustness of sanctions, or they may concern the 'transmission' of economic impact into political pressure. Technocratic reports involve inter-institutional coordination, legal adjustments and other regulatory issues as part of concrete policy advice.

The review focuses on two main themes. First, it discusses the contributions and limitations of the existing literature on the relationship between coercive international sanctions and conflict development. The review traces the disconnected theorizing that is present in the literature. Conceptualizations remain mostly isolated across different levels of analysis, theorizing either international conflict or domestic politics, and they do not systematically connect insights gained at the different levels. Furthermore, across levels, conceptualizations subscribe to a simplistic sender–receiver model of communication. At the international level, sanctions and demands unambiguously 'transmit' to a 'target'; at the domestic level, the effects of sanctions unfold one-dimensionally along an input/output model of economic impact, translating into political pressure. As a consequence of such compromises, conceptual approaches treat imposed sanctions as exogenous to putatively constant conflict perceptions, resulting in a 'static' understanding of sanctions conflicts.

Second, the review notes a research gap concerning the systematic consideration of different sanctions strategies. Particular sanctions strategies are either not considered at all, or they are presumed to be mere logical opposites. The focus then remains mostly on negative sanctions, as the strategy that is more widely empirically observable. Also, as an obvious consequence of the presumption, a systematic theorization of a combined sanctions strategy is conspicuously absent.

The review proceeds in three steps. It begins by assessing the key theoretical contributions to international sanctions, discussing their conceptual image of sanctions and their theorization of how sanctions work. Furthermore, the review takes note of additional influence factors in sanctions conflicts that have been identified in the literature. In the second section, it discusses empirical evaluations and the work on regulatory procedures which together make for a technocratic empiricism. The third step summarizes and discusses the findings of the literature review and outlines the challenges of theorizing coercive international sanctions.

2.1 Sanctions theory: current state of the art

This section critically evaluates existing contributions that conceptualize sanctions and that theorize how they work. First, in conceptual terms, these contributions take a position on the logic of sanctions, on the instruments that sanctions consist of, on the relationship between particular sanctions strategies and on which of them to include in analyses. Second, the contributions theorize how coercive sanctions work in international conflict. The early roots of conceptual treatments as well as of theories on international sanctions can be traced to Albert Hirschman's work on foreign trade as a source and instrument of national power. Many of the field's defining challenges and issues were noted by Johan Galtung in his theorization of sanctions against Rhodesia. The section takes the basic conceptual parameters formulated by these authors as a point of departure for a comprehensive discussion of existing conceptualizations and theorizations of international sanctions.

Hirschman provided the common idea of how coercive international sanctions work. He simplified his argument as follows: the "influence which country A acquires in country B by foreign trade depends in the first place upon the total gain which B derives from that trade", and further depends on the painfulness of substituting trade restrictions and the 'strength of vested interests' on this trade in country B (Hirschman 1969:18). Thus, the potential influence of economic sanctions on a country is directly related to the profits that country gains from an economic exchange relationship. In the field's jargon, the 'sender' aims, with sanctions, to manipulate the utility calculus of the 'target' to the extent that a formerly dis-preferred policy option becomes more attractive than the initially preferred option.

Johan Galtung called the assumed direct relation between trade manipulation and political influence the 'naïve theory' of sanctions: The pressure that negative sanctions put on a country stems from "a limit to how much value-deprivation the system can stand and . . . once this limit is reached (resulting in a split in leadership or between leadership and people) . . . political disintegration will proceed" (Galtung 1967:388). Implicitly, the 'naïve theory' assumes the existence of a 'societal transmission belt' as an unproblematic given, which directly transforms economic impact into political pressure (Portela 2010). Galtung was quick to discount this view as resting on a simplistic notion of society. Instead, he proposed to consider the target society as "an organism with a certain self-maintaining potential" (Galtung 1967:409), having the potential to adapt in the face of hardship.

Hirschman was concerned with the exploitative potential of dependence in trade relations. Besides manipulating trade, coercive international sanctions can, however, entail a large variety of other instruments. Galtung recognized this, and while he also subsumed capital restrictions to trade relations, he distinguished more broadly between economic, diplomatic and communication sanctions. By taking sanctions to be basically any actions which aim to make a target comply with norms promoted by a sender, Galtung (1967) in addition included both negative and positive sanctions in his definition. Subsequently, however, Galtung focused on negative economic sanctions. In doing so, though, he by no means denied the conceptual and practical significance of non-economic and positive sanctions, as he clarified.

Galtung formulated the persisting key challenges and issues in conceptual research on coercive international sanctions. First, sanctions may occur in different strategies: The use of negative or positive sanctions may bear specific conceptual implications; the use of particular instruments may affect a conflict differently. Second, when theorizing coercive international sanctions, there is the fundamental issue of the transmission of impact into political pressure and consequences.

The theory review will look at these issues in turn. In the first part, it addresses existing conceptualizations of coercive international sanctions. It critically assesses notions of what sanctions are: their basic logic and the instruments and strategies of which they are presumed to consist. The review illustrates specific solutions to conceptual challenges and considers their merits and limits. In the second part, the review assesses how existing research substantially theorizes coercive sanctions in international conflict. This work falls into three categories: theorizing sanctions either at an international level, or at a domestic level or a combination of both. Particular contributions concern specific positions on the conceptual issues outlined in the first part. The review notes that many issues of existing conceptual work evolve around the 'societal transmission belt' and the underlying assumptions predicated on it, resulting in a disconnected theorizing.

2.1.1 Conceptualizations of sanctions

When examining different sanctions strategies, like Galtung, scholars mostly focused on negative economic sanctions. This considerably restricts the underlying notion of sanctions. Positive sanctions are abundant in international relations as well. For example, trade concessions have often been linked to political issues, and similarly to the granting of development assistance (Hazelzet 2001). Conceptually, the presumed operational logic of coercive international sanctions manipulating the utility of a target's policy options is in principle indiscriminate towards costs and inducements. Galtung (1967), aware of this non-clarified issue, questioned whether positive sanctions work in the exact reverse way to negative sanctions. Nonetheless, Galtung effectively theorizes negative sanctions only, despite calling his work a 'general theory of economic sanctions'. The question essentially remains to be settled of how positive sanctions work, and whether and to what extent there is an analogous 'transmission belt' between economic impact and political pressure.

Generally, the mere existence of positive sanctions brings conceptual challenges. The investigation of sanctions raises the issue of setting a 'reference point' (Baldwin 1971; cf. Davis 2000): Is the ending of a granted incentive already a negative sanction, and vice versa? Senders and targets may differ in their perceptions of such developments, so their respective reference points need to be acknowledged. Negative and positive sanctions are relative notions, and they may develop dynamically. Baldwin notes that reference points evolve over time: "Today's reward may lay the groundwork of tomorrow's threat", once the reward becomes expected (1971:24). Indeed, what seems to distinguish positive sanctions from their negative counterparts is their orientation towards future cooperation (Haass and O'Sullivan 2000).[2] However, any such differences remain mostly neglected and conceptually unexplored.

Scholarly inattention is even stronger concerning the combination of negative and positive sanctions in international conflict. While Galtung described the possibility of combining negative and positive sanctions as among the most far-reaching questions in his conclusions, it has remained hitherto almost entirely neglected. A supposed merit of combining positive incentives with negative sanctions has often been claimed, though, particularly in the research conducted on positive sanctions. Haass and O'Sullivan (2000:175) describe these merits as the "subtle lessons about combining honey and vinegar", but the lessons remain anecdotal. Such research has mostly committed and restricted itself to demonstrating the general usefulness of incentives, in a less theoretically guided manner (Crumm 1995; Long 1996; Cortright 1997; Newnham 2002).

Hadewych Hazelzet's dissertation (2001) is a notable exception to this absence of explicit research activity regarding the combination of negative and positive sanctions. Her work documents the widespread use of combined sanctions by the European Union and, to a lesser degree, the United States. Focusing strongly on senders, she undertook an extensive quantitative investigation into the reasons, goals and robustness of different sanctions policies. Although it was pioneering research on the combination of negative and positive sanctions, her work is not primarily theory-oriented. It does not include a conceptual treatment of the distinct qualities of negative and positive sanctions and their combination. Overall, conceptual sophistication thus remains limited. Alexander George's (1991) claim that the addition of positive to negative sanctions may attain what negative sanctions alone would fail to achieve continues to rest on assumptions that such a combination increases flexibility and bargaining potential, and on maximizing the spread between costs and benefits.

In line with the broadly restricted view of sanctions strategies, most but not all conceptual treatments have concentrated specifically upon economic instruments,[3] neglecting non-economic ones.[4] David Baldwin provides a rationale for a focus on economic instruments and not on other types. With a specific interest in providing a conceptual account of the variety of uses and effects of economic statecraft, he notes that "conceiving of economic sanctions in terms of the intended effects on the receiving state is no help at all in distinguishing economic from noneconomic tools of statecraft" (1985:36). Baldwin's work precisely builds on the premise of a foreign policy perspective that explores a specific instrument (*economic* statecraft) and aims to remain open to a variety of potential consequences.

Accordingly, there may be well-founded conceptual reasons for a restriction on economic instruments. Quite often, however, a simple definition substitutes for a conceptual justification. There are two variants. In the first variant, definitions squarely reflect the 'naïve theory' of sanctions and include the presumption of a 'transmission belt'. Robert Pape neatly summarizes this general rationale-cum-definition: "Economic sanctions seek to lower the aggregate economic welfare of a target state by reducing international trade in order to coerce the target government to change its political behaviour" (1997:93f.). In a second variant, the state possesses proper interests, independent of society to a certain degree (Kirshner 1997). Thus, a short-cut 'transmission belt' no longer is a conceptual premise as Portela rightly observes, but the basic concept/definition in the form 'economic impact → political pressure' remains in place (Portela 2010). Now the difference is merely that the state, or rather its government, itself acts as a rational utility maximizer and sanctions target specifically the leadership's calculus.

When the conceptual premise of an investigation of coercive international sanctions presumes a 'transmission belt', a focus on economic instruments seems suggestive. However, such reasoning would be somewhat tautological and ultimately in itself unsustainable. First, economic *impact* may very well stem from political sanctions, as Baldwin noted. Second, the presumed impact of sanctions on the target state, or rather, its society, which then transmits into political pressure, need not be necessarily of an economic nature in the first place. There is no *a priori* reason which would exclude non-economic instruments. Rather, since the aim of coercive sanctions supposedly was to affect the *political goals* and *policies* of a rational, utility-maximizing target, it strictly follows that such utility would include non-economic factors[5] when policies are in fact part of any such calculation. This applies all the more to conceptual approaches of the 'impact → pressure' rationale that assume independent state interests: Target governments may care more about political costs to them than about the economic impact on society, as Blanchard and Ripsman (1999) observe.

Of course, such utility of non-economic factors lends itself less to quantification, and their consideration may thus be less open to certain methodological approaches. Moreover, the inclusion of non-economic factors will put more demand on a theoretically-sound conceptualization of the impact → pressure rationale. While the availability of adequate economic indicators may warrant a focus on economic instruments on methodological grounds, a research interest in the *political effectiveness* of coercive international sanctions decidedly does not justify such a restriction. As Audie Klotz observes, politically, "costs and benefits are measured in social as well as economic and military terms. Thus international pressures can create incentives far beyond the strictly economic" (1995:155). In fact, a growing strand of the literature on international sanctions does incorporate non-economic instruments, testifying to their systematic application in practice (George 1991; Klotz 1995; Haass and O'Sullivan 2000; Hazelzet 2001; e.g. Cortright and Lopez 2002; Portela 2010), and the point is that there is no basic conceptual reason not to do so. Far from it, non-economic diplomatic and cultural instruments may incur costs and bring political consequences no less effectively than economic instruments may do (Crawford and Klotz 1999a).

To sum up the review of existing conceptual work on sanctions strategies and instruments, different strategies are frequently treated as logical opposites, with only limited recognition of positive sanctions and their potential idiosyncrasies. In a utilitarian rationale conceiving of sanctions as instruments to manipulate cost/benefit ratios, negative and positive sanctions are logically interchangeable. An important insight into the conceptual challenges of dealing with different strategies of sanctions concerns the setting of the reference point that makes sanctions positive or negative. In any case, conceptual examinations of different sanctions strategies remain limited, with no existing theorization of the particularities of combined sanctions. In terms of instruments, restricting these to economic measures rests more on definitional grounds than well-founded conceptual premises or empirical observation. While there are no conceptual reasons to exclude non-economic measures even in terms of the 'naïve theory', including them only raises additional questions regarding their supposed transmission mechanism.

2.1.2 Theories of international sanctions as coercive instruments

Ever since, the literature on international sanctions has struggled with the link between economic impact and political pressure, when conceptualizing sanctions and accounting for their political (in)effectiveness. Theoretical treatments can be divided into three categories, with two of them privileging particular 'levels of analysis', whereas the third category seeks to transcend such analytical boundaries. Research into the first category focuses on relational factors at an international level between senders and target states. Such accounts of coercive international sanctions proceed with a top-down approach. They rest on the premise that, ultimately, these factors are decisive to an extent that justifies treating target states as unitary rational actors and putting domestic factors into a black box. Effectively, this approach rejects the transmission issue as an analytical problem. Conversely, contributions to the second category embark on a bottom-up approach. They fully focus on the transmission process and regard domestic factors as the decisive ones. Relational factors between sender and target are at best of secondary importance and are of no interest analytically. The final category of work seeks to incorporate or transcend these different analytical levels, by maintaining that both the other perspectives produce incomplete accounts of international sanctions.

Sanctions and international relations

One approach with a top-down perspective that is exemplary in its parsimony and stated explanatory power is Daniel Drezner's game-theoretical analysis which considers negative economic sanctions and positive incentives, but rather in an either/or mode than as combined sanctions strategies. The insights flowing from his analysis are remarkable, because they are somehow counter-intuitive: Successful cases of economic coercion are often instances of negative sanctions between allies, not between adversaries. More precisely, apart from a target state's opportunity costs of deadlock, the success of an economic coercion attempt seems to be linked to the target state's given expectations of future conflict, with a 'giving-in' signifying a weakening of its relative bargaining position in future conflicts (Drezner 1999:307).

Harrison Wagner (1988) analyzed the differences in economic strength between sender and target and the latter's economic dependency on the former as another factor at the inter-state level.[6] By engaging bargaining theory, Wagner challenges the common wisdom as first coined by Hirschman that dependence translates into more influence. Rather, both sender and target need to consider themselves to be better off for cooperative results. On the other hand, Eaton and Engers (1992), in a sophisticated way of extending the common sense of the 'naïve theory', find senders' and targets' 'relative toughness' (i.e. their ability and patience to endure costs) to influence the outcomes of sanctions impositions as well. Moreover, Valentin Krustev (2010) finds that senders take into account their own and a target's strategic position when setting their political goals and engaging in economic coercion. Accordingly, political demands and decisions on coercion are endogenous to conflict processes. In a similar relational vein, Ang and Peksen (2007) describe the influence of relational differences in perceived issue salience. Again, relational differences in perceptions significantly matter for the outcome of sanctions impositions.

These top-down approaches outline how the sanctions conflict situation informs the actions of opponents. In order to illustrate how such game-theoretical approaches theorize 'conflict' at the international level in the first place, it is worthwhile examining their conceptual bases. Historically, game-theoretical analyses of sanctions conflicts have significant connections to the notions of deterrence and compellence, which were propelled by strict game-theoretical concepts up until their heyday during the Cold War. With their interest in conceptualizing conflicts as situations of interdependent decision-making between opponents that effectively seek to influence behavior through threats and promises, they are fundamentally about coercion.

In his seminal study of deterrence, Thomas Schelling (1960) put forward a notion of conflict that shares some basic traits with the ones informing game-theoretical analyses of sanctions. Examining these traits of Schelling's conception, and of subsequent works in the same spirit that followed it, is instructive for a precise understanding of the premises and of the limitations of such notions of conflict. Schelling's work had a defining influence on the field. The depiction of conflict using game-theoretical deterrence theory rests on the notion of rational agents shaping the system (Freedman 1998). It is ultimately a product of a radical reduction of 'conflict' to the behavioral choices of opponents, based on their relational position vis-à-vis each other: "adversaries watch and interpret each other's behaviour, each aware that his own actions are interpreted and anticipated, each acting with a view to the expectation that he creates" (Schelling 1960:21).

A basic element of deterrence as well as of coercion is thus about influencing expectations on the part of an opponent through certain behavior. This exercise decisively rests on the idea of manipulating 'choice': An agent aiming to deter may seek to influence or stabilize the expectations of an adversary *by limiting its own freedom of choice* to essentially having no other option but to retaliate. Schelling (1960:22) calls this a "paradox that the power to constrain an adversary may depend on the power to bind oneself".

With actually imposed sanctions, the situation differs slightly. The sender has already acted on what perhaps was a threat initially, and it seeks to compel a target to make a change of course that the latter has already embarked on. Yet both conceptions, that of deterrence and of sanctions, share a common trait which enables their depiction in game-theoretical logic in the first place: the idea that adversaries retain freedom of choice. As Lawrence Freedman emphasizes, 'coercion' aims at the actions of an opponent as a voluntary agent, shifting choice from the coercer to the coerced (Freedman 1998).

Deterrence-inspired game-theoretical conceptions of conflicts make additional crucial assumptions about opponents. Despite the use of threats and coercion as a means of influencing a conflict, "the roles of deterrer and challenger are considered unproblematic", as Richard Ned Lebow observes (2005:767). The perspective of the target, which, as Freedman (1998) concedes, might differ fundamentally as to whether it is 'deterrence' (or coercion, respectively) and not perhaps an offensive move that it is being confronted with, contributes little to the analysis, even while the phenomenon in question, deterrence (or coercion) ultimately rests with the receiver. Instead, the conviction held by 'would-be deterrers' that their defensive motives in the use of such means are self-evident remains mostly unquestioned (Lebow 2005).

The analysis furthermore remains largely unconcerned with any impediments related to interpretation or perception effects interfering with the assumption of perfectly rational actors. Although, as Alexander George notes, whether a strategy will work in any situation "rests heavily on the correctness of the policymaker's assessment of the opponent's perceptions and strategic reasoning", it is an assessment that is intermediated by the policymaker's own perceptions, as should be noted again. Robert Jervis meticulously outlined the weight and extent of intervening perceptual issues, concluding that "it is often impossible to explain crucial decisions and policies without reference to the decision-makers' beliefs about the world and their images of others" (Jervis 1976:28). It is a daring and highly idealtypical move to propose that players act on perfect information and pure rationality (cf. George 1991). In effect, the entire problem posed by perceptual bias, skewed interpretation and uncertainty, all fairly characteristic of conflicts and crises, is assumed away.

At the bottom of these game-theoretical conceptions of conflict lies a simplistic notion of communication. Although Schelling had reflected on varieties of communication (e.g. verbal communication, written communication), 'anticommunicative' strategies, problems of perception and the need for players to arrive at some understanding of each other (Schelling 1960), its complexity remains underappreciated. As Freedman acknowledges, there is indeed a need "to take into account not only of the messages delivered by A but also of those actually received [by B]" (Freedman 2004).

Irrespective of some radical methodological choices, top-down treatments of sanctions conflicts demonstrate that there is a crucial relational component to coercive international sanctions and their outcomes. Yet the decisions of opponents as rational agents are informed by *given relational properties*: While Drezner's unit of analysis are dyads of states and their foreign policies directly implicated in the sanctions instances, his ultimate sources of explanation are the general relationship and the distribution of capabilities between the states involved. These factors are intermediated through future-oriented calculations by the states. In other words, external relational properties inform the target state's expectations of future conflict. Moreover, authors treat factors such as specific configurations of asymmetrical interdependence or issue salience in a similar way to relational properties. Target states thus have a concern for the relational conflict development, just as senders consider their relational position in conflict escalation. Sanctions need to be considered as part of a larger conflict setting. However, although conflict perceptions are essential explanatory elements, there is neither a concept of their formation, nor of conflict communication in a broader way that appreciates the complexity of the social processes involved. Finally, it must be noted that only Drezner considers sanctions other than negative ones. Yet to what extent other sanctions strategies relate more broadly to these important relational aspects of sanctions conflicts has thus far remained unexplored.

Sanctions and domestic politics

Other studies follow a decidedly different approach, taking the domestic politics of target states into exclusive consideration. They focus on the 'transmission belt' in pursuance of a *bottom-up* perspective. The public choice model developed by William Kaempfer and Anton Lowenberg in 1992 represented a major step forward, formulating some of the conclusions pointing to the expediency of targeted sanctions that years later would be drawn on empirical grounds. With their strict public choice perspective, a state or government would not be assumed to have independent interests. Rather, it is assumed that they result entirely from the relations of dominant interest groups within a country. Thus the principle of targeted sanctions is to focus on key groups within a target state who are either directly involved in the regime or who benefit from the status quo.

In a related bottom-up perspective on international sanctions which aims to explore 'how they function', Jonathan Kirshner seeks to specify more thoroughly the 'microfoundations' of sanctions. Kirshner clarifies at the outset the reasons for his interest in examining the 'transmission belt', locating the cause of ineffective sanctions in the "failure of . . . economic effect to translate into the desired political outcome" (1997:41). As with Kaempfer and Lowenberg's public choice approach, the microfoundations are based on the differential impact of sanctions on particular groups within the target state. Yet Kirshner in part inverts the relationship between target state and society. Moving the state leadership to the center, he focuses on clientelistic relations between the government and supporting groups. In his view, sanctions that weaken the government may create specific political interests for some particular groups in the first place. Besides affecting the utility calculus of the government directly, influence attempts may thus occur through two additional 'mechanisms': Overthrowing the government and shifting the balance of power between different factions *within* the wider political elite, including the government.

Subsequently, other authors brought additional insights to this bottom-up perspective. Most of these studies further investigated the impact of sanctions, comparing democratic and autocratic states. Generally, negative economic sanctions can be expected to succeed less against authoritarian target states because their leadership relies on smaller core support groups and is less constrained (Lektzian and Souva 2007; Allen 2008).[7] However, a closer look reveals that different effects on autocracies may also relate to different sanctions instruments (Brooks 2002), or to the type of autocracy (personalist vs. single-party and military regimes) on which sanctions are imposed (Escribà-Folch and Wright 2010). Still, these findings basically all embrace a 'microfoundations' approach and add little additional substantive theoretical aspects to the bottom-up perspective.

Lee Jones' social conflict analysis of sanctions adds a broader take on the social forces at work in the target state's society and the lines of conflict existing therein, based on a Gramscian perspective (Jones 2015). Contrary to the public choice model's lean focus on the economics of interest group dynamics and the 'microfoundations' approach's addition of state interests, the approach inspired by

Antonio Gramsci puts forward a more extensive notion of governance that includes the state itself as well as civil society. Governance reflects the hierarchical configuration of social relations and political coalitions present in a society. The socio-political coalitions involved are the focus of the main analytical interest of Jones' social conflict analysis of sanctions, which evaluates "how the material effects of sanctions condition [these] socio-political conflicts" (Jones 2015:44). The resulting approach delivers a broader response to the issue of the transmission belt, putting emphasis on political discourse: Its notion of 'political coalitions' as key domestic agents comprises 'power, interests, resources, ideologies and strategies' and provides a proper concept of the way in which distributive economic impact translates into political effects. However, despite this extensive inclusion of non-economic factors composed of political coalitions, Jones' analysis remains limited to the impact of negative economic sanctions.

In principle, both a public choice and a microfoundations approach, as well as Jones' social conflict analysis, would readily invite the inclusion of positive incentives. Indeed, Kaempfer and Lowenberg observe (1992:8) promisingly:

> [A]n important implication emerging from the analysis . . . is that sanctions will often fail to achieve their intended political objectives, and might even be counterproductive, unless they are designed to hurt or benefit specific groups selectively within the target polity. The notion of 'sanction' should be interpreted to include positive as well as negative measures.

Approaches that disaggregate the 'transmission belt' seem particularly well suited to deliver on this proposition. However, like Jones' Gramscian model, Kaempfer and Lowenberg's and Kirshner's contributions consist solely of selective negative measures. Any 'benefit' to domestic political forces more strongly devoted to sender demands within the target states would then result, first, from the comparative relative gains resulting from the losses produced by negative sanctions to other pressure groups. Second, such benefit may result from the symbolic value carried by negative sanctions as imposed onto the forces profiting from the objectionable behavior in question and their motivating impact on oppositional groups. Viewed this way, it becomes essentially unnecessary to apply genuinely positive incentives – the same effect would be attainable through negative sanctions, as long as they are strong enough in terms of the two criteria just mentioned.

This view is over-simplified. First, negative sanctions carry with them the risk that they will trigger a 'rally around the flag' effect, of a symbolism gone wrong, so to speak. In consequence, sanctions would make the situation even worse from the senders' perspective: they would face a country firmly determined to resist this coercive influence attempt. Kaempfer and Lowenberg (1988) noted this (see also Lopez and Cortright 1997; Selden 1999). It remains entirely unclear why positive sanctions should have a similar effect. Second, in conceptual terms of both public choice and a 'microfoundations' approach, what amounts to negative sanctions against a particular social group may be perceived entirely differently by another group. It is thus a matter of context and perspective. Third, and related to this, such a view basically denies that there is much difference between coercive actions and more conciliatory and cooperative measures in international relations, in the interaction between one state and another.

Furthermore, a comparison of Kaempfer and Lowenberg's work with Drezner's model quickly reveals that much of their unawareness of the particularities of negative and positive sanctions stems from the approach itself. With such bottom-up perspectives, the 'system' is, ontologically speaking, the target society, and the 'units' within this system are the given individual interest groups (with or without including the state), which are the sources of explanation. The target policy is viewed as entirely resulting from these interest group dynamics. Remarkably, under consistent application of Kaempfer and Lowenberg's model the mentioned 'rally-around-the-flag' effect could stem *only* from the mobilizing potential of certain interest groups and not from genuine aspects of the international relationship between sender state and target state *per se*.

It is exactly this link between relational aspects between sender and target at the international level that is an integral component of Drezner's research. Top-down arguments, on the other side, are blind to the diverse processes and effects of sanctions domestically. Thus, in Drezner's analysis, conflict expectations trump calculations of utility – and the resulting disutility of noncompliance in the case of high conflict expectations must be sold domestically. It thus necessarily results in domestic internalization processes. It remains unclear, though, how such internalization proceeds. Instead, 'expectations of future conflict' depend solely on the general relationship between senders and targets, with the perception of this relationship assumed to be non-dynamic, statically given. Nevertheless, perceptions in top-down approaches are fairly relevant for the success or failure of sanctions.

International relations and domestic politics

Research in the final sub-category seeks to transcend some of the limitations that stem from restricting conceptualizations to either a top-down or a bottom-up perspective. In aiming for a more holistic approach, Frank Schimmelfennig, Stefan Engert, and Heiko Knobel (2006) incorporate explanatory factors from both interstate and domestic levels in their research on European socialization. They are interested in the promotion of norms and of 'constitutive rules' more broadly through positive sanctions and conditionalities. However, Schimmelfennig and his colleagues maintain that even with a constructivist notion of norm promotion within an 'international community' it is appropriate to observe both socializing senders and target state actors as acting strategically, instead of subscribing to a logic of internalization and appropriateness. In this configuration, they find the 'material' coercion of strategically acting agents – a classical microfoundations perspective – a more important initial socialization mechanism than legitimacy effects. As a caveat to this latter claim though, Pelc (2010) finds that the perceived legitimacy or illegitimacy of coercion attempts does indeed have a significant effect on target state cooperation.

The approach of strategic adaptation assumes "no logically or theoretically necessary connection between the assumptions of a community environment and of appropriate action" (Schimmelfennig et al. 2006:17). In the course of a developing relation, no domestic actors would change, learn or internalize new preferences.[8] Arguably, such a process even excludes interest change as occurring "slowly and as a function of the new incentive structures" (Checkel 2001:556) which would result out of an evolving social environment. Consequently, neither the social environment evolves (only rules do), nor do identities. One is left wondering where exactly the constructivist value added is supposed to lie when agents produce an international community *entirely* out of material cost/benefit calculation.

Like Schimmelfennig et al., Thomas Bernauer and Dieter Ruloff (1999) include explanatory factors from both the inter-state and the domestic level in their work on positive incentives and arms control. However, they focus on the contingency of actions and their uncertain bases. These involve not only incomplete information regarding the other state's preferences, but include also the fact that preferences in themselves are often contested and potentially dynamic. Thus, as indicated before, perceptions matter, and they do so in the strategic situation between states, but also through the process of their domestic formation as bases of the political articulation of preferences. Bernauer and Ruloff further implicate a more direct relationship between the choice of sanctions strategy and the formation of perceptions when noting the often markedly negative effects of negative sanctions on perceptions (e.g., they "smack of extortion" [1999:5] and are more confrontational [1999:21]). However, their research was dedicated to proving the merits of positive incentives in general. Thus their work neither focused on combined sanctions strategies, nor did it pursue the link between choice of strategy and perceptions more explicitly.

Investigations into the non-economic impact of sanctions may shed more light on the differences between negative and positive sanctions and the specific effects of incentives. In her research on sanctions and the promotion of norms, Klotz identifies a different operational logic, based on legitimation and the socialization effects of sanctions instead of economic impact. Contrary to the skepticism of Schimmelfennig et al., Klotz (1995) demonstrated that sanctions may also affect a target state through social transformation: By granting or denying legitimacy to certain political positions, sanctions can promote a socialization which subsequently contributes to re-defining interests. Since such sanctions rely primarily on political rather than economic impact, their 'impact → pressure' rationale is significantly different, though. While it may operate through distributing costs and/or benefits across groups with different normative political positions, socialization and re-defined interests may also occur through normative communication: "Sanctioners aim to affect the worldviews of the target's elite decision makers and general population. Thus, for sanctions to work, decision makers must understand and be persuaded by normative arguments" (Crawford and Klotz 1999a:27f.). There is thus another important 'mechanism' of influence attempts available in the 'domestic structural component' of norm-promoting international sanctions.

Pre-existing conflict relations between sender and target at the international level may significantly influence – positively and negatively – notions of legitimacy and the prospect of normative influence attempts, as Crawford and Klotz (1999a) observe. The interplay between domestic politics and international relations can represent a complex pattern of interdependent conflict perceptions between sender positions and particular groups at the domestic level of the target state, influenced by specific sanctions instruments (Crawford and Klotz 1999b). By implication, legitimacy effects would add to the differences between particular sanctions strategies. For example, positive incentives may be more persuasive with regard to the legitimacy of a certain normative position than punishments alone may be. However, Crawford and Klotz do not theorize this more extensively.

Studies bringing political discourse that revolves around ideological positions closer to the center of analysis represent a significant extension to the notion of coalitions of socio-political groups. Etel Solingen outlines the interplay of sanctions and domestic coalitions differentiated by 'outward-looking' and 'inward-looking' socio-political positions, particularly on national security (Solingen 2012). Depending on this context, target states' sensitivity to political and economic costs varies. Interestingly, some of the contributions to the volume edited by Solingen explore the interaction between negative and positive sanctions and domestic context. They find that the choice of sanctions strategy may affect the national security stance and that the domestic context in turn influences the political response to coercion attempts (Kreps and Pasha 2012; Nincic 2012): Negative sanctions may aggravate an already inward-looking target state stance that emphasizes national security, whereas positive sanctions may not necessarily have an opposite effect. The contributions to this volume on sanctions strategies and domestic context in the area of nuclear proliferation bring fresh insights and ideas. However, they do not result in a systematic overarching model of sanctions strategies and domestic politics, nor is there a conceptual justification as to why the decisive discursive positions of socio-political coalitions should be limited to an in-ward/out-ward looking national security nexus.

In sum, research in all three categories identifies important aspects and problems that contribute to our conceptual knowledge of sanctions conflicts. A top-down perspective highlights important aspects stemming from a focus on the relational interaction between sender and target. Perceptions of relations and the expectations linked to them exert an influence on the merits of particular sanctions strategies. There is thus a crucial relational component to international sanctions, which consequently need to be considered as part of a wider conflict. The top-down perspective remains silent, though, on the processes involved in the formation of perceptions and expectations. Instead, it assumes away these processes by seeing states as unitary, rational actors.

Contributions with a bottom-up perspective disaggregate the target state and show that it matters greatly what kinds of sanctions affect which domestic actors and groups of a target state – economically, and non-economically. The work of Klotz and others investigating the non-economic impact of sanctions adds further insights, with potential implications also extending to the relational level.

Bottom-up contributions, however, similarly exclude important aspects of sanctions that pertain to the international conflict dimension between sender and target. In addition, bottom-up approaches unnecessarily neglect the potential particularities of different sanctions strategies.

Contributions with a third perspective, seeking to transcend the restrictions of the former two, aim to extend a rationalist 'microfoundations' approach in a way that incorporates to a limited extent aspects from both the top-down and bottom-up perspective. Ultimately, however, these approaches refrain from decisively going beyond the 'transmission belt' of the naïve theory, although they acknowledge certain aspects of coercion with international sanctions in tension with it. Either these tensions are minimized by restrictively accommodating non-economic aspects to a 'microfoundations' approach, or the additional factors and their impact upon a static cost/benefit model, such as the impermanence of preferences and the formation of perceptions, are recognized but not consequently pursued further.

2.2 Technocratic empiricism

Apart from theoretical work that sets about conceptualizing coercive international sanctions, the literature increasingly focuses in an empiricist manner on evaluating sanctions, and in a technocratic manner on optimizing regulatory procedures in the application of sanctions. In contrast to some of the theoretical work, this literature variously takes the basic conceptual issues around international sanctions such as the 'economic impact → political pressure' rationale as settled, or it subscribes to a broad heuristic that seeks to link a larger variety of 'input' factors to 'outcomes'.

Both of these positions are reflected in large quantitative analyses that seek to assess first and foremost the effectiveness of economic sanctions. There are three particularly notable collections of large data. First, the data set created by Hufbauer, Schott and Elliott in 1985 (revised and updated in 1990, 2007) remains to date among the most ambitious in this respect. Their study aims at identifying the factors that increase the successful contribution of sanctions to the realization of the goals of senders. The number of factors included is extensive, ranging from economic indicators to political variables such as a target's regime type, economic and political stability, and prior relations between sender and target. In terms of results, Hufbauer et al. (2007) concluded from their analysis that roughly a third of international sanctions cases more or less 'worked' from the view of the senders and in accordance with the naïve theory. The data set consists of 174 cases of economic sanctions covering nearly a century, from 1914 until 2007, including 13 preliminary assessments of cases that began after 2000.

However, as much as it covers such an impressive time span this analysis of economic sanctions is also a product of a certain time. In fact, the historical contingency of the HSE database is proven most strongly through its basic conception of the economic indicators of sanctions: they rest on a view that is centered on an understanding of sanctions as comprehensive economic instruments whose application indiscriminatingly aims to do a maximum of economic damage to a national economy (Hufbauer et al. 2007:chap. 4). Theoretically, the underlying assumption that general economic costs directly and effectively translate into political pressure has never gone uncontested, nor is the assumption that economic costs are the sole determinative factor warranted in itself, as the conceptual analysis above demonstrated. In addition, the conception of sanctions applied simply as indiscriminate economic instruments limits the analytical value particularly of included regime type variables. Effectively, it precludes any assessment of the 'microfoundations' of sanctions, of 'how they function'. More generally, the HSE analysis has been criticized for its controversial coding of cases, which has a major influence on their overall assessment. When assessed more restrictively, the success rate of sanctions drops considerably below the claimed third of all cases (Pape 1997).[9] This has also been noted by Morgan and Schwebach (1997), who expressed detailed criticism on further methodological grounds that puts the results of Hufbauer, Schott and Elliott into perspective.[10]

The assessment of the 'outcome' variable of sanctions instances in the HSE database has also received serious criticism regarding two broad aspects. The first aspect concerns the basis against which the outcome is evaluated. Hufbauer, Schott and Elliott chose as this basis the extent to which the target acquiesced to the original demands of the senders. These original demands of the senders are divided into five different categories (modest target policy change, regime change, disruption of military adventure, impairment of military potential, change of target policies in another major way) which is supposed to reflect the fact that senders' goals in imposing sanctions vary in their level of ambition (ibid. 2007:52). This approach in effect mixes the subjective perspective of senders with the subjective evaluation of the investigator. The perspective of the target on the conflict is thus excluded. Moreover, there is no benchmark of how ambitious the self-defined goals of the senders are in relation to the particular conflict at hand, apart from the very rough assignment into the above-mentioned different categories by the researcher (Portela 2010:15f.).

Another, particularly large data set was created by Clifton Morgan, Navin Bapat and Valentin Krustev, including 888 cases from 1971–2000. It is also the most up-to-date collection of data and the most recently published (2009). Morgan et al. emphasize particularly the inclusion of 'threats' of sanctions: in the existing literature it was plausibly argued that in many cases, sanctions would already work at the threat level. A state that will acquiesce would rationally do so before sanctions were actually imposed and actual costs materialized (Smith 1995; Drezner 2003; Lacy and Niou 2004). Excluding the threat level from analysis then leads to biased results in underestimating the real political effectiveness of sanctions. Morgan et al. thus cited the beginning of a case of sanctions when the mere utterance of a concrete threat from a sufficiently high official (executive or legislative) to this end was made. In addition, the data set embraces a broad understanding of sanctions and includes not only the negative economic sanctions instruments[11] but also those of positive sanctions[12] (if any) and diplomatic sanctions[13] (if any) mentioned at the pre-imposition phase.

The high number of cases included also results from more controversial factors, however: Morgan et al. believe that it is also possible to define as sanctions those cases where the aim is to change the *economic* policies of a target state, something that other authors exclude as cases of trade war (e.g. Pape 1997). Depending on the notion of 'success' applied to the data, 20–45 per cent of sanctions are cases deemed to be successful coercion (Morgan, Bapat, and Krustev 2009). Finally, the outcome of sanctions instances was coded in a different way from the questionable HSE approach. It is captured in a set of variables that looks first at whether and to what extent the sender or target acquiesced at one point, and then evaluates the nature of the settlement from the perspectives of the senders and the targets separately on two ten-point-scales. This allows generally for two different definitions of 'success': Success can either be defined in terms of categorical acquiescence, or, in a more nuanced way, in terms of the sender achieving more of its objectives than the target.

What is lacking in the TIES data set is the conception of the costs sanctions, real and anticipated: it imports the HSE weaknesses on this point and evaluates the economic costs to the whole target state economy. For sanctions that discriminatively seek to target particular groups and political actors in a target state, this indifferent cost evaluation is therefore not appropriate. To be fair, Morgan et al. report that their analyses suggest that the strong relation between sanctions' costs and the political success of the coercer that was found in some of the earlier studies is generally supported (Bapat and Morgan 2009:101f.). The variable then is useful for assessing *comprehensive* sanctions, and limited to them.

A third large data set was created by Hazelzet (2001), who undertook an extensive quantitative analysis of EU and US usage of sticks or carrots exclusively in the field of human rights violations, covering 246 cases. She further focused her research on the senders and their particular reasons for applying (or not applying) different sanctions strategies. Of specific interest to her was the variation in type of measures across targets and over time, and the particular variation in types of responses between the US and the EU. A detailed examination of the effects of sanctions on target states, or an assessment of their political effectiveness with regard to the latter, was beyond the scope of the study.

Both the HSE and TIES data sets individually contain a rich set of valuable information on coercive international sanctions. However, such basic assessments as linking specific input factors (say, economic impact) to certain outputs (political effectiveness) remain descriptive presentations of certain patterns of correlations. As much as such descriptions are valuable in themselves, they have obvious limits in terms of the conclusions that may be drawn from them. First of all, the input–output design of such basic analyses generally limits any obtainable insights on the actual 'transmission' assumed in between. More specifically, any inferences are limited by the variables that are included in or left out of the data. Thus, a basic assessment of the HSE and TIES data offers a very rough estimate of the effectiveness of sanctions in coercing a target state, and of the possible contribution of particular factors, on the assumption that no important intervening variables or interaction effects are omitted. This, however, is hard to substantiate without a proper background theory.

HSE, and the TIES data set to a lesser extent, reproduce the problems found in the conceptual discussion that stem from a limited appreciation of both domestic and international processes involved in sanctions conflicts. Thus, while HSE include information on prior conflict relations and regime type, their lack of a more sophisticated notion of sanctions (different strategies) limits the use of the data beyond a simpler assessment of the 'naïve theory'. This also applies to a lesser degree to the TIES data set. Broader contents such as the inclusion of threats, different sanctions types and a more elaborate notion of outcomes are set off by a similarly simple notion of sanctions.

Clara Portela's analysis of the determinants of success of EU negative sanctions represents a different empirical approach (Portela 2010). Her analysis rests on a careful assessment of existing research and a consideration of factors deemed relevant for the outcome of sanctions policies. Her work can be characterized as 'qualified heuristic': It aims to determine those conditions or combinations of conditions that decisively influence the independent effect of sanctions and uses a Qualitative Comparative Analysis design for inductive hypothesis generation.

Departing decisively from existing research, most prominently the HSE analysis, allows Portela to avoid many of the existing flaws by carefully revaluating the merit of individual factors on their continued plausibility. She hence aims to correct the crude and outdated measurement of broad economic disruption as a 'harm indicator' in the HSE database through replacing it with 'extent of disutility' to account for targeted measures as well as other selective EU measures that are still based on more broad economic disutility (Portela 2010:35ff.).[14] Another modification is made to common approaches in the treatment of the 'nature of the target society' as a potentially influential factor. Portela contests its relevance in this shape, since sanctions (at least in her research) are almost always directed against undemocratic states. Inspired by George (1991) she focuses instead on how sanctions goals endanger the target state government's survival, based on the observation that regimes may hardly be persuaded to commit suicide (Portela 2010:40ff.). In Portela's Qualitative Comparative Analysis, all of the three ways in which negative sanctions may contribute towards a successful outcome contain, as a necessary condition, that sanctions must not threaten the target state leadership's grip on power.

Portela succeeds in developing a more systematic analysis out of somehow piecemeal analyses that struggle to formulate any coherent conclusions, basically through overlapping correlations over one another (Hufbauer et al. 2007). However, her specifically inductive heuristic also demarcates the limitations of her work. Relations between individual factors are established to a much more concrete extent than had taken place before. However, a comprehensive theoretical explanation that captures the conditional relations remains beyond the scope of the chosen methodology. Generally, she has focused on the domestic impact of sanctions but excluded the relational dimension of international conflict. Furthermore, Portela's decision to stick with the usually narrow definition of sanctions neglects the relevance (empirically as well as theoretically) of different sanctions strategies and prevents their systematic inclusion into the analysis. Also, and specifically in relation to her actual analysis, it is regrettable that while she did report on combinations of conditions that are conducive to the success of negative sanctions, an enquiry into the conditions or combinations of conditions that inhibit success would have been equally as interesting.

As a note on a final kind of work on international sanctions, there are contributions that investigate, and often aim to optimize, the regulatory procedures concerning their implementation. Some of this work is related to efforts by governmental agencies that have sought to systematically assess and learn from policy experiences on imposing targeted sanctions. These efforts occurred in subsequent exchanges between scholars and practitioners, most prominently as part of the Interlaken Process (Swiss Federal Office for Foreign Economic Affairs 1998, 1999), the Bonn-Berlin Process (Brzoska 2001) and the Stockholm Process (Wallensteen and Staibano 2003). Further, there are a number of papers that similarly engage with regulatory procedures and their implications (Fitzgerald 2001; Brzoska 2003; e.g. Biersteker and Eckert 2006; Van Elsuwege 2011). Without going into the particularities of specific contributions, what they all have to some extent in common as a working hypothesis is that they presume that the main conceptual issues of how sanctions 'function' is settled. The impact of sanctions on individuals and social groups is supposed to result in political pressure. However, many targeted sanctions and their adjacent procedures do not aim to coerce a target state, but seek to limit the operational possibilities of non-governmental organizations such as terrorist networks and organized crime. As such, these contributions – although reproducing to a certain degree the more broadly assumed operational logic of sanctions – are not relevant to this research on coercive international sanctions against states.

2.3 The challenges of theorizing international sanctions

Treatments in the literature of the political effectiveness of coercive international sanctions and, more substantially, of 'how they function' are able to shed light on important consequential factors located at specific levels of analysis. Yet they leave as many issues unaddressed as they raise new ones. These issues broadly evolve around disconnected theorizing that remains restricted to different 'levels of analysis'. There is a gap when the inquiry remains limited to one level of analysis. Top-down approaches render it impossible to investigate the domestic formation processes of perceptions. Bottom-up approaches, which focus on target states' domestic politics, neglect the relational aspects of the international conflict.

Disconnected theorizing remains unable to cover the full interplay between the international conflict and domestic processes involved in the formation of political views, and hence incapable of providing a full account of the social conditions within sanctions conflicts that are conducive to either cooperation or non-cooperation. The existence of this interplay, however, is a conclusion that must inevitably be drawn. At the same time, much of the reproduction of simplistic economic cost/benefit common sense constantly acknowledges the significance of perceptions and estimations. However, it fails to systematically theorize these essentially non-economic aspects.

To reiterate the main conceptual tensions found in the review, first, conflict perceptions matter, but there is no concept of their formation in the first place. Actually, sanctions are generally held to be exogenous to perceptions of the conflict itself. Even when some studies take senders' demands and decisions about coercion as endogenous to conflict, i.e. conflict exerting an influence on them, they largely ignore the possibility that sanctions in turn might also affect conflict perceptions. Yet why would the imposition of strong negative sanctions leave target perceptions of the conflict unaffected?

Second, the choice of strategies of sanctions supposedly matters with regard to different expectations on international conflict development, but particular sanction cannot be presumed *a priori* as 'negative' or 'positive', as Baldwin's observations about setting a *reference point* highlighted. Whether sanctions are positive or negative may rest in the eye of the beholder. Insofar as authors simply take the senders' viewpoint and do not take the targets' perspective into account, the conceptual premise conveniently eliminates the potential existence of an issue in the first place.

Third, sanctions may create political interests in the first place and affect tentative preferences, yet these continue to be broadly treated as given properties. Although mostly neglected, sanctions do affect the interests, resources and strategies of social groups within a target state. Hence, their material context influences political discourse. Studies that recognize the role of domestic political discourse, however, do not draw a systematic conceptual link to the international conflict dimension. Furthermore, it remains unclear why exactly political sanctions are frequently excluded, even with analyses that focus on discourse.

The review traced the disconnected theorizing that is present in the literature. There are a number of problematic disconnections. First, the theorizing of most conceptualizations is isolated across different levels of analysis. Typically, contributions focus either on the international conflict and reduce domestic society to a rational black box, or they seek to account for the political outcomes of sanctions efforts solely by dissecting the domestic politics of 'target' states in the sense of a closed system that is supposed to react to external stimuli. Second, and to some extent as a consequence of this point, existing conceptual approaches treat the meaning that sanctions acquire and conflict development as exogenous to each other. These disconnections effectively remove the relation between the development of conflict and the political meaning of sanctions out of consideration altogether.

Besides testifying to the relevance of both aspects of international conflict and domestic aspects of a target state, a number of factors from both levels indicate that basic and on-going formations of perceptions, expectations and, indeed, intersubjective meaning, matter much more than is appreciated by existing conceptualizations of international sanctions. Even though top-down approaches mostly treat perceptions and expectations as relational properties, subjective estimations and perceptions of conflict would by all means play an important role. Although 'strategic positions' may rely on capability estimates based on quantified measures, they are still ultimately subjective. There is at best an intersubjective consensus on positions. A daring conceptual premise in this context is the notion of the voluntarism of the target in face of coercion. To what extent the targets of coercive sanctions see themselves as indeed retaining freedom of choice is an open question that remains entirely unaddressed. Exploring it further though would imply opening up the domestic black box. There, social groups will indeed conceive particular sanctions differently. As Kirshner implied, such discriminating effects are apt to politicize social groups and to create new political interests. These developments are liable to influence perceptions of international conflict and of the legitimacy of sanctions, and they will contribute to the development of any preferences attributed to a target state.

Generally, what is missing from research on international sanctions is conflict opponents' construction of social reality. Indeed, studies keep the notion of opponents, of their positions/preferences and of sanctions firmly transfixed, even when the social phenomenon described is fundamentally dynamic. Sanctions seek to change conflict – at least that is the premise of studies of sanctions as coercive instruments. Accordingly, the main criticism raised in the review of existing literature goes against a *'static' understanding* of sanctions conflicts.

The numerous individual observations pertaining to the identified issues point to a larger problem. Existing conceptualizations of coercive international sanctions generally subscribe to a rationalist-positivist research program.[15] There are two aspects to this problem. First, assumptions that are limited, on the one hand, more generally to the prevalent operational logic of coercive international sanctions of cost/benefits manipulating a target state's utility calculus and, on the other hand, to a societal transmission belt of 'economic impact → political pressure', both rely on a simple sender-receiver model of 'communication'. That is, the economic measures together with a 'sender's' stated conditions unambiguously 'transmit' to the 'target'; the same goes for the domestic 'transmission' of economic impact into political pressure, and political pressure into political consequences. However, this model is put into doubt already by the basic issue of the reference point from which a sanction appears as either a negative or positive one. Conceptually, sanctions are part of engagement in foreign policy, coercive diplomacy and communication in international conflict. That is, they are contextual to a wider social phenomenon and need to be conceptualized accordingly.

Second, as Jeffrey Checkel (2001) observes, the underlying methodological individualism effectively prevents any substantial conceptualization of the bases of the implied formation processes.[16] It effectively precludes any comprehensive appreciation of an endogenous relation between conflict and sanctions; it limits the extent to which the formation and development of perceptions and interests can be appreciated as a dynamic social process beyond an input/output scheme; and it limits the recognition of interactions between relational processes of international conflict and domestic political processes. Thus, for example, game-theoretical approaches popular in the sanctions and bargaining literature have clear structural limits, with their focus set on *given* properties, players, rules and payoffs.

What *meaning* sanctions and a conflict may acquire is not a trivial matter to be cast aside, as numerous investigations of sanctions conflicts strongly suggest. It is thus first necessary to thoroughly *understand how sanctions work* in order to approach the question of when they might be successful, and when they might fail. Coercive international sanctions are part of relational conflict processes and the domestic social construction of these conflict relations. The issues identified in the literature review suggest a more holistic theorizing regarding how international sanctions conflicts are socially constructed in the first place.

Notes

1 This is a very simple illustration using sheer numbers, which does not include any consideration of the significance and meaning of particular cases.
2 Even in a purely econometric analysis, negative and positive sanctions are not identical, once the attitude of a target (assumed a unitary rational actor) towards risk as unitary rational actor is taken into account (Bergeijk 1994).
3 Since Galtung's paper, scholars have observed different instruments of negative sanctions and examined them extensively. Most of this work indeed focused on trade sanctions, while other instruments, such as financial and monetary sanctions, came increasingly under scrutiny. Notably, Jonathan Kirshner (1995) produced a careful conceptual examination of monetary sanctions. Broadly speaking, however, examinations of different instruments generally did not aim to scrutinize the validity of the basic operational logic of sanctions, but rather ascertained their effectiveness under various empirical settings. In consequence, this research can be classified as technocratic empiricism and some of its results are discussed below.
4 Non-economic instruments include the evocation/revocation of diplomatic recognition, international isolation, travel bans (personal, tourism), suspension of negotiations/agreements, political encroachment (declarations, military intimidation).
5 Blanchard and Ripsman (1999) explicitly note the importance of incurring *political* costs and include non-economic sanctions at least as 'compound' sanctions.
6 There is additional literature exploring the role of multilateral cooperation but its significance remains controversial (Martin 1993; Bapat and Morgan 2009; McLean and Whang 2010).
7 Depending on such constraints arising from dependence on public support, even 'innocent bystanders' in fact may sometimes make for effective target groups in order to 'transmit' impact into pressure, contravening the ethics of 'targeted' sanctions (Major and McGann 2005).
8 For Schimmelfennig et al. the trick is that with the adoption of norms and rules, reinforcement increasingly occurs through 'domestic enforcement mechanisms'.
9 Pape's restrictive evaluation of the success rate of economic sanctions, however, is at least as questionable as the original HSE assessment (see Baldwin and Pape 1998).
10 Nevertheless, Morgan and Schwebach used individual indicators of the HSE data set for their own analysis after making some modifications.
11 Sanctions are classified into ten different types: 1. Total Economic Embargo, 2. Partial Economic Embargo, 3. Import Restriction, 4. Export Restriction, 5. Blockade, 6. Asset Freeze, 7. Termination of Foreign Aid, 8. Travel Ban, 9. Suspension of Economic Agreement, 10. Other.
12 Carrots are classified into five different types: 1. Economic Payments, 2. Trade Concessions, 3. Removal of Previous Sanctions, 4. Military Aid, 5. Political Concessions (e.g. diplomatic recognition).
13 Diplomatic Sanctions are classified into four different types: 1. Expulsion of Ambassador, 2. Recall of Ambassador, 3. Temporary Closing of Embassies, 4. Ending Diplomatic Contact.
14 The 'disutility' caused by targeted sanctions like financial restrictions or even flight bans is, of course, rather difficult to capture. Information and assessment is not entirely given in a formalized manner and is in part only accessible through interviews.

15 In fact, of the literature reviewed, only Klotz's work on norms as promoted by sanctions advances a significantly different, constructivist ontology.

16 Irrespective of possibly included factors such as different regime types – this would only affect impact, pressure and consequences but does not change the sender–receiver model.

Bibliography

Allen, Susan Hannah. (2008) Political Institutions and Constrained Response to Economic Sanctions. *Foreign Policy Analysis* 4: 255–274.

Ang, Adrian U-Jin, and Dursun Peksen. (2007) When Do Economic Sanctions Work? Asymmetric Perceptions, Issue Salience, and Outcomes. *Political Research Quarterly* 60: 135–145.

Baldwin, David A. (1971) The Power of Positive Sanctions. *World Politics* 24: 19–38.

Baldwin, David A. (1985) *Economic Statecraft*. Princeton, NJ: Princeton University Press.

Baldwin, David A. (2000) The Sanctions Debate and the Logic of Choice. *International Security* 24: 80–107.

Baldwin, David A., and Robert A. Pape. (1998) Evaluating Economic Sanctions. *International Security* 23: 189–198.

Bapat, Navin A., and T. Clifton Morgan. (2009) Multilateral versus Unilateral Sanctions Reconsidered: A Test Using New Data. *International Studies Quarterly* 53: 1075–1094.

Bergeijk, Peter A. G. van. (1994) *Economic Diplomacy, Trade and Commercial Policy: Positive and Negative Sanctions in a New World Order*. Aldershot: Elgar.

Bernauer, Thomas, and Dieter Ruloff. (1999) *The Politics of Positive Incentives in Arms Control*. Columbia: University of South Carolina Press.

Biersteker, Thomas J., and Sue E. Eckert. (2006) *Strengthening Targeted Sanctions through Fair and Clear Procedures: White Paper*. Providence, RI: Watson Institute for International Studies, Brown University.

Blanchard, Jean-Marc F., and Norrin M. Ripsman. (1999) Asking the Right Question: When Do Economic Sanctions Work Best? *Security Studies* 9: 219.

Brooks, Risa A. (2002) Sanctions and Regime Type: What Works, and When? *Security Studies* 11: 1.

Brzoska, Michael. (2001) *Smart Sanctions: The Next Steps: The Debate on Arms Embargoes and Travel Sanctions within the "Bonn-Berlin Process"*. Bonn International Center for Conversion, Nomos.

Brzoska, Michael. (2003) From Dumb to Smart – Recent Reforms of UN Sanctions. *Global Governance* 9: 519.

Checkel, Jeffrey T. (2001) Why Comply? Social Learning and European Identity Change. *International Organization* 55: 553–588.

Cortright, David. (1997) *The Price of Peace: Incentives and International Conflict Prevention*. Lanham: Rowman & Littlefield Publishers.

Cortright, David, and George A. Lopez. (2002) *Smart Sanctions: Targeting Economic Statecraft*. Lanham: Rowman & Littlefield Publishers.

Crawford, Neta C., and Audie Klotz. (1999a) How Sanctions Work: A Framework for Analysis. In *How Sanctions Work*, edited by Neta C. Crawford and Audie Klotz. London: Macmillan.

Crawford, Neta C., and Audie Klotz. (1999b) *How Sanctions Work: Lessons from South Africa*. London: Macmillan.

Crumm, Eileen M. (1995) The Value of Economic Incentives in International Politics. *Journal of Peace Research* 32: 313–330.
Davis, James W. (2000) *Threats and Promises: The Pursuit of International Influence*. Baltimore: Johns Hopkins University Press.
Drezner, Daniel W. (1999) *The Sanctions Paradox: Economic Statecraft and International Relations*. Cambridge: Cambridge University Press.
Drezner, Daniel W. (2003) The Hidden Hand of Economic Coercion. *International Organization* 57: 643–659.
Eaton, Jonathan, and Maxim Engers. (1992) Sanctions. *The Journal of Political Economy* 100: 899–928.
Escribà-Folch, Abel, and Joseph Wright. (2010) Dealing with Tyranny: International Sanctions and the Survival of Authoritarian Rulers. *International Studies Quarterly* 54: 335–359.
Fitzgerald, Peter L. (2001) Managing Smart Sanctions against Terrorism Wisely. *New England Law Review* 36: 957.
Freedman, Lawrence. (1998) *Strategic Coercion: Concepts and Cases*. Oxford: Oxford University Press.
Freedman, Lawrence. (2004) *Deterrence*. Cambridge: Polity Press.
Galtung, Johan. (1967) On the Effects of International Economic Sanctions: With Examples from the Case of Rhodesia. *World Politics* 19: 378–416.
George, Alexander Lawrence. (1991) *Forceful Persuasion: Coercive Diplomacy as an Alternative to War*. Washington, DC: US Institute of Peace Press.
Haass, Richard N., and Meghan L. O'Sullivan. (2000) *Honey and Vinegar: Incentives, Sanctions, and Foreign Policy*. Washington, DC: Brookings Institution Press.
Hazelzet, Haldewych. (2001) *Carrots or Sticks? EU and USA Sanctions in Reaction to Human Rights Violations*. Florence: European University Institute.
Hirschman, Albert. (1969) *National Power and the Structure of Foreign Trade*. Berkeley: University of California Press.
Hufbauer, Gary, Jeffrey Schott, and Kimberly Ann Elliott. (2007) *Economic Sanctions Reconsidered*. 3rd ed. Washington, DC: Institute for International Economics.
Jervis, Robert. (1976) *Perception and Misperception in International Politics*. Princeton, NJ: Princeton University Press.
Jones, Lee. (2015) *Societies Under Siege: Exploring How International Economic Sanctions (Do Not) Work*. Oxford: Oxford University Press.
Kaempfer, William H., and Anton David Lowenberg. (1988) The Theory of International Economic Sanctions: A Public Choice Approach. *The American Economic Review* 78: 786–793.
Kaempfer, William H., and Anton David Lowenberg. (1992) *International Economic Sanctions: A Public Choice Perspective*. Boulder: Westview.
Kirshner, Jonathan. (1995) *Currency and Coercion: The Political Economy of International Monetary Powers: The Political Economy of International Monetary Power*. Princeton, NJ: Princeton University Press.
Kirshner, Jonathan. (1997) The Microfoundations of Economic Sanctions. *Security Studies* 6: 32–64.
Klotz, Audie. (1995) *Norms in International Relations: The Struggle against Apartheid*. Ithaca: Cornell University Press.
Kreps, Sarah, and Zain Pasha. (2012) Threats for Peace? The Domestic Distributional Effects of Military Threats. In *Sanctions, Statecraft, and Nuclear Proliferation*, edited by Etel Solingen. Cambridge: Cambridge University Press.

Krustev, Valentin L. (2010) Strategic Demands, Credible Threats, and Economic Coercion Outcomes. *International Studies Quarterly* 54: 147–174.

Lacy, Dean, and Emerson M. S. Niou. (2004) A Theory of Economic Sanctions and Issue Linkage: The Roles of Preferences, Information, and Threats. *Journal of Politics* 66: 25–42.

Lebow, Richard Ned. (2005) Deterrence: Then and Now. *Journal of Strategic Studies* 28: 765–773.

Lektzian, David, and Mark Souva. (2007) An Institutional Theory of Sanctions Onset and Success. *Journal of Conflict Resolution* 51: 848–871.

Long, William J. (1996) *Economic Incentives and Bilateral Cooperation*. Ann Arbor: University of Michigan Press.

Lopez, George A., and David Cortright. (1997) Economic Sanctions and Human Rights: Part of the Problem or Part of the Solution? *The International Journal of Human Rights* 1: 1.

Major, Solomon, and Anthony J. McGann. (2005) Caught in the Crossfire "Innocent Bystanders" as Optimal Targets of Economic Sanctions. *Journal of Conflict Resolution* 49: 337–359.

Martin, Lisa L. (1993) *Coercive Cooperation: Explaining Multilateral Economic Sanctions*. Princeton, NJ: Princeton University Press.

McLean, Elena V., and Taehee Whang. (2010) Friends or Foes? Major Trading Partners and the Success of Economic Sanctions. *International Studies Quarterly* 54: 427–447.

Morgan, T. Clifton, Navin Bapat, and Valentin Krustev. (2009) The Threat and Imposition of Economic Sanctions, 1971–2000. *Conflict Management and Peace Science* 26: 92–110.

Morgan, T. Clifton, Valentin Krustev, and Navin A. Bapat. (2013) Threat and Imposition of Sanctions (TIES). Available at: www.unc.edu/~bapat/TIES.htm. (Accessed July 10, 2013).

Morgan, T. Clifton, and Valerie L. Schwebach. (1997) Fools Suffer Gladly: The Use of Economic Sanctions in International Crises. *International Studies Quarterly* 41: 27–50.

Newnham, Randall. (2002) *Deutsche Mark Diplomacy: Positive Economic Sanctions in German-Russian Relations*. University Park, PA: Pennsylvania State University Press.

Nincic, Miroslav. (2012) The Domestic Distributional Effects of Sanctions and Positive Inducements. In *Sanctions, Statecraft, and Nuclear Proliferation*, edited by Etel Solingen. Cambridge: Cambridge University Press.

Pape, Robert A. (1997) Why Economic Sanctions Do Not Work. *International Security* 22: 90–136.

Pelc, Krzysztof J. (2010) Constraining Coercion? Legitimacy and Its Role in U.S. Trade Policy, 1975–2000. *International Organization* 64: 65–96.

Portela, Clara. (2010) *European Union Sanctions and Foreign Policy: When and Why Do They Work?* London: Routledge.

Schelling, Thomas C. (1960) *The Strategy of Conflict*. Cambridge, MA: Harvard University Press.

Schimmelfennig, Frank, Stefan Engert, and Heiko Knobel. (2006) *International Socialization in Europe: European Organizations, Political Conditionality, and Democratic Change*. Basingstoke: Palgrave Macmillan.

Selden, Zachary. (1999) *Economic Sanctions as Instruments of American Foreign Policy*. Westport, CT: Praeger.

Smith, Alastair. (1995) The Success and Use of Economic Sanctions. *International Interactions: Empirical and Theoretical Research in International Relations* 21: 229.

Solingen, Etel. (2012) The Domestic Distributional Effects of Sanctions and Positive Inducements. In *Sanctions, Statecraft, and Nuclear Proliferation*, edited by Etel Solingen. Cambridge: Cambridge University Press.

Swiss Federal Office for Foreign Economic Affairs. (1998) *Expert Seminar on Targeting UN Financial Sanctions*. Interlaken.

Swiss Federal Office for Foreign Economic Affairs. (1999) *2nd Interlaken Seminar on Targeting United Nations Financial Sanctions*.

Van Elsuwege, Peter. (2011) The Adoption of "Targeted Sanctions" and the Potential for Inter-Institutional Litigation after Lisbon. *Journal of Contemporary European Research* 7: 488–499.

Wagner, R. Harrison. (1988) Economic Interdependence, Bargaining Power, and Political Influence. *International Organization* 42: 461–483.

Wallensteen, Peter, and Carina Staibano. (2003) *Making Targeted Sanctions Effective: Guidelines for the Implementation of UN Policy Options*. Uppsala, Sweden: Department of Peace and Conflict Research, Uppsala University.

3 A sociological theory of coercive international sanctions

Coercive sanctions are social facts constructed in conflict communication. Relations in sanctions conflicts are part of, and are (re)produced in, social processes. This chapter presents a sociological theory of international sanctions conflicts. It unfolds in a triad its conceptualization of sanctions conflicts. Each of the sections in this part represents an element of the triad, addressing one of the specific research questions raised: the meaning of sanctions, the social construction of sanctions conflicts and conflict transformation and the influence of sanctions upon it. The elements of the conceptual triad are interconnected. Each individual element refers to the other elements and remains incomplete without them.

The first element of this triad conceptualizes sanctions as inherently relational phenomena. Coercive sanctions, as a means of enforcing a decision in international conflict, convey a tension in their potential meaning in conflict communication. On the one hand, coercive sanctions appeal to cost/benefit calculations, offering a decision in a utilitarian rationale; on the other hand, they reflect a power rationale in seeking to enforce a decision. Sanctions imposed as a means of coercing decisions imply a distinction between decision-makers and those affected by the decision, corresponding to Niklas Luhmann's distinction between risk and danger: If agents attribute possible future conflict developments to their own decisions, then that reflects an observation of risk, whereas an external attribution of such decisions amounts to an observation of danger. Negative, positive or combined sanctions strategies convey this tension in their potential meaning differently. The selection of a particular meaning depends on their social construction in conflict communication.

The second element of the triad introduces and builds on a model of conflict based on communication. The kind of meaning that sanctions will ultimately acquire is endogenous to the conflict they are part of, there is a need to enquire into the peculiarities of on-going conflict communication. In other words, in order to address what meaning sanctions effectively communicate, it is necessary to take into account how international conflict constructs adversaries in the first place. Sanctions conflicts consist either of communicated interest or identity incompatibilities. Issue conflicts that communicate incompatible interests are susceptible to a utility rationale. Once conflicts have escalated to communicating identity incompatibilities, agents ascribe responsibility, attribute causality and question the legitimacy of the Other in a way that makes cooperation unviable. Depending on on-going conflict communication, sanctions are more likely to communicate either a utility or a power rationale. Yet at the same time, sanctions as actions in conflict communication influence what meaning conflict acquires and may in turn promote conflict transformation. Thus the meaning of sanctions and conflict communication are in a dialectical relation.

Finally, the third element of the triad is about conflict transformation. The concept of securitization allows conflict escalation to be delineated as a qualitative shift in communication that is decisive for prospects of cooperation and non-cooperation in sanctions conflicts. I establish securitization as a theory of agency and posit it as a causal mechanism. As a theory of agency, securitization represents a particular engagement with contingency. In applying the pragmatist conception of agency developed by Mustafa Emirbayer and Ann Mische, securitization indicates how agency provides for its own necessity through securitizing moves that construct a crisis in meaning and contingency, to which it is offered as a solution. Securitization rejects a communicated power rationale and the implied deprivation of agency and decision by providing a rival solution: as an assertion of agency in claiming a 'threat'. It thereby effectively links the meaning of sanctions along a power rationale to conflict transformation. As a causal mechanism, securitization goes beyond the causal attributions made by agents in social practice to an analytical level: a securitized sanctions conflict implies non-cooperation.

Demarcating the theory's scientific ontology

The theory presented in the subsequent chapters heterogeneously draws on conceptual elements that can be assigned to different research paradigms. Its sociological perspective posits an understanding of sanctions that rest on the "intersections and interactions among multiple social processes in different domains of social reality" (Sil and Katzenstein 2010:12) – or, rather, 'images' of different domains – that contribute to the development of the meaning in international conflict. The emphasis the theory puts on social processes of communication and its notion of conflict as exhibiting intrinsic dynamics aims to capture consequential factors that resist a reduction to individualist accounts; its pragmatist notion of agency, however, underscores the role of human actors in the unfolding of social processes. Such an analytic eclecticist approach "allows us to ask questions about features of international politics that are assumed away by other paradigms" (Finnemore 1996:328).

There are pitfalls involved, though, in any attempt at an inter-paradigmatic stance, if we neglect the inherent tensions involved in synthesizing concepts from different theoretical edifices (Harvey and Cobb 2003). In the remainder of this introductory section, I will therefore outline the terms of the theory's scientific ontology. These are the basic terms upon which the theory is built. The section eclectically introduces Niklas Luhmann's notion of communication as the basic denominator of social reality, along with a pragmatist notion of agency as engagement with contingency. It thereby also illustrates the bases of the theory's decisive departure from existing rationalist, methodological individualist approaches to coercive international sanctions.

The sociological theory of international sanctions conflicts follows a social ontology. It maintains that in international sanctions conflicts, much of the politics revolves around the construction of meaning. Whatever their material base may be, sanctions acquire relevance through their meaning and operation as social facts. This view is part of a sociological, 'communicative' turn in IR that foresees agency and causality as communicative artefacts (Albert, Kessler, and Stetter 2008). Social reality is entirely subsumable to communication. The social construction of meaning thus becomes the primary subject of social scientific investigation.

'Communication', as established by Niklas Luhmann, consists of contingent social selection processes that construct phenomena as well as actors and agency in a socially meaningful way. Reality is continuously reproduced in communication and is inseparable from it. 'Social facts' are synthetic products, endogenous to social context: "What counts for a socially meaningful object or event is always the result of an interpretive construction" (Guzzini 2000:159; cf. Palan 2000; Friedrichs and Kratochwil 2009). This directs the research interest towards investigating the social processes involved in the formation of social facts and their development.

There is no simple sender–receiver communication. Meaning tends to be pluralistic, context-dependent and dynamic (cf. Wittgenstein 1974). Communication as the underlying process reflects a situation of double contingency: In any initial encounter between *Alter* and *Ego*, their respective range of possible meaning determination remains potentially unlimited (Luhmann 1995:106). This raises two immediate problems. First, there is the problem of action: When it comes to interaction between agents there is the possibility of refusing to interact. Such an option does not exist for communication, however. Given a proper medium, it is not possible to not communicate. A refusal to interact already communicates something. Action and agency are artefacts in communication. Their interpretation is endogenous to social process, their recognition depends on the social: "The terms of individual agency remain very much the product of the ongoing relations in which they are embedded" (Nexon 2010:101; cf. Guzzini 2000).

Second, there is the problem of unintended consequences: When communicating (or acting, as part of communication), there is no way of guaranteeing that the proposed consequences will materialize. Unintended consequences are just as much part of an action as are intended consequences. Thanks to double contingency, the attribution of consequences to an action is an entirely social process: Action is not satisfyingly captured when its analysis solely focuses on individualistic authorship and the pursuance of preconceived ends. Rather, "communication among all those concerned plays an essential role" (Joas 1993:24). Unintended consequences inevitably raise the question of social process.

These issues suggest that reducing social reality to interaction is limiting and insufficient. A conception of the social in terms of interaction already takes as given what is actually not without presuppositions. Most prominently, it reifies the notion of action and agency. Such a step already implicates other highly meaningful attributions such as intentionality, responsibility, consequences and causality. This means foreclosing an investigation into the conditions under which such meanings emerge. Thus, a full-fledged consideration of the consequences of such attributions is no longer possible.

Communication as the denominator of social reality refers to the synthesis of the difference between information, utterance and understanding (Luhmann 1995:145–154). In Luhmann's conceptualization of this process as the basis of all sociality, an utterance refers to an observer's selection of understanding that inherently includes the possibility of a competing selection. Accordingly, communication exists only once there is a particular *understanding*, which constructs actors, meaning and agency. In this recursive process, communication suggests a meaning, which can either be accepted or rejected by producing another, competing meaning in communication.

With a perspective that is committed to communication as its analytical base, meaning does not reside with objects or subjects. What is decisive is the *social processing* of meaning: "Meaning ('Sinn') then forms the general medium of communication" (Albert 2010:52). Meaning emerges out of a communicative process comprising intersubjective attributions, whether intentionally made or not. Meaning promotes certain 'views', a certain 'reality', and puts them center stage, while demoting others. It is never fully fixed. I will refer to this un-owned selection of meaning as *social process*.

It is analytically of interest to such an approach to look at the specific ways of socially constructing meaning: how observers draw distinctions, make selections and how communication eventually constructs actors. In systems theory terminology, analyzing social reality "shift[s] from observing objects to observing observations" (Jaeger 2010:70). In other words (although this is inevitably a re-interpretation), the analysis focuses on the concrete patterns of social objectification. I will refer to these concrete patterns, which perform the attribution of meaning, agency and causality as *social practices*.

I will highlight two ontological implications that stem from this communicative turn, one for contingency and expectations and the other for the notion of agency. First, the double contingency in social relations leads to a significant potential for uncertainty for those involved. 'Action', 'consequences' and 'intentions' are all endogenous to process and become expressed in practices. However, we obviously do not observe that 'anything goes'. On the contrary, repeated communication permits the development of expectations, which in turn reduce contingency. Iterative patterns of common distinctions, 'symbols' (Mead), or 'semantic forms' (Luhmann) socially stabilize and objectify meaning, enabling intersubjective understanding. In that sense, they ensure a socially objectified relation among a sequence of social actions (Herborth 2004:78).

The second implication is that the communicative turn suggests a repositioning of agency. Agency resides with the "creative solution of problems by an experimenting intelligence" (Joas 1993:248). Of course, for such creative solutions to *social* problems to exist, they need social recognition, since agency and social action depend on social attribution. That is, agency socially exists only as ascription of meaning in communication. However, contrary to Luhmann, who was interested in a macro-sociological theory of social systems, this approach to international sanctions conflicts retains an interest in actor-reproducing social practices. The distinction between social process that reflects the abstract notion of meaning emergence in communication and social practices that reflect concrete patterns of social objectification extends to the notion of 'agents' and 'actors'. I refer to 'agents' as meaning content that emerges through social ascription processes. Agents are abstractions in communication. By contrast, 'actors' are entities reified in patterns of social practices.

The study takes a conception of agency as creative intelligence and connects it with the notion of contingency in communication.[1] That is, contingency is potentially always present in practices, resting on the fact that any selection in communication includes on principle the possibility of its alternatives. Whenever tensions emerge, or situations are socially constructed as such, iterative practices no longer work and contingency becomes prevalent: "the specifically political emerges when action takes place in a situation in which no reference to a common value system can be established, but a choice is made" (Guzzini 2010:306; cf. Kratochwil 1971). In a way, in questioning established ways of processing actions by challenging their constitutive bases, i.e. established symbols, such situations represent a crisis in meaning communication. What is decisive for such crises is if, and to what extent, formerly accepted routinized meanings are questioned (Herborth 2004:79); these crises denote a radical openness and represent an opportunity for political agency in a moment of contingency (cf. Jackson 2006:32f.). They require a political intervention to establish meaning; a selection has to be made to provide closure.

Taken together, both the 'un-owned' processing of meaning centered on communication and the notion of creative agency in a moment of contingency rest on meaning emergence as an inherently social phenomenon. Yet they seem to differ in their notion of the wider system in which the production of meaning is embedded. Proponents of a pragmatist view describe it as an open system. Indeed, the notion of agency as creative intelligence (Joas 1993) builds on an understanding that meaning is never fixed. However, even if meaning is inherently pluralistic, and even if any communicated meaning suggestion can be accepted and rejected, meaning always concatenates with further meaning (Luhmann 1995:62). 'Meaning' cannot be followed by no meaning (*Un-Sinn*). Social process thus ensures closure in communication. Social process is on the one hand fundamentally open; closure occurs through selecting a *meaningful* follow-up operation in communication (Luhmann 1995:154).

Structure of the chapter

The above discussion has presented the basic terms of a social ontology of the sociological theory of international sanctions conflicts that I will later develop in more detail. It has clarified the points of departure from existing rationalist, methodological individualist approaches to coercive international sanctions. With social reality emerging entirely out of communication and the consequent methodological shift from 'truth' to 'meaning', the social construction of meaning involved and the practices that attribute agency and causality become of primary theoretical interest.

The sections that follow below unfold in a triad the sociological theory of international sanctions conflicts. The triad develops an analytical model of coercive sanctions with a focus on conflict transformation. Each element of the triad addresses one of the specific research questions that were raised: the meaning attached to sanctions, the social construction of conflict and the influence of particular sanctions strategies on conflict transformation. The theory argues that conflict relations and the meaning of sanctions are endogenous to each other. Negative, positive and combined sanctions strategies promote different meanings within on-going international conflict and affect subsequent conflict development differently.

Whether sanctions are conducive to non-cooperation or to cooperation depends on how conflict communication constructs adversaries and on how agents conceive of sanctions as decisions within conflict. The concluding section draws the main insights of the individual elements together and formulates the prospects of non-cooperation and cooperation for particular sanctions strategies in international conflicts.

3.1 The meaning of sanctions in conflict communication

> One man's risk is another man's danger.
>
> – Niklas Luhmann[2]

Coercive sanctions are social facts relationally constructed in international conflict. Whatever their potential material base, sanctions do not simply transmit their meaning from a 'sender' to a 'target'. To reflect that, this theory of coercive international sanctions deliberately departs from the usual terminology in the sanctions literature of 'sender' and 'target' in favor of 'initiator' and 'addressee'. This section conceptualizes the way in which agents socially construct the meaning of coercive sanctions in mutual conflict. It addresses the first of the specific research questions, regarding the meaning that coercive sanctions acquire as actions concerning the position of an opponent. The study theorizes the meaning of sanctions as communicated actions constructed as decisions in mutual conflict. As communicated actions, sanctions contain a tension between the offering of a choice to the addressee and the imposition of an initiator's decision on a conflict. Coercive sanctions are thus particular kinds of actions with a tension regarding their meaning in conflict communication between opponents. The section further outlines how particular sanctions strategies promote different meaning potentials in conflict communication.

The notion of coercive sanctions as actions that are relationally constructed takes a significantly different conceptual starting point to the one taken by existing concepts of coercive sanctions. In conceptualizing economic statecraft as an instrument of foreign policy, David Baldwin preferred it to the notion of 'economic coercion' when discussing conceptual merits. Baldwin did so on the grounds that the latter was a 'relational concept' whereas the former was a 'property concept': "To describe an influence attempt of [A upon B] as 'coercive' says as much about B's perceptions and value system as it says about A's policy choice" (Baldwin 1985:39). As a property concept, 'economic statecraft' depends for its meaning solely on the initiator's intent.

Likewise, reductionist approaches to international sanctions such as rationalist and game theory conceptions largely factor out communication. These approaches assume rational states-as-players who act strategically. Utility calculation on external stimuli substitutes for communication. Yet it remains entirely inconceivable how addressees, or 'targets', could realistically conceive of the whole plot as 'sanctions' in the first place, when conflict communication (or social construction in general) is simply presumed away, out of the enquiry – when is the action of another player a coercive sanction? When is it merely a part of its economic policy?

This theory takes exactly the opposite approach to the one that Baldwin suggested and to the one upon which rationalist approaches rest. In keeping with the social ontological bases of this investigation, the meaning that sanctions acquire is inherent to conflict communication. Based on the conclusions that the study drew from the critical review of the literature on coercive international sanctions, this sociological conceptualization addresses three specific conceptual issues. First, the conceptualization recognizes the idiosyncrasies of negative and positive sanctions strategies, and it also addresses combined sanctions strategies. Combined sanctions strategies refer to the simultaneous use of negative and positive sanctions. They are, in other words, neither purely negative, nor purely positive.

Second, there is the issue of the reference point. What the initiator of positive sanctions might see as a mere reduction to an incentive that is still positive, the addressee may interpret as a different development. Whether it is indeed positive or negative is in the eye of the observer. Whether a measure is coercive – negative or positive – depends on the meaning it acquires in conflict communication.

Third, the conceptualization should not be biased against non-economic instruments. When sanctions are a means to coerce *politically*, the conceived costs and benefits are *per definitionem* not limited to economic terms. And neither should be the means associated with these costs. Whether agents conceive of measures as coercive sanctions lies with the meaning they acquire in communication.

This investigation builds conceptually on the notion that coercive international sanctions are a means of enforcing a decision in conflict. It takes the meaning of sanctions as endogenous to social process. That is, meaning neither resides exclusively with the initiator nor with the addressee. The analytical shift of attention towards meaning in communication shifts conceptual focus on the distinctions and attributions that construct both sanctions as decisions and the agents involved. In order to illuminate this, the study takes up Niklas Luhmann's distinction between risk and danger in the observation of actions as communicated decisions on possible future outcomes.

The first part of this section presents the concept of sanctions as coercive actions in communication along two dimensions. First, on an agency dimension, coercive sanctions are actions constructed as decisions by agents in international conflict. Sanctions as decisions on conflict may conform either to observations of risk or to observations of danger. In short, if agents attribute possible future conflict developments to their own decisions, then that reflects an observation of risk, whereas an external attribution of such decisions amounts to an observation of danger. Such meaning potential exists on both 'sides' of the conflict. Second, on a relational dimension, coercive sanctions communicate a tension in meaning between a utility rationale suggesting that there is a choice for the addressee to decide upon, and a power rationale, where the initiator's decision is imposed upon the mutual conflict. The section addresses each dimension in turn. The two dimensions are conceptually entwined with one another.

In the second part, I connect the developed conceptualization of the meaning of sanctions in general to particular sanctions strategies. Particular sanctions strategies relate differently to the inherent tension in the meaning of sanctions. Negative sanctions suggest an external decisional attribution and emphasize a power rationale. By contrast, positive sanctions emphasize a utility rationale and suggest an observation of decision as risk to an addressee. Combined sanctions strategies are initially indifferent. Overall, the conceptualization takes the meaning of sanctions as contingent upon its construction in conflict communication. It lays the basis of the sociological approach to international sanctions conflicts for understanding the conditions of possibility for cooperation and non-cooperation.

3.1.1 Sanctions, risk and danger

Coercive sanctions are social facts. They are socially constructed by agents in a conflict. There are two conceptual dimensions involved in constructing coercive sanctions. First, agents construct coercive sanctions as a particular type of action. Sanctions as *coercive* actions are about decision on a conflict, decisions that influence the further course of a conflict. Second, coercive sanctions are relational phenomena. Imposed by an initiator on an addressee, sanctions are communicated actions in a mutual conflict. As communicated actions, their meaning is subject to a double contingency. That is, it depends as much on the addressee's understanding as it does on the initiator's actions. The meaning that sanctions acquire as relational actions emerges from how agents construct them as decisions on conflict. In constructing meaning, the first dimension of agency and decision and the second, relational dimension, are closely interrelated. This section conceptualizes each dimension in turn.

Agency dimension

The theory conceptualizes coercive sanctions in terms of the relational construction of actions as decisions in international conflict. In the first dimension, taking coercive sanctions as social facts, agents construct sanctions as actions in terms of a decision on further conflict development. Sanctions constructed as a means of coercing decisions convey a potential distinction between decision-makers and those affected by the decision. Coercive sanctions imply that one side decides on a mutual conflict that includes an 'Other'. To elucidate these circumstances, it is helpful to analyze how agents observe action and decision in a sanctions conflict and the social ascriptions involved therein.

Niklas Luhmann's sociology of risk advances a notion of action constructed as decision. 'Risk' makes potential future developments contingent upon decisions in the present: "losses that may occur in the future are attributed to decisions made" (Luhmann 1993:101). In this notion, the other side of the form of risk is not the rejection of this contingency, but rather the *external* attribution of decision.

Coercive sanctions communication reflects a similar logic. For the initiator as an agent in communication, decisions on sanctions concern the imposition of measures to influence possible developments and outcomes in the *future*. Initiators of coercive sanctions conceive of conflict development as contingent on and susceptible to their decision.[3] Agency thus emphasizes a projective dimension: "What can occur in the future . . . depends on decisions to be made at present" (Luhmann 1993:16). In other words, to the initiator of coercive sanctions, they are a means of effectively exerting a decision on further conflict development to the extent that they make the addressee cooperate.

A few examples may illustrate how initiators introduce coercive sanctions as proposed observations of decision in international conflict. Multilateral sanctions as imposed by the United States, the European Union and the UN on Iran broadly seek to enforce a decision on the conflict regarding the country's nuclear program. The initiators of sanctions regard the future existence of Iranian nuclear capabilities as contingent and seek to avert its development. Similarly, sanctions in the context of the OECD Harmful Tax Practices Initiative against offshore financial centers are a means of enforcing a decision on the conflict on 'unfair' financial practices that encourage tax evasion, in the view of initiators. Even sanctions in the form of conditional development assistance to promote democratization and human rights (e.g. EU enlargement policies in Eastern Europe; EU, OECD DAC development policies) subscribe to the form of risk as a coercive means by initiators to promote a decision on a conflict. Thus coercive international sanctions largely reflect a form of risk as a means of enforcing a decision in conflict across a wide range of contexts.

Such a perspective on risk as contingent decision-making does not merely point to the uncertainties and information limits involved (Beck 1992); rather, it rests on analytically observing distinctions, selections and attributions made in communication. From such a perspective, it is irrelevant whether an agent 'consciously' perceives the context of decision as a risk.[4] What effectively matters from this perspective is that the construction of meaning follows the *form* of risk: "The only requirement is that the contingent loss be itself caused as a contingency, that is to say, it be avoidable" (Luhmann 1993:16).

In the attribution of consequences to decisions, coercive sanctions rest on "a controlled extension of rational action" (Luhmann 1993:13–14). The addressee of coercive sanctions as an agent in communication may full well subscribe in a similar way to a construction of action as a decision in the sense of risk, deciding on future outcomes. Accordingly, addressees would likewise conceive the future development of the conflict as contingent upon their decision as agents in communication.

However, there is another side to the distinction of the form of risk implicated in coercive international sanctions. This other side is the absence of attributing future consequences to one's own decision. When addressees attribute consequences *externally*, as being affected by the decisions of the Other, it represents a 'danger': "The affected party . . . sees himself as endangered by decisions that he neither makes himself nor controls. Self-attribution is not possible for him. He is dealing with dangers – even when he sees and reflects that, from the point of view of the decision maker . . . , it is a matter of risk" (Luhmann 1993:107). Most importantly then, risk allows the attribution of possible future outcomes to own decisions. With the observation of danger, addressees see future outcomes no longer as contingent upon their own decisions, that is, they attribute decisions externally. Risk as a semantic form marks a boundary with completely different conditions given on either side of the distinction: "the distinction risk/danger is constructed asymmetrically. . . . [O]nly in the case of risk does decision making (that is to say, contingency) play a role. One is exposed to dangers" (Luhmann 1993:23).[5] This makes 'decisional attribution' a decisive element. It separates decision-makers from those merely affected by the decisions, and it connects them in terms of observing risk and danger.

In the first dimension of coercive sanctions as social facts, the construction of sanctions as decision involves a distinction regarding the form of risk. Agents may construct their actions in terms of risk, engaging in decisions on potential future conflict developments. However, agents may also construct a danger from being only affected by externally-attributed decisions. Sanctions communicate both sides of the form, giving rise to potentially different relational meanings in a mutual conflict.

Relational dimension

The way in which agents construct sanctions as decision is entwined with the second dimension, the meaning sanctions acquire as relational phenomena in conflict communication. Sanctions as communicated actions are about decisions on a *mutual* conflict. Thus, there is a relational component to the meaning of sanctions concerning decision. Initiators of coercive sanctions aim to impose a decision on conflict, yet the observation of actual decision is conditional on a change in the addressee's political position. Coercive sanctions seek to manipulate the cost-benefit calculation of the Other, promoting a utility rationale. An addressee constructing a risk decides on the utility of its position in the conflict in the face of changing underlying political premises. In other words, when an addressee self-attributes a decision in a sanctions conflict in observing a risk, sanctions acquire a relational meaning in terms of a utility rationale.

So far, the notion of sanctions as a means of enforcing decision in conflict does accord to a significant degree with other, rationalist approaches to coercive international sanctions. Coercive sanctions promote a utility rationale to the extent that they are conditional on an addressee's political position towards cooperation in mutual conflict. However, it would also be premature to conclude the analysis here. There is a crucial precondition for such a construction of decision as 'risk' to prevail across sanctions conflicts. Conceiving of sanctions as promoting a utility rationale in the construction of action as decision is merely a *suggested meaning imposition in communication*. However, there is no simple sender–receiver communication; a utility rationale cannot be simply 'transmitted'. Communication subjects agents to a condition of double contingency, a situation wherein "what different observers consider to be the same thing generates quite different information for each of them" (Luhmann 1993:21).

Coercive sanctions are inherently relational phenomena in conflict communication and this second dimension needs to be fully considered. Sanctions as a coercive means of enforcing a decision on a conflict potentially convey a different meaning for the addressee, as one merely affected by the decisions of the initiator. In the end, coercion refers to one agent effectively influencing the range of political options that an addressee considers available in a mutual conflict; it thus takes both sides of this relation for an action to emerge as a coercive decision (Baldwin 1985:38–39). The form risk/danger delineates a communication of decision concerning the Other and highlights a power rationale, reflected in the distinction between decision-makers and those affected. At this point, contingency emerges as a crucial element. As noted above, the recognition of action is subject to a double contingency. If actions are communicated as decisions concerning the Other's actions, then there is a power necessity. Power thus emerges only in situations of double contingency, i.e. when decisions represent selections that could also be made differently (Luhmann 2000:59).

At first glance, the notion of sanctions communicating a utility or a power rationale may appear similar to the notion of relative and absolute gains prevalent in rationalist and neo-neo approaches to conflict and collaboration in international politics (e.g. Baldwin 1993) and in certain game-theoretical models of sanctions conflicts. To recapitulate, these approaches build on a highly idealized setup, assuming pre-given interests and, indeed, opponents' freedom of choice. The latter however depends on addressees observing consequences as being contingent upon their own decisions. Sanctions as exhibiting a meaning potential both along a utility and a power rationale thus qualify the notion of relative/absolute gains as being an artefact of an underlying conflict communication process that is analytically prior.

In terms of the meaning that coercive sanctions acquire as social facts, the dimension of action and decision and the relational dimension are closely linked. For agents in conflict communication, sanctions are intricately linked to attributing decision-making: to attribute outcomes to decisions made. Thus a key dimension to this sociological theory of coercive international sanctions is the observation of decision in communication, with its attribution of risk or danger. When agents attribute a possible future outcome to present decisions, a risk observation prevails. The use of sanctions to coerce in conflict aims to manipulate the cost/benefit calculation of the Other; it communicates a utility rationale. At the same time, however, it communicates a power rationale as coercive action that suggests an external attribution of decision. In the end, sanctions are a means of enforcing a decision in conflict, and one which subjects the addressee to that decision.

3.1.2 Sanctions rationales and sanctions strategies

The meaning potential of sanctions in communication conveys a tension. Coercive sanctions as a means of enforcing a decision in international conflict convey both a utility and a power rationale. On the one hand, coercive sanctions appeal to cost/benefit calculations, offering a decision in a utility rationale; on the other hand, they reflect a power rationale in seeking to enforce a decision on the conflict. Particular sanctions strategies promote different meaning potentials in terms of two intertwined dimensions of risk/danger, utility/power rationale (see Table 3.1). The tension between the two rationales of sanctions does not lead to an *a priori* selection of meaning, though. The presence of both rationales does, however, imply that specific sanctions strategies may promote either rationale differently.

The observation of negative sanctions strategies invites a distinction between decision-makers and those affected. When the addressee sees a basic necessity or right at issue, negative sanctions strategies, through their emphasis on denying, emphasize a power rationale. In following a power rationale, for the addressee "future losses are seen not at all as the consequences of a decision that has been made, but are attributed to an external factor" (Luhmann 1993:101f.). The addressee sees itself only in terms of being affected by the decisions of the Other in a situation that does not offer much of a 'choice' to the addressee but presents a *danger* to it, thus implying external decisional attribution. Thus, the notion that 'coercion' aims to influence the actions of an opponent as a 'voluntary agent' may not quite register with the opponent as Freedman (1998) presupposed.

Most straightforwardly, in their potential to challenge the addressee as decision-maker, negative sanctions touch upon a foundational institution of the modern state in a similar way to international interventions (Finnemore 2003:7). If state sovereignty means 'omnicompetence in power', then negative sanctions strategies

Table 3.1 Meaning potentials, sanctions rationales and sanctions strategies

Strategy	*Agency dimension*	*Relational dimension*
Negative sanctions	**External attribution: Danger** Self-attribution: Risk	**Power rationale** Utility rationale
Positive sanctions	**Self-attribution: Risk** External attribution: Danger	**Utility rationale** Power rationale
Combined sanctions	**Open**	**(Power + utility rationale)**

readily offer the grounds for constructing a danger. Generally, negative sanctions strategies provide an enabling condition of a meaning of sanctions as a danger to the addressee.

Positive sanctions strategies do not convey to the same extent the potential attributional consequences of negative sanctions. In positing an offer on which the addressee is in a position to decide, they emphasize much more a utility rationale. Their meaning potential in international conflict is thus decisively different. With positive sanctions strategies, the sides of the form no longer consist of risk to the initiator and danger to the addressee. Instead, both sides are represented: with the use of positive sanctions, risks may well turn into dangers for initiators, e.g. when observing a decision by the addressee not to make good on a commitment agreed to in exchange for an incentive that was offered previously. With the possibility of such an attribution occurring, "the distinction fails. The risk is the danger. The space distinguished is the same" (Luhmann 1993:121). From this perspective, as soon as the initiator has granted an incentive, the decision not to resume the conflict lies with the addressee (cf. Haass and O'Sullivan 2000:4).

In terms of constructing decision, negative and positive sanctions thus vary significantly. The reasoning that threats are cheaper than promises when they work, and promises are cheaper than threats when they fail, does not hold true for imposed sanctions, as is sometimes implied (Baldwin 1971:28).

A third type of sanctions strategies are combined sanctions. There is no longer the inevitable consequence of a strict distinction between sanctions decision-makers (who decide upon a risk) and those affected (by an external decision). In offering incentives and relying on costs at the same time, combined sanctions represent an openness and exhibit a logical 'undecidedness'. In their indeterminacy, their meaning potential between 'risk' and 'danger' as actions and decisions in conflict communication is open. Combined sanctions strategies are different from negative or positive sanctions strategies in their initial indifference toward both utility and power rationale. For combined sanctions strategies it is no longer possible to exclude *a priori* particular possibilities.

Particular sanctions strategies, with their status as 'negative' or 'positive' itself being conditional on social construction, promote certain meanings more than others. Thus, the selection of specific sanctions strategies in social practice bears consequences for subsequent conflict development. Some sanctions strategies may promote a construction of decision as risk; others will promote an observation of danger. To this extent, the selection of particular strategies in social practice amounts to enabling a certain meaning potential; they are not deterministic. Conversely, however, in enabling some possibilities, these selections also impede certain other possibilities. They thus discriminatively promote varying meaning potentials in the ensuing conflict communication.

3.1.3 Conclusion

Coercive sanctions are a means of enforcing a decision in international conflict. Agents that self-attribute such decisions in relation to future conflict development subscribe to a construction of decision as 'risk'. Conversely, an external attribution of decision amounts to an observation of 'danger'. In principle, sanctions carry the meaning potential of both sides. Decisional attribution, however, means drawing a boundary, between decision-makers responsible for a situation or an outcome, and those merely affected by the decision. Sanctions as relational phenomena in communication give rise to a tension between a utility rationale and a power rationale that centers on the construction of action as decision. A persistent external attribution of agency, however, challenges the constitutive basis of a political agent; it is irreconcilable with self-determination as a constitutive principle (Margalit and Raz 1990; Luhmann 2000:339ff.). In a crucial sense, 'danger' is about the *absence of agency and decision*.

The conceptualization of coercive sanctions communicating actions as decisions in international conflict takes a distinct position on the three above-mentioned ambitions of this sociological theory. First, the two dimensions involved in conceptualizing sanctions as a means that aims to enforce decisions in conflict lend particular characteristics to negative, positive and combined sanctions strategies. Negative and positive sanctions promote meaning of decision on conflict differently. Second, in terms of a reference point for judging a sanction as being either negative or positive, this issue consistently resides with communication in international conflict. In other words, independent of the possible intentions of an initiator, whether a sanction is positive or negative depends on social construction involving the addressee. Importantly, however, so does their more profound meaning as actions in international conflict. Finally, this concept does not privilege economic or non-economic instruments but remains open to diverse measures that are designed to enforce a decision. Trade or financial instruments may coerce as much as diplomatic or travel sanctions. The particular instrument does not count as much as it being an attempt at relational influence that conforms to the logic of communicated action seeking to impose a decision on a conflict.

Particular sanctions strategies promote different meaning potentials. Negative sanctions strategies emphasize a power rationale. By contrast, positive sanctions strategies emphasize a utility rationale. As a third kind, combined sanctions strategies are initially indifferent towards both utility and power rationale. The selection of specific sanctions strategies by the initiator as agent in communication thus has constitutive effects. Yet with the infeasibility of a simple sender–receiver model of communication between the initiator of sanctions and an addressee, sanctions communicate both sides of the two dimensions as meaning potentials. Accordingly, decisional attribution remains essentially contingent. It is a question of social construction.

Individual sanctions strategies relate differently to processes of attribution of decision-making. However, it is only the consideration of sanctions strategies within wider conflict communication that makes it possible to specify the particular meaning suggested by a certain sanctions strategy: whether it is closer to a power or a utility rationale. In other words, it is impossible to state what meaning a certain sanctions strategy will acquire without taking conflict communication and the processing of meaning by the addressee into account. It is possible, however, to narrow down the meaning potential, which particular sanctions strategies to promote more strongly. Even then, however, it is crucial to emphasize that irrespective of strategy, sanctions, on principle, convey both sides of the two dimensions.

What meaning coercive international sanctions will actually acquire in international conflict, and to what effect, is endogenous to the social processing of meaning and the pertinent social practices in communication. Such a conceptualization raises particular requirements for substantive theorizing on the relevant social conditions within sanctions conflicts conducive to either cooperation or non-cooperation. It is first necessary to address the question of how the international conflict is socially constructed as part of a more general model of conflict communication. Second, such a broader conceptualization further needs to theorize how the addressees of coercive sanctions may reject an observed meaning imposition attempt along a power rationale. The possibilities of rejecting this communication and its corresponding meaning imposition will advance a rival solution in terms of the defining features of the form risk/danger: contingency, decision and agency.

3.2 International conflict and coercive sanctions

Sanctions do not occur in a relational vacuum. Conceptualizing sanctions as actions aimed at enforcing a decision on conflict indicates their intrinsic connection to a broader notion of international conflict. This section addresses the second of the specific research questions: how international conflict and the positions of opponents are socially constructed. The section introduces a conception of international conflict that, first, contextualizes sanctions that communicate actions as decisions and, second, accommodates the notion of a utility and a power rationale as communicated meaning potential in conflict. The conception of conflict lays the basis of accounting for coercive sanctions in the transformation of international conflicts. It posits conflict as a dynamic social process and focuses on the evolving meaning of conflict communication.

Coercive sanctions occur across a broad variety of international conflicts, ranging from trade disputes and the enforcement of international norms such as human rights or nuclear non-proliferation, to disputes on competing territorial claims. As the existing literature on coercive sanctions in international conflict has broadly demonstrated, there are different conflict conditions that exert an influence on the prospects of cooperation and non-cooperation in the use of certain sanctions strategies. However, evolving conflict conditions may dynamically affect the meaning of sanctions themselves. With sanctions as part of international conflict, the relational construction of conflict will affect the meaning that particular sanctions acquire. 'Positive' sanctions introduced as part of official development assistance may become perceived as illegitimate infringement on sovereignty, as happened with the US aid disbursement to Bolivia during the government of Evo Morales (Fuentes 2008).[6] Thus, the meaning that sanctions will acquire cannot be assumed independently of what kind of conflict emerges. Accordingly, an approach to coercive sanctions in international conflict needs to account conceptually for the relational construction of conflict that sanctions take part in.

Similarly, sanctions as a means of enforcing a decision in conflict are not actions that are neutral to the on-going development of conflict perceptions. A 'harmless' trade issue may end up being observed as coercive sanctions that convey a power rationale, as in the case of NAFTA (North American Free Trade Agreement) and the uprising in Southern Mexico by the EZLN (Ejército Zapatista de Liberación Nacional) (Vargas 1994; Ross 1995; Russell 1995).[7] Thus, the meaning that sanctions in fact acquire will in turn bear diverging implications for subsequent conflict communication.

The meaning that sanctions acquire is closely linked to the broader conflict of which they form part. At the same time, sanctions can actively shape conflict perceptions. Conceptually, there are three possible avenues down which to proceed on the two-way relation between sanctions and conflict meaning. First, we could conceive of the relation as circular, with all the ensuing difficulties in determining where exactly to 'enter' the circle analytically and how to 'exit' it again. Second, the relation could be analytically excluded, treating the meaning of sanctions instead as pre-given and similarly treating conflict as a given configuration of relational properties. Existing top-down approaches to coercive international sanctions do exactly that. However, when perceptions of the broader conflict are not independent of the meaning of sanctions, it is not possible to develop a priori a typology of different conflicts and then test different strategies in a classical variable-based design against this. Rather, it is necessary to take into account the transformative processes involved and analyze their constitutive effects.

Finally, a third possibility is to conceptualize the relation between sanctions and conflict meaning as a dialectical process. 'Conflict' then is a broader, ubiquitous phenomenon. Sanctions occur as part of already on-going conflict communication – that is, in the context of an established conflict meaning. Consequently, it is necessary to provide a conception of the social processes involved in the construction of conflict. Later, I will take up a concept of international conflict that adheres to Luhmann's notion of communication as analytical base. The conception of conflict proposed and introduced to IR by systems theory scholars conceives of conflict meaning as an evolving process. It is able to incorporate a notion of sanctions as actions observed as decisions in communication. The conception of international conflict delineates specific stages of conflict escalation and suggests how sanctions introduced, in obtaining a specific meaning, may promote either the iterative continuance of established conflict communication, or its transformation.

3.2.1 Conflict as communicated incompatibilities

Sanctions are instruments that are intrinsic to conflict. They occur only in conflict: without conflict, sanctions are not conceivable. Such a view rests on a broad understanding that does not associate conflict exclusively with violence. Rather, it takes conflict as a ubiquitous phenomenon of social life. Countless political institutions serve the purpose of regulating conflict, give recognition to legitimate differences or provide stable mechanisms of conflict resolution. Democratically elected parliaments are exemplary of this in providing in one body all of the aforementioned functions for society. From a historical point of view, the institution of the parliament is a formidable achievement of human society. Not all societal conflicts are dealt with in such a way, though, and one of the features of international politics is the limited presence of conflict-processing institutions that provide the abovementioned functions. Some of them serve basic regulatory purposes to prevent the worst, such as the Geneva Conventions; others are highly sophisticated regimes formalized in organizations such as the WTO. Against the limited presence of such institutions, international politics is characterized by state sovereignty. This has significant implications for the legitimacy of any other authority as well as problematic consequences for social conflict. Many areas are marked by the absence of regimes with binding authority for the processing of conflict, with state authorities themselves left to judge on their conflicts with other states.

This broad perspective takes any kind of social conflict to consist of a communicated 'incompatibility of subject positions' (cf. Galtung 1969; Albert, Diez, and Stetter 2008:15). It is rooted in taking communication as an analytical base. To reiterate, communication aims for an imposition of meaning on the addressee (Luhmann 1995). The addressee for its part may accept or reject the suggested meaning – either way, there is a processing of meaning on its part and communication proceeds. Rejection in this case marks incompatible subject positions and when these incompatibilities begin to be reproduced, conflict is manifest. From that basic conceptual notion, systems theory scholars proceeded towards developing a more comprehensive model of social conflict and subsequently introduced it into IR. This analysis largely adopts the developed conflict model along with slight adaptations to make it suitable to the analysis of coercive international sanctions.

What do these subject positions consist of? In line with the argument concerning coercive international sanctions conveying potential meaning along a utility and a power rationale, subject positions are taken to consist of two components: the constructed interests and identity of a subject. 'Subject' can of course mean any political entity. Ultimately, conflicts consisting of communicated *interest* incompatibilities can be mediated. Based on the mutual orientation of conflict subjects towards a utility rationale, such conflicts express the possibility of settling differences through political-economic means including coercion.[8] By contrast, conflict communication that centers upon questioning basic shared meanings, norms and identities, articulates incompatibility to a much more serious extent. Through explicitly rejecting fundamental commonalities, such conflicts formulate non-negotiability and resist their "political reduction to interest incompatibilities" (Luhmann 2000:218f., author's translation). Therefore, the more communication constructs a conflict as interfering with basic shared meanings, the more protracted the conflict becomes. I will subsequently develop this notion as a basis for understanding sanctions conflict in more detail.

Heinz Messmer (2003) developed a model inspired by Luhmann's systems theory that conceptualizes the features internal to conflict communication as social process. It is not the incompatibilities that affect conflict, but conflict communication itself that produces the incompatibilities in the first place: "[T]he main elements and structures of conflict development are self-referentially produced by conflicts themselves. Hence, what characterizes conflicts is the ongoing internal procession of 'contradiction' and 'opposition'" (Messmer 2007:101), independent of particular context. Accordingly, neither a meaning imposition nor its rejection or their sources as antagonistic agents precede this communication process. Instead of simple sender–receiver communication, there are essentially ascribed, incompatible meanings.

Messmer's model of conflict communication distinguishes several conflict stages of growing conflict intensity, each of which has its own specific structure, which sets them apart from the others. Conflict processes of different intensities "can be separated roughly in terms of the extent to which they – iteratively – reproduce a communicated contradiction at the very same process stage, or whether they transform the conflict towards a different level of intensity" (Messmer 2003:293, author's translation). As its duration increases, conflicts gain in structural weight and become more persistent in the sense that communicated contradictions become mutually expected. In conflicts as social process, communicated incompatibilities play out differently at certain points of conflict development.

Messmer's systems-theoretical model has subsequently been adapted by Albert, Diez, et al. (2008) to the study of political conflict more specifically. Four conflict stages aim to comprehensively capture completely the possible spectrum of conflicts in increasing intensity, ranging from a temporary articulation of disagreement to a ruthless attempt to assert one position over another by any means (see Figure 3.1). The first stage marks a *conflict episode*, the passing rejection of a

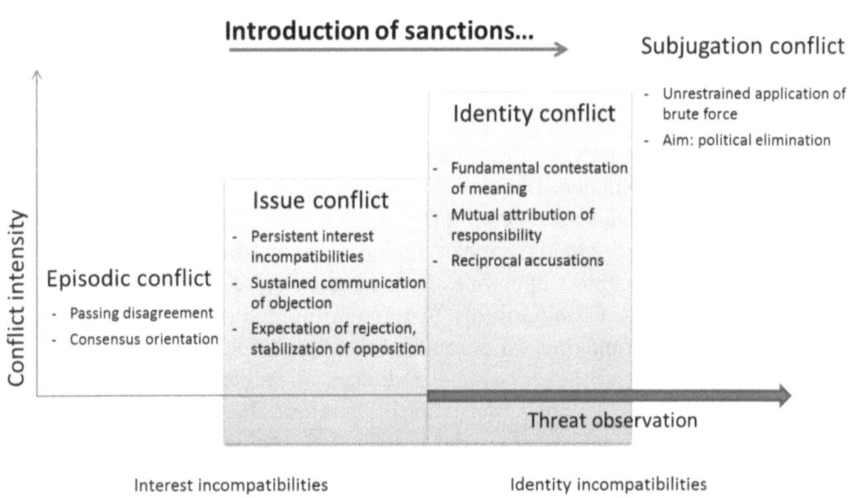

Figure 3.1 Conflict escalation and international sanctions

(adapted from Diez, Thomas, Stephan Stetter, and Mathias Albert [2006]; Messmer [2003]) proposition or disagreement over meaning on a particular issue and subsequent dissolution of incompatibility with an overall 'consensus orientation' (Messmer 2003:289). For a theory of international sanctions, this stage is by and large uninteresting – it is interesting only to the extent that it indicates the part of conflicts that play hardly any role in sanctions conflict. For sanctions to occur, incompatibilities must be more persistent and the intensity of a conflict stronger.

The articulation of interest incompatibilities becomes persistent once political conflicts reach the stage of *issue conflicts*. Conflicts are characterized by a sustained communication of mutual objection regarding a specific issue, together with opponents' attempts to convince one another of their particular views (Messmer 2003; Albert, Diez, et al. 2008). Dissent stabilizes between opposing actors who basically agree to disagree on a specific issue. Thus, conflict communication tends towards institutionalizing interest incompatibilities, it expresses not a consensus orientation but rather expectations of rejection and dissent (Messmer 2003:290). This development is a silver bullet towards the imposition of sanctions: The utility rationale of coercive sanctions rests on affecting the addressee's calculative base, in order to 'convince' the Other that interests are in fact compatible. This goes for negative as well as for positive sanctions strategies. Such a utilitarian perspective observes sanctions as instruments used to deal with situations of protracted conflict, where on the one hand bargaining seems to lead nowhere and has effectively failed, but on the other hand the importance of the issue makes this unacceptable to the sanctioning entity. Thus, coercive international sanctions are a typical phenomenon of protracted issue conflicts, applied to them in order to solve the conflict through dissolving a perceived interest incompatibility of subject positions.

However, as Albert et al. note, the re-orientation of issue conflicts towards expectations of rejection implies another crucial tendency (2008:18): "the conflict starts to develop structurally more stable notions of 'opposition', which facilitates collective groups to relate communications to the other party". With communicated rejection beginning to refer to the opposing 'Other', the potential of identity incompatibilities thus already exists as an emergent possibility at this stage of a conflict. Against this background it is important to emphasize that particular conflict stages are not strictly separate, manifesting in exclusive isolation through completely replacing each other (Diez, Stetter, and Albert, 2006, p. 568). Predominant conflict observations can be contested by competing views. Nor are sanctions an instance limited to one particular conflict stage.

With the trace of an identity component already insinuating itself in issue conflicts, it becomes the definitive element at the next stage, *identity conflicts*. At this stage, dissent and rejection fully concentrate on identity incompatibilities. Any particular issue drops behind a fundamental contestation of meaning and a corresponding "self-referential perception of [conflict]" (Albert, Diez, et al. 2008:18). Addressees do not simply differ on a specific issue, but disagree on the meaning they ascribe to each other as subjects in social relations. Identity conflicts communicate a mutual attribution of responsibility for the problematic situation and reciprocal accusations (Messmer 2003:290). Conflict parties question the legitimacy of the position of the Other. Accordingly, the meaning entailed in discriminatory communication is not exactly likely to be met with acceptance. On the contrary, conflicts become entangled in the reproduction of subjects themselves and these discursive dependencies can easily lead to the institutionalization of identity incompatibilities: "they are part of the (re-)production of subject positions, the articulation of which in turn reproduces the conflict" (Albert, Diez, et al. 2008:16). In consequence, identity issues do not only deepen a conflict, but also fuel its continuance.

At the stage of identity conflicts, sanctions play a different role. Sanctions as communicated actions tend to be observed in relation to subject identities and not in the context of interest incompatibilities. The meaning attached to sanctions as communicated actions may reflect an observation that reproduces identity incompatibilities. Sanctions, communicating a power rationale as decisions concerning the addressee, impugn its identity by questioning its legitimacy as agent in social relations. Sanctions thus reinforce a "victim-offender relation" (Messmer 2007:107). Interest incompatibilities and a conflict decision along a utility rationale then play at best a subordinate role.

The more a focus on interest incompatibilities regarding a specific issue is in retreat against identity issues and related questions of basic norms and shared meanings defining commonalities across conflict, the more the prospects of a solution to the conflict dwindle. As Ronald Krebs and Jennifer Lobasz (2007:423) point out, accusations in identity conflicts often follow similar rhetorical patterns: "'we' were attacked because of 'who we are,' not because of 'what we have done'". With the increased saliency of constructing the Other as a threat, conflict communication may deteriorate definitively.

At this point, social conflict may escalate into *subjugation conflicts*. Mutual attribution of responsibility for the crisis, and threats and sanctions as communicated decisions contingent upon compliance give way to the actual application of direct physical violence with the aim of politically eliminating the Other. There is no longer much concern for the political position of the Other, or its potential cooperation. Cooperation – with whatever kind of addressee is left – will be realized by other means. Coercive international sanctions play if anything a secondary role; military force becomes the preferred instrument of conflict solution.

Having introduced these four conflict stages in order to conceptualize international sanctions conflicts, a few words are in order on the small, but nonetheless significant differences to the model suggested by Messmer (2003, 2007) and to its adaptation by Albert et al. (2008). These differences concern specifically the fourth stage of conflict communication, termed here 'subjugation conflicts', and they concern more abstractly the notion of power in communication. Messmer, and to a lesser extent Albert et al. as well, originally restrict coercion in general to the final stage of conflict escalation. Messmer argues that at this final stage, the conditionality of coercion effectively replaces communication. By contrast, issue incompatibilities communicate argumentative disaccord and identity incompatibilities communicate relational contradictions (Messmer 2003:108). Similarly, Albert et al. (2008:19) suggest that the change of the primary function of communication from demarcating the Other to its subordination or possible extinction is the main distinctive feature between the third and the fourth conflict stage.

There are three reasons as to why the slight revision proposed by this model of conflict communication has increased cogency. First, for both of the other models their distinction between third and fourth stage rest in part on linking 'questioning legitimacy' to 'coercion' and 'subordination'. However, 'identities' operate by suggesting a devaluation of the Other, at a social psychological level as well as a macro-sociological level (Tajfel and Turner 1986; Campbell 1998). Such devaluation might easily include 'legitimacy', with ensuing attributions of threats along a 'victim-offender relation'. Still, depending on the purpose of the particular model, distinctions pointing in either direction may certainly be justified.

Second, at a more abstract level, there is a tension between power as a symbolic medium of communication ('actions communicated as decisions') and power as 'ending communication' as part of coercing compliance. There are a number of reasons for favoring a notion of power as a symbolic medium of communication. A threat, by itself, does not introduce power into conflict communication, only its relational observation in terms of submission. To the extent that coercion is a relational phenomenon, sanctions communicate a power rationale. In addition, physical violence is not the main expression of power adopted by this theory, as imposed meaning selection in a condition of double contingency in communication. Rather, physical violence is indeed the "culmination point of social conflict" that 'ends communication' (cf. Messmer 2007:107f.).

Third, and most importantly, coercive international sanctions transcend various stages of conflict communication. True, at the stage of issue conflicts, the addressee conceives of sanctions precisely not as coercing a decision in terms of a power rationale. However, when conflict communication escalates towards observing identity incompatibilities, addressees will understand sanctions accordingly. For this theory of international sanctions conflicts, it is analytically more appropriate to adopt a relational notion of power. It allows for sanctions to communicate a power rationale that questions the identity of the other, instead of restricting coercion to the fourth conflict stage and blurring the difference between sanctions and war as the application of brute physical violence.

3.2.2 Conclusion

The stage model of sanctions conflicts presented here shows how conflict escalates from communicating interest incompatibilities towards an increasing reference to identity incompatibilities with an observation of threats. International sanctions feature most strongly in medium-heavy conflicts, being introduced in protracted issue conflicts and replaced by military means at the extreme end of subjugation conflicts. Coercive international sanctions occur as part of two significantly different kinds of conflict communication. Conflicts resting on interest incompatibilities remain limited in as much as they provide a common focus on an issue and are susceptible to a utility rationale with which sanctions are often associated.

However, conflicts become qualitatively different when communication predominantly exhibits identity incompatibilities. A utility rationale depends on commonly accepted *bases of interest*, a mutual agreement on the meaning of the conflict situation.[9] To the extent and in the sense that incompatibilities become more fundamentally about meaning, they will resist political reduction to interest incompatibilities that could be solved with a utility rationale: Conflict communicates profound differences in the meaning adversaries ascribe to each other as subjects, attributing responsibility to the Other and denying the Other's legitimacy as agent in communication. In consequence, sanctions, observed along a power rationale, as communicating discrimination between decision-makers and those affected, will reinforce existing identity incompatibilities and lead to non-cooperation.

This is not to imply that sanctions are in themselves in principle unfit to deal with identity conflicts, nor is it to suggest that sanctions do not have non-utilitarian effects. Rather, it illustrates that different kinds of conflict indeed have potentially vast implications for international sanctions and their rationales. Hence, it is important to understand the type of conflict in which international sanctions occur. Further, it is important to know how a conflict transforms from one that is about interest incompatibilities on a specific issue into a much deeper and more comprehensive conflict of identity, norms and values. It will be argued in the next part that securitization theory not only provides a means of capturing a core trend in conflicts with their tendency across conflict stages towards perceiving the Other as a threat, but that it essentially allows the capturing of this transformation of conflict which is crucial to international sanctions.

3.3 Securitization: theory of agency and causal mechanism

The concept of securitization allows the capturing and modeling of a key transformation of conflict communication involving international sanctions. This section addresses the third of the specific research questions, on conflict transformation and the influence of sanctions upon it. In that transformation, securitization interlinks conflict communication and coercive sanctions constructed as decisions therein. On the one hand, conflict escalation occurs as a process of securitization: away from communicated issue incompatibilities towards communicated identity incompatibilities, mutual recriminations and constructing the Other as a threat. On the other hand, coercive sanctions either suggest a utility rationale or impose a power rationale in conflict communication. Securitization rejects a communicated power rationale and the implied deprivation of agency and decision by providing a rival solution: as assertion of agency in claiming a 'threat'. Securitized sanctions conflicts imply non-cooperation.

As proposed by Diez et al. (2006), securitization can serve well as a way of tracing the way in which a conflict unfolds. Their conflict stage model views securitization as an on-going process, which allows the development of a conflict to be followed over time. Another advantage is that such a process-centered approach allows for the analysis of counter-moves, contestations and de-escalations of conflict over time ('de-securitization'). This sociological theory's analytical model of international sanctions adheres to the notion of securitization as a process. However, it requires a slightly different characterization of that process.

For prospects of cooperation in international sanctions conflicts, the difference between issue conflicts and identity conflicts is a crucial one. I will take up the concept of securitization to theorize this transformation of conflict in more detail. The discussion below argues for a repositioning of securitization as a theory of agency and a causal mechanism in conflict transformation.

As a theory of agency, securitization represents a particular engagement with contingency. In applying the conception of agency developed by Mustafa Emirbayer and Ann Mische (1998), conflict escalation becomes apparent from a discontinuity in on-going issue conflict communication that exhibits an open, precarious future. The radical openness produced in the disruption of meaning creates the opportunity for agency in a situation of contingency. It provides a viable basis for securitizing moves. Securitization represents not only the culmination of such a crisis in meaning, but its successful closure through agency and decision. Importantly, such a situation emerges only in a process of social construction at the end of which the situation presents itself as a crisis, a moment of contingency involving the opportunity for agency. In other words, securitizing moves construct a crisis in meaning and contingency, to which 'security' then offers a solution in instantiating agency and realizing closure. Securitization, by asserting agency, effectively links the meaning of sanctions along a power rationale to conflict transformation.

Besides introducing securitization as a theory of agency, I posit securitization as a causal mechanism that traces the decisive transformation from an issue conflict into an identity conflict. There are two dimensions to securitization as a causal mechanism in sanctions conflicts. First, in social practice, securitization links an external cause (a threat) to a specific effect (security). Agents in securitization thus engage in a momentous causal attribution that results in communicating an identity conflict. Second, at an analytical level, a securitized sanctions conflict implies non-cooperation. Securitization thus amounts to a causal mechanism on cooperation and non-cooperation in international sanctions conflicts.

Given the crucial function served by securitization in the sociological approach to international sanctions conflicts that has been developed, a careful treatment of the concept is essential. Apart from outlining what securitization is and does, it is equally important to establish the limits of the concept, clarifying what it is not and what it cannot do. Critics persistently point to the limits of securitization theory beyond the immediate process of securitization: that the notion lacks a broader concept of social context and society, and hence is unable to grasp such influences. Indeed, securitization is not a theory of social processing of meaning more generally, let alone a theory of society. Arguably, that is not its aspiration in the first place. Put differently, securitization represents a very specific element in a broader social context. The introduced notion of conflict as communicated subject incompatibilities and the concept of sanctions as actions constructed as decisions in conflict communication established a specific vision of a broader social context.

Subsequently, the chapter first reviews the conceptual development of 'securitization'. In the literature, there is a controversy between on the one hand, securitization proposing a performative notion of what security does and, on the other hand, its emphasis on intersubjectivity and social context. The review critically reflects on this discussion with its ensuing 'externalist' focus on social context, which ultimately neglects the notion of a securitizing act. In a second step, the chapter develops securitization as an agential engagement with contingency. There are two dimensions involved. On a temporal dimension, securitization asserts agency in constructing a contingent future as a crisis. On a social dimension, securitization re-locates causes and attributes responsibility for the crisis. In claiming an external threat, securitization consequentially transforms an issue conflict into an identity conflict. A third step positions securitization as a causal mechanism. Analytically, securitization transforms sanctions conflicts to such an extent that cooperation becomes unviable.

3.3.1 Securitization, concept development

Securitization theory develops a notion of security as being socially constructed in communication. For any security problem to exist, be perceived and of political consequence it needs social verification. Hence, threats exist only as social facts through ascriptions in communication.[10] Accordingly, across diverse issue areas its defining logic can be described as a linguistic process, as a speech act: security emerges "when an issue is presented as posing an existential threat to a designated referent object" (Buzan, Wæver, and de Wilde 1998:21). The presentation is a securitizing move; securitization happens only once a relevant audience accepts this security speech act.

With the notion of securitization as originally proposed by the Copenhagen School, the first thing that is remarkable is that social verification plays a critical role. It highlights how security as meaning is socially produced. The security speech act does not only establish the reality of an existential threat, however. A securitizing move claims the need for extraordinary means and the justification of actions beyond the 'normal rules of the game' (Buzan et al. 1998:25), granting legitimacy to measures which exceed the boundaries of established accepted procedures. This elucidates the second remarkable element of securitization: in delineating security as a speech act, the concept focuses on what security does in terms of political consequence and further emphasizes the performative aspect of securitization. By all means then, securitization marks a disruption and an escalation that transforms meaning and the way political problems are perceived. It is a disruption of routine political procedures; at the same moment it denotes a crisis, securitization offers a solution.

The initial concept of securitization, though very useful in offering new insights in the social construction of threats and the practices involved, was subsequently criticized for taking into account social context only in passing. It is mostly addressed through the notion of 'facilitating conditions' of the security speech act (Stritzel 2007),[11] and while this on the one hand acknowledges the relation between securitization and its context, it on the other hand stops short of consequently integrating this relation (McDonald 2008:571). In addition, the audience and its role remain equally under-theorized (Balzacq 2005): Whereas its role is crucial in demarcating securitization as an intersubjective construction, first generation work neither elaborated more thoroughly upon who the relevant audience is and how to identify it (Vuori 2008), nor did it specify what audience acceptance would entail (McDonald 2008).

Starting from that perspective, second generation securitization scholars such as Thierry Balzacq (2005, 2010), Holger Stritzel (2007, 2011) and Felix Ciută (2009) opted for developing securitization theory strictly along an 'externalist' vein towards comprehensively conceptualizing and integrating context. Thus, externalist work explores the particular discourses that make securitization possible, the socio-political context in which actors are discursively embedded and points to the context-sensitivity of meaning. However, such interpretation of the concept of securitization further promotes a division between the context-fused externalist practices of socially constructing threats and the performative 'internalist' security speech act centered on the intervention.

Arguably, though, the very dividing of securitization into an internalist and externalist part is itself problematic. The critique against the internalist part rests on a specifically structuralist, socially detached take on speech acts as purely textual, taking language almost as a Hegelian universal that essentially neglects the basic sociality of language and meaning in the first place (cf. Palan 2000). As a rather immoderate shortcut, it excludes the few (externalist) elements of context actually included in the original notion of securitization. With such a division between the two conceptual parts of securitization established, it is easy to see how the restrictive delineation of an internalist part leads to claims that security as a speech act misses out on intersubjectivity.

Nevertheless, the critique put forward by second generation scholars puts the limitations of the original notion of securitization into the spotlight: while it provides a specific conception of how security issues are socially established as an existential threat through agency, it says nothing about "how and why that particular intervention became possible" (McDonald 2008:576). Therefore, along with the internalist/externalist divide is a plea to downgrade the internalist part and focus instead upon the externalist elements of securitization and its relation to a broader social context.

To a significant extent, externalist work focuses on 'social practices' at the cost of 'social process'. By subscribing to an externalist position, theoretical treatments have concentrated on embedding securitization in social context, but have neglected the notion of social agency that is so prominently present in the original framework as part of what security does. Somewhat ironically, Stritzel declares at the end of such a treatment that a "clearer and more elaborated theory of the securitizing act" was needed (Stritzel 2007:376).

Viewed in this way, the strict division into internalism/externalism is an unfortunate development. The securitization concept, as initially proposed by the Copenhagen School, enables a remarkable perspective on social process and transformation. The concept outlines how agency provides for its own necessity through securitizing moves that construct a crisis in meaning and contingency, to which it offers a solution in realizing closure by way of a simple, binary choice: either recognize the threat and legitimize the use of extraordinary means, or the referent object will not survive. Along with that solution, securitization transforms social relations.

This elaboration of securitization takes a different road than the path chosen by many second-generation scholars. It rejects the strict division of securitization into internalist/externalist parts, which puts a purely textual notion of speech act against social context. Instead, securitization is a particular operation in communication, one that instantiates agency. Subjected to double contingency, securitization is in principle social. That is, the security speech act depends as much on social recognition on the one hand as it transforms social relations on the other. Accordingly, as Stefano Guzzini suggested, securitization is much better understood as a process, one that is "directed to the understanding of why certain moves can be expected in given national security discourse, why some of them may find a receptive audience . . ., and indeed why certain action-complexes can then follow" (Guzzini 2011:331). The contained references to social context make only lean mention of its conditions of possibility.

Beyond that, securitization theory does not have the ambition to capture comprehensively social practices and the processing of meaning in general; it is simply not "a shorthand for the broader construction of security" (McDonald 2008:564). Thus, central to this take of securitization as a theory of social agency is the relation between the social construction of an existential threat, agency and specific political effects. Securitization, understood this way, is only applicable to social processes and practices in which agency plays a key role. For in considering a security speech act, the audience not only makes or breaks securitization but also potentially attributes agency. Agency in this sense is socially (re)produced in and through securitization.

In fact, the first generation work on securitization focused so heavily on the basic relation between constructed threat, agency and political effects that it implicitly adopted a rather restricted notion of communication: Communication somehow stops at the 'borders' of unquestioningly reified political entities (Dunn Cavelty and Jaeger 2015). Any relational developments beyond such borders could make it at best as 'facilitating conditions' into securitization proper. Instead of challenging such focused attention, the delineation suggested here sticks to that focus but conceptually embeds 'securitization' in a wider notion of relational conflict as part of a broader construction of security. Securitization transforms issue conflicts into identity conflicts and amounts to a causal mechanism in disputes involving coercive international sanctions.

The chapter subsequently builds on securitization, first, as a theory of agency and, second, as a performative act that transforms conflict. Within broader conflict communication, securitization thus assumes a double role. I develop securitization as a theory of agency by positing agency as engagement with contingency, building on the conceptual work of Emirbayer and Mische. Securitization connects a certain interpretation of past developments to a precarious future. In on-going social processing of meaning, it constructs a crisis, a moment of contingency. Securitization is an instantiation of agency that offers 'security' as a solution to this crisis. Conflict transformation becomes apparent through the way in which social process reproduces agency, either in iterative meaning communication, or in a discontinuity that exhibits an open, projected future. Developing securitization more thoroughly as a theory of agency allows for a revised view of its performative aspect, and its operational meaning in conflict communication.

The involvement of securitization in conflict transformation raises a two-fold causality dimension. Securitization promotes a particular meaning selection, against possible alternative ways of conceiving a political issue. Thus, in socially recognizing a securitizing move, the audience does not merely ascribe agency but grants the power to define reality. In social practice, securitization links an external cause (a threat) to a specific effect (security). Such causal attribution results in communicating an identity conflict. Moreover, a securitized sanctions conflict implies non-cooperation.

3.3.2 Agency and temporality

Securitization presents an instantiation of agency in communication. To recapitulate, agency refers to an engagement with contingency, in the ability to modify or change preconceived meaning in communication. Meaning selections always communicate the possibility of a different selection. Therefore, contingency at all times remains present in communication, even when tamed by routinized meanings that allow for expectations to develop. Conflict communication routinely reproduces markedly different kinds of rejection at both conflict stages. Securitization transforms an issue conflict into an identity conflict, which in consequence requires a conceptualization of the qualitative shift that the escalation entails.

By transforming conflict, securitization breaks with common meaning expectations in communication. Securitization creates an opportunity for agency in constructing a moment of contingency. In the moment of heightened contingency, securitization exerts a defining force over its context. Without communicative context, it is hard to tell whether securitization transformed a conflict communication or whether it is part of a continuing identity conflict. It is thus crucial to explore carefully the relation between agency and context in order to capture precisely the qualitative shift that securitization entails.

In on-going issue conflict communication, claiming an existential threat to a referent object stands out as a crisis that transcends and disrupts routinized meanings and adjacent expectations. Whereas securitization on an ontological level intersubjectively establishes the perception of an existential threat, it presents a temporal re-orientation at an operational level in how contingency appears in social process. As Mustafa Emirbayer and Ann Mische elaborated in their comprehensive social theorization of agency, such temporal orientation is a core element, if not the defining dimension, to understanding agency in its social operation.

Inspired by Hans Joas' work, Emirbayer and Mische set about further developing a pragmatist notion of agency as a creative intervention in the social processing of meaning. They conceptualize agency as "temporally constructed engagement" (Emirbayer and Mische 1998:970), along two temporal concentrations: iteration and projectivity.[12] These elements characterize human agential engagement with contingency.

To recapitulate, in confronting contingency, expectations rest on shared symbolic meanings. Expectations then provide the bases of meaning selection in the follow-up operations of on-going social interaction. The reduction of contingency is largely expressed through *iteration*, the selective reactivation of past patterns of meaning (Emirbayer and Mische 1998:971). Iteratively reproduced meanings make routinized social practices possible. There is thus a temporal orientation towards the past, enabling selections in communication that extrapolate routine and stability.

Crucially, whereas iteration emphasizes routinization, a selection in iteration nonetheless occurs that exhibits agency. Considering this circumstance against securitization, it highlights once again that there is no determinacy – selections could also be made differently. To stay within the iterative dimension of routine expectations and its imprinting of the past in commitment to continuity thus is also a meaningful expression of agency.

For their part, selections always take place in the present. Selections rest on interpretations of the past either in a reiterative updating, or in constructing a discontinuity. Such discontinuity marks a crisis in the communication of meaning through which contingency, otherwise kept in check by mutual expectations, comes to the fore. That way, follow-up operations are called into question. With the future now essentially open, indeterminate and precarious, agency changes its temporal orientation and emphasizes a different, *projective* concentration: "the locus of agency here lies in the hypothesization of experience . . . by generating alternative possible responses to the problematic situations" (Emirbayer and Mische 1998:984).

Continuing issue conflicts reiteratively communicate interest incompatibilities, and the common expectation in communicating decisions is to observe acceptance or rejection according to a utility rationale. These expectations thus constitute the 'normal rules of the game' which stabilize expectations by providing a common frame of reference *within* which the suggested meaning in communication will be accepted or rejected.

In escalating conflict, securitization represents a qualitative shift in the engagement with contingency, away from iteration towards projectivity. A securitizing move breaks with iterative patterns of communicated meaning by constructing a crisis. It rejects established conflict communication, and the alternative meaning that reflects iterated expectations: of communicated issue incompatibilities and of decisions conforming to a utility rationale as 'common rules of the game'. Thereby, in constructing a moment of contingency, a securitizing move creates an opportunity for projective agency. Securitization exerts a transformative force on its context by offering a projected future with a choice of binary alternatives: survival or non-survival of the threatened referent object. By playing on contingency, agency in conflict escalation firmly adopts a projective concentration in favor of a particular response to the constructed crisis.

In sanctions conflicts, agency plays a key role in constructing actions relationally as decisions. Agency, as temporal engagement with contingency, reflects the tension in the two competing meaning potentials of sanctions, along a utility rationale and a power rationale. Securitization in sanctions conflicts constructs a crisis: one that is affected by the decisions of the Other. The crisis amounts to a danger in the absence of agency and decision. In rejecting a power rationale, securitization allows the recuperation of agency in conceiving the future again as contingent upon a proper decision. Securitization proposes a decision on what *will* occur in a contraction of decision-making potential that essentially *downplays* contingency. The logic, after all, is one of binary choice towards the survival of a referent object.

Agency as temporal engagement with contingency thus generally plays an important role in sanctions conflict communication. In the iterative, routine social processing of meaning, the past is a source of stabilization that links to the future through agency in the present, mostly by giving clear expectations (Emirbayer and Mische 1998:579). In the words of Søren Kierkegaard, "Life can only be understood backwards; but it must be lived forwards".[13] As agency becomes more prominent and its role more explicit in social process, so does the role of the future along its evocation in the hypothetical resolutions promoted by creative, projective hypothesization on the part of actors of future possibilities informing choice in the present. In consequence, this decisive re-orientation towards a projected future means that there is an important additional element to agency, one of a logic of meaningful possibilities (Berenskoetter 2011). While the importance of temporality is without question, the temporal orientation in agency however is merely a symptom, an artefact of the real issue: contingency. Generating the mutual bases for robust expectations as the common 'rules of the game' in issue conflicts helps to reduce contingency; delineating the future in terms of a binary choice in response to a threat in the securitization of conflicts first exposes and then downplays contingency, since it rests on a specific reconstruction of events and it reduces an essentially open multitude of possibilities.

3.3.3 Agency, causes and responsibility

Besides the two temporal elements of agency as engagement with contingency there is a third social-causative element however, without which a conceptual account would remain incomplete. The most significant qualitative shift in escalating conflict communication does not occur as a temporal re-orientation of agency, but as a social contingency, in locating causes and attributing responsibility.

Agency involves social recognition. In securitization, however, the role of the audience exceeds a characterization of simply establishing intersubjectivity. Or, more precisely, in accepting a security speech act, there is more to what the audience does than consenting to a perception of threat which then constitutes a security issue. The security speech act, with its positioning of securitizing speaker and confirming or disconfirming audience, contains in itself the notion of intersubjectivity. However, treatments of the security speech act typically focus entirely upon what security does: in terms of establishing a threat and its adjacent political implications. The constellation between securitizing speaker and audience in establishing agency has received less attention in the literature. Accordingly, the audience's conceptual role is mostly one of passive acceptance or rejection, although it is decisive in establishing intersubjectivity.

In accepting a security speech act, the *audience attributes agency to the speaker*. It is a situation of double contingency. To appreciate this contestability and its consequences, "one must observe . . . the process of attribution" (Luhmann 1993:xliii). A perspective on agency that misses the role of social recognition is thus not entirely relational all the way down. Essentially, through social ascription agency is constitutive to 'action': in socially recognizing an action, agency undergoes a process of attribution.[14] In a similar vein, Jackson and Nexon (1999:318) see agency as "created by networks of relations", which are dynamic constellations that exhibit social recognition and attribution.

The security speech act delineates agency as part of communication, and there is more to this process in communication than just the ability of agency to define its context. The security speech act defines its context, yet the securitizing actor depends on social recognition. In essence, the audience does not only accept a speech act, but at the same time socially recognizes an utterer as the securitizing actor. This is a crucial operation with immense political implications: In social recognition, the audience grants the securitizing actor the power to define reality. Likewise, this power can be contested or denied in rejecting a securitizing move or by de-securitization.

Defining reality in securitization in its turn consists of the "construction of narratives that locate [binary] future possibilities in relation to more or less coherent causal and temporal sequences" (Emirbayer and Mische 1998:989). Whereas 'danger' in sanctions conflict communication implies a resignation of agency as the attribution of consequences to decision, 'security' allows such meaning imposition to be depicted as a threat to identity and the (recuperation of) self-attribution of decision-making in a single operation, effectively transforming the 'danger' into a 'threat'.[15] Securitization establishes a specific reality by causally linking a particular interpretation of past developments to a projected future. Securitization thus allows analysis of the attribution of causes and responsibility in conflict communication.

A securitizing agent's power to define 'what is' makes 'causality' a meaning selection made in social practice. Causality here is an attribution made by political actors in social practice. In attributing a particular cause (a threat) to a specific effect (security) out of a universe of possible (past) causes and (future) effects, securitization represents a politically consequential selection. In securitizing an identity conflict, agents attribute causes and responsibility for the deteriorating conflict externally, voicing recriminations unequivocally against the adversary. At the same time, securitizing claims erode the legitimacy of the Other's position. There is thus a social-causative selection of meaning through social agency *within* securitization.

Agents attribute causes and responsibility differently in non-securitized issue conflict communication. Causes and responsibilities may vary, but in any event, they do not become the subject of conflict communication in a mutual observation of issue incompatibilities. In securitizing conflict transformation, agency thus engages in a decisively distinct re-location of causes and responsibility. Accordingly, the social-causative element of engaging contingency in agency firmly denotes conflict communication in issue and identity conflicts, linking possible future states to particular causes in particular ways.

Securitized sanctions conflicts imply non-cooperation. Securitization in sanctions conflicts instantiates agency and constructs threats, against a renunciation of agency in an exposition to dangers (on threats, one can act; one is exposed to dangers) as the insinuated alternative. Therefore, cooperation on sanctions that communicate a power rationale would amount to submitting to decisions of the Other, violating the very bases on which securitization as engagement with contingency rests. Substantive cooperation presupposes de-securitization or non-securitization, subscribing to self-attributed decisions along a utility rationale in issue conflict communication.

As a consequence of such an analytical approach, "who promotes [causality claims] and to what typical constrictions to the generally implied infinity in subsequent operations" (Luhmann 1996:4, author's translation) becomes of primary interest. Agency is not just simply a neutral temporal engagement that connects the past to the future, expressing more or less continuity. As becomes apparent along these lines of reasoning, there is an intimate relation between the social recognition of agency, temporality, power and causality. Causality is entirely bound up with and endogenous to social practice. It is a meaning selection made by political agents in social practice. Securitization is not only politically meaningful through the ontological establishment of a threat, but is also highly consequential in devising the power to define what is. The concept allows such selection to be traced through the lens of social agency.

The attribution of responsibility in sanctions conflicts is intricately linked to their social construction as threats: With the securitization of sanctions, there is an implication of responsibility for the situation towards the initiator of sanctions, together with an allegation of illegitimacy. Sanctions in identity conflicts thus inevitably raise the issue of the attribution of responsibility (cf. Messmer 2003:290).

The implied drawing of boundaries between a state and a threatening external Other, however, may also occur in a different way, between a domestic opposition and a state's government. Conceptually and practically, there is no inherent reason for associated boundaries in social conflict to align to *state* boundaries. In one sense, the 'addressee' in coercive international sanctions may be a state as a referent object at which 'cooperation' as the outcome of sanctions is aimed; in another sense, whether in terms of a utility rationale centered on 'interest' (cf. Kaempfer and Lowenberg 1992) or in a power rationale centered on 'identity', the definition processes involved in the social processing of meaning require a much broader view than a limited perspective on 'the state' as a unitary decision-making unit. 'The addressee' may then be 'the government' of a state, but there might be rifts in how the conflict is observed that extend beyond the government or even reach into government. There is thus another side to the drawing of boundaries: For the government of a state addressed in the imposition of sanctions, 'external' decisional attribution in the social processing of danger may concern not so much the initiator of sanctions but (also) the domestic opposition. Similarly, a political opposition may dissociate from the construction of conflict suggested by state agents, and either engage in securitizing or de-securitizing conflict communication.

3.3.4 Securitization as causal mechanism

When considering securitization as transformative of sanctions conflicts, there are two dimensions of causality, a practical and an analytical one. The practical dimension, as a social-causative element of agential engagement with contingency, refers to how agents within the conflict attribute causality. The analytical dimension of causality pertains to whether we can observe cooperation or non-cooperation through sanctions. While the first dimension connects sanctions to how the conflict is socially constructed and perceived politically, the second dimension is about a general statement on conflict development (see Figure 3.2). The view advanced here is that both dimensions are closely connected. How political agents attribute causality is of crucial importance for eventual cooperation in international sanctions conflicts.

At the *first dimension*, securitization transforms an issue conflict into an identity conflict. The rise of a crisis in the disruption of common meaning, the prevalence of accusations and rejection of responsibility for the conflict, illustrates how particular meaning in communication and its rejection provide a viable basis for securitizing moves (Albert, Diez, et al. 2008). Conflicts escalate beyond seeking the solution to an issue. In the self-referential perception of conflict by the addressee of sanctions as one in which the initiator is denying legitimacy to the Other, closure is subsequently realized through securitization: Denial of legitimacy provides ample grounds for the construction of a security threat. The conflict transforms into one centered on identity.

Dimension of causality	Practice (first dimension)	Analytical (second dimension)
	<u>Identity conflict</u> Construction of threat: Denial of legitimacy External attribution of cause	Securitization: → Non-cooperation
	<u>Issue conflict</u> Basic agreement on meaning of conflict	Non-securitization: → *Possibility* of cooperation

Figure 3.2 Securitization as causal mechanism

The *second dimension of causality* refers to the transformation of the conflict through securitization to such an extent that cooperation becomes unviable. Thus, on the question of the social conditions within sanctions conflicts that are conducive to cooperation, securitization represents a causal mechanism. When conflict communication no longer focuses on issues but upon the Other and accordingly a utility rationale is rejected, this marks a crisis in meaning: basic understandings and common definitions are questioned or refused. Meaning becomes fundamentally contested.

What is remarkable about the concept of securitization is the focus it lays upon the performative aspect – what 'security' does in terms of political consequences. In the case of sanctions conflicts, the political consequences consist of the difference between conflict observations centering on controversy about particular issues, but largely remaining oriented towards *cooperation*, and conflict observations centering upon a fundamental irreconcilability with the Other, leaving *non-cooperation* as the only political option possible. Securitization thus represents a causal mechanism in conflict development.

Delineating the selection of meaning that occurs through securitization as decisive for prospects of cooperation highlights that such selection in social practice is contingent. In this conception the study follows Guzzini's proposition of securitization as a causal mechanism and his characterization of securitization as "a process that can lead to the anticipated effects, but does not do so necessarily" (Guzzini 2011:331). This approach therefore differs decisively from a model based on cause and effect that assumes, first, a static relation between cause and effect and, second, their realization as law-like or probabilistic, simply depending on a certain fit of 'external' conditions (Falleti and Lynch 2009). What is of interest is their *meaningful* connection (Goertz 1994:28). Context and meaning are intricately linked.

Endogeneity of context means that mechanisms are not necessarily determinate (Elster 1998:45). As Guzzini (2011) summarizes, there are generally two ways in which causal mechanisms relate to determinacy and indeterminacy: Either the processes of social causation or the resulting effects remain contingent, whereas the respective other side of the equation can be established determinatively. In this theory of international sanctions in social conflict, securitization is the mechanism that may lead to an identity incompatibility and trigger non-cooperation. The effects of this process are determinate. It marks the death sentence to the outcome that is sought when a conflict party introduces sanctions in order to coerce.

Delineating securitization as a causal mechanism in conflict involving international sanctions is a means of reducing complexity, and of establishing *analytical* regularity. Yet it is not at all some sort of ultimate foundation, an "unmoved mover" serving as a crutch to compensate an alleged empirical obscurity with abstraction (cf. Mahoney 2003:5). Likewise, it obviously does not rest on methodological individualism as a substitute (cf. Hedström and Swedberg 1998). 'Causal mechanism' here simply refers to "recurrent processes generating a specific kind of outcome" (Mayntz 2004:237). What is essential to this enquiry is that mechanisms cover dynamics, qualitative changes of significant consequences in on-going social processes. The process of securitization, for its part, is as much relational as the social reality of its actors and stems from processes in communication. The intimate relation between context, meaning and, ultimately, agency is true to an analytical perspective that considers mechanisms as contingent processes in communication.

The delineation of securitization as causal mechanism emphasizes the contingency of selection in practice. There are no abstract, law-like relations independent of social process and historical contingency. The definition of causality patterns through the connecting of an interpretation of the past to a hypothetical future emphasizes the exposed position of the present and the need for continuous updating thereof. However, in the iterative need to meaningfully connect the past to future directedness, meaning selections indeed become consequential.

3.3.5 Conclusion

As the third element of the triad, this section completes the conceptual development of the analytical model of the sociological theory of coercive international sanctions conflicts. It has addressed the third of the specific research questions, on conflict transformation and the influence of sanctions upon this process. The section introduced the notion of securitization to delineate conflict escalation as a qualitative shift in communication that is decisive for prospects of cooperation and non-cooperation. Securitized sanctions conflicts imply non-cooperation.

In the transformation of sanctions conflicts, securitization interlinks conflict observation and coercive sanctions constructed as communicating decisions. It connects the meaning of sanctions along a power rationale to conflict transformation. Securitization rejects a communicated power rationale and the implied deprivation of agency and decision by providing a rival solution: as assertion of agency in claiming a 'threat'.

Securitization represents a particular engagement with contingency. In conflict communication, securitizing moves evoke a crisis in meaning and contingency, exhibiting an open, precarious future. The radical openness produced in the disruption of meaning creates the opportunity for agency. First, in a projective temporal re-orientation of agency, securitization represents not only the culmination of such a crisis in meaning, but its successful closure through decision on an imagined binary future. Second, in a social dimension, securitization ascribes causes, and attributes responsibility for the crisis by constructing and external threat.

The meanings of conflict and of sanctions are closely intertwined with each other. On the one hand, sanctions as communicating a power rationale are securitized in reasserting agency and attributing causes and responsibility externally, constructing the Other as a threat. The conflict transforms towards communicating identity incompatibilities. Thus, depending on their social construction, sanctions may escalate an issue into an identity conflict. On the other hand, when conflict communication is already about identity incompatibilities, addressees observe sanctions potentially along a power rationale, contributing to an already existing securitization of conflict.

There are two dimensions to securitization as causal mechanism in sanctions conflicts. In social practice, securitization links an external cause (a threat) to a specific effect (security) that results in communicating an identity conflict. Second, at an analytical level, a securitized sanctions conflict implies non-cooperation. Securitization thus amounts to a causal mechanism for cooperation and non-cooperation in international sanctions conflicts.

3.4 Conflict, sanctions strategies and cooperation

International conflicts, and the meaning of sanctions applied as part of them, evolve dynamically. The meaning that sanctions ultimately adopt is dialectically linked to on-going conflict development. The preceding chapters conceptualized social conditions of international sanctions conflicts that are conducive to either cooperation or non-cooperation. The chapters addressed conceptually three specific research questions, regarding the meaning attached to sanctions, the construction of conflict and the influence of particular sanctions strategies. The sociological conceptualization adopted a dynamic notion of international conflict consisting of communicated issue or identity incompatibilities. Sanctions obtain their specific meaning through the way agents ascribe responsibility, legitimacy and causality in social practice. Particular sanctions strategies may either promote the continuance of expected conflict communication, or its transformation.

The conclusion draws on the insights gained in the individual chapters of the conceptual triad and outlines the mutual influence of on-going conflict communication and particular sanctions strategies on prospects of non-cooperation and cooperation. It formulates expectations regarding the impact of specific sanctions strategies upon conflict transformation. Sanctions conflicts can be divided into either communicating interest incompatibilities in issue conflicts or, more fundamentally, communicating identity incompatibilities, with the latter amounting to the securitization of conflict. In the case of interest incompatibilities, there is the possibility of reconciliation, whereas securitization leads to non-cooperation. This difference in social conflict therefore matters. Remarkably, both utility rationale and power rationale, which are implicit to issue conflicts and identity conflicts respectively, are reflected in the distinction risk/danger as a form of observing decision-making through sanctions. Coercive sanctions however cannot be considered *a priori* external to how incompatibilities are constructed in international conflict. Sanctions themselves may contribute to securitization processes. It is thus necessary to take the effects of coercion on the social construction of incompatibilities into account for understanding the development and the outcome of sanctions conflicts.

Sanctions relate differently to issue conflicts and identity conflicts (see Table 3.2). With identity conflicts amounting to non-cooperation, securitization as the process of conflict transformation becomes of primary interest. While there is no linear relation between international sanctions and a particular construction of subject incompatibilities, the effects of securitization are determinate. As long as the sanctions conflict remains securitized, non-cooperation will ensue.

Table 3.2 Sanctions strategies and conflict development

Conflict communication	*Negative sanctions*		*Positive sanctions*		*Combined sanctions*	
	(Utility)	***Power***	***Utility***	***(Power)***	***Utility***	***Power***
Issue incompatibility	. . .	+	. . .	+	. . .	+
Identity incompatibility	-	. . .	-	. . .	-	. . .

Securitization: + ; Continuity . . . ; De-Securitization: –

Accordingly, securitization represents a causal mechanism that establishes the relation between international sanctions and on-going international conflict as contingent. Importantly, the effects of securitization as causal mechanism are only determinate in one direction. By contrast, a non-securitized conflict does not deterministically lead to cooperation. In the absence of securitization, international sanctions do not lead straightforwardly to cooperation by an addressee. A utility rationale still prevails and addressees construct decisions on its basis.

When sanctions are in a contingent relation to conflict observations, the constitutive role of meaning in conflict communication becomes decisive. A simple sender–receiver model of communication between the initiator of sanctions and an addressee is unfeasible. Rather, the meaning potential of sanctions in international conflict conveys a tension. On the one hand, coercive sanctions aim to manipulate cost-benefit calculations, reflecting choice in a utility rationale; on the other hand, they reflect a power rationale in seeking to enforce a decision on the conflict. Both rationales are about agency and the social attribution of decisions; sanctions communicate both rationales as meaning potentials.

Negative sanctions strategies emphasize a power rationale. In questioning the addressee as an agent in conflict communication, they offer ready-made grounds for securitization. The addressee sees itself only as being affected by the decisions of the Other in a situation that does not offer much of a ‘choice’ to the addressee but presents to it a *danger*, thus implying external decisional attribution. However, such meaning potential need not be taken up by a securitizing agent in the processing of meaning by the addressee. It depends on social construction. An addressee may well observe the conflict as one of interest incompatibilities and make a decision based on a utility rationale. However, negative sanctions strategies provide an enabling condition of a meaning as danger. Likewise, with a securitized international conflict an introduced negative sanctions strategy is unlikely to foster cooperation since its power affinity reinforces an identity incompatibility.

Positive sanctions strategies are of a different kind; they emphasize a utility rationale. Accordingly, positive sanctions strategies are unlikely to contribute to conflict securitization. On the contrary, they may offer an enabling condition for non- or even de-securitization, communicating an offer on which the addressee may decide. With that offer, positive sanctions strategies are also true to Schelling’s (1960) notion that promises (or commitments) may become more expensive than threats. For initiators, risks may well turn into dangers with a subsequent decision by the addressee not to cooperate in exchange for a previously offered incentive.

As a third kind, combined sanctions strategies are initially indifferent towards utility and power rationales; they are open and contingent. They may lead to de-securitization, yet they may also enable securitization, depending on their construction in on-going conflict. Combined sanctions strategies thus make a multifaceted appearance, one that promises a more complex and perhaps controversial relation between prevailing conflict communication perceived as sanctions by opponents in practice.

Particular sanctions strategies have constitutive effects insofar as they make certain meanings possible. Conversely, in enabling some possibilities, particular strategies also impede certain other possibilities. When an identity conflict is already given, negative sanctions likely feed into the logic of such conflict communication. They barely enable the de-securitization of a securitized conflict. Positive sanctions strategies, for their part, are unlikely in themselves to enable the securitization of an issue conflict, since they do not suggest the referential linkage. Accordingly, by enabling some meaning possibilities and making other possibilities unlikely, particular sanctions strategies have a dispositional quality.

Crucially, the kind of strategy – whether sanctions are positive or negative – remains a matter of social construction. Thus, an addressee may differ from an initiator in conceiving sanctions and their suggested meaning potential. This demands a reconsideration of agency and decision-making to approach the question of communicated meaning and unintended consequences. As becomes evident, meaning in sanctions is indeed bound to context. Meaning is context-dependent and only by putting sanctions strategies into context can we identify analytically the meaning potential that a particular sanctions strategy suggests. There is no reason to expect an initiator of sanctions to be *a priori* able to decide upon meaning in sanctions episodes. The processing of meaning in sanctions episodes is a highly situational affair. The use of power, it seems, often works against its own ends. Yet the odds are different in different sanctions strategies. Unintended consequences (for initiators, that is,) thus seem particularly prevalent with negative sanctions strategies. The analysis into potential securitization processes allows for an investigation into the social construction of situated meaning and the observation of unintended consequences. Non-securitization becomes a necessary condition for any prospect of cooperation.

Notes

1 The theory of sanctions conflicts selectively takes up specific notions developed by Luhmann that it finds analytically advantageous in sorting out the basic terms of social reality. Different research interests warrant different solutions for substantive theoretical issues.

2 (Luhmann 1993:153).

3 Once the initiator as agent in communication conceives the future conflict development as contingent, there is no escape from the full implications of the form of risk, since not taking action is of course also a risky decision.

4 Luhmann builds his notion of second-order observation on the "assumption that every observer [of reality] has to make use of a distinction to be able to indicate what he wishes to observe. Observations are nothing more or less than distinguishing indications" (Luhmann 1993:15). What matters then is that observers draw distinctions, make selections and attributions that reflect the notion of risk, irrespective of whether they consciously refer to their construction of decision as 'risk'.

5 Following Luhmann's methodology, the concept of risk is acquired through second-order observation "by determining the counter concept and thus by distinguishing distinctions" (Luhmann 1993:23).

6 Morales' Movimiento al Socialismo (MAS) accused USAID of materially supporting existing oligarchic structures and the prevailing social injustice. After assuming the presidency, Morales' government, in a certain ironic twist, asked USAID to finance its own state-centered development campaign 'Evo Cumple'. See Los Tiempos, July 28, 2008: 'Evo quiere dinero de Usaid para plan "Bolivia cambia"'.

7 The EZLN claimed NAFTA to be a deliberate move towards the final straw that would eliminate the livelihood of millions of peasants and their families, forcing them to abandon the remaining traces of indigenous culture.

8 Delineating a utility rationale of cost/benefit calculation as the mutual orientation of subjects in conflict communication is not a statement on human nature. It is not to claim that humans are 'intrinsically' and ineluctably utility-maximizers (or satisfiers) of objectively who simply take into account cost/benefit relations. Rather, a utility rationale as part of common expectations is a social systemic effect, one that asks for decisions to be retrospectively interpretable as utility-centered. It is a socially common ascription that introduces such evaluative bases as the benchmark of decision (Luhmann 1993:47, 1997:108). Instead of over-relying on the rather difficult assumption of subjective preferences' temporal stability against a dynamic social context (cf. Hindess 1988:39), a utility rationale itself is taken to be a social expectation (and rational choice to have a clear normative connotation) that represents a specific demand on the evaluation of a decision within a social/temporal context. This touches upon what Emirbayer and Mische (1998:966) called the "problem at the heart of rational choice explanations": the question of how socially embedded actors, who are subject to a temporal contingency – located in a complex social context that evolves over time – can reach decisions which in hindsight may be called 'rational'. Thus, the demand is that decisions be evaluable in a plausible reconstruction as following a cost/benefit rationale.

9 The bases of utilitarian approaches, rational choice and game theory alike, clearly reflect this, as John Harsanyi's remarks on these bases emphasize: "Whatever the merits of the rationality concept of Bayesian decision theory may be, it is still in need of further generalization, because it does not adequately cover rational behavior in game situations, that is, in situations where the outcome depends on the behavior of two or more rational individuals who may have partly or wholly divergent *interests*" (Harsanyi 1977:322).

10 This is not to say that a threat as a physical fact may not exist, but rather, that such existence is without social consequence in the absence of social recognition. Take the crude example of a space rock on a collision course with Earth: it is of social consequence as a threat only once it is socially identified as such. This even holds for the scenario of an unanticipated impact, which would be the actual manifestation of catastrophe, not the threat of it. It is further perfectly possible and probable that in such a case the space rock would be constructed as a threat in hindsight. If there is still someone left to do so, that is.

11 The essentialist element of 'sectors' as proposed by the Copenhagen School in 1998 is considered here as being barely compatible with a social constructivist approach, as Doty (1998) argues.

12 Emirbayer and Mische delineate agency along three constitutive dimensions: iteration, projectivity and practical evaluation. I take up the first two dimensions as the primarily temporal elements. In integrating their conceptualization of agency into securitization,

my approach differs slightly from the one taken by Emirbayer and Mische with regard to their third element, 'practical evaluation', as the discussion will indicate.

13 An abbreviation of the full statement: "It is quite true what philosophy says; that life must be understood backwards. But then one forgets the other principle: that it must be lived forwards. Which principle, the more one thinks it through, ends exactly with the thought that temporal life can never properly be understood precisely because I can at no instant find complete rest in which to adopt a position: backwards" (Kierkegaard 1996 [1843]:63, 161).

14 Emirbayer and Mische (1998:1004) recognize this by advancing an analytical distinction between agency, action and structure, with social action to result from a synthesis of context and agency. Social context thus enters the equation (in the guise of 'structure'). However, this of itself still stops short of a full apprehension of the 'relational' in agency, since what in principle remains controversial is to what extent context shapes action in particular instances.

15 'Security' thus draws a conceptual boundary with significant analogies but also decisive differences to the form of risk (cf. Luhmann 1993): Like 'risk', the other side of the conceptual boundary consists of 'danger' as absence of agency and decision. Unlike 'risk', though, 'security' downplays contingency in its projective concentration of agency, by reducing the future to a merely rhetorical, binary choice – conveying an element of 'decisionism'.

Bibliography

Albert, Mathias. (2010) Modern Systems Theory and World Politics. In *New Systems Theories of World Politics*, edited by Mathias Albert, Lars-Erik Cederman, and Alexander Wendt. Basingstoke: Palgrave Macmillan.

Albert, Mathias, Thomas Diez, and Stephan Stetter. (2008) The Transformative Power of Integration: Conceptualising Border Conflicts. In *The European Union and Border Conflicts: The Power of Integration and Association*, edited by Thomas Diez, Stephan Stetter, and Mathias Albert. Cambridge: Cambridge University Press.

Albert, Mathias, Oliver Kessler, and Stephan Stetter. (2008) On Order and Conflict: International Relations and the "Communicative Turn". *Review of International Studies* 34: 43–67.

Baldwin, David A. (1971) The Power of Positive Sanctions. *World Politics* 24: 19–38.

Baldwin, David A. (1985) *Economic Statecraft*. Princeton, NJ: Princeton University Press.

Baldwin, David A. (1993) *Neorealism and Neoliberalism: The Contemporary Debate*. New York: Columbia University Press.

Balzacq, Thierry. (2005) The Three Faces of Securitization: Political Agency, Audience and Context. *European Journal of International Relations* 11: 171–201.

Balzacq, Thierry. (2010) Constructivism and Securitization Studies. In *The Routledge Handbook of Security Studies*, edited by Myriam Dunn Cavelty and Victor Mauer. London: Routledge Chapman & Hall.

Beck, Ulrich. (1992) *Risk Society: Towards a New Modernity*. London: Sage Publications.

Berenskoetter, Felix. (2011) Reclaiming the Vision Thing: Constructivists as Students of the Future. *International Studies Quarterly* 55: 1–22.

Buzan, Barry, Ole Wæver, and Jaap de Wilde. (1998) *Security: A New Framework for Analysis*. London: Lynne Rienner.

Campbell, David. (1998) *Writing Security: United States Foreign Policy and the Politics of Identity*. Revised ed. Minneapolis: University of Minnesota Press.

Ciută, Felix. (2009) Security and the Problem of Context: A Hermeneutical Critique of Securitisation Theory. *Review of International Studies* 35: 301–326.

Diez, Thomas, Stephan Stetter, and Mathias Albert. (2006) The European Union and Border Conflicts: The Transformative Power of Integration. *International Organization* 60: 563–593.

Doty, Roxanne Lynn. (1998) Immigration and the Politics of Security. *Security Studies* 8: 71–93.

Dunn Cavelty, Myriam, and Mark Daniel Jaeger. (2015) (In)Visible Ghosts in the Machine and the Powers That Bind: The Relational Securitization of Anonymous. *International Political Sociology* 9: 176–195.

Elster, Jon. (1998) A Plea for Mechanisms. In *Social Mechanisms: An Analytical Approach to Social Theory*, edited by Peter Hedström and Richard Swedberg. Cambridge: Cambridge University Press.

Emirbayer, Mustafa, and Ann Mische. (1998) What Is Agency? *American Journal of Sociology* 103: 962–1023.

Falleti, Tulia G., and Julia F. Lynch. (2009) Context and Causal Mechanisms in Political Analysis. *Comparative Political Studies* 42: 1143–1166.

Finnemore, Martha. (1996) Norms, Culture, and World Politics: Insights from Sociology's Institutionalism. *International Organization* 50: 325–347.

Finnemore, Martha. (2003) *The Purpose of Intervention: Changing Beliefs about the Use of Force*. Ithaca: Cornell University Press.

Freedman, Lawrence. (1998) *Strategic Coercion: Concepts and Cases*. Oxford: Oxford University Press.

Friedrichs, Jörg, and Friedrich Kratochwil. (2009) On Acting and Knowing: How Pragmatism Can Advance International Relations Research and Methodology. *International Organization* 63: 701–731.

Fuentes, Jorge. (2008) Evo Morales:"Nosotros Somos Gobierno, No Somos Poder, Lo Que Sí Estamos Tratando de Construir El Poder Del Pueblo". *Casa de las Américas*: 114–126.

Galtung, Johan. (1969) Violence, Peace, and Peace Research. *Journal of Peace Research* 6: 167–191.

Goertz, Gary. (1994) *Contexts of International Politics*. Cambridge: Cambridge University Press.

Guzzini, Stefano. (2000) A Reconstruction of Constructivism in International Relations. *European Journal of International Relations* 6: 147–182.

Guzzini, Stefano. (2010) Imposing Coherence: The Central Role of Practice in Friedrich Kratochwil's Theorising of Politics, International Relations and Science. *Journal of International Relations and Development* 13: 301–322.

Guzzini, Stefano. (2011) Securitization as a Causal Mechanism. *Security Dialogue* 42: 329–341.

Haas, Richard N. and Meghan L. O'Sullivan. (2000) *Honey and Vinegar: Incentives, Sanctions, and Foreign Policy*. Washington, DC: Brookings Institution Press.

Harsanyi, John. (1977) Advances in Understanding Rational Behavior. In *Foundational Problems in the Special Sciences*, edited by Robert E. Butts and Jaakko Hintikka. Dordrecht: D. Reidel.

Harvey, Frank, and Joel Cobb. (2003) Multiple Dialogues, Layered Syntheses, and the Limits of Expansive Cumulation. *International Studies Review* 5: 144–147.

Hedström, Peter, and Richard Swedberg. (1998) Social Mechanisms: An Introductory Essay. In *Social Mechanisms: An Analytical Approach to Social Theory*, edited by Peter Hedström and Richard Swedberg. Cambridge: Cambridge University Press.

Herborth, Benjamin. (2004) Die via media als konstitutionstheoretische Einbahnstraße. Zur Entwicklung des Akteur-Struktur-Problems bei Alexander Wendt. *Zeitschrift für Internationale Beziehungen* 11: 61–87.

Hindess, Barry. (1988) *Choice, Rationality, and Social Theory*. London: Unwin Hyman.

Jackson, Patrick Thaddeus. (2006) *Civilizing the Enemy: German Reconstruction and the Invention of the West*. Ann Arbor: University of Michigan Press.

Jackson, Patrick Thaddeus, and Daniel H. Nexon. (1999) Relations before States: Substance, Process and the Study of World Politics. *European Journal of International Relations* 5: 291–332.

Jaeger, Hans-Martin. (2010) Modern Systems Theory and/as Historical Discourse Analysis. In *New Systems Theories of World Politics*, edited by Mathias Albert, Lars-Erik Cederman, and Alexander Wendt. Basingstoke: Palgrave Macmillan.

Joas, Hans. (1993) *Pragmatism and Social Theory*. Chicago: University of Chicago Press.

Kaempfer, William, and Anton David Lowenberg. (1992) *International Economic Sanctions: A Public Choice Perspective*. Boulder: Westview.

Kierkegaard, S. (1996) *Papers and Journals: A Selection*. New York: Penguin Classics.

Kratochwil, Friedrich. (1971) Politik und Politische Wissenschaften. Ein Diskussionsbeitrag zum Begriff des Politischen. *Zeitschrift für Politik* 18: 113–123.

Krebs, Ronald R., and Jennifer K. Lobasz. (2007) Fixing the Meaning of 9/11: Hegemony, Coercion, and the Road to War in Iraq. *Security Studies* 16: 409–451.

Luhmann, Niklas. (1993) *Risk: A Sociological Theory*. Berlin: Gruyter.

Luhmann, Niklas. (1995) *Social Systems*. Stanford: Stanford University Press.

Luhmann, Niklas. (1996) Das Risiko der Kausalität. In *Kreativität – Wirtschaft – Recht, Zürcher Hochschulforum*, edited by Najib Harabi. Zürich: vdf Hochschulverlag AG.

Luhmann, Niklas. (1997) *Die Gesellschaft der Gesellschaft*. Frankfurt am Main: Suhrkamp.

Luhmann, Niklas. (2000) *Die Politik der Gesellschaft*. Frankfurt am Main: Suhrkamp.

Mahoney, James. (2003) *Tentative Answers to Questions about Causal Mechanisms*. Philadelphia. Annual Meeting of the American Political Science Association.

Margalit, Avishai, and Joseph Raz. (1990) National Self-Determination. *The Journal of Philosophy* 87: 439–461.

Mayntz, Renate. (2004) Mechanisms in the Analysis of Social Macro-Phenomena. *Philosophy of the Social Sciences* 34: 237–259.

McDonald, Matt. (2008) Securitization and the Construction of Security. *European Journal of International Relations* 14: 563–587.

Messmer, Heinz. (2003) *Der soziale Konflikt: Kommunikative Emergenz und systemische Reproduktion*. Stuttgart: Lucius und Lucius.

Messmer, Heinz. (2007) Contradiction, Conflict and Borders. In *Territorial Conflicts in World Society: Modern Systems Theory, International Relations and Conflict Studies*, edited by Stephan Stetter. London: Routledge.

Nexon, Daniel H. (2010) Relationalism and New Systems Theory. In *New Systems Theories of World Politics*, edited by Mathias Albert, Lars-Erik Cederman, and Alexander Wendt. Basingstoke: Palgrave Macmillan.

Palan, Ronen. (2000) A World of Their Making: An Evaluation of the Constructivist Critique in International Relations. *Review of International Studies* 26: 575–598.

Ross, John. (1995) *Rebellion from the Roots: Indian Uprising in Chiapas*. Monroe: Common Courage Press.

Russell, Philip L. (1995) *The Chiapas Rebellion*. Austin: Mexico Resource Center.

Schelling, Thomas C. (1960) *The Strategy of Conflict*. Cambridge, MA: Harvard University Press.

Sil, Rudra, and Peter J. Katzenstein. (2010) *Beyond Paradigms: Analytic Eclecticism in the Study of World Politics*. Basingstoke: Palgrave Macmillan.

Stritzel, Holger. (2007) Towards a Theory of Securitization: Copenhagen and Beyond. *European Journal of International Relations* 13: 357–383.

Stritzel, Holger. (2011) Security as Translation: Threats, Discourse, and the Politics of Localisation. *Review of International Studies* 37: 2491–2517.

Tajfel, Henri, and John Turner. (1986) The Social Identity Theory of Intergroup Behavior. In *Psychology of Intergroup Relations*. Chicago: Nelson-Hall.

Vargas, Jorge A. (1994) NAFTA, the Chiapas Rebellion, and the Emergence of Mexican Ethnic Law. *California Western International Law Journal* 25: 1–79.

Vuori, Juha A. (2008) Illocutionary Logic and Strands of Securitization: Applying the Theory of Securitization to the Study of Non-Democratic Political Orders. *European Journal of International Relations* 14: 65–99.

Wittgenstein, Ludwig. (1974) *Philosophical Grammar*. Oxford: Basil Blackwell.

4 Methodology and methods

The choice of the appropriate method depends on several key orientations and decisions made in the course of a scientific inquiry. In order for the findings to be valid, it is crucial that there should be conceptual coherence between, first, the essential theoretical components, second, the methodological stance and third, the methods applied. The justification of the choice of methods depends not just on the obvious relationship to the research puzzle, but to an equal extent on a clarification of the methodological position and on ensuring the overall coherence of the three above-mentioned components. To reiterate, this theory explores the conditions within sanctions conflicts that are conducive to either cooperation or non-cooperation from a sociological perspective. First, what is the meaning of coercive sanctions as actions concerning the position of an opponent? Second, how are such positions constructed in international conflict? Third, what influence do coercive sanctions have on conflict transformation? These three questions are so closely interlinked that their individual contributions to the overall issue – cooperation/non-cooperation – cannot be isolated from each other and treated in separation. Accordingly, they do not pertain to different causal factors that could be treated as independent variables, precisely for the reason that they are not independent of each other (cf. Hall 2003:381–383).

Viewed from a comprehensive perspective, methodology is about, first, the relationship between researcher and the reality of the world and, second, that between knowledge and observation (Jackson 2011). It is of critical importance to clarify the position of a scientific project with regard to both issues since these issues are decisive for the rationale of its evaluation (Hall 2003:374). The rationale of evaluation consists of the logic of observation and the logic of case comparison. Regarding the former, the perspective upon which this theory of sanctions conflicts rests conceptualizes reality as consisting of communication. Far from being limited to a substantive claim about the nature of (social) reality, this claim also extends to the relationship between researcher and the world. It amounts to a rejection of a simple correspondence theory of truth. Facts do not speak for themselves. All observation is theory-dependent. This 'analyticism' conforms to a monist worldview. On the logic of case comparison, cases studies serve to designate those elements critical to causation and to demonstrate the utility of differences between individual analytical configurations of the model.

The decision regarding the preferred methods for empirical investigation rests upon, first, the basic theoretical orientation of the study and, second, the substantive conceptual elements put forward within the theory. Regarding the first aspect, the theory privileges the notion of meaning in communication and social process. It considers individuals not as being entirely independent of their social world; quite to the contrary they *are* only in relation to this social world. With regard to the second aspect, this endeavor has laid out several key components. The most fundamental of these components is the ontological primacy that is given to the notion of meaning in communication and the subsequent focus on how meaning is processed socially. What matters for the choice of methods, according to this perspective, is social process. The scientific interest is in how distinctions are drawn, how meaning emerges and how selections are subsequently made in social practice.

These conceptual factors suggest two choices regarding methods. First, a framing analysis within discursive fields will garner the substantive meaning content in the relevant political discourse. The more focused approach of framing analysis is justified on the grounds that the posited model – contrary to a more inductive approach resting on a broader discourse analysis – generates clear orientations that can readily serve as a guide to the analysis of frames located within specific discursive fields. Second, the notion of a social process that temporally unfolds and comprises social attributions and causation in social practice quite naturally suggests process tracing to carefully reconstruct the unfolding of developments and locate decision in discourse and more concretely in its socio-political environment. Securitization and its contestations unfold in a process, but it is also crucial to connect this to the observation of the materiality of sanctions and their political-economic effects.

The logic of comparison within the methodological position of the study furthermore influences its case selection rationale. As case studies serve to demonstrate the utility of differences between analytical configurations, the case selection rationale will present an analyticist re-interpretation of a most similar systems design.

Subsequently, the chapter describes each of the three components – methodological stance, decision on methods and case selection rationale – in a more detailed manner.

4.1 Methodology: analyticism

Theories construct a reality. The formation of knowledge "is not a passive registration . . .; it is an active conceptualisation" (Guzzini 2010:313). Theories are world views, not in the sense of an image that is taken of something that is 'more real', but rather to the extent that theories in themselves constitute the world to which researchers readily have access (Jackson 2011:114). Any system of meaning as consisting of abstractions and inferences is constitutive of further conceptualizations that are intersubjective and semantic (Davis 2005).

Defining reality as essentially social and assigning primacy to meaning as constitutive of social objects are statements about the world as part of a *scientific ontology* (Patomäki and Wight 2000). Taking a position on *scientific access* to reality in turn decides the logic upon which any evaluation of scientific theories rests in the first place (Bunge 1996). The importance of this latter issue of *philosophical ontology* can hardly be overstated. Two issues will be clarified, therefore: first, the relation between researcher and the world and, second, between knowledge and observation (Jackson 2011).

The position of this investigation into sanctions conflicts, that all observation is inherently theory-dependent, is a statement on the nature of science. It first of all rejects a correspondence theory of truth that rests on taking objects unproblematically as given, independent and external to any significant mediation, be it mental or social (Lakoff 1988). Along with this rejection goes the Cartesian dualist position of separating world and mind, resulting in the dismissal of a positivist input–output scheme of conjunctive causation (King, Keohane, and Verba 1994), as well as of critical realism's proposition of mind-independent *facts* about unobservables (Wight 2006; Snidal and Wendt 2009).

The sociological theory of coercive international sanctions rests on a *philosophical ontology* of 'Analyticism' that combines two particular methodological positions on the issue of access to reality. It depicts the relation between researcher and the world as a monist one, wherein reality is a theory-driven construct. Based on synthetic facts, analyticist researchers construct analytical models, wherein relevant factors are specified and evaluated on their role in the configurative causation of an outcome (Jackson 2011:142). In that sense, the developed sociological approach to international sanctions posits a model, and not a correspondence-driven representation. The notions advanced within that model, such as causal mechanisms, or the relation between emerging meaning and effective consequences, are strictly limited in their ontology to their logical function *within* the model, or to the wider system of meaning of a specific social constructivist scientific ontology.

What, then, is the relation between knowledge and experience? The pertinent philosophical-ontological issue is about *access* to reality. Scientific facts are synthetic. They stem from the conceptual tools provided by science, and relate to empirical phenomena. Accordingly, "[i]t is the observable implications of theory-dependent concepts that we call 'data' or 'facts'" (Davis 2005:48). This relation of synthetic facts links knowledge to actual experience, to the 'sphere of the perceivable'. In turn, it fundamentally alters the characterization of the task and the standards of evaluating research. "What researchers do is to order analytically the empirical data in accord with a model the worth of which lies *not* in its correspondence to the world, but in its pragmatic consequences for ordering the facts of the world" (Jackson 2011:115, emphasis in original). Scientific models are logical instruments within analytically available images. Analyticism thus subscribes to a phenomenalist view of the relation between knowledge and observation. Evaluation proceeds in terms of the criteria of the system of meaning to which a theory belongs, in terms of 'explanatory utility'.

For this model of coercive sanctions conflicts, the aim is the innovative ordering of synthetic facts, judged on its usefulness for granting new insights in making sense of the world. Similarly, the logic of comparison does not aim at empirical generalization through the comparative evaluation of case studies. Consequently, the rationale of case studies does not subscribe to a 'the more, the better' approach. Instead, the aim is to compare particular configurations *for the specific purpose of highlighting the utility of the effective differences between analytical configurations*.

The goal of analytical comparison is to *demonstrate how differences matter and offer new insights* into understanding the phenomenon of coercive sanctions in international conflict. Case studies thus serve to demonstrate the utility of these differences between analytical configurations and to "ascertain which factors are critical to the causal configuration" (Jackson 2011:148). This depiction of the relation of analytical models and case studies differs from the position of Patrick Thaddeus Jackson, who restricts analyticism to 'singular causal analysis', i.e. an investigation into the peculiarities of individual cases (Jackson 2011:154). However, this seems to be fairly dependent on the scope of the proposed model. A model may be general enough to cover a range of different analytical configurations (which is what the present model of coercive sanctions in international conflict does). The analysis of multiple cases instead is about the depiction of different analytical configurations in terms of an outcome.

To summarize, this study employs an analyticist research strategy in its proposition of an analytical model to understand the way in which meaning of coercive sanctions in international conflict is processed. Individual case studies serve to demonstrate the utility of differences between various configurations of meaning that sanctions and conflicts acquire, and how they relate to outcomes.

4.2 Methods: framing analysis and process tracing

The introductory part of this chapter has outlined the logic of observation and the logic of comparison that form the bases of the empirical investigation. This part outlines the methods of substantive empirical analysis and presents the rationale for their choice. Several additional factors are of relevance for the choice of methods. These factors either emanate from the conceptual elements of the theory, or they are assumptions and scope conditions that set out its explanatory horizon. This outline of the decision on methods will thus initially summarize the relevant conceptual factors, before presenting the rationale for the specific choice of framing analysis and process tracing. The discussion of these methods precedes the concrete outline of the empirical analysis.

The developed theory formulates particular conceptual elements that are important for the choice of method. Among them, the broad notion of communication put forward is highly significant in several respects. First, there are several media of communication. Communication does not solely consist of statements made in discourse, but – highly relevant to an analysis of coercive international sanctions – also of symbolically coded material transfers. Moreover, once sanctions are introduced in conflict in order to coerce, they are the main form of communication; when this occurs negotiation has failed. Accordingly, the material bases of coercive sanctions matter, although they do not translate directly into a specific policy.

This plays into a second aspect, the absence of simple sender–receiver communication. Since communication centers upon the difference between message and understanding, the analysis is about observing observations and not about the observation of objects. In short, meaning is decisive. Both aspects permit, even force, the analysis to be focused on the addressee of international sanctions. The initiator of sanctions is of course partaking in the social conflict as well. However, and related to the second aspect, how the initiator observes conflict is observed by the initiator or, in other words, what meaning it acquires for the initiator does not simply travel to the addressee. What the initiator may observe as an issue conflict may represent to the addressee a conflict of identity.

In addition, this theory focusses solely on sanctions introduced in order to coerce. Here is where the assumptions come in: the aim of such sanctions is to bring about cooperation. Sanctions introduced with different political ends, for example the economic deprivation of an adversary, are not covered by the study. This is significant in two ways. First, the two aspects of a broad notion of communication imply what needs to be covered in empirical analysis and thus suggest the methods that may be chosen. Accordingly, the empirical analysis must go beyond an investigation of text associated with a narrow definition of discourse. The declared goals of sanctions, as well as their material robustness, need to be evaluated when they are the main form of communication. When sanctions are declared to serve coercive purposes, but are implemented in ways that strongly lack any such attributes, then they are inconsistent with what this study is about.

Second, these considerations reveal the scope of the approach developed. Apart from excluding sanctions that serve non-coercive purposes, an extensive analysis of the observation of sanctions by their initiator is not necessary, according to the argument made here. The analysis includes the technical particularities of sanctions policies. However, the initiator's observation of conflict as part of its partaking in conflict communication does have to be taken into account. Nonetheless, the main focus of the empirical analysis is on the social processing of meaning by the addressee of sanctions, the addressee's observation of conflict and of sanctions therein.

In consequence, there are two specific methods favored for empirical analysis, each of which covers the specific requirements of the developed perspective on international sanctions in conflict. The first method, framing analysis, is aimed at the meaning content which is particularly reflected in the first two specific research questions, the observation of conflict and the meaning of sanctions. Framing analysis serves as a common parenthesis that allows the capturing of the construction of reality and emergent meaning with a focus on agency and contention (Benford and Snow 2000:614). Particularly in the context of highly salient coercive sanctions conflicts, "politics involves contestation between relatively clearly defined positions, which compete to find resonance among a number of carriers" (Neumann 2009:71).

Whereas a framing analysis aims to capture empirically the substantive meaning content, process tracing is a crucial second method used in the empirical investigation. In addition to the argument regarding the significance of meaning in sanctions conflict, the theory draws *connections between individual conceptual elements that describe the specific developments as a process* (i.e. observation of conflict, meaning of sanctions and influence of sanctions strategies on conflict development). Process tracing thus contributes to the empirical tracing of the first two research questions – how a specific meaning is attached to sanctions and how the conflict is observed – but it is especially important to the third question, that is, the influence of certain sanctions strategies and change rationales in the processing of meaning. The analysis traces these connections as developments that unfold along a temporal sequence as a social process. In being connected, they meaningfully interact with one another. That is, observing a conflict in a specific way interacts with the meaning that sanctions acquire; both are further connected to the impact that particular sanctions strategies will have.

The following two sub-chapters discuss in more detail both framing analysis and process tracing in the context of this research. With framing analysis, there is a certain tendency in the literature to paint this method in individualistic hues. However, there are no compelling reasons for such an interpretation, and alternative, non-individualistic interpretations do indeed exist. I will take these up and adapt them to suit the concepts advanced in the theory. Likewise, process tracing is a widely used technique applied across diverse research contexts. Regarding this study, the main bone of contention concerns claims of a required methodological dualist perspective and a correspondence theory of truth for process tracing. Again, there are no compelling reasons for an exclusionary view; alternative standpoints on this issue have already been articulated, and convincingly so. Accordingly, I will locate the method within the analyticist methodology and specify it along the requirements of the empirical analysis.

4.2.1 Framing analysis

The advancement of framing analysis[1] as a method of empirical analysis denotes a particular understanding of frames that may seem unconventional at first. Despite this unconventionality, 'frames' have been so widely applied that the actual use of the term is often ambiguous and ridden with conceptual inaccuracies. An explication of the particular understanding of frames advanced here is thus in order. Viewed as a method, frames do not do the significant conceptual work, that is, this is not about a *framing theory*. Frames are not part of the analytical model of sanctions conflicts. Nor does this understanding entail a *theory about frames*, wherein frames are considered as 'real ontological entities' (in the dualist sense) that empirically *do* something, e.g. influence social action, which would then be traced in the analysis of the material.

Instead, framing analysis as a *method* does something in empirical analysis: it organizes the empirical material. This view is still in line with more general notions wherein frames organize knowledge through categories and distinctions

(Autesserre 2009:254). Contrary to these notions, it is not frames themselves that shape understandings of the world and it is not frames that establish conditions of possibility. Framing analysis as a method takes this relation the other way around in tracing and reflecting meaning through organizing phenomenological knowledge. In line with a monist view, framing analysis is a tool that gives a focus to empirical observation, a method which – like all methods – provides particular lenses with which to highlight those phenomena that are of significance to the analytical approach.

In the theory of sanctions conflicts that has been developed, meaning emerges through the interplay of several elements, such as associating sanctions with a utility or a power rationale, or observing conflicts in terms of issue or identity incompatibilities. Ultimately, however, the shift in meaning that is decisive in sanctions conflicts – securitization – is an agency-driven process. Besides the inherently projective securitizing move itself, social recognition as instantiation of agency and the attribution of responsibility are the substantive parts of the transformation of meaning into an identity conflict. The aim thus is to "investigate the workings of power in the production of [meaning] by exploring the struggle over who gets to speak authoritatively" (Dunn 2009:81).

Accordingly, framing analysis as a method seeks to enable the empirical localization of these substantial parts of the meaning of sanctions conflicts. It is preferable to a more open discourse analysis, because a properly specified framing analysis empirically provides what the analytical approach conceptually proposes. Framing analysis is also preferable to a narrower focus on securitization directly because sanctions conflicts may also remain fully non-securitized. We want to know whether agency stays iterative and how meaning remains delimited along established rules against the background of different sanctions policies.[2]

Frames capture and densify the discursive processes of meaning negotiation (cf. Gamson 1992); first, there is a diagnostic part that consists of the identification of a specific problem and involves social attributions; second, the proposed solutions to the problem are covered by the prognostic part of frames (Benford and Snow 2000:616). In the context of securitization processes, 'threat frames' are conceptualized as establishing the issue that threatens a certain referent object and proposing actions towards a solution (Dunn Cavelty 2008:30–33). Although the concept of threat frames covers an important part of meaning emergence in sanctions conflicts, the outline of frames ultimately needs to reflect both the developed notion of securitization more directly as a theory of agency, and the wider conceptual environment.

- Diagnostic framing: By substantively establishing the issue that threatens a certain referent object, a respective threat frame is projective; it *illustrates* a departure from its alternative, an iterative reproduction of established patterns of meaning in line with a utilitarian approach to conflict solution. Threat frames capture the attribution of responsibility towards the Other and the view of being only affected by escalating decisions of the Other. Diagnostic framing is thus about the causes of the conflict or its escalation and establishes whether and to what extent addressees view sanctions as part of these causes.

- Prognostic framing: A conflict securitization proposes a way forward in a distinct, binary manner that consists of either survival or non-survival of the referent object. Hence it differs markedly from prognostic framings in a non-securitized issue conflict with no references to survival and no necessary reduction of contingent choices and solutions to a binary selection. A prognostic framing also covers the articulation of actions associated with the proposed solution to the problem.

The linkage between the content of the diagnostic and prognostic parts of frames is fairly obvious. Any proposed way forward depends of course on a certain diagnosis of what the issue is about.[3] Again, this highlights that the distinction is purely synthetic, organizing the empirical material in a way that helps to identify and distinguish the content that is relevant to the emergence of meaning according to the theory developed.

For capturing social recognition as instantiation of agency, it is of interest to look at how well the contents of frames resonate with their audience. Unlike Benford and Snow's (2000:619–622) notion of resonance, particular factors like consistency and credibility are not of direct interest here. These elements are part of a theory about frames; they may certainly contribute to audience acceptance, but both the research interest and the way in which framing analysis is employed here as a method of empirical analysis are different.[4] In highlighting the role of the audience, frame resonance highlights the intersubjectivity of meaning.

- Frame resonance: Social recognition plays a dual role. On the one hand, diagnostic framing contains an attribution of responsibility, and therein *agency*, either as self-attribution or towards the Other. On the other hand, prognostic framing illustrates a solution to the identified problem in terms of actions which at the same time would mark a reproduction or recuperation of initiative and, crucially, agency. For this to materialize, the theory sees social recognition as the key factor. Consequently, it is important to trace empirically how prognostic/diagnostic framing resonates with the politically relevant audience.

Closely related to the issue of the resonance is the potential existence of competing frames. The social generation of meaning is a continuously contested process and this is well reflected in framing analysis (Steinberg 1998).

- Frame competition: Competing frames describe coherent alternative diagnoses and prognoses. The salience of competing frames is directly related to the resonance of a particular framing (cf. McAdam 1996) in that it affects its political predominance and acceptance among the relevant political audience.

The notion of frame competition allows the social contestation of meaning to be organized by means of identifying coherently linked alternative diagnoses and prognoses. Frames and competing frames thus capture different existing diagnoses and prognoses in a struggle to become the predominantly accepted meaning of sanctions and conflict. Analogously to the use of 'representations' in discourse analysis, if there is only one framing, for example a securitization, then the discourse on the meaning of sanctions and conflict is closed. However, analysis then of course does not become uninteresting, since "this does not mean that it is not political, because it takes a lot of discursive work to maintain [such] a situation" as Neumann (2009:70) observes.

The fact that there might be more than one empirically identifiable framing, indeed several competing frames, indicates the need to consider framings as situated in a wider *discursive field*. Put differently, if frames are supposed to capture emerging meanings, and resonance serves as an indicator of meaning contestation, then this requires that they be located in a relational field wherein contestation between different problem diagnoses and prognoses occurs. Discursive fields delineate meaning contestation around a common issue: the sanctions conflict by the addressee. Accordingly, their most basic dimension pertains to the discourse on the meaning of sanctions and conflict: it is *open* when competing frames can be identified; it is *closed* when there is a lack of competing frames.

Given the role of social recognition in the instantiation of agency, the social contextual circumstances of framings become important. Social context can be characterized by long-established, institutional actors with equally saturated relations. Social context is different and much less structured for newly emerging discursive fields where new understandings of an issue must first be developed and positions established. As part of a method for empirical analysis discursive fields are instruments for organizing the empirical environment of framings.[5]

Fields are located between the concrete contested framings and a common orientation that resembles stability. However, fields are not static: "One must think flow, not control" (Neumann 2009:70). One dimension along which discursive fields vary is the aforementioned openness or closure of discourse, i.e. frame contestation. The second dimension is relational and illustrates social and temporal properties of discursive fields, i.e. whether a field is emergent with not yet institutionalized agencies and unstable actor relations or whether a field is highly structured wherein agencies are reproduced and actor relations are established and stable (see Figure 4.1).

Discursive fields of meaning contestation in conflict help to empirically organize the broader analysis of how agency is assigned in communication and how actors emerge and are reproduced as agents:

- Discursive fields consist of particular framings and eventually competing frames with a common orientation towards the social conflict involving international sanctions. Furthermore, the discursive environment comprises significant institutions[6] and historical repertoires to which framings resort. The relational component encompasses the political struggle, how agency is reproduced: it thus integrates frame resonance and processes of social recognition.

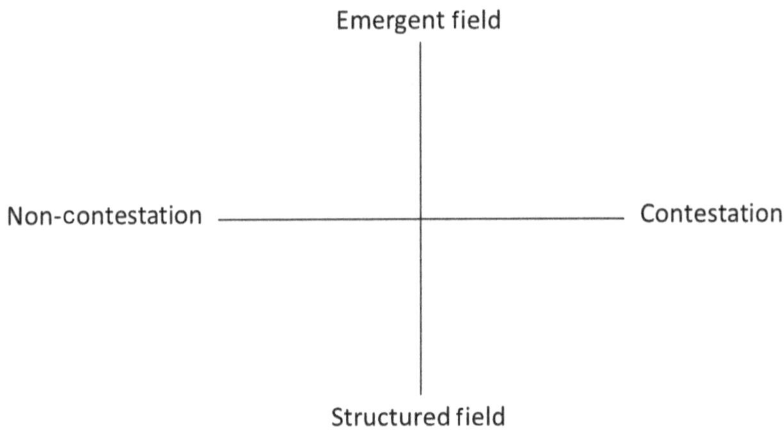

Figure 4.1 Discursive fields (cf. Snow 2008:11)

Discursive fields also encompass the eventual embedding of sanctions and conflict in a broader history of antagonisms, through 'historical repertoires'. These are, in their stronger and more explicit versions, similar to what Hilton and Liu termed a 'historical charter', "a foundational myth for a society, defining rights and obligations" (Liu and Hilton 2005:538). Charters consist of key elements of historical repertoires persistently invoked in the processes of identification constitutive of a social group. There need not be consensus on the meaning of these elements, which can be contested, but the general significance of these elements is uncontroversial (Liu, Sibley, and Huang 2013).

Discursive fields are therefore also vital in assessing whether securitization signifies a qualitative change between an issue conflict and an identity conflict. To restate, the conflict between the initiator of sanctions and the addressee can already be securitized before the introduction of sanctions. In addition, conflict history can pertain to the sanctioning entity but may also have a domestic component and include oppositional groups. Competing frames may well be linked to such societal conflicts.

Although fields denote an element of stability, they are not clearly defined but fuzzy and dynamic (Steinberg 1998:856). Additional actors may appear and meaning potentials cannot be strictly limited beyond their common subject of the sanctions conflict. This is more cautiously meant as a caveat, however. What can be expected as the usual situation is that fields are reasonably stable because institutions, legitimacy and power are supportive factors.

In summary, framing analysis as an empirical tool is used to organize phenomenological observations on the social processes of meaning emergence. Its individual elements each cover a particular theoretical proposition (see Table 4.1). Diagnostic framing captures how the conflict is observed, whether there is a threat

Table 4.1 Conceptual elements in empirical analysis

Conceptual Element	Empirical Analysis
History Of Conflict Initiator-Addressee • Issue Conflict • Identity Conflict • Historical Repertoires	→ Discursive Field
Meaning in Sanctions Conflicts: Causes • Causes of Conflict o Iteration: established rules o Threat to referent object (sanctions) • Attribution of Responsibility (Decision-Makers/Affected)	→ Diagnostic Framing
Meaning in Sanctions Conflicts: Policies • Proposed actions • Non-securitization: Issue-centred • Securitization: survival, binary choice	→ Prognostic Framing
Meaning in Social Contestation • Audience acceptance • Social recognition • Alternative meanings	→ Frame Resonance → Frame Competition
Discursive Environment of the Addressee • Contestation • Institutions • Actors • Political agency	→ Contested/non-contested discursive field → Emergent/structured discursive field

and the attribution of responsibility, and whether sanctions are viewed as a significant cause. Prognostic framing is about a respective way forward and eventual securitization. Frame resonance and competition cover social contestation, with the former focused on social recognition and the latter on the substantive content of meaning contestation. Framings are embedded in fields which capture the broader discursive environment of the sanctions conflict.

All in all, framing analysis is thus applied as a method for empirically tracing the emergence of meaning. To recall, in the theoretical approach, meaning represents the condition of possibility for particular actions and, by implication, outcomes of sanctions conflicts. With the method of framing analysis, a conceptual core component is covered in empirical inquiry.

4.2.2 *Process tracing*

The sociological theory of international sanctions conflicts delineates how certain actions and decisions become possible, but it does not stop there: the selection processes in the social processing of meaning amount to causation in social practice. Securitization represents the decisive conceptual piece in the unfolding process of sanctions conflicts; it is *the* causal mechanism. Other factors posited by the theory, like the observation of the conflict and sanctions themselves, feed into the processing of meaning and contribute to social causation. None of these elements however possesses in itself decisive causal powers. Causation resides in practice and remains an agency-driven process which is modeled as securitization. At this point process tracing comes in. Framing analysis is a heuristic method that captures meaning emergence. Process tracing is the necessary temporal complement that covers the linkage of meaning with agency in social practice.

Process tracing as a method serves to illustrate explanations that make reference to causal mechanisms (Mayntz 2004). Oftentimes, process tracing as a technique of empirical investigation is associated with positivist methodology. There, it has a complementary role for transcending the limitations encountered with complex interaction effects in existing methods of testing hypotheses (Hall 2003). Instead of erecting a black box between 'cause' and 'effect', within-case observations are "linked in particular ways . . . [and it] is this very lack of independence among these observations that makes them a powerful tool of inference" (George and Bennett 2005:207). The instigation of process tracing to open the black box indicates where its main clout as a method lies: in the investigation of causal mechanisms (Bennett and Checkel 2014), and causal mechanisms feature prominently in non-positivist methodologies. Pragmatist notions of agency and of consequences as enablers of causality refer to causal mechanisms (Johnson 2006; Kratochwil 2007).

Process tracing is also useful to analyticist investigations in that it is able to transform "a historical narrative into an analytical causal explanation couched in explicit theoretical forms" (George and Bennett 2005:211). In a monist view, process tracing encompasses "mechanisms [that] are theoretical constructs or heuristic devices, which we apply to our observations in order to classify them" (Pouliot 2007:373). Process tracing in an analyticist inquiry is an analytical construct around a causal mechanism, giving a dynamic account of social developments.

In the empirical analysis of this study, process tracing is the method used to capture social causation. Causation always implies a temporal sequence. The interplay between meaning and social practice develops as a temporal sequence, as a process. As Jeff Checkel (2008) notes, process tracing alone cannot account for the whole of this interplay: "Process tracing is strong on questions of interactions" (p. 116) but is seen as "missing the broader forces that enable and make possible human agency" (p. 124). Process tracing thus stands in a relation of complementarity to framing analysis which, taken in isolation, is equally impotent to account for causation. Framing analysis captures meaning as a condition of possibility for social causation, but for the latter "[w]e must ask, Who constructs knowledge and truth claims, for what purposes, and against what resistance?" (Dunn 2009:81). In short, social practice is the pivotal concern, and it is agency-driven.

Ultimately, it is actors who engage in practice, even when 'agency' is a collective affair, a product of social attribution. Consequently, the aim is to draw connections between emerging meanings, actions and decisions along a temporal sequence. To paraphrase Machamer, Darden and Craver (2000:3), process tracing as an analyticist technique in a constructivist inquiry focuses upon causal mechanisms that are composed of meanings and practices. This means reconstructing unfolding developments in a theoretically informed way, centered upon the notion of securitization as theory of agency and as eventually a causal mechanism. Securitization and the involved attribution of causality are brought about mainly by institutional practices involving those actors socially recognized as competent agents.[7] The public and the media observe government bodies, parties, politicians, factions and social movements as political actors; furthermore, these entities themselves observe each other as actors in their relational references. This will subsequently guide the empirical analysis accordingly. The statements of these different entities are socially elevated and processed in a way leading to the ascription and recognition of distinct political positions in a discursive field. For securitization as a causal mechanism in sanctions conflicts the decisive factor is in what ways these political actors attribute causal responsibility. The aim is to trace the emergence of meaning and to locate decisions in discourse as social practices, as processes amongst actors (see Table 4.2).

The theory of sanctions conflicts formulates clear relational positions (initiator, addressee; securitizer, audience). On the side of the initiator of sanctions we are interested in what kinds of sanctions are actually imposed. Importantly, this potentially includes not only negative sanctions but also positive ones. We are in addition interested in the temporal pattern of imposed sanctions: are there different strategies occurring separately, or is there a combination of negative and positive sanctions? Accordingly, the analysis should not only focus upon the immediate

Table 4.2 Actors in empirical analysis

	Actors	Sources
Initiator	**Administration**	
	• Executive (includes Ministries)	→ Official statements, texts → Supporting documents
	• Legislature (includes sub-groups)	→ Statements → Supporting documents
	Executing organizations	
	• Special Agencies	→ Statements → Supporting documents
Addressee	Government	
	• Executive (+ Key Ministries, Military)	→ Official statements, texts → Supporting documents
	Opposition	
	• Parliamentary	→ Statements, speeches, debates
	• Non-parliamentary (+ Business)	→ Opinion polls (when available) → Statements → Academic analyses
	Media	
	• Local Newspapers	→ Articles, editorials, op-eds
	• International News Agencies	

government bodies such as the executive, legislature and the like; depending on the specifics of the initiator, other executing organizations such as development agencies also need to be taken into account.

On the addressee side of sanctions conflicts the social processing of meaning takes center stage. It is reflected in particular frames and is conceptualized as occurring within a discursive field. This suggests a focus upon specific groups of actors. Obviously, the government is in a highly privileged position in the observation of conflict. It legitimizes state action. Moreover, governments observe each other relationally as main addressees. The discourse on the meaning of foreign policy issues revolves around claims made by the government. The media are important bearers of frame resonance. They may also convey competing frames, but contestation in the discursive field on a sanctions conflict is mainly driven by the policy statements of opposition parties or, in certain cases, by non-parliamentary opposition groups and social movements. The latter increase in importance in the case of authoritarian regimes. The interplay between the framings of sanctions, resonance and potential contestation is carried out by these political actors. Though frame resonance is also reflected in the positioning of other political groups in the discursive field, elections are the most straightforward revelation of frame resonance with the public as a main audience. The interplay between these factors is decisive in whether a conflict is securitized or not and whether cooperation may ultimately ensue.

Besides the attention to text in the emergence of meaning this study rests on a broad notion of communication that needs to be reflected in process tracing. Sanctions regularly contain material aspects, symbolically coded bindingly in terms of money. This needs to be included in the analysis. Both the meaning and the material are consequential. Process tracing documents the material attributes of the sanctions imposed by an initiator as part of a process development in conflict communication. For negative sanctions, it is necessary to distinguish coercive sanctions from other types of sanctions. Furthermore, and especially in the case of positive sanctions, the manipulation of material flows is an important contribution to fostering or inhibiting the capacity of particular social groups. Consequently, the specific targeting of sanctions is part of the communication process that needs to be traced.

4.3 Case selection rationale

The study opts to analyze empirically the sanctions conflicts between China and Taiwan and between the US and Iran on the Islamic Republic's nuclear program in order to illustrate its developed sociological theory of sanctions conflicts. The case selection rests on two main motives. First, these conflicts allow a comparative illustration of the occurrence of negative, combined and positive sanctions strategies in six individual cases within two most similar systems designs. Both conflict systems, China–Taiwan and the US–Iran, offer a great opportunity for a disciplined comparison to highlight the utility of the analytical configurations that the developed conceptualization suggests.

Second, the conflicts between China and Taiwan as well as between the US and Iran present interesting challenges for the investigation's propositions on the relation between sanctions, conflict observation and securitization as causal mechanism. Since the end of the civil war, China and Taiwan have never signed a peace treaty but have instead continued to define their political identities in ways that mutually exclude the existence of the Other. Such a conflict poses a challenge to any prospects of de-securitization. Since the Islamic Revolution, the conflict between the US and Iran is similarly prone to communicating identity incompatibilities, between 'oppressive imperialists' and 'supporters of terrorism' that are part of an 'axis of evil'. This section looks further at the two reasons for the case selection.

Why conduct the empirical analysis in a most similar systems design? A number of reasons favor such an arrangement. Yet there are also some methodological issues in need of clarification. Generally, a most similar systems design is a method proposed for the handling of complexity. It seeks a comparison between cases as similar as possible to focus on a central, distinguishing feature to account for empirically observed developments. In the words of Przeworski and Teune, who formally introduced the concept (1970:33): "The number of common characteristics sought is maximal and the number of not shared characteristics sought, minimal". The design thus imitates the logic of an experiment that deliberately strives to control complexity.[8]

The substantive interpretation of a most similar systems design as 'controlled experimentation' reflects a positivist methodology. Its comparative political analyses focus on a 'macro-level' to assess similarities across political systems (De Meur and Berg-Schlosser 1994). Specific case characteristics are interpreted as variables in an effort to eliminate variation to all but one, explanatory factor: "Common characteristics are conceived of as 'controlled for,' whereas intersystemic differences are viewed as explanatory variables" (Przeworski and Teune 1970:33). The precise challenge to a positivist most similar systems design, however, consists exactly of ensuring that all differences are covered and minimized, a usually impossible task (Faure 1994). In consequence, results are overdetermined by too many remaining differences. Within positivist political science, scholars aim to attenuate the problem by assessing the conclusion reached in the comparison through within-case analysis such as process tracing (Collier 1993; George and Bennett 2005:252). In addition, whether there is in fact variation or not depends on the conceptual lenses applied to examine cases. In other words, it is a question of the theories used: "Theory guides the choice of independent variables to vary and extraneous variables to be kept constant" (Anckar 2008:395). Obviously, the theories used also determine the match of cases. As David Collier (1993:112) observes, "cases that are closely matched from one point of view may contrast sharply from another".

From an analyticist point of view, the premises of a positivist most similar systems design mimicking an experiment are already problematic. As has been mentioned, with all observations theory-driven, the assumption of independently given evidence against which to evaluate propositions becomes untenable (see also

Davis 2005). Theory thus guides the identification of case characteristics, the assessment of match across cases and the evaluation of empirical data. That may offer some relief to the concept of most similar systems design, but it also raises the question of its usefulness to an analyticist methodology.

This investigation argues that the merits of a most similar systems design transcend a positivist methodology. First and foremost, the concept serves to reduce the complexity of empirical data, whether conceived from a positivist or from an analyticist-phenomenalist perspective. Conceptually, any reductionist model, which by its very nature essentially subsumes many, more fine-grained details, will profit from circumstances where many of these details remain akin when demonstrating its utility.

Second, the study's sociological approach and its analyticist methodology can accommodate a notion of 'system' as well, although one that differs from its interpretation in many comparative political analyses as a 'political system'. In an investigation into the sanctions conflicts between, first, China and Taiwan and, second, the US and Iran over the Islamic Republic's nuclear program, interest lies in the relational conflict dyad. The study has conceptualized conflict as a relational process of communication, with both opponents communicating, instead of merely reacting to external stimuli. Thus, the most similar systems design encompasses the whole conflict, not merely the political system of one of the opponents.

Third, the theory developed by this investigation, the possible analytical configurations it proposes and its notion of a causal mechanism, are interested in how particular conditions and developments relate to the causal mechanism of conflict transformation. In other words, the interest is in how common characteristics and differences, as proposed by theory, contribute to conflict development. Whether such characteristics consist of processes and practices or independent and dependent variables remains immaterial to this basic motive for a most similar systems design.

As a most similar systems design, the concrete analysis of the sanctions conflicts between, first, China and Taiwan and, second, the US and Iran, has additional analytical advantages. Generally, there are two immediate possibilities of distinguishing particular cases in such a design, spatially and temporally (Lijphart 1971:689; George and Bennett 2005:166). Of the two, the challenges for a spatial distinction are disproportionately larger. Finding spatially-distinct most similar cases, with cultural and many other possibly dissimilar characteristics playing into social practices, is difficult and doubtlessly relies on a compromise that presents a greater liability than a neat diachronic analysis of one international conflict divided into successive cases. Of course, with conflict and social relations generally part of an evolving process, there will still be differences between temporally divided cases. However, applying detailed process tracing ensures that any changes in conceptually relevant characteristics are analytically recognized. In consequence, the specific constellation of three successive distinct sanctions strategies both in the conflict between China and Taiwan, and in the conflict over Iran's nuclear program make them even more suitable for analysis in terms of a most similar systems design.

The aim of the empirical analysis is to illustrate the utility of differences between particular analytical configurations of the developed model for understanding how cooperation and non-cooperation become possible in international sanctions conflicts. For that purpose, a most similar systems design provides an appropriate constellation.

Besides, the conflict systems between China and Taiwan as well as between the US and Iran also present interesting cases for exploring the proposed relation between sanctions, conflict observation and its transformation towards (non-)cooperation. For greater China, the civil war between the communist People's Republic of China and the Republic of China's nationalist Kuomintang, who retreated to Taiwan, did not end in the mid-20th century with one side declaring victory and the other side conceding defeat, or with a peace treaty. Instead, military hostilities stopped and the PRC unilaterally declared victory. The ROC never recognized the PRC or the Communist Party as a legitimate political actor, let alone as representing China. Neither did the PRC recognize the ROC. Instead, both the PRC and ROC kept their mutually exclusive claims to represent China, including the island of Taiwan. Such a conflict of communicated but literally incompatible identities presents a challenge to any prospects of conflict transformation towards issue incompatibilities. Yet in the 1990s, the PRC increasingly sought to impose its notion of the *status quo* and its vision for reunification on the ROC, with the use of various coercive sanctions strategies.

In general, relations between the US and the Islamic Republic are characterized by deep suspicion or outright enmity, non-recognition and a refusal to establish official diplomatic channels or to engage in direct dialogue, fueled by mutual observations of fundamental identity incompatibilities. The Iranian narrative of the Islamic Revolution as an assertion of independence against the US imperialist oppressor stands against traumatic US experiences and an image of a regime that supports terrorism and is willing to disregard the universal norms of the US-backed global order. The dispute over Iran's nuclear program takes place against this broader conflict setting, with equally high stakes for the opponents involved, making any enduring solution to this dispute a daunting proposition.

The empirical analysis of both the China–Taiwan and the US–Iran conflict systems illustrates the relation between on-going conflict, sanctions and conflict transformation. It includes negative, combined and positive sanctions strategies and focuses on conflict transformation between communicated issues and identity incompatibilities. On the developed theory's own terms, the six individual cases taken together are certainly representative of many sanctions conflicts that involve conflict transformation. The fact that both conflict systems are challenging in terms of prospects of transformation towards issue incompatibilities increases the analytical utility gained from the empirical analysis.

Finally, a few words on the feasibility of conducting an empirical analysis of the Cross-Strait conflict without proficiency in the Chinese language and the dispute over Iran's nuclear program without proficiency in *Farsi*. In the case of the Cross-Strait conflict, important local media sources are available in English. Both the PRC and ROC press publish English editions. Also, the conflict is very well reported in international media. As an additional source, BBC Monitoring offers translation of local media content. For Iran, I rely mostly on the BBC Monitoring translation services of major Iranian media (newspapers, radio, television), which provides a rich collection of Iranian sources across the discursive field. Conceptually, the analysis aims at the broad processes of conflict observation and the respective developments of the main political positions in Taiwan's and Iran's discursive fields. It does not aim to meticulously analyze particular statements in every detail or any possible discursive facets. The analysis is interested in the main statements of the main positions in the discourse. Inevitably, media reports already present interpretations of particular statements. However, given the conceptual bases of this investigation with its emphasis on intersubjectivity and social ascription, such an objection misses the point and does not matter. There are no significant constraints to the empirical analysis.

Notes

1 The study uses the terms 'framing' and 'frames' interchangeably.
2 Finally, this also militates against a discourse analysis centered entirely upon identity representations as proposed by Lene Hansen (2006). The obsession with the notion of 'identity' and its exclusive binding to 'representations' basically allows for no 'neutral' or even 'positive' observations of relationships, only hierarchical and more or less 'negative' ones. This is a questionable position. Irrespectively, the developed theory of sanctions conflicts formulates a clear distinction between issue conflict and identity conflict. Consequently, a blurring of this distinction on methodological grounds is, if anything, disadvantageous.
3 The linkage is also disclosed in that *norms* transcend the two parts of frames: as much as a diagnostic framing can disclose a norm violation, a prognostic framing will contain a way forward that transforms diagnosed difference into otherness in references to that normative claim. This transformation equals a securitization into an identity conflict.
4 Contrary to the notion of framing put forward by Benford and Snow (2000), there is no additional distinction of 'motivational framing' that would address the 'call for action' separately as a component of agency. A diagnostic frame in the logic of securitization, and especially the prognostic part, already discloses an action rationale. In addition, the notion of agency advanced in the theory significantly differs from Benford and Snow's ultimately individualist and, at least in terms of trend, reifying concept of agency.
5 Discursive fields have been used to conceptualize the discursive environment of framings (Spillman 1995; Steinberg 1998; Snow 2008). Individual approaches vary: Their intellectual roots either lie with structuralism or symbolic interactionism, and Pierre Bourdieu's notion of fields exercised a varying additional influence (Bourdieu 1998). Both scholars engage in significant theoretical work on the notion of 'fields'. Here, fields are considered as "analytical constructions, rather than empirical objects" (Hansen 2006:51), as tools of empirical analysis.
6 In the sociological sense of the word; 'sovereignty' is one example of such an institution.
7 This depiction builds on the notion of social practice suggested by Barry Barnes (2001), but emphasizes more firmly the relational component as constitutive of actors and agents. Again, this is not to engage in a perspective that would build upon an ethnography of social practices as its main analytical focus.
8 As Ernest Nagel expressed in one concise sentence, such "controlled investigation consists in a deliberate search for contrasting occasions in which the phenomenon is either uniformly manifested (whether in identical or differing modes) or manifested in some

cases but not in others, and the subsequent examination of certain factors discriminated in those occasions in order to ascertain whether variations in these factors are related to differences in the phenomena – where these factors as well as the different manifestations of the phenomenon are selected for careful observation because they are assumed to be relevantly related" (Nagel 1979:453).

Bibliography

Anckar, Carsten. (2008) On the Applicability of the Most Similar Systems Design and the Most Different Systems Design in Comparative Research. *International Journal of Social Research Methodology* 11: 389–401.

Autesserre, Séverine. (2009) Hobbes and the Congo: Frames, Local Violence, and International Intervention. *International Organization* 63: 249–280.

Barnes, Barry. (2001) Practice as Collective Action. In *The Practice Turn in Contemporary Theory*, edited by Theodore R. Schatzki, Karin Knorr Cetina, and Eike von Savigny. London: Routledge.

Benford, Robert D., and David A. Snow. (2000) Framing Processes and Social Movements: An Overview and Assessment. *Annual Review of Sociology* 26: 611–639.

Bennett, Andrew, and Jeffrey T. Checkel. (2014) Process Tracing: From Philosophical Roots to Best Practices. In *Process Tracing in the Social Sciences: From Metaphor to Analytic Tool*, edited by Andrew Bennett and Jeffrey T. Checkel. Cambridge: Cambridge University Press.

Bourdieu, Pierre. (1998) *Practical Reason: On the Theory of Action*. Stanford: Stanford University Press.

Bunge, Mario. (1996) *Finding Philosophy in Social Science*. New Haven, CT: Yale University Press.

Checkel, Jeffrey T. (2008) Process Tracing. In *Qualitative Methods in International Relations: A Pluralist Guide*, edited by Audie Klotz and Deepa Prakash. Basingstoke: Palgrave Macmillan.

Collier, David. (1993) The Comparative Method. In *Political Science: The State of the Discipline II*, edited by Ada W. Finifter. Washington, DC: American Political Science Association.

Davis, James W. (2005) *Terms of Inquiry: On the Theory and Practice of Political Science*. Baltimore: Johns Hopkins University Press.

De Meur, Gisèle, and Dirk Berg-Schlosser. (1994) Comparing Political Systems: Establishing Similarities and Dissimilarities. *European Journal of Political Research* 26: 193–219.

Dunn, Kevin C. (2009) Historical Representations. In *Qualitative Methods in International Relations: A Pluralist Guide*, edited by Audie Klotz and Deepa Prakash. Basingstoke: Palgrave Macmillan.

Dunn Cavelty, Myriam. (2008) *Cyber-Security and Threat Politics: US Efforts to Secure the Information Age*. Abingdon: Routledge.

Faure, Andrew Murray. (1994) Some Methodological Problems in Comparative Politics. *Journal of Theoretical Politics* 6: 307–322.

Gamson, William A. (1992) *Talking Politics*. Cambridge: Cambridge University Press.

George, Alexander L., and Andrew Bennett. (2005) *Case Studies and Theory Development in the Social Sciences*. Cambridge, MA: MIT Press.

Guzzini, Stefano. (2010) Imposing Coherence: The Central Role of Practice in Friedrich Kratochwil's Theorising of Politics, International Relations and Science. *Journal of International Relations and Development* 13: 301–322.

Hall, Peter A. (2003) Aligning Ontology and Methodology in Comparative Research. In *Comparative Historical Analysis in the Social Sciences*, edited by Dietrich Rueschemeyer and James Mahoney. Cambridge: Cambridge University Press.

Hansen, Lene. (2006) *Security as Practice: Discourse Analysis and the Bosnian War*. Abingdon: Routledge.

Jackson, Patrick Thaddeus. (2011) *The Conduct of Inquiry in International Relations: Philosophy of Science and Its Implications for the Study of World Politics*. Abingdon: Routledge.

Johnson, James. (2006) Consequences of Positivism: A Pragmatist Assessment. *Comparative Political Studies* 39: 224–252.

King, Gary, Robert O. Keohane, and Sidney Verba. (1994) *Designing Social Inquiry: Scientific Inference in Qualitative Research*. illustrated ed. Princeton, NJ: Princeton University Press.

Kratochwil, Friedrich. (2007) Of False Promises and Good Bets: A Plea for a Pragmatic Approach to Theory Building (the Tartu Lecture). *Journal of International Relations and Development* 10: 1–15.

Lakoff, George. (1988) Cognitive Semantics. In *Meaning and Mental Representations*, edited by Umberto Eco, Marco Santambrogio, and Patrizia Violi. Bloomington: Indiana University Press.

Lijphart, Arend. (1971) Comparative Politics and the Comparative Method. *The American Political Science Review* 65: 682–693.

Liu, James H., and Denis J. Hilton. (2005) How the Past Weighs on the Present: Social Representations of History and Their Role in Identity Politics. *British Journal of Social Psychology* 44: 537–556.

Liu, James H., Chris G. Sibley, and Li-Li Huang. (2013) History Matters: Effects of Culture Specific Symbols on Political Attitudes and Intergroup Relations. *Political Psychology*. Available at: http://onlinelibrary.wiley.com/doi/10.1111/pops.12027/abstract. (Accessed May 16, 2013).

Machamer, Peter, Lindley Darden, and Carl F. Craver. (2000) Thinking about Mechanisms. *Philosophy of Science* 67: 1–25.

Mayntz, Renate. (2004) Mechanisms in the Analysis of Social Macro-Phenomena. *Philosophy of the Social Sciences* 34: 237–259.

McAdam, Doug. (1996) The Framing Function of Movement Tactics. In *Comparative Perspectives on Social Movements: Political Opportunities, Mobilizing Structures, and Cultural Framings*, edited by John D. McCarthy, Mayer N. Zald, and Doug McAdam. Cambridge: Cambridge University Press.

Nagel, Ernest. (1979) *The Structure of Science: Problems in the Logic of Scientific Explanation*. Cambridge: Hackett Publishing Company.

Neumann, Iver B. (2009) Discourse Analysis. In *Qualitative Methods in International Relations: A Pluralist Guide*, edited by Audie Klotz and Deepa Prakash. Basingstoke: Palgrave Macmillan.

Patomäki, Heikki, and Colin Wight. (2000) After Postpositivism? The Promises of Critical Realism. *International Studies Quarterly* 44: 213–237.

Pouliot, Vincent. (2007) "Sobjectivism": Toward a Constructivist Methodology. *International Studies Quarterly* 51: 359–384.

Przeworski, Adam, and Henry Teune. (1970) *The Logic of Comparative Social Inquiry*. New York: Wiley-Interscience.

Snidal, Duncan, and Alexander Wendt. (2009) Why There Is International Theory Now. *International Theory* 1: 1–14.

Snow, David A. (2008) Elaborating the Discursive Contexts of Framing: Discursive Fields and Spaces. *Studies in Symbolic Interaction* 30: 3–28.
Spillman, Lyn. (1995) Culture, Social Structures, and Discursive Fields. *Current Perspectives in Social Theory* 15: 129–154.
Steinberg, Marc W. (1998) Tilting the Frame: Considerations on Collective Action Framing from a Discursive Turn. *Theory and Society* 27: 845–872.
Wight, Colin. (2006) *Agents, Structures and International Relations: Politics as Ontology*. Cambridge: Cambridge University Press.

Part II

Analysis

Sanctions and conflict (de-)escalation

One of the key traits of the current sociological theory is its ability to describe evolving sanctions conflicts and the implication of sanctions in the eventual transformation of conflict communication. The two conflict systems focused upon in the empirical analysis, between China and Taiwan and between the US and Iran, are among the most protracted, sensitive disputes in international politics, with strong security implications for the opponents involved. Both conflict systems provide an exceptionally rich setting for observing evolving sanctions conflicts. They provide a complete variety of observed sanctions strategies. In the conflict between China and Taiwan, negative, combined and positive sanctions strategies were imposed. Apart from one case of negative sanctions, the dispute over Iran's nuclear program involves two cases of combined sanctions – yet there was a significant difference in conflict development in these two cases. It is thus most remarkable that in both the Cross-Strait conflict and the dispute between the US and Iran, conflict communication evolved significantly, moving towards a securitized conflict and then on to eventual conflict de-escalation.

The empirical analysis of each of the two conflict systems is broadly divided into three parts that address the more specific research questions on the observation of conflict, the meaning that sanctions acquire and how sanctions impact on conflict development. The first part of the empirical analysis aims to capture the wider conflict of which sanctions are a part. Analyzing the broader history of conflict reveals the kinds of communicated incompatibilities of which the conflict consists. This knowledge of how conflict participants view and understand the conflict forms the bases for assessing the main research interest of this project: cooperation and non-cooperation in sanctions conflicts. In the case of the initiator, knowledge of conflict observation is important if we are to be able to ultimately judge whether or not there is cooperation on an 'issue conflict'. In the case of the addressee of sanctions, this first part establishes the historical dimension of what was termed the 'discursive field' in the methodology section. In other words, to be able to assess the development of a conflict in this way, it is necessary to know what 'cooperation' and 'non-cooperation' would entail in a particular conflict. One component of this discursive field is the immediate history of the conflict: what is the conflict about? Another component consists of historical repertoires, elements that are not part of the immediate history, but which are invoked artefacts of past relations. Then, in the next step, the characteristics of the addressee's discursive field are laid out more specifically. These are the foundations for assessing how social conflict is observed by the addressee. I will establish a) lines of contestation in the discursive field, and b) to what extent the field is emergent or structured. At this point, the aim is to capture the basic elements of contestation so as to obtain a broad picture of the political discourse, divisions and actors.

The second part of the empirical analysis then establishes what sanctions policies were pursued by the initiator, and traces, in a detailed analysis, the influence these policies had on the addressee's conflict observation. The periods when different sanctions strategies were observed are viewed as separate cases, resulting in three distinct cases of sanctions for the conflict between China and Taiwan, and three cases of sanctions for the conflict over Iran's nuclear program. I will analyze each of the six cases in the two conflict systems in two steps. In a first step, I will trace the sanctions that were introduced and establish the corresponding conflict observation by the initiator. The analysis thus takes the understanding of conflict outlined in the preceding part not only to contextually embed sanctions policies but also to further trace the way in which the initiator's conflict observation has evolved over time. Again, this is important if we are to be able to make an assessment on a possible conflict transformation. In a second step, I will trace the impact of sanctions on the addressee's conflict observation. This will involve addressing the more specific research questions regarding the meaning attached by observers to sanctions and how the sanctions imposed impact on their understanding of the conflict. In so doing, I will again take the findings established in the preceding part and use them to trace the way in which the addressee's discursive field on conflict observation has evolved over time and how the lines of contestation between the particular positions in the discursive field have developed.

I will use the two techniques presented in the methodology section of this book – process tracing and framing analysis – to investigate the addressee's observation of conflict and sanctions. In applying framing analysis and process tracing, I will analyze in detail the interplay between sanctions and conflict observation. First, I will trace in detail the temporal evolution of the discursive field by documenting statements from the main political groups. Second, in a framing analysis, I will examine more explicitly the particularities of each group's position and the lines of contestation between different positions by focusing upon a) the diagnostic framing (the alleged causes of the conflict, the role of sanctions, the attribution of responsibility), and b) the prognostic framing (the proposed actions/solutions). These are the two crucial steps for analyzing the process of securitization as a causal mechanism. They potentially contain not only one diagnostic framing that dominates how the conflict is observed, but also competing frames advanced by the political opposition, as part of a contested discursive field. In the actual analysis, I will use the two techniques, with some overlaps. Both techniques are applied in equal measure, though, to ensure that the content as well as the temporal development of conflict observation becomes evident.

Finally, the third part of the empirical analysis draws together and summarizes the insights gained in the analysis of the six cases to give the big picture. It provides an overview of the different sanctions strategies, securitization and (non-) cooperation in the conflict systems being analyzed: between China and Taiwan and over Iran's nuclear program. Based on the results of the analysis of the six cases, this part presents the interplay that has been observed between the conceptual elements of the theory, as observed in practice, and extends to the overall findings of that interplay.

5 Sticks, carrots and conflict transformation

China's sanctions against Taiwan

The conflict between the People's Republic of China (PRC, in this chapter also Mainland China) and the Republic of China (ROC, in this chapter also Taiwan) is prone to identity incompatibilities. Ever since the end of the Chinese Civil War in 1949, the very notion of whether there indeed exists a state called 'Taiwan' has given rise to an identity conflict. Yet relations between Mainland China and Taiwan from the middle of the century onwards have not shown a linear deterioration. Instead, observation of conflict has varied, and has currently stabilized along a delicate notion of temporary co-existence: There is one China which is able to tolerate different systems of governance.

In the past, this particular idea of 'One China' was challenged. After a few years of détente, by the mid-1990s, conflict observation began to emphasize and reinforce identity incompatibilities: In Taiwan, the continuing rise of the initial proponents of democratization created further potential identity incompatibilities. China, for its part, forcefully articulated reunification as a political goal.

Chinese sanctions policies can be divided into three cases of different strategies. In the first case, from 1995 to about 2002, negative sanctions contributed to a securitization of the conflict. In the second case, from around 2003 to 2005, some negative sanctions combined with some positive incentives, contributed to the conflict becoming deadlocked and to a stand-off between competing conflict observations within Taiwan. From 2005 onwards, positive sanctions contributed to a transformation of the conflict. Securitization processes represented a causal mechanism in the observation and transformation of the conflict.

The next part establishes the broader setting and history of this conflict system. Based on this understanding, the second part traces initiated sanctions and conflict development in three distinct cases, each addressing the research questions on conflict observation, the meaning of sanctions therein and the influence of sanctions on conflict development.

5.1 Delineating the conflict between China and Taiwan

This first part of the empirical analysis aims to capture the wider conflict of which sanctions are a part. The history of the conflict focuses on persisting incompatibilities in conflict communication. It outlines these incompatibilities by analyzing the historical understanding of the conflict by the initiator and the addressee of sanctions. Moreover, in the case of the initiator, knowledge of how the PRC observes the conflict is important in order to be able to ultimately judge whether or not there is cooperation on an 'issue conflict'. In the case of the addressee of sanctions, this first part establishes the historical dimension of what was termed the 'discursive field' in the methodology outline. One component of this discursive field is the immediate history of the conflict: what is the conflict about? Another component consists of historical repertoires, elements that are not part of the immediate history, but which are invoked artefacts of past relations. Then, in the next step, the characteristics of the addressee's discursive field are laid out more specifically. These are the foundations for assessing how social conflict is observed by the addressee. I will establish a) lines of contestation in the discursive field, and b) to what extent the field is emergent or structured. At this point, the aim is to capture the basic elements of contestation so as to obtain a broad picture of the political discourse, divisions and actors.

The conflict between what is now known as the People's Republic of China on the mainland and the Republic of China on Taiwan is one of persistent and comprehensive identity incompatibilities. Essentially, the self-observations of the antagonists mutually exclude the existence of the respective Other. Put differently, the PRC and the ROC construct their own identities in a way that challenges and even denies the existence of the Other. The conflict consists of communicated identity incompatibilities that result in a strict mutual securitization.

Communicated identity incompatibilities basically go back to the early days of the Republic of China (established in 1912) at the beginning of the 20th century and, more specifically, to China's civil war (1927–1949). The confrontation between Communists and the right-wing nationalist Kuomintang consisted not only of ideological differences but of competing claims to exclusive representation of China. The civil war ended with the factual military victory of the Communist Party of China on the mainland and the retreat of Kuomintang forces to Taiwan. Communist forces were able to secure around 99 per cent of China's territory and population. However, despite the fairly unambiguous end of military confrontation, the conflict itself was institutionalized in its contemporary spatio-territorial expression. Neither the Communist Party of China on the mainland, nor the Kuomintang in Taiwan gave up their claim to exclusively represent China. Crucially, this also meant that none of the antagonists questioned China's unity. Rather, the PRC regards Taiwan to be a defective province whereas the Republic of China considers the communist reign on the mainland to be a 'communist rebellion' (Chou and Nathan 1987; Lee 1995).

In greater China, the past 100–150 years are viewed as a traumatic time of deep humiliation. Compared to the great, 5,000-year history of the Chinese nation, it is considered a period of hitherto-unseen disgrace, with foreign imperialist powers intervening almost at will, dissecting and occupying parts of imperial China and shattering the Sino-centric worldview (Croizier 1990). Along with the separatist activities of some movements during Republican China (Crossley 2004), this helped to make the image of a unified, sovereign nation one of the most cherished political principles in modern China. It also creates a salient historical repertoire for the securitization of 'separatism' and other attacks on the national integrity.

Why is it valid to take a closer look at the historical narratives about this particular period in history? There are several reasons, some of them conceptual, others empirically grounded. First, this tumultuous time is perhaps the most important, but in any event a key source for the idea of the modern Chinese nation. It is simply unthinkable to engage in historical discourse regarding the emergence of the modern nation in China without reverting to a specific interpretation of the events of this era that defines the present. Interpretations of historical events advance a particular reconstruction of the past in order to define the present, from the present. The events of the 'Century of Humiliation' represent a historical repertoire. They are invoked as a 'historical charter', "defining rights and obligations for society and legitimizing social and political arrangements" (Liu, Sibley, and Huang 2013:3).

Second, the conflict between China and Taiwan emerged from events at this time, not only as part of particular historical constructions but quite literally from the confrontation between the Kuomintang and the CCP. Thus, it is hardly possible to properly understand the meaning of 'One China' as part of conflict communication without a basic knowledge of the historical narratives pertaining to this period. Finally, while the securitization of the sanctions conflict by the addressee (Taiwan) is on principle sufficient for resultant non-cooperation, it is analytically appropriate to have a broader view of conflict communication, including the basic meaning ascribed to it by the initiator (Mainland China). Such a view is necessary if we are to be able to positively establish what kind of incompatibilities develop and to better understand the eventual identity incompatibilities.

5.1.1 Mainland China's idea of the Chinese nation

A particularly poignant view of the 'Century of Humiliation' (百年國恥, *bainian guochi*) is prevalent in Mainland China, positing key elements of historical repertoires. Official discourse constructs history from the mid-19th century onwards as an 'internal' and 'external' struggle for the integrity and sovereignty of the Chinese nation, endangered by foreign imperialist powers and corrupt, incompetent domestic governments. Besides detailed accounts in historical textbooks, there is a 'National Humiliation Day', and 'a forest of monuments' (Wang 2008) is dedicated to commemorating humiliation, promoting a return to greatness, and the sacrifices made.

The historical accounts subscribed to by the PRC do not just attribute agency and responsibility to foreign imperialist powers and their bullying of China; they also blame the 'corrupt', 'ignorant' and 'decadent' Chinese governments of the time for China's fall from former greatness. Thus, 'humiliation' is a 'social practice', its 'othering' is deeply political (Callahan 2004). The CCP is the savior of China, and the respective emphasis on the two parts of this image of history provides the benchmark upon which the CCP's policies are to be judged. "Use the past to serve the present, use the foreign to serve China", as Mao advised.

After the CCP's victory in 1949, historical accounts focused heavily on the domestic dimension. Essentially, the CCP advanced what Zheng Wang calls a 'victor narrative' in class struggle (2008:789): "China's decline and suffering in modern history were caused mainly by the internal corruption and incompetence of the feudal or capitalist rulers, the Qing Court and the nationalist Kuomintang (KMT). Foreign invasions thus became a secondary factor in explaining China's traumatic national experience". In post-1949 historical accounts of the PRC, "the century of national humiliation ends with the national salvation of China in 1949 when Mao and the Chinese Communist Party (CCP) finally put 'China' back together again" (Callahan 2004:205).

Now, the historical repertoires provided by the dark century conjure up a different image. The 'Century of Humiliation' today is one of national humiliation at the hands of foreigners in a discourse of patriotic nationalism (see Zhao 2004).[1] Instead of accusing the Kuomintang of playing a disreputable role in the struggle against foreign rule, these newer accounts pay tribute to the efforts of other Chinese agents such as the Kuomintang in the patriotic fight for the nation (Wang 2008). Nevertheless, the CCP is the author of China's 'rejuvenation' (Wang 2012:129f.).

PRC & Taiwan

In Mainland China, historical repertoires of the humiliation narrative are consistently linked to the 'Taiwan issue'. In the political discourse of the PRC, Taiwan is considered an inalienable part of China. Official statements portray Taiwan's contemporary status as one of the last obstacles to the final restoration of territorial integrity, shaking off the scars of the 'Century of Humiliation'. The reunification of China is the great nationalist project.

In the early 1990s, late efforts to undermine the legitimacy of the Taiwanese government were still explicitly linked to the Kuomintang. In his speech on the 70th anniversary of the CCP in 1991,[2] General Secretary Jiang Zemin made some reconciliatory moves that essentially proposed a path towards cooperation on an issue conflict. Despite the openness of the invitation, however, the CCP's vision for reunification comes with particular conditions. These conditions rest on the principle of 'One Country, Two Systems', outlined in the early 1980s under Deng Xiaoping:[3] The 'Taiwan White Paper' of 1993[4] re-invokes the principle that there is only one sovereign government of China, but Taiwan would be granted autonomy and could retain its own 'capitalist' system allowed to coexist with Mainland China's 'socialist' system; in 1995, Jiang stated that Taiwan would even be able to keep its own armed forces.[5] Nonetheless, as the Taiwan White Paper emphasizes, "there is only one China in the world, Taiwan is an inalienable part of China and the seat of China's central government is in Beijing".

The 'One China' principle more generally, and the Taiwan White Paper specifically, have recourse to the humiliation narrative. The Paper refers explicitly to China's modern history as a 'record of humiliation' and invokes both the foreign and domestic dimensions in pointing to the causes of Taiwan's separation. It states that "unless and until this state of affairs is brought to an end, the trauma to the Chinese nation will not be healed and the Chinese people's struggle for national reunification and territorial integrity will continue". In this context, Taiwanese independence is entirely out of the question. The PRC categorically rejects 'Taiwan independence' or any similar construct involving more than one government of China. However, the paper states that "the Chinese government is convinced that Taiwan compatriots want national reunification and that this is also true of most of the political forces in or out of office in Taiwan".

In sum, the way in which the PRC observes Cross-Strait relations has recourse to historical repertoires of humiliation at the hands of domestic and foreign agents. In the first decades of the PRC, the CCP authorities attributed responsibility both to foreign imperialist powers and to the Kuomintang in securitizing an identity incompatibility. However, over the years, historical accounts have put more of the blame on foreign imperialists while acknowledging to some degree the contributions of Kuomintang forces to the fight for the Chinese nation. Reunification was defined as the great national project, politically enshrined in the 'One China' principle. The primary means of pursuing reunification is the 'One Country, Two Systems' doctrine. Thus, with this evolving conflict observation the PRC moves towards observing an issue conflict with the possibility of cooperation under the 'one country, two systems' formula. However, the PRC does not exclude military force as *ultima ratio* in pursuing this goal, and in particular as a means of averting secession. There is a caveat regarding a possible transformation into an issue conflict: overall conflict communication may still perpetuate a securitized conflict involving identity incompatibilities. In the end, a conflict is simply not defined by one of its actors, but conflict communication defines the antagonists.

5.1.2 Taiwan's idea of nation

Having outlined how the People's Republic of China imagines the Chinese nation and depicted the historical repertoires put forth in observing Cross-Strait relations, this part describes the historical dimension of the discursive field on the way in which Taiwan observes Cross-Strait relations. The ROC's self-observation similarly contributes to a securitized identity incompatibility. As in Mainland China there is a discourse on 'humiliation' in Taiwan as well, which creates historical repertoires. These historical accounts inevitably attribute causes and agency differently. The 'humiliation' of China ends earlier: in 1943, with the Republic of China's renegotiation of the 'unequal treaties' by Chiang Kai-shek (Callahan 2004).

Effectively, during the years of the Kuomintang's Nationalist dictatorship, historical accounts of the era of 'humiliation' closely resembled those in Mainland China (Mitter 2003). The involvement of the 'rebelling communists' and 'foreign powers' in humiliating China is as profound and fatal in the Kuomintang-Taiwanese historical account as it was, conversely, in the PRC. With Taiwanese democratization, historical accounts and the repertoires that they use diversified and shifted significantly.[6] Thus, since the late 1980s, the 'humiliation era' has been most remarkable for its notorious muteness in, if not absence from, political discourse, compared to its massive evocation on the mainland. Certainly, a narrative of humiliation with domestic and foreign dimensions does exist, but it does not serve to the same extent as historical repertoire in political discourse on the Cross-Strait conflict.

What historical repertoires do, then, inform the Taiwanese discourse on the conflict with Mainland China? In Taiwan, monuments are built to commemorate other events, in particular the February 28 Incident (also: 2/28 Incident). The event that gained a central position in Taiwanese accounts of political history took place in 1947, two years after Taiwan was 'retroceded' from Japan to the Republic of China. When the Kuomintang took over the administration of the island, the corruption, economic mismanagement and 'mutual distrust'[7] between the newly-arrived Mainlanders who were now in charge and the island residents (Lai, Myers, and Wei 1991) finally culminated in an uprising on February 28. Subsequently, after military reinforcements arrived from the Mainland, the Kuomintang forces quelled the uprising and enforced martial law. During the years of the dictatorship, the 2/28 Incident was a non-event, hardly reported on.[8] Political campaigns[9] and large annual demonstrations on February 28 in Taiwanese cities from 1988 onwards pushed the government to officially recognize and shed light on the Incident. In 1988, President Lee Teng-hui (Kuomintang) acknowledged the 'tragedy'; finally, in 1995, President Lee apologized to the families of the victims on behalf of the state.[10] Although perhaps not immediately obvious, the wider politics of the 2/28 Incident is of immense relevance for the Cross-Strait conflict. Contemporary political discourse in Taiwan around the 2/28 Incident comes with its proper *problematique* of foreignness. It was the Taiwanese democracy movement which strongly promoted public recognition and investigation into the 2/28 Incident (Gold 1994). The democracy movement later formed the Democratic Progressive Party (DPP) in 1986 (Rigger 2001). However, besides democratization and reappraising the past, a significant share of Taiwanese political discourse revolves around independence, and this came together in debates about the Incident.

Essentially, the rise of the DPP is part of a discourse on identity. Competing accounts of the 2/28 Incident in Taiwan were already linked to the legitimacy of Mainland rule in the name of the Republic of China during the 'White Terror' years of dictatorship. Such contestation found a particularly strong expression in the 'Declaration of Formosan Self-Salvation', which challenged the legitimacy of Mainland rule on principle, either by Communists or the Kuomintang, and called for independence (Peng Ming-min, Hsieh Tsung-min, and Wei Ting-chao 1964).[11] Equally, in the 'Kaohsiung Incident' of 1979 (also: Meilidao Incident, Formosa Magazine Incident), political opposition publicly challenged Kuomintang rule on the grounds of its human rights record. Its leaders and the defendants were convicted to years in prison on the basis of the Sedition Law (Articles 100 & 101 of the Criminal Code), which furthermore criminalized any form of promoting independence (Winn and Yeh 1995). Years later, some of the convicted activists became leading figures of the DPP.

In sum, historical narratives in Taiwan contribute to the observed Cross-Strait identity incompatibilities in diverse ways. The traditional official narrative sees the Republic of China as the sole legitimate representative of greater China, thus denying a legitimate existence of the PRC. However, the joint propositions of democracy promoters and independence advocates challenge the ROC government not merely as undemocratic but as illegitimate Mainland rule, basically questioning the notion of 'One China' as a whole.

Discursive field of Taiwan's politics on Cross-Strait conflict

This section proceeds to trace the development of Taiwan's discursive field on observing Cross-Strait relations. It establishes different positions on relations and the conflict with the Mainland and presents lines of contestation between these positions. As is readily apparent, historical repertoires in Taiwan are more diverse than on the mainland. They are selectively invoked in producing a discursive field on Cross-Strait relations, with positions varying between the extremes of reunification and independence. In other words, controversy in conflict observation within Taiwan revolves around the notion of 'One China'.

In the discursive field on observing Cross-Strait relations in Taiwan, three main political positions emerged in the first half of the 1990s. In general, these positions vary and relate systematically to one another regarding the notions of 'unification' and 'independence' at either end of the spectrum. That is, observation of Cross-Strait relations is contested along this continuum. However, the meaning that particular positions attach to both 'unification' and 'independence' itself changes and evolves over time, making the field a significantly emergent one.

More substantially, the observing of Cross-Strait relations in Taiwan moved significantly in the early 1990s towards an emphasis on the island as a proper political entity, either basically as the Republic of China, or as Taiwan proper. This is also reflected in the election results (see Table 5.1). The contestation between advocates of unification, a continuing status quo and independence became institutionalized politically into different parties, with parties themselves consisting of multiple factions covering a delimited range of the spectrum from 'unification' to 'independence' (see Table 5.2). Contestation also became increasingly intense,

Table 5.1 Election results, 1991–1994

ELECTION	*Kuomintang*	*DPP*	*New Party*	*Others*
1991: National Assembly	69	23	–	7.5
1992: Legislative Yuan	53	31	–	16
1994:				
– Taiwan Province Governor	56	39	4	
– Taipei Mayor	26	44	26	
– Kaohsiung Mayor	54	39	3	

Sources: Nohlen, Grotz, and Hartmann (2001); South China Morning Post, December 4, 1994: 'Gains for opposition in Taiwan Elections'.

Table 5.2 Taiwan's discursive field on Cross-Strait relations: political groups, positions and figures

	DPP	*Kuomintang*	*New Party*
Factions & positions	*Formosa faction:* • democratic reform • de-facto independence • Cross-Strait exchange *New Tide faction:* • radically democratic • formal independence	*Liberals:* • democratic reform • pragmatic diplomacy • status quo • Cross-Strait exchange *Conservatives:* • no direct presidential elections • reunification	• no direct presidential elections • anti-communism • strictly pro-reunification • no pragmatic diplomacy

with other issues such as democratic reform becoming in part observed through the lens of Cross-Strait relations.

At the beginning of the 1990s, the incumbent Kuomintang government of President Lee Teng-hui moved significantly away from its position that the ROC was the sole legitimate representative of China. By and large it developed a view of 'one China, two governments', thus leaving behind the old hitherto securitized identity incompatibility. The element of continuity in Kuomintang statements is the observing of Taiwan as part of the Chinese nation. While slowly distancing itself from claims to Mainland China and even Outer Mongolia, the Kuomintang continued to promote the Republic of China as a legitimate political entity. This positioning covered a range of conflicting policies: The view of 'one China, two governments' itself was prone to raise questions about how both notions could possibly go together; the quest for recognition did not just aim for reciprocity in PRC observations, but 'pragmatic diplomacy' extended this aim towards broader international recognition.

In concrete proposals as well as in general statements, the Kuomintang formulated preconditions for engagement and for eventual unification. To begin with, the 'first stage', that of 'ending hostilities', was not just a suggestion as to how the unification process might evolve; any further steps were made ultimately conditional upon a renunciation of the use of force by the PRC.[12] A further, far-reaching precondition was the democratization of the Mainland. As Lee emphasized, the aim of the Kuomintang is China's reunification specifically under freedom and democracy.[13]

Besides the renunciation of the use of military force as a political option, 'recognition' is another of President Lee's Kuomintang government's basic preconditions for a dialogue on reunification. Recognizing the PRC was quite explicitly based on an expectation of reciprocity. The Kuomintang government made 'dual recognition' another precondition of unification dialogue. As President Lee put it bluntly in 1995, China may "pursue unification based on the reality that the two sides are governed respectively by two governments".[14]

The quest for recognition of the Kuomintang, however, extends further than the eventual dialogue on the conflict between the PRC and the ROC. In addition to this demand, the Lee government actively sought to promote the international recognition of the Republic of China by third states,[15] and it sought to gain membership in international organizations. Among these international institutions were the APEC,[16] GATT[17] (and later the WTO[18]), the WHO[19] and most prominently the United Nations.[20]

In 1995, a visit to the United States by President Lee finally elevated the controversy over Kuomintang positioning and polarization to unprecedented heights. Lee took the opportunity to speak at his *alma mater*, Cornell University. Though officially considered 'private', Lee's visit to the United States represents a highly symbolic culmination of pragmatic diplomacy. His speech[21] at Cornell, where Lee was introduced as 'President of the Republic of China', was a political address, which Lee opened by calling his visit "an honour for the 21 million people of the Republic of China in Taiwan".

Kuomintang policies on Cross-Strait relations were thus a delicate balance of reiterative and projective observations. In addition, the Kuomintang government embraced democratic transition and took up the political demands of the democracy movement; some Kuomintang policies such as legislative reform and direct presidential elections were observed across the whole discursive field as making the Republic of China more representative and thus Taiwanese. Moreover, the Lee administration was quick to take up the advancement of 'democracy' as a newly distinctive feature between the PRC and the ROC. By announcing that it was a precondition for unification, the Kuomintang government prepared the ground for the observation of new identity incompatibilities in Cross-Strait relations. Though the Kuomintang government categorically rejected any aims of formal independence, President Lee's reference to the Republic of China *in Taiwan*, on a not-so-private visit to the United States, clearly represented the unprecedented step of asserting the existence of a quite separate political entity in Taiwan.

Conservative nationalists rejected the repositioning on the observation of Cross-Strait relations by the Lee administration. Instead, they sought to continue with the position of One China, the Republic of China. As their observations became irreconcilable with the liberal Kuomintang government, they embarked on an institutionalization of their own observation in the New Party after Premier Hau Pei-tsun resigned in February 1993. The New Party positioned itself as staunchly unificationist, refusing any policies which could be viewed as casting doubt on a commitment towards One China, such as those of the Lee government. To this end, New Party politicians rejected direct presidential elections. The New Party's strong promotion of direct links and the expansion of Cross-Strait relations not only added distance from the Kuomintang in the discursive field, but even amounted to a modification of its observation of the PRC – an enemy of the ROC, but an ally in the cause of One China.

The DPP recruits many of its members from the democratization movement, and from independence activists: people, who have committed their political lives to resisting the Nationalist dictatorial government. A significant number of its influential politicians are dissidents who were politically persecuted. Accordingly, it is the DPP which most vocally pushed for the recognition of the 2/28 Incident, for democratic reform and popular elections.

Generally, DPP members took issue with Taiwan's status, with views ranging from a firm commitment to independence that is as much means to an end as it is an end in itself, towards views that reject independence as impractical. These differences notwithstanding, Taiwan's status vis-à-vis greater China is at least 'still undecided' for the DPP.[22] Different factions promote competing views which politicize independence in different ways. More radical stances aim to include an independence clause in the DPP platform, whereas a moderate approach abstains from such a move but seeks the legalization of its advocacy.[23] Here again, 'independence' politically relates to democracy promotion.

The DPP exhibited the most dynamic and heterogeneous of positions in the discursive field. For all its heterogeneity, though, the DPP was committed to independence as much as to democracy. Whether this meant a democratic Republic of China or a democratic Taiwan varied across factions, as did the meaning of independence itself. The Formosa faction, in observing 'de-facto independence', tended towards supporting the status quo and a reiterative approach to Cross-Strait relations. Effectively, there was considerable common ground between the Formosa faction and the Lee administration's view of two governments across the Strait, with his own administration representing the people of Taiwan. Both the positioning of the DPP's Formosa faction and of Kuomintang liberals on Cross-Strait relations thus tended towards a center in the discursive field. Yet the DPP as a whole, composed also of the New Tide faction, together advanced a stronger notion of independence. De-facto independence was the conservative notion of Cross-Strait relations, with New Tide members clearly advocating a formal declaration of independence. Thus, to some degree, the conflict over mutually exclusive claims to represent greater China does not extend to the DPP positioning. Taiwan was not part of China, and the Kuomintang government the legacy of foreign occupation.

Accordingly, the discursive field around the conflict changed significantly from the 1990s on. What was once a largely uncontested observation (the one promoted by the Kuomintang and Mainland elites) of a 'communist rebellion' on the Mainland now emerged into a field where conflict observations were fiercely contested politically by clearly identifiable competing articulations. By and large, the observation of Cross-Strait relations had moved towards one of two distinct political entities.

5.2 A conflict with three different sanctions strategies

This is the second part of the empirical analysis of the sanctions conflict between China and Taiwan. Mainland China's policies during the period of democratic consolidation and the rise of pro-independence parties can be divided into cases of three different sanctions strategies. First, during the years of Jiang Zemin, from 1995 to 2002, China used a negative sanctions strategy. The second strategy, from 2003 to 2005, involved negative sanctions combined with some emerging positive incentives in the PRC's Cross-Strait policies. Third, from 2005 onwards, during Hu Jintao's presidency, China switched to a largely positive sanctions strategy.

Generally, these different sanctions strategies reflect changing Chinese conflict observations during the three cases.

I will analyze each of the three cases in two steps. In a first step, I will trace the sanctions that were introduced and establish the corresponding conflict observation by the PRC. It thus takes the PRC's understanding of conflict as outlined in the preceding part, not only to contextually embed sanctions policies, but also to further trace the way in which the PRC's conflict observation has evolved over time. Again, this is important to enable an assessment on a possible conflict transformation. In a second step, I will trace the impact of PRC sanctions on Taiwan's conflict observation. This will involve addressing the more specific research questions regarding the meaning attached by Taiwanese observers to sanctions and how the sanctions imposed impact on their understanding of the conflict. In so doing, I will again take the findings established in the preceding part and use them to trace the way in which Taiwan's discursive field on observing Cross-Strait relations has evolved over time and how the lines of contestation between the particular positions in the discursive field have developed.

During the first case, the primary concern was clearly reunification on Mainland China's terms, which amounted to a reaffirmation of the claim of exclusive representation. Jiang Zemin consistently insisted on the 'One Country, Two Systems' position. In his Eight Point Speech in 1995 on reunification,[24] Jiang envisaged the steps that would be necessary to achieve reunification and made it clear that China was prepared to protect this position by force. In the face of any opposing Taiwanese claims to represent China, this position easily lends itself to the observation of an identity conflict. Thus, sanctions were applied as much to contain the rise in Taiwanese nationalism and pro-independence sentiments as to coerce Taiwan towards a path to reunification. The stated purposes of sanctions thus went beyond what both the PRC and the ROC considered to be the official status quo, which was 1) a mutual commitment to 'One China', with disagreements as to what exactly this notion would entail; and 2) the absence of any political 'roadmap' or timeline for reunification.

The second case represents a combination of continuing negative sanctions with emerging positive sanctions. That is, overall the PRC reduced negative sanctions, discontinuing some measures while, at the same time, introducing some positive sanctions, with plans for additional positive incentives at a later date. In that sense, the second phase of combined sanctions policies marks a period of transition. It also marks a shift in China's observation of the Cross-Strait conflict: the PRC began to recognize, albeit still to a very limited extent, the legitimate needs and political interests of their Taiwanese 'blood brothers'. Nonetheless, the PRC's stated aim remained a timely reunification, and the doctrine of 'one country, two systems' strongly prevailed.

In the third case of sanctions, when policies switched to an emphasis on positive incentives, they were accompanied by a re-articulation of China's political position. The Four-Point Guidelines set out by President Hu Jintao in 2005[25] relax the goal of reunification, but strongly emphasize the idea of 'One China'. Hu further called for a commitment by the Taiwanese authorities to the 'Five No's', which directly pertain to concrete political steps that are considered to be secessionist. Arguably, ambitions thus became more modest (Wang 2007), and by focusing on commonalities and maintaining the status quo, this position is about observing an issue conflict. Interestingly, as William Norris (2016) notes, the different sanctions policies rest on the perception of differing temporal contingencies: the earlier position, formulated by Deng and Jiang, promoted the need to act towards the goal of unification within a shorter timeframe, whereas with Hu's reformulation, time was not so much an issue. Accordingly, there were different temporalities in observing decisions on the conflict, both in the form of 'risk'.

5.2.1 One China, diverging visions: negative sanctions fueling discord

When the PRC embarked on its "One Country, Two Systems" formula, prompted by the patriotic nationalism of the early 1990s, it advanced a conflict observation that raised the possibility of dialogue. Reunification with Taiwan represents the final, necessary step for ending the 'Century of Humiliation', now imagined as a common Chinese goal pursued across different systems that included the ROC, even in its unfortunate role as ultimately an agent of foreign aggressors in bringing about China's division.

Negative sanctions occurred in the Cross-Strait conflict at a time when evolving political positions reinforced incompatibilities with new vigor, as outlined in the preceding chapters. While old views of mutually exclusive claims of representing greater China became more restrained, political positions in Taiwan were increasingly assertive towards promoting Taiwan as a proper political entity. The ROC government accompanied its efforts towards enhancing its international recognition by emphasizing democracy as a distinct achievement. Compared to the old conservative nationalism in Taiwan which centered on greater China, discourse began to conceive of democracy either as a precondition for reunification or as a reason for de-facto independence.

In the context of developments in Taiwan, the PRC's approach was one of containment and coercion, reasserting its conflict position of 'One China, Two Systems' as a temporally-limited transition mode towards full reunification.

Mainland China's conflict observation and sanctions against Taiwan

The first case included four different categories of economic and political sanctions: a) political encroachment through declarations, white papers, and laws in respect of Taiwan's status; b) military exercises and intimidation; c) international isolation and the undercutting of diplomatic relations; and d) direct economic disruption and business intimidation. Throughout the entire first case, some measures were applied on a continuous basis, the majority of which were related to international recognition. The PRC consistently thwarted Taiwanese ambitions to join international organizations, membership of which imply statehood, such as the United Nations (averted every year from 1993 onwards) and the WHO (Larus

2006). Beyond this, sanctions in the first case can be analytically divided roughly into two waves. The first wave peaked in summer 1995, the second in the second half of 1999.

The first wave of sanctions began shortly after President Lee's visit to the United States. It centered mostly on military intimidation, accompanied by increasing political encroachment. PRC officials had already repeatedly voiced strong disapproval in public statements ahead of Lee's visit, observing it as a step towards 'two Chinas'.[26] Already suspicious and disapproving of the Kuomintang's pragmatic diplomacy,[27] a foreign ministry statement claimed that the planned visit was an attack on Chinese sovereignty and the aim of reunification, for which "the Chinese government and people are ready to stand up against any odds".[28] Remarkably, most statements addressed the government of the United States, thus reiterating a rejection of the legitimacy of the ROC government.

Chinese state media attributed actions which undermined Cross-Strait relations to Lee Teng-hui, stating that such actions "helped Taiwan's pro-independence forces run amok" with the aim of making the split "fixed or permanent".[29] Another critical article, published in 'People's Daily', the official newspaper of the CCP, lays out the wider stakes of Lee's US visit and invokes the historical repertoire of China's fight for national integrity and sovereignty: "Chinese people have fought against aggression, exploitation and humiliation for the past 100 years. For the sovereignty of the country and dignity of the Chinese nation, the Chinese will not bow before any kind of bullying but strike back no matter how poor they are and what hardship they endure".[30] The article concludes by noting the PRC's explicit opposition to "two Chinas" or "one China, one Taiwan", and warns that "if Taiwan declares 'independence', China will not sit idly by". A few weeks later, PRC media comments sought to discredit Lee personally, playing on the very same salient historical repertoires: Lee's father was accused of being "100 per cent a traitor", stating that he had worked as a policeman for the Japanese government in the 1920s; reports also cited a Japanese weekly as stating that Lee had "a heart that is more Japanese than a Japanese".[31] It is thus safe to infer that, besides strongly rejecting any sort of international recognition of the ROC, PRC authorities would have welcomed President Lee's removal as head of the Taiwanese authorities, and considered him an obstacle to timely reunification.

Coercive measures initially took the form of military exercises conducted in close vicinity to Taiwan's coast and included the firing of missiles close to Taiwanese shores. During the ramping up of military exercises, Jiang advised the PLA to heighten its 'combat-readiness' and be prepared to deal with the 'Taiwan independence movement'.[32] In early July 1995, military drills began with air and sea exercise 'East Sea Number 5', conducted about 400km off Taiwan's north coast.[33] Later that month, the PLA ran missile tests in the waters roughly 130km off the north coast of the island, forcing almost 150 civilian flights to change course.[34] The tests were accompanied by the extensive mobilization of land, air and sea forces in the Fujian and Zhejiang provinces at the Strait, while the state radio broadcaster announced that a declaration of independence would trigger an invasion right away.[35] The mobilization exercise included main combat forces and was reported to have been the largest mobilization seen in over 20 years.[36] A second series of missile tests, fired at a distance of around 90km, came even closer to Taiwan. This round of tests was publicly announced by Xinhua in the evening news, a move that was noted by international media as unusual.[37] The joint exercise spanned several weeks and was reported to 'simulate an air-and-sea blockade' against US intervention in a potential military conflict with Taiwan, and "to prepare for an actual attack on the island if that proved to be necessary", according to newspaper reports citing PLA sources.[38]

In addition to their symbolism, these military exercises amount to sanctions for two reasons. The first and conceptual reason lies in the way in which they influence politics by economic means: around the time of the military exercises in 1995, the TAIEX stock index suffered heavy losses, falling from around 5,550 points in early July, when plans for military exercises were reported, to around 4,500 points on August 14,[39] right before a second round of military exercises began (see Figure 5.1).[40] Further, close to 150 commercial flights had to be re-directed, and alternative shipping routes had to be used.[41] Taiwanese fishermen were actively harassed and had to suspend operations;[42] business confidence was undermined, with Taiwanese investments on the mainland between July and August reduced by almost half.[43] A second, related empirical reason is that the military exercises were *observed* as coercive. The economic implications mentioned above and the political statements by the Taiwanese authorities, examined in greater detail below, testify to this.

Military exercises were accompanied by political encroachment and public condemnation of Taiwanese observations of Cross-Strait relations and in particular of ROC President Lee,[44] and by statements that underlined the PRC's willingness and

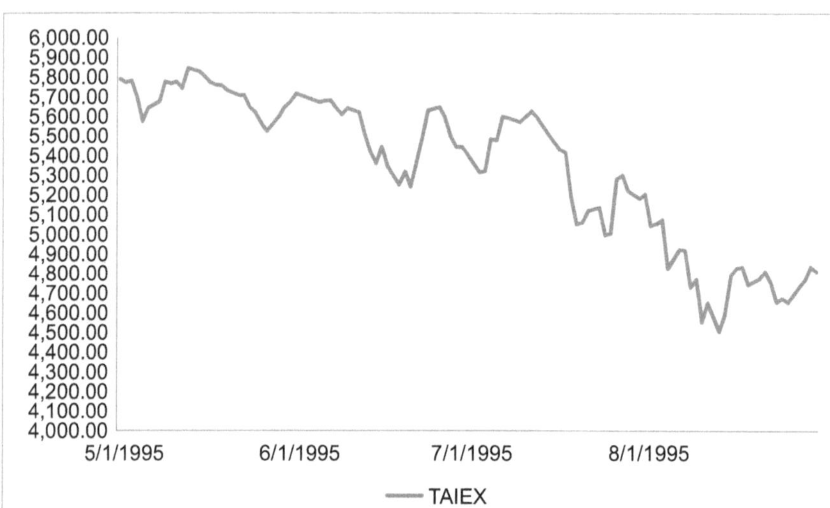

Figure 5.1 Taiwan stock exchange performance, May–August 1995. Data: twse.com.tw

capability to take Taiwan by force if necessary.[45] In early 1996, with the presidential election approaching, Chinese media reported on a proposed timetable for reunification.[46] Inevitably, such a commitment would expose differences in the observation of Cross-Strait relations and put the conflict under the microscope. The impact of such rumors in the media on Taiwan's economy was quickly apparent, with the TAIEX losing 3.6 per cent on the day of the news report.[47]

A few days later, the PRC announced a resumption of joint military exercises, amassing troops in Fujian[48] and, according to reports, also included Nanjing and Guangzhou in its 'war zone' this time round.[49] The military drills were carried out in the weeks leading up to Taiwan's presidential election.[50] Missile tests effectively encircled Taiwan, conducted only 50km away from the northern coast of Taiwan and 100km away from its southern shores,[51] and in areas close to the ROC islands of Kinmen and Matsu and in Keelung in northern Taiwan.[52] In addition to these large-scale exercises, the PRC issued more explicit official statements proposing an economic blockade scenario against the island.[53] About 300 flights again had to be re-directed.[54]

The second wave of negative sanctions saw a pattern not too different from the first. However, the emphasis this time was clearly not so much on military intimidation, but more on political encroachment and to a slightly greater extent on business intimidation. In summer 1999, the PRC once again began to stage massive military exercises, announced in response to particular Taiwanese observations of Cross-Strait relations.[55] These military exercises did not involve close-by missile tests as was the case in 1996; nonetheless, the overall mobilization of forces continuously from July until September was extensive.[56] Forces in Zhejiang, Fujian and Guangdong were combat-ready, with the 'war zone' extending to Gansu province. Newspapers reported the PLA moving some of its elite officers, experts in amphibious and urban warfare, to these regions.[57] Furthermore, military forces were reportedly granted 'first strike approval' in any confrontation with Taiwanese forces,[58] with a large number of warplane sorties closing in on a demarcation line across the Strait.[59]

Exercises began in July and lasted until September; they included drills in Guangdong,[60] as well as navy maneuvers[61] and most notably a large joint exercise off the coast of Zhejiang province. As part of the maneuver, PLA forces simulated an invasion of Taiwan, as Xinhua reported: "The military exercise provided a spectacular sight of a straits-crossing and landing operations by Chinese forces armed with high-tech weapons".[62] Contrary to previous exercises, the purpose of this exercise was to demonstrate 'fighting a big war', according to reports in the Chinese press.[63] At the time of these coastal exercises, the PRC also tested a long-range intercontinental missile and claimed to possess the capability to build neutron bombs – news commentaries saw Taiwan as the indirect addressee of these latter announcements, with the US as transmitter.[64] In addition to these military measures, the PRC ordered a "total mobilization in diplomacy" to further isolate Taiwan internationally.[65]

In addition to the PRC's announcement of military exercises in July 1999 and reports of troop movements, heavy losses were recorded on the TAIEX, falling by over 1,000 points from 8,462 to 7,411 points between 12 and 16 July, 1999.[66] Similar to in 1996, some civilian flights had to be diverted during the exercises[67] and there were some reports of ship harassments.[68] Besides the announcement and start of military exercises, the response of the PRC authorities to Taiwanese observations on Cross-Strait relations further consisted of issuing threats that the country would resort if necessary to military force, warning of 'monumental disaster'.[69] In addition, there is some evidence that in summer 1999 the PRC authorities approached Taiwanese business investors in Mainland China, the *Taishang*, 'lobbying' them to advocate pro-China positions and to condemn Taiwanese politicians who reject unification and the 'One China' principle. However, as Tanner points out, analyses of public discourse "conclude that very few *Taishang* spoke up. . . . Instead, most kept silent" (Tanner 2007:114).

After the end of the military exercises in September 1999, the PRC consistently stepped up political encroachment and continued to issue threats of using military force. Alongside the threats, China was reported to have embarked on steadily increasing the number of missiles it had pointing at Taiwan.[70] According to comprehensive media reports, the PLA embraced a three-pronged approach towards Taiwan's presidential election in March 2000:

> the use of force against Taiwan right away if the new Taiwanese leadership after the March 2000 presidential election continues to carry out a policy of splitting; the use of force as the only way to deter the seeking of independence from Mainland China by Taiwan; and preparation to fight against the United States and its Western allies if they engage in military intervention in a war between Mainland China and Taiwan.[71]

Chinese officials further declared that a presidential candidate who advocates Taiwan's independence is unacceptable to China.[72]

In February 2000, with the presidential election drawing close, the PRC's Taiwan Affairs Council issued a White Paper on Taiwan entitled 'The Taiwan Question and the Reunification of China'. In the paper, the PRC declared Taiwan part of Chinese territory "under both domestic and international law" and rejected any legitimate basis for a referendum on Taiwan's status.[73] However, in the paper the PRC also refused to renounce the use of military force. Instead, it strongly tightened the conditions which would trigger such use of force if Taiwan refused indefinitely to negotiate unification.[74] Around the time of the publication of the White Paper, news reports in the Hong Kong media were circulating possible deadlines for reunification.[75] In early March 2000, the Central Military Commission asked the PLA to 'actively prepare' for the use of force, while President Jiang refused to set any explicit deadline for reunification.[76] Finally, at a televised press conference on 15 March 2000, PRC Premier Zhu Rongji embarked on laying down China's 'bottom line': "I want to make clear here that whoever comes into power in Taiwan after the election must not go about 'Taiwan independence', nor will 'Taiwan independence' in whatever form be allowed".[77] Zhu went on to directly address Taiwanese voters: "The people of Taiwan are standing at a very critical historical juncture, so let me give advice to all the people of Taiwan: Do not act just on impulse".[78] Otherwise, Zhu declared, "they will have no other opportunity to regret".[79]

Around the time of the 2000 presidential election, negative sanctions began to focus more strongly on the *Taishang's* business relations. Such sanctions were less public than the military exercises and are not as easy to trace.[80] Empirical research indicates that the PRC authorities exerted 'persuasive' pressure through organizing voting initiatives especially during the 2000 presidential elections (Tanner 2007). In cases where voting 'recommendations' were ignored, "mainland Chinese authorities penalize, or at least threaten to penalize, those *Taishang* by limiting their business opportunities and conveniences on the mainland" (Wu 2007:307).

In the wake of the elections, negative sanctions against the *Taishang* were observed, with those who were considered to be supporters of pro-independence parties pressurized and subjected to harassment.[81] Among the targets were large, prominent companies such as computer manufacturer Acer, Chi Mei Petrochemicals and Evergreen.[82] Reports cited sources from China's Taiwan Affairs Office as having threatened to revoke preferential trade agreements and investment privileges.[83] Measures included company visits by intimidating Chinese officials, the breaking of engagements, surprise inspections of factories, delays in business dealings as well as "aggressive, selective investigations of [company] compliance with Beijing's notoriously vague tax, labor, industrial, and environmental regulations" (Tanner 2007:115).

Conflict observation and social processing of meaning of sanctions in Taiwan

This section connects the sanctions applied in conflict with their meaning and the observation of the conflict by the addressee. The driving questions are: first, what meaning do Taiwanese observers attach to sanctions, and second, in what ways did conflict observation in Taiwan develop in the wake of the sanctions that were introduced? The temporal interplay between the sanctions introduced, emerging meanings and their eventual contestation is approached by tracing the process of the evolving conflict observation along the corresponding evolvement of the competing framings presented above. This part then analyses a) the diagnostic framing (alleged causes of the conflict, role of sanctions, attribution of responsibility), and b) the prognostic framing (proposed actions/solutions).

When China fired missiles directly off the Taiwanese coast in July and August 1995, this led to popular confrontations that confirmed competing conflict observations. In demonstrations, unificationists protested against 'separatist actions' as posing a threat to the Republic of China, while advocates of independence claimed there was a threat against the Republic of Taiwan (Huang 2000:143). Those who took to the streets for independence observed Chinese military exercises as sanctions applied to intimidate Taiwan as a separate state into changing its position.[84] Others personally denounced President Lee's quest for international recognition and attributed a pro-independence position to him; these right-wing protesters considered Lee responsible for the threat to Taiwan and demanded his resignation.[85] With public protests divided between those advocating independence and those in favor of unification, public polling results indicated that support for independence, albeit in decline against the backdrop of the military exercises, was only slightly weaker than support for reunification. While support for the latter remained stable at 30 per cent, maintaining the status quo became more popular; close to 60 per cent subscribed to further strengthening military capabilities to oppose Chinese threats.

Indeed, in spite of competing conflict observations, there was blanket condemnation by all political groups covering the main positions in the discursive field of the 'intimidating' military exercises which were observed as sanctions attempting to influence Taiwanese politics. DPP politicians saw the exercises as raising tensions and deemed them to be in violation of international agreements, urging the PRC "to respect each other's sovereignty".[86] Similarly, the New Party protested against the exercises as being counterproductive and endangering peace.[87] Kuomintang politicians called the threat to security in the region an "act of pirates"[88] that was designed to intimidate the people.[89] Moreover, there was also considerable agreement across the parties in essentially claiming a security threat. Shih Mingteh, the chairman of the DPP, observed that "the largest threat to Taiwan is China",[90] a view that was also expressed by President Lee in a state-of-the-nation address at the National Assembly, during which he claimed that Chinese communists "pose a severe threat to Taiwan"[91] and to the stability of the whole region.[92] In face of such a threat, both Kuomintang and DPP politicians made pledges to further strengthen Taiwan's military forces.[93] They even publicly discussed eventually investigating the feasibility of nuclear weapons as an 'effective deterrent'.[94]

New Party politicians also observed a security threat, but their perception differed significantly from other claims. While joining in on the broad condemnation of PRC missile tests, New Party members ultimately attributed responsibility for the threat to the advocates of Taiwanese independence.[95] New Party members considered Lee and other Kuomintang liberals to be among those in the pro-independence camp. Consequently, already in the initial stages of mutual condemnation of PRC military exercises, differences in conflict observation were apparent in the diagnostic framing advanced by the various political groups.

The differences in the immediate reactions to the PRC military exercises indicate a basic continuity in the competing observations of the Cross-Strait conflict in Taiwan's discursive field. This is further confirmed by the prognostic framing of statements which subscribe to the particular positions. The Kuomintang was quick to note that such actions as the missile tests would mean putting the goal of unification at risk.[96] President Lee reiterated the aim of reunification and his opposition to secessionism, but at the same time vowed to continue with Taiwan's search for extended international recognition.[97] Lee elaborated that such recognition remained a precondition for any political dialogue with the PRC: "Refusing to accept the split and separate regimes only serves to obstruct reunification. If there is no split, there can be no reunification".[98] The Kuomintang government also continued to rule out reunification under communism.[99] Even while striking a more reconciliatory tone and proposing to improve bilateral relations,[100] President Lee referred to his unyielding commitment to reunification as coming with wider, similarly unyielding, preconditions: China must "unify under democracy, freedom and general well-being".[101]

Yet, this continuity in conflict observation expressed by the Lee government and Kuomintang liberals in face of Chinese threats was contested by some prominent conservative party members. Former Prime Minister Hau Pei-tsun and former Parliament Speaker Liang Su-jung joined public demonstrations demanding peaceful reunification, in which many protestors attributed responsibility for the crisis to President Lee.[102] Differences in conflict observation also surfaced at a Kuomintang congress to nominate the presidential election candidate in 1996, where Lee was challenged by Lin Yang-kang, vice chairman of the party, former president of the Judicial Yuan and member of the conservative faction.[103] Hau, now also party vice chairman, also reportedly refused to support Lee. These conservative members of the 'Chinese Alliance for Democratic Reform' were of the opinion that Lee should be replaced by Lin since Lee's Cross-Strait policies leaned too much towards pro-independence.[104] When the Kuomintang nominated Lee, Lin announced he would run for election outside of the party.[105] He declared that when elected president he would make a public pledge that Taiwan would never pursue independence, in contrast to Lee, fearing that President Lee's re-election would spark even tenser relations with the Mainland.[106]

Statements by DPP members similarly exhibited a prognostic framing that confirms a general continuity in conflict observation. Already the appeal by DPP members calling on the PRC to respect sovereignty indicated a certain degree of continuity in the DPP's agenda for the future of Taiwan: international recognition of what is already a political fact, Taiwan's independence.[107] Indeed, the DPP fully questioned any grounds for revising its stance on the Cross-Strait conflict, contesting that the PRC's military exercises meant any change at all in conflict communication "because the military threat has existed a long time".[108] The strongest testimony to this desire for continuity was perhaps the nomination of Peng Ming-min as presidential election candidate in 1996. The independence advocate won the nomination against Formosa faction member Hsu Hsin-liang.[109]

The New Party considered this as confirmation of its suspicions about the Lee government and the Kuomintang liberals. Of the major political groups in the discursive field, its prognostic framing remained the most reconciliatory towards Mainland China. In its firm commitment to reunification, the New Party continuously advanced a competing conflict observation that it saw as being in strong contrast to not only that of the DPP, but more significantly to that of the Kuomintang. When the title 'Republic of China on Taiwan' appeared in official correspondence by overseas missions in October 1995, New Party leader Jaw Shau-kong was quick to denounce it as yet another deliberate step towards independence: "If such a name change is widespread among our overseas offices, it would suggest that President Lee Teng-hui has engaged in activities to promote another version of an independent Taiwan".[110] In fact, conflict observations by New Party members and by Kuomintang conservative 'rebels' such Lin and Hau converged considerably. Once Lin and Hau had announced their plans to run for presidential elections, the New Party even rallied behind its 'ideological mentors'.[111]

In general, besides these rearrangements, the conflict observations of all the major parties exhibited a basic continuity in face of continuing PRC military exercises, with particular positions becoming more pronounced. As the parliamentary elections in December 1995 and presidential elections in March 1996 drew closer, competing conflict observations became increasingly distinctive. Ahead of the parliamentary elections on 2 December, the New Party sought to position itself as the 'peace promoter' in Cross-Strait conflict, aiming at an '*unconditional* and immediate peace agreement'.[112] It was precisely preconditions like mutual recognition that continued to be upheld by the Kuomintang government: "I'm sorry, you are the boss, but so am I. There is no room for compromise", Lee remarked on Deng Xiaoping's 'One Country, Two Systems' formula.[113] On the other hand, the Kuomintang sought to position itself as the guarantor of stability[114] to distinguish its position decisively from that of the DPP. The DPP in turn reiterated its claim that the military intimidation did not contribute in any way to the existing conflict and disputed that China would actually attack even if independence were officially declared (which was basically unnecessary, thanks to Taiwan's de-facto independence).[115]

The voting results of the 1995 legislative elections did not indicate any decisive public shift in either direction in terms of conflict observation. However, with the Kuomintang (46 per cent) losing its absolute majority and the DPP making only marginal gains (+5 seats, 33 per cent), most public commentaries saw the New Party, which tripled its seats (13 per cent), as the winner in the election.[116] While other matters such as local issues of course played a major role in parliamentary elections,[117] politicians across all parties nonetheless connected the outcome of the elections to the Cross-Strait conflict. Prime Minister Lien interpreted the result as an indication of broad support for the government; DPP politicians saw the result as confirmation that voters were unimpressed with Chinese threats and vowed to continue pursuing independence.[118] New Party politicians 'admitted' that China's threats helped their cause: "Communist China's military exercises drew some votes for us from people who supported Taiwan independence before".[119]

Justificatory statements are fairly typical in post-election declarations, but what is interesting here is that subsequent statements during the presidential election campaign confirmed that the parties continued to subscribe to their expressed position. The Kuomintang and President Lee even offered renewed justification for insisting on their preconditions to Cross-Strait dialogue in the wake of the intimidating experience of PRC military exercises in the run-up to the elections. Lee called the intimidation an attack on democracy, stating that "the ballot is stronger than the bullet".[120] Lee insisted on this position in face of continuing military exercises [121] and further argued that Chinese intimidation actually reflected the PRC's fear of democracy, and not so much of independence.[122] At the same time, Lee's pledges to pursue international recognition became noticeably fewer in the months prior to the presidential elections, while he continued to reiterate his opposition to secessionism. Likewise, Lee's remarks on the Cross-Strait conflict became more reconciliatory. The Kuomintang government repeatedly emphasized its promotion of peace (in ending the status of a 'communist rebellion' and recognizing the PRC)[123] and underlined its willingness to sign a peace agreement.[124] With peace as the common aspiration across the Taiwan Strait, the Kuomintang further proposed an expansion of commercial, cultural and information links.[125] Yet the Lee government's reconciliatory gestures insisted, on principle, on preconditions: substantially expanding the 'three links' would require peace in the first place[126] and reunification would only be feasible under democracy.[127] Overall, the Lee ticket sought to describe itself as the guarantor of stability and balanced policies, as well as the promoter and defender of democracy.[128]

In its campaign for the presidential elections the DPP's position on Cross-Strait relations was neatly reflected in its slogan: 'Independence Yes, Unification No'.[129] Unlike the position taken by the Kuomintang, the DPP did not retreat from its position in any way which could be considered reconciliatory. To the contrary, presidential candidate Peng confirmed that his views had not changed since his writing of the 'Declaration of Formosan Self-Salvation'.[130] Advancing further an observation of native Taiwanese identity, the DPP even ran a televised advertisement stating that "[o]ver the past century we have seen 50 years of colonisation by the Japanese and then 50 years of domination by the Kuomintang. Now is the time to return Taiwan to the Taiwanese".[131] Relatively in line with this, Peng insisted that the government should indeed fight against reunification "to safeguard the country's security and sovereignty", and not to have it confused "as part of China".[132] DPP politicians called Lee's ignoring of Chinese military threats inadequate,[133] and stressed that threats would only "increase our determination to work for an independent Taiwan".[134] Defiant of this "terrorism from China",[135] Peng sent a letter to Beijing asking for the recognition of Taiwanese sovereignty and demanding an end to intimidation.[136] The DPP thus continued to observe Taiwan as defacto independent but contested there being an actual invasion threat in the event of its winning the elections as "KMT brainwashing".[137]

In their statements, New Party politicians consistently expressed most concern of a serious threat of invasion or other kinds of retribution by the PRC, yet they attributed responsibility for the situation to the Kuomintang government and President Lee in particular. When presidential candidate Lin declared that "China will certainly act if Taiwan declares itself independent",[138] he was also referring to the independence stance taken by the DPP, but his remarks were more explicitly aimed at the pursuance of recognition policies by the government and its pragmatic diplomacy.[139] Despite his condemnation of the PRC for its military exercises as posing a threat to the security of the Taiwanese people,[140] it was Lee's actions, according to vice-presidential candidate Hau, which brought Taiwan to the brink of war.[141] Lee betrayed the Kuomintang's mission to reunify China.[142] Now, Lee was refusing to acknowledge the extent and severity of the tensions: "Lee Teng-hui cannot continue to deceive the public by saying there is nothing to worry about", New Party chairman Chen Kuai-miao claimed.[143] In its self-characterization, the New Party, by contrast, was the only viable promoter of peace and Cross-Strait reconciliation.

Taiwan's 1996 presidential elections produced a distinct victory for Lee Teng-hui. The incumbent president was able to secure a clear majority of 54 per cent of the popular vote. The DPP candidate Peng Ming-min came in second with 21.13 per cent, followed by the New Party-endorsed candidate Lin Yang-kang, who received 14.9 per cent of the ballot.[144] Having been re-elected, President Lee was quick to contextualize the election result accordingly: "At this critical moment when our nation faces danger and provocation, we completed this election. The glory belongs to all 21 million people here. We wrote a new page in Taiwan's 400 years of history".[145] In addition to assigning this to Taiwan's rather than to China's history, Lee again cited democracy as a distinguishing feature: "They fire missiles and stage military exercises to scare us, but we are not afraid at all . . . . We are showing the world that democracy and freedom are more valuable than anything else".[146] Such views have fairly close parallels with DPP observations on the presidential election and its result. Party Chairman Shih concluded that "[b]eing able to choose our own leader is a victory in itself. It proves we are indeed an independent, sovereign state".[147] DPP officials were split, however, on whether the result really was a vote in support of independence. While the defeated vice-presidential candidate Frank Hsieh stated that "Mr Lee was clearly for unification, so the anti-unification campaign failed", Shih believed the opposite to be true. This was similar to former DPP Chairman Hsu, who interpreted the combined votes for Lee and Peng as indicating "a clear choice by the Taiwanese to oppose Chinese intimidation and threats and to continue to support Taiwan's effort to build its international status".[148] Reactions by New Party officials were more muted, with Chen urging Cross-Strait reconciliation.[149] However, Hau offered a particularly gloomy outlook of continuing tensions in Cross-Strait relations involving an eventual economic blockade, calling Lee a 'traitor' in favor of independence.[150]

Conflict observation after the first wave of negative sanctions

After the presidential elections, the first wave of Chinese sanctions, military exercises in the vicinity of Taiwan, ended. Conflict observation on the Taiwanese side, however, remained largely unchanged. The 'new old' Kuomintang government continued to make reconciliatory statements in keeping with the rhetoric of its recent presidential election campaign, without compromising its position.

Pledges and invitations to resume talks across the Taiwan Strait by government officials were advanced more formally by President-elect Lee in his inaugural address, during which he emphasized dialogue as a path towards conflict resolution and offered "to embark upon a journey of peace to Mainland China [. . .] to meet with the top leadership of the Chinese Communists for a direct exchange of views in order to open up a new era of communication and cooperation between the two sides".[151] Lee mentioned commonalities such as the 5,000 years of Chinese history but insisted on the sovereignty of the Republic of China and vowed to continue with its 'pragmatic diplomacy'. Accordingly, foreign trips by government officials continued in the following years,[152] frequently involving 'stopovers' in the US.[153] Also, the campaign to join the UN continued at first,[154] albeit at a lower profile.[155] Efforts to expand dialogue,[156] with the aim of also eventually signing a peace accord at the turn of the millennium[157] and of fostering economic exchange[158] in a limited and controlled manner were accompanied by calls for caution and restrictions on economic investments on the Mainland[159] as part of a 'no haste, be patient policy' (Tanner 2007:47f.). The Kuomintang government also announced further restrictions on such investments should the conflict escalate.[160] Despite these efforts, Taiwanese investment in China was reportedly continuing to grow unhindered.[161] The Lee administration continued to raise its unchanged preconditions,[162] while reiterating its commitment to reunification.[163] At the same time, the government continued to refer to the division[164] in a particular way, as 'one divided China', restating its intention to promote the sovereignty of the Republic of China.[165] In addition, the Kuomintang government relinquished historical Republic of China claims to Outer Mongolia. Together with constitutional changes that suspended provincial Taiwan and National Assembly (i.e., Taiwan + Mainland) elections, such moves could contribute to interpretations of Taiwan as a separate state.[166] The visit to Taiwan of the Dalai Lama, who was called a separatist by conservatives,[167] and announcements regarding opening a representative office in Taipei, also potentially furthered this image, despite assurances to the contrary.[168]

On several points, the DPP's position on matters related to the Cross-Strait conflict was in considerable accordance with that of the Kuomintang government. DPP politicians vowed to return to dialogue with China[169] but demanded that a cross-party consensus be established on the content of the dialogue.[170] The DPP assented to the constitutional changes and the revocation of claims to Outer Mongolia.[171] DPP member Lu Hsiu-lien even led Taiwan's official delegation to the UN to make known Taiwan's wish to return to the organization.[172] In addition to such agreements, DPP statements continued to favor independence, with different party factions either more or less in favor. DPP politicians disagreed on how to promote independence politically: some, like Chen Shui-bian, pushed for a referendum, while others, such as party chairman Hsu Hsing-liang, rejected this idea and supported a more toned-down approach.[173] The visit of the Dalai Lama, broadly welcomed by DPP members, further prompted demands to accord him the honor of state guest and not just to treat him as a ROC citizen,[174] calling into question any claims the ROC might hold over Tibet. Yet, despite such statements endorsing independence, persisting differences among DPP politicians on the party's stance on independence and an overall dominance of the 'toned-down' pragmatic stance taken by Formosa faction members[175] had already led to a split. In late 1996, discontent members split from the DPP and established the Taiwan Independence Party (TAIP).[176] The new party went on to promote independence: "Our goal is to set up the Taiwan Republic. We will mobilize all social forces to fight China's hegemony" according to a statement.[177]

New Party statements on the Cross-Strait conflict displayed a general continuity in opposition to independence and pragmatic diplomacy.[178] New Party politicians took a more cautious approach and voiced reluctance to renouncing claims to Outer Mongolia, questioning the larger implications for the Republic's claim to

Mainland China.[179] They voiced similar concerns about and disagreement with constitutional changes that would change Taiwan's provincial government,[180] viewed as a step towards independence.[181] When the Dalai Lama visited Taiwan, New Party politicians also insisted he did so as a citizen of the Republic of China.[182] Besides the preoccupation with protecting the ROC's designated circumference beyond the island of Taiwan, the New Party specified its own vision for the political status of contemporary China as 'one China, two Chinese states'.[183] Accordingly, New Party politicians also insisted that the PRC would need to give up its pretense of exclusively representing China.[184] Yet the New Party seemed far less principled regarding its stated position, favoring a pragmatic turnaround on expanding exchange to reduce tensions and improve relations across the Taiwan Strait. Such efforts focused particularly on expanding economic relations[185] and 'direct links',[186] but amounted to seeking an understanding to have military observers in the PRC to build up trust.[187] Propagated by New Party chairman Jaw as a more informal 'second channel', this engagement included establishing a liaison office in Beijing for Cross-Strait business and informal talks.[188] The eagerness of the New Party's offer to act as 'mediator' may reflect a concern expressed by party members that time would actually play into the hands of the PRC in the Cross-Strait conflict.[189]

Summary and analysis

As is evident from the process tracing following the PRC's introduction of negative sanctions, general conflict observation in Taiwan became more strongly securitized (see Table 5.3). Conflict communication consisted of amplified identity incompatibilities that essentially evolved around challenges to the PRC's 'One China, Two Systems'. All three major parties in the discursive field claimed a security threat in their diagnostic framings. For both the Kuomintang and the DPP, the PRC, in pursuing its illegitimate attempt to enforce its observation of Cross-Strait relations decisively on the island, bears causal responsibility and is the source of the threat. Of the parties, only the New Party attributed responsibility differently, pointing at the Taiwanese independence movement more broadly and

Table 5.3 Taiwan's discursive field on conflict observation, 1996

Political party	*New Party*	*Kuomintang*	*DPP*
Diagnostic framing	Security threat	Security threat	Security threat
Attribution of responsibility	Mainly independence promoters	PRC	PRC Unification promoters
Prognostic framing	Dialogue Reunification	International recognition Military build-up	Formal independence Military build-up
Conflict observation	Issue incompatibility	Identity incompatibility	Identity incompatibility

at President Lee Teng-hui's policies and statements in particular as the cause of the conflict escalation.

Prognostic framing in conflict communication similarly reflected in general an increasingly securitized identity incompatibility. Both the Kuomintang and the DPP decidedly refused to acquiesce and begin reunification talks, or indeed to even embrace the PRC's 'One China' principle. Instead, the Kuomintang insisted on its preconditions and continued to pursue its goal of international recognition for the democratic Republic of China, observing it as a distinct political entity. As was the case with the Kuomintang, the DPP promoted the expansion of Taiwan's military capabilities as a means to counter the threat. In addition, the DPP considered pursuing formal independence as the correct measure for handling the conflict. Again, only the New Party, having securitized a primarily local threat, consistently subscribed to 'One China' in a sense closer to the one promoted by the Mainland and aimed for timely negotiations on reunification.

Given these developments on positions on the observation of Cross-Strait relations, only a strong result (if not an outright victory) by the New Party in the presidential election in 1996 could have amounted to a development of conflict observation in line with PRC policies. The actual election results made for a decisively different conflict observation, which essentially perpetuated a newly amplified identity incompatibility. In the years after the election, conflict observation by and large displayed continuity.

As the analysis demonstrates, China's negative sanctions strategy clearly contributed to increasing securitization of the conflict and to identity incompatibilities. The PRC's negative sanctions strategy failed spectacularly in this first wave.

Second wave of negative sanctions, presidential election 2000

The Cross-Strait conflict became more confrontational again in 1999 when PRC officials began making threats and China resumed military exercises in areas close to Taiwan. On the island, this was preceded by remarks by President Lee Teng-hui less than a year ahead of the presidential elections, whereby he stated that ever since 1991, Cross-Strait relations had not been conducted between 'two political entities', but on a 'special state-to-state' basis. In an interview with German radio Deutsche Welle, Lee further added that given these 'historical' and 'legal facts', "there is no longer any need to declare Taiwanese independence".[190] Lee also warned of a threat to the region due to Chinese nationalism and the Mainland's failure to implement democracy.[191] These assertions regarding Taiwan's status followed earlier observations in a book authored by Lee who, instead of advocating hasty reunification or independence, favored keeping the status quo or seeking a third option in the form of decentralizing China into seven regions.[192] Lee indicated that his remarks were a necessary clarification for "dialogue and negotiations with the Chinese communists on an equal footing".[193]

Despite the general commitment of Kuomintang politicians to dialogue and conditional reunification, they remained wary of the PRC and denounced any security threat, pledging to defend their position against any coercive pressure.

In his radio interview with Deutsche Welle, President Lee had again claimed that the PRC and its refusal to renounce the use of force posed a key threat to Taiwan's security and interpreted subsequent military maneuvers accordingly (Lee 1999).[194] Other Kuomintang politicians reiterated similar observations in relation to Chinese threats. Defense Minister Tang Fei insisted that to resolutely counter the PRC's military threat, defense spending would need to increase from 2.6 to 3–3.5 per cent of GDP.[195] The ROC's Defense Ministry described PRC military exercises, which are intentionally announced as such, as being designed "to undermine the morale of our people" and to scare.[196] Vice President and Kuomintang presidential nominee Lien Chan noted that "Chinese communists have deployed a number of missiles threatening Taiwan",[197] but played down Chinese military threats, emphasizing dialogue as the method of conflict resolution and alleging that the government of the PRC had not investigated carefully enough its Cross-Strait policy propositions.[198] Yet Lien proceeded to demand a further strengthening of military capabilities to "let the Chinese communists know if they want to settle disputes by resorting to force, they would pay dearly".[199]

President Lee's reassertion of the status of Cross-Strait relations subsequently defined the Kuomintang position until the presidential elections the following year, as well as some of the wider controversy on the conflict in Taiwan. Lien Chan endorsed Lee's statements as merely clarifying Taiwan's political existence and called the PRC's 'One China' policy a ploy to block and denigrate Taiwan to a province.[200] Accordingly, Lien considered Lee's statements as not amounting to any changes in Taiwan's position,[201] a view seconded by Prime Minister Vincent Siew: "President Lee's definition mainly affirms reality and underscores parity between the two sides of the Taiwan Strait".[202] In line with this, the government renewed its bid to join the UN.[203] Lien said that Taiwan's policies towards the Mainland would continue to be guided by the 'three no's' and 'three wants': 'no independence, no hasty reunification, no confrontation', but instead 'peace, exchanges and a win-win situation'.[204]

Kuomintang politicians, however, generally remained committed to reunification.[205] Provided the recognition of parity, Lien pledged explicitly to remain open-minded on the method of eventual reunification.[206] Confirming its continuing commitment to reunification, the Kuomintang rejected revising the constitution to declare Taiwan as an independent state.[207] Although preconditions for reunification, such as initiating democratic reform, were upheld,[208] they were relaxed as obstacles to official dialogue.[209] Lien extended this more 'constructive' approach to his stance on general Cross-Strait exchange. He vowed to embark on a 'journey of peace' to the Mainland and to seek the establishment of a hotline between the two governments.[210] Lien even pledged to engage in direct dialogue with PRC President Jiang: "I think we can meet to talk about the promotion of bilateral exchanges and cooperation. We can even exchange views on any political issues", provided that the PRC demonstrates "goodwill toward Taiwan".[211] Lien's campaign platform exhibited a more pragmatic approach centering on broader exchanges while also keeping to a principled stance on Taiwan's status (quo) and reunification.[212] In resuming dialogue, investment and trade should be facilitated and exchanges expanded with the goal of establishing 'three little links';[213] yet mutual participation in international organizations should be also discussed, as should a peace agreement.[214]

In contrast to President Lee's more pronounced declaration of Taiwan's status, Lien's public statements as presidential nominee were notably lower key, emphasizing continuity[215] and rejecting the need to reaffirm Lee's position. Instead, Lien vowed to aim for stability and cooperation under parity,[216] possibly in the form of a confederacy[217] but definitely not as part of the PRC's 'One Country, Two Systems' formula, as he declared at his nomination.[218] Subsequently, Lien elaborated: "The two sides have come up with different interpretations of the 'one-China policy' . . . In the future we can continue negotiations . . . but at this point we can only go on in our own way".[219] At best, such a formula could be 'One China, respective interpretations', Lien remarked in another reconciliatory statement.[220] Yet in face of PRC Prime Minister Zhu Rongji's 'advice' to voters on the eve of Taiwan's elections not to "just act on impulse at this juncture, which will decide the future course that China and Taiwan will follow. Otherwise I'm afraid you won't get another opportunity to regret", Lien firmly observed that "other countries should respect the fact of Taiwan's independence and its sovereignty".[221]

In the elections in 2000, Vice President Lien Chan was not the only Kuomintang politician to formulate a Cross-Strait conflict observation as part of a bid for the presidency. A competing observation was advanced by popular former Taiwan governor James Soong, who quit the party after he was denied the official ticket due to the party's top-down style nomination.[222] Unrestrained by President Lee's statements on Cross-Strait relations, Soong offered an observation of conflict that was slightly more 'pro-China' and reconciliatory. Claiming that "Taiwan needs a leader who is not reckless",[223] Soong aimed for de-escalation. He stated that when elected president, he would sign a "mutual non-aggression peace treaty", established between the 'nation' of "the Republic of China and the People's Republic of China", which would last for 30 years.[224] Upon its expiration, "the two sides, both as a sovereign state, would continue their ties for 20 more years modelling after the European Union, if they do not oppose their status quo", with the people of Taiwan deciding on the island's fate in a referendum.[225] Soong also iterated a distinct version of 'relative sovereignty' in Cross-Strait relations, calling them "'quasi-international' because it would neither be domestic, nor would it be international".[226] Soong's running mate Chang Chao-hsiung paraphrased this positioning with the formula "one is no less than one, and one plus one is bigger than two".[227]

Along similarly reconciliatory lines, Soong argued a need to recommence dialogue and proposed to seek 'direct communication' by inviting the PRC's chief official for Cross-Strait relations – based on the condition of parity, however.[228] In order to promote de-escalation, Soong declared himself "willing to embark on a peaceful journey to the mainland before the inauguration"; faced with the possible political obstacles of conflict resolution (read: transformation), Soong proposed "to enhance friendship and peace through economic and cultural exchanges".[229] Remaining critical of the existing restrictions on economic investment and the ban on the 'three links', Soong vowed to establish direct links in a breakaway from the Lee administration's Straits exchange policies: "We prefer to develop cross-strait economics on a positive and constructive basis, instead of the on-going 'go slow, be patient' course," Chang elaborated.[230] Such a development would include opening 'mini' direct links between the PRC and the frontline Quemoy (also: Kinmen, 金門) and Matsu islands, as well as a greater level of free trade as part of the PRC's and the ROC's eventual joint membership of the WTO.[231]

Even while Soong's statements clearly displayed reconciliation and a commitment to sideline differences by focusing on expanding exchange, Soong neither embraced the PRC's 'One Country, Two Systems'[232] – indeed he explicitly rejected it – nor were his statements in favor of (timely) reunification. His proposed peace agreement would more likely have meant postponing the question for decades and, in addition, deciding on it in a popular referendum, also referring to the conflict as a 'human rights' issue.[233] Taiwan's people "cannot accept Mainland Chinese rule and are strongly concerned about Taiwan's security and freedom", which will be defended against military threats, Soong maintained, rejecting to rule out the eventual development of surface-to-surface missiles and proposing increased investment in national defense.[234] Intimidation attempts would also mean ruling out any dialogue on Cross-Strait relations: "Taiwan does not take any threat, does not bow to pressure and we will not negotiate out of fear",[235] and this also means that "[a]ny timetable [for reunification] would not be accepted by the Taiwan public".[236] Summing up his positioning, Soong stated that "most people in Taiwan favor a policy against immediate unification and immediate independence. The correct policy has been formulated to reduce hostilities between the two sides".[237]

James Soong's positioning in the discursive field on the Cross-Strait conflict was considered more reconciliatory and de-escalatory than the one taken by Lien and it was sufficiently so to have conservatives and New Party politicians endorse his candidacy. On election day, New Party Chairman Lee Ching-hua together with New Party presidential nominee Li Ao stated at a press conference: "Anti-Taiwan independence forces cannot be divided. Therefore, all the anti-independence voters should support James Soong".[238] Li Ao had no prospect of winning the election.[239] Prior to that, a number of Kuomintang members and other conservatives had already declared their support for Soong, among them former Prime Minister Hau Pei-tsun.[240]

A great deal of the concern expressed by the "anti-Taiwan independence" camp was linked to the possibility that DPP candidate Chen Shui-bian might win the election. Initially, compromise in any direction was deemed unlikely by commentators in light of intra-party differences on the DPP's stance on independence between the various factions. Yet after some election defeats, prominent former pro-independence politicians, among them Chen Shui-bian, began to make less principled statements.[241] Instead of aiming for a referendum on independence, Chen voiced support for the 'status quo'. Subsequently, this stance was specified in a party resolution as Taiwan being "an independent sovereign state and that any move that changes the status quo can only be taken after gaining the consent of the people of Taiwan through a referendum".[242] The resolution also accepted 'Republic of China' as the official name but denied the necessity to insist on it in official matters. Remarkably, however, the referendum requirement to any change to the observed de-facto independence of Taiwan covers an official declaration of independence as well as reunification. Consequently, despite some toning down, the DPP nevertheless called itself "the guardian of Taiwan independence".[243]

As DPP presidential nominee, Chen Shui-bian fully embraced this resolution in his proposition to engage constructively in Cross-Strait relations, with the aim of achieving "peace, stability, prosperity and mutual trust in the Taiwan Strait under the premise of firmly maintaining Taiwan's sovereignty, independence and national dignity".[244] In order to advance this fourfold goal of peace, stability, prosperity and trust, Chen suggested the following steps. First, the creation of a 'special buffer peace zone' and mutual military monitoring, followed by a peace agreement which is committed to a peaceful settlement of the dispute and based on the recognition of parity.[245] Second, Chen proposed to reconvene dialogue with the PRC: "we are eager to engage in dialogue and contact with China. We do not exclude any issue including possibly political issues", even reunification.[246] Third, he recommended that "ongoing restrictions on transportation, commerce and investment be lifted providing that national security is ensured";[247] DPP party chairman Lin Yi-hsiung went even further to suggest open-ended economic cooperation: "Economically the two sides could establish a customs alliance, a free trade zone and a common market".[248] Yet all these offers were clearly based "on the premise of ensuring Taiwan's national security and according to our strategic goals on economic security".[249] Any expansion of economic exchange should thus occur gradually and reflect that "national security is the top priority".[250]

Despite fairly far-reaching offers of intensified dialogue, exchange and cooperation, Chen's statements nonetheless reflected a definite sense of threat. As much as Chen made overtures to eliminate restrictions on Cross-Strait trade and investment, he had already observed in terms of existing exchange that "to a Taiwan that is confronted by military intimidation from China, such a high degree of trade and investment dependency is definitely risky".[251] In the face of these threats and intimidation, Chen further sought to ensure increased defense through participation in the proposed US theatre missile defense system.[252] As reflected in the party resolution, the DPP presidential nominee's statements were based on "a platform for safeguarding the right of the Taiwan people for self-determination"[253] and any stated aims to seek dialogue and expand exchanges were to be contingent on 'parity' and were not to pose a threat to Taiwan's de-facto independence. Accordingly, Chen elevated this claimed right to self-determination to a distinct conditionality: "We will not declare independence unless China wants to use force against us".[254] The principles of democracy, human rights and the right to self-determination would also become the elements of a "new internationalist" foreign policy which would replace the existing 'pragmatic' diplomacy with the aim of promoting Taiwan as a sovereign state internationally.[255] To this end, Chen proposed that Lee Teng-hui travel the diplomatic world as Taiwan's official 'envoy of peace'.[256] In fact, Chen repeatedly stated his agreement with President Lee's description of Cross-Strait relations as 'special state to state' relations,[257] and even suggested "reaching consensus internally in Taiwan helpful to promoting cross-strait peace and stability".[258]

The Republic of China's presidential election in 2000, a close race for the most part, was won by DPP candidate Chen Shui-bian. He secured 39.3 per cent of the popular vote, closely followed by James Soong, who received 36.8 per cent of the ballot. Much of the remaining vote went to Kuomintang candidate Lien Chan, with 23.1 per cent.[259] In his victory speech, Chen claimed its historical significance as "not a victory for myself and Annette Lu, or the DPP; it's is a victory for the people of Taiwan and for democracy".[260] Chen subsequently reiterated his reconciliatory aims, along with the links set out during the campaign: "In order to maintain national security and the benefits of all the people, we would like to immediately negotiate with China on the issues of direct links, direct commerce, investment and military confidence-building measures". He further reaffirmed his offer to visit the PRC ahead of his inauguration.

Nonetheless, Chen also observed widespread public opposition to the 'One Country, Two Systems' formula, reaffirming his position on Taiwan's independence: "our authority and sovereignty should be forever protected".[261] In turn, Kuomintang nominee Lien Chan conceded defeat. Congratulating the president-elect, Lien expressed his hope that Chen would "very carefully govern this country and the pressing issues that need a lot of attention".[262] James Soong congratulated Chen and, more so, the Taiwanese people; he stated his intention to establish a new party in response to the wishes of his supporters.[263] New Party politicians were quick to announce their sympathy, attracted by the prospect of forming an opposition alliance.[264] Yet their common cause to save the Republic of China was not entirely limited to the fact that advocates of independence had won the election. Indeed, major issues in the 2000 presidential election were the proliferation of crime and 'black gold', as well as links between organized crime and politics.

Following the negative PRC sanctions and the 2000 presidential election in Taiwan, President-elect Chen Shui-bian in his inauguration address entitled 'Taiwan stands up', offered a general outline of his proposals on finding a solution to the Cross-Strait conflict. Chen established his policy of 'Four No's and One Without', (also referred to as 'Five No's'), stating that

> as long as the CCP regime has no intention to use military force against Taiwan, I pledge that during my term in office, I will not declare independence, I will not change the national title, I will not push forth the inclusion of the so-called 'state-to-state' description in the Constitution, and I will not promote a referendum to change the status quo in regards to the question of independence or unification. Furthermore, the abolition of the National Reunification Council or the National Reunification Guidelines will not be an issue.
>
> (Chen 2000)

Based on such commitment, Chen reiterated his intention to seek political dialogue with the PRC, one which did not exclude any topic, and also to promote increased economic exchanges. However, the DPP politician pledged as President of the ROC to "maintain the sovereignty . . . and security of our country" – the recognition of parity would remain the precondition for substantive political dialogue. Chen further clarified the meaning of 'sovereignty' to exclude the notion of 'One China' as being the present situation, declaring that it could only refer to a possible future state of affairs (ibid.). Chen continued to observe Taiwan as a fully sovereign state, rejecting the PRC's proposed compromise of 'One China, two "equal" political entities', wherein the PRC would nonetheless effectively represent China internationally.[265] Therefore, also in the context of the presidency, there is continuity in DPP conflict observation, amounting to an identity incompatibility.

Despite this continuity in conflict observation, offers of dialogue initially continued,[266] but in face of political deadlock the DPP administration concentrated on promoting Cross-Strait exchange.[267] Expanding the 'three links', however, also remained politicized. This was not just because of the occasional demand by the PRC that they be discussed only on condition that the DPP government subscribe to 'One China'.[268] In connection with Taiwan's conflict observation more directly, the DPP government frequently linked such negotiations to the start of wider government dialogue.[269] In the end, only 'mini-links' were approved, which only established air, transport and postal links between outlying islands (Kinmen, Matsu) and the Mainland.[270]

The DPP government also sought to limit economic dependence on China and to expand international economic ties, aiming to sign a free trade agreement with Japan. In yet another drive to promote Taiwan's presence internationally, the Chen administration embarked on its own version of 'pragmatic diplomacy'. Termed 'neo-internationalism', the government announced its policy to expand development assistance as well as ties to major powers through unofficial visits.

Summary and analysis

Similar to the run-up to the presidential elections in 1996, conflict communication in 2000 also was characterized by amplified identity incompatibilities, which evolved as a result of the attempted imposition and rejection of PRC's 'One China, Two Systems' principle. The tracing of conflict observation in Taiwan reveals that, in general, it became more strongly securitized ahead of the presidential election (see Table 5.4). The Kuomintang, most prominently President Lee but also

Table 5.4 Taiwan's discursive field on conflict observation, 2000

Political party	*Soong/New Party*	*Kuomintang*	*DPP*
Diagnostic framing	Security threat	Security threat	Security threat
Attribution of responsibility	Mainly independence promoters	Mainly PRC Independence promoters	PRC Unification promoters
Prognostic framing	Dialogue Military build-up	Dialogue Military build-up	International recognition Military build-up
Conflict observation	Issue incompatibility	Identity incompatibility	Identity incompatibility

presidential candidate Lien Chan, denounced an on-going security threat from the PRC in diagnostic framings. The DPP and its candidate Chen Shui-bian, as well as presidential candidate James Soong, concurred with such diagnosis. Again, there were also important differences in diagnostic framing. The Kuomintang and the DPP largely agreed that the PRC was the source of the threat, yet in both cases, there were particular twists to the narrative. In Lien's statements, moves towards formal independence were a contributing factor; in Chen's statements, the factor contributing to the security threat to Taiwan was a change in the status quo in the opposite direction, i.e. towards unification. Soong on his part pointed to irresponsible advocates of independence and the 'reckless' actions of President Lee as being significant causes of the threatening situation.

In addition, the commonalities in their observation of Cross-Strait relations were greater between the Kuomintang candidate and the DPP candidate. When Lien subscribed to Lee's depiction of relations as 'special state-to-state' and de-facto independent, differences between the Kuomintang's observation and that of the DPP as two equally independent, sovereign states became negligible. Both candidates also aimed to strengthen this status quo, notwithstanding their aforementioned differences on potential threats to it. By contrast, Soong's observation of relations as (merely) 'quasi-international' between 'relative sovereigns' was de-escalatory, possibly transforming the dispute into an issue conflict.

With regard to prognostic framing, the commonalities between the Lien and the Soong ticket were greater. Both candidates advanced an essentially bi-directional prognostic framing, with one consisting of proposals to promote peace through dialogue and increased exchange and the other consisting of pledges to increase military spending to counter the security threat. This latter proposition was also voiced by Chen. The DPP candidate similarly vowed to pursue dialogue, but his pledges to pursue international recognition for Taiwan were more pronounced. A more significant difference, however, was the way in which he articulated his statements which amounted to a somewhat hypothetical, but in a sense 'projective', securitization. As presented above, Chen most frequently raised security issues in connection with either proposed policies (i.e. expanding economic exchange), or hypothetical forced changes to the 'status quo' of de-facto independence. Overall, the prognostic framing in Chen's statements emphasized the aim to pursue and advance common Cross-Strait interests and to sideline differences. In effect, Chen's stated policy proposals would, if anything, strengthen this observed status quo – depending, of course, on the prospect of an eventual popular referendum.

Given the three positions on observing Cross-Strait relations during the 2000 presidential election campaign, James Soong clearly was the candidate considered the most pro-China by the Taiwanese public. By contrast, Chen Shui-bian was the strongest advocate of a de-facto independent, sovereign Taiwan, one which was described ahead of the elections by PRC officials as somewhat unacceptable. Accordingly, Chen's victory was a Cross-Strait political disaster for the PRC. On the face of it, negative sanctions again contributed to amplifying identity incompatibilities in the Cross-Strait conflict observation. However, to analytically contextualize the election results, more than 60 per cent of the electorate voted for Soong and Lien and not for the DPP or an eventual independence vision. ROC market fluctuations in the days around the election may be a further indication that, ultimately, the result seemed to reflect support for the Cross-Strait political status quo.

5.2.2 'System' vs 'government': polarizing combined sanctions

Despite promoting the observation of an identity conflict during the run-up to the presidential elections, at the beginning of his term in office President Chen's ROC government advanced overtures to the PRC regarding dialogue and expanding exchanges. Yet much of the conflict observation during Chen's first term revolved around his intention to introduce a referendum on Cross-Strait relations. By contrast, Kuomintang politicians called for expanding exchanges with Mainland China. They clearly stated their commitment to unification as guiding such dialogue.

In turn, the PRC continued to denounce what it considered 'movements towards independence' such as proposals for a referendum, constitutional changes or changes to the name of the Republic of China. Vice President Hu Jintao observed Taiwanese separatism as "an element of sabotage to peace and stability in the Asian-Pacific region" and declared that the PRC would "never allow the independence of Taiwan nor would it tolerate the harm caused by separatist forces in Taiwan to China's sovereignty and territorial integrity".[271] The PRC reiterated this position in November and December 2003 on suspecting further separatist moves.[272]

Mainland China's conflict observation and sanctions against Taiwan

The different approach is taken in the second case, with its combined sanctions strategy, sets it apart from the previous two waves of negative sanctions. Besides a notable reduction in military exercises and intimidation, the second case of sanctions involved a combination of both negative and positive economic and political measures. These combined sanctions fell into five categories. Negative sanctions included a) some political encroachment through declarations and laws; b) international isolation; and c) business intimidation. Positive sanctions included a) limited recognition of basic needs and interests; and b) initial offers of some economic incentives.

To begin with, during the legislative elections in December 2001 the PRC largely refrained from staging extraordinary military exercises or from engaging in extensive political encroachment. If anything, it was this inaction which was notable. Although the PRC continued with its military exercises, by and large these were annual routine drills. However, these maneuvers routinely involved practicing landing operations, or simulated attacks on aircraft carriers.[273]

The PRC continued to reiterate its commitment to eventually resorting to military force to prevent such an outcome. In response to this perceived move by the

ROC government in August 2002, the PRC stepped up its rhetoric in various media outlets, stating that 'separatist action' would bring disaster and equating a declaration of independence with a declaration of war.[274] Given such developments, "peace will have to be safeguarded and won through the use of force", an article in the People's Daily stated.[275]

At first glance, these statements do not seem much different from political encroachment in the second wave of negative sanctions. Yet, contrary to statements made by Zhu and others when addressing Taiwan's public on the use of force as last resort, PRC declarations began to differentiate between the ROC government and 'the people of Taiwan'. In addition, they began to explicitly recognize the right of their 'blood brothers' to self-determination, on the premise that the integrity of China be preserved.[276] In line with this, President Hu Jintao (Hu became Jiang's successor in November 2002) further differentiated between the ROC government and its people when he met with Taiwanese investors, courting them as 'patriots': "The central government believes the Taiwan people, who have a long tradition of patriotism, will contribute to the peaceful reunification".[277] In his New Year's address 2004, Hu stated that the PRC is "very much concerned about [Taiwan compatriots'] interests and happiness" and vowed to adhere "to the basic principle of peaceful reunification" while reiterating that separatist activities would not be tolerated.[278]

Whereas the PRC abated military intimidation considerably over the course of this case and statements on the Cross-Strait conflict became less oriented towards unrestrained threats, the PRC redoubled its efforts to isolate Taiwan internationally. Besides preventing the ROC from joining international organizations, the PRC involved Taiwan's partners such as the United States, its key ally, and France, an important arms supplier. In December 2003, after receiving PRC Premier Wen Jiabao, US President Bush stated: "We oppose any unilateral decision by either China or Taiwan to change the status quo. And the comments and actions made by the leader of Taiwan indicate that he may be willing to make decisions unilaterally to change the status quo, which we oppose".[279] Bush's statement was 'appreciated' by the PRC government.[280] In late January 2004, French President Chirac stated after a meeting with President Hu in Paris: "France condemns an initiative such as the [Taiwanese] referendum which can appear as aggressive. Anything that raises tensions is dangerous; any initiative that can be interpreted by one party or the other is dangerous for everybody and therefore irresponsible".[281] In addition, Chirac called for lifting the arms embargo which had been imposed against China after the Tiananmen Square Massacre in 1989.[282]

With the ROC presidential election approaching in March 2004, PRC officials reiterated statements that emphasized commonalities with its 'Taiwan compatriots' and differentiated between the people of Taiwan in general and the Taiwanese government and its disruptive actions.[283] Alongside these statements, officials also reiterated the 'bottom line' that separatist actions could not be tolerated.[284] Accordingly, a Taiwan Affairs Office official declared that "[p]eace and stability across the Taiwan Straits will be determined by what happens in the next three months".[285] However, apart from this 'bottom line', statements emphasized a peaceful reunification and openness to dialogue.[286] In a call for dialogue on reunification, Premier Wen invoked two native Taiwanese poets to highlight common bonds.

Apart from the usual invitations to expand the three links based on Taiwan's acceptance of the 'One China' principle, the PRC began to offer its first substantive economic incentives in January 2004, also on condition that Taiwan accept the principle. Taiwan Affairs Office officials announced an incentive "to offer Taiwan farmers more privileged access to the mainland's agricultural market as well as investment opportunities".[287] After a visit by former pro-unification DPP Chairman Hsu in November 2004 the PRC added an additional seven kinds of fruit to the five fruit types which had already been granted import permission (Norris 2016).

However, at the time of Taiwan's 2004 presidential election sanctions were again imposed on the *Taishang* in the form of pro-China voting initiatives (Schubert 2013), harassment and intimidation.[288] Ahead of the elections, more than 20 *Taishang* were arrested and publicly charged with spying (Tanner 2007:118f.). After the presidential election, suspected pro-independence *Taishang* were subjected to threats and penalties, culminating in the intimidation of Chi Mei founder Hsu Wen-lung who was considered to be politically close to the DPP.[289] In a subsequent newspaper publication, Hsu endorsed the 'One China' position, perceived as "an attempt to protect his company's mainland operations" (Schubert 2013:72f.). Although the measures against *Taishang* amounted to negative sanctions, their extent needs to be put critically into perspective. However, notwithstanding this caveat, what is necessary here is that, again, these measures have been socially observed in Taiwan itself as negative sanctions. Furthermore, these negative sanctions did not go as far as to factually blacklist Taiwanese companies, and more comprehensive trade sanctions were never actually introduced, as Tung Chen-yuan (2002) notes in his extensive analysis of the politics of economic Cross-Strait exchanges.

Finally, similar to retaliation against *Taishang*, other negative sanctions did not end with the 2004 presidential election. Instead, and related to retaliation against *Taishang*, plans for trade sanctions and new military exercises appeared in news media, triggering a stock market plunge of 3.48 per cent on June 3, 2004.[290] Political encroachments were also strongly reinforced, with Jiang, still chairman of the Central Military Commission, envisaging 2020 as the deadline for reunification.[291] Negative sanctions policies found their spectacular conclusion in the official promulgation of the Anti-Secession Law in March, 2005. Effectively, the law legalizes the use of force in case of secession. Yet PRC officials denied that the law was any form of 'law mobilization order'.[292] Instead, the law aimed to strengthen and advance relations and exchanges across the Strait, Premier Wen declared[293] (for an assessment of the law's articles, see Lin 2008:7). Again, to what extent the law amounts to a negative sanction depends upon whether or not it is observed as such.

Sanctions conflict observation in Taiwan

Despite overtures to enter into dialogue and expand exchanges, much of conflict observation during Chen's first term in Taiwan was dominated by his intention to introduce a referendum on Cross-Strait relations, declared in August 2002. Shortly before, Chen had again called on the PRC to begin dialogue whereby he indicated that when offers of dialogue were continually turned down, "[we]'ll have to seriously consider whether to walk down our own road to strive for Taiwan's future".[294] In announcing his plans for a referendum "on Taiwan's future and destiny", Chen further observed that "each side (of the Taiwan Strait) is a country", and Taiwan "does not want to become the second Hong Kong or Macau".[295] In Taiwan, Chen's statements were widely considered a departure from his more moderate, dialogue-seeking approach, even when DPP politicians claimed that there had been no change in the government's position.[296] After repeated debate and speculation on the date of the referendum, in June 2003 the DPP started to consider having it coincide with the 2004 presidential election.

Kuomintang politicians advanced different views on the idea of a referendum, as they did on the Cross-Strait conflict following their defeat in the 2000 presidential election. In contrast to the election campaign, differences in the observation of Cross-Strait relations and conflict became more distinct during the first DPP presidential term. As was the case with the DPP, Kuomintang politicians pledged to expand exchanges with Mainland China, with some travel to the Mainland to meet CCP politicians.[297] By contrast, however, Kuomintang politicians clearly stated their commitment to unification as guiding such dialogue.[298] In a step to draw both sides of the Strait closer towards that goal, Kuomintang politicians continued to promote and discuss the idea of a confederation.[299] This also included embracing the '1992 Consensus' of 'One China, different interpretations'.[300]

True to their commitment to reunification, Kuomintang politicians were initially quick to demand an explanation when President Chen hinted at Taiwan going its 'own road' and criticized Chen's referendum proposal,[301] denouncing his 'one state on either side' observation: "Chen's reckless remarks have tied the future and the well-being of Taiwan's 23 million people to the gunpowder keg of Taiwan independence",[302] as Kuomintang chairman Lien Chan claimed. Similarly, James Soong, chairman of the newly-established People First Party (PFP), stated that Chen's observation was in conflict with the constitution[303] and rejected a referendum as polarizing society.[304] Both opposition parties declared their intention to cooperate with one another against the ruling DPP and entered into an alliance, known as the 'Pan-Blue Coalition'.[305] Like their Kuomintang counterparts, PFP politicians endorsed this '1992 Consensus' and similarly called for direct links, based on mutual acceptance of this consensus.[306]

However, the entire political opposition did not express disagreement with Chen's observation of Cross-Strait relations and his announcement of his intention to seek a referendum. Instead, the discursive field on the Cross-Strait conflict saw the (re)surfacing of former President Lee Teng-hui, backing a new political group, the Taiwan Solidarity Union (TSU), in mid-2001. In Lee's words the aim of this new group was "cementing democracy and strengthening Taiwan".[307] Furthermore, according to the leader of the TSU, Huang Chu-wen, the group regards Cross-Strait relations as 'special state-to-state' relations and rejects a relaxing of the 'go slow, be patient' policy.[308] In addition, in Lee's words, the DPP government was "exerting its best efforts" on Cross-Strait relations.[309] In the course of his support for this new political group, the Kuomintang revoked Lee's party membership.[310] According to TSU politicians, because they share relatively similar political positions, the new party "hopes to co-operate with the Democratic Progressive Party".[311] In the parliamentary elections in December 2001, the TSU succeeded in obtaining 5.78 per cent of the vote, while the DPP gained a majority (38.67 per cent) for the first time, together forming the 'Pan-Green Coalition'. The Kuomintang (30.22 per cent) lost its majority while PFP received 20.44 per cent, with the Pan-Blue Coalition effectively retaining an absolute majority.

Hence this broad continuity in the Taiwanese conflict observation was nonetheless accompanied by substantial change in the discursive field, which saw renewed, more subtle efforts by the Chinese to exert influence ahead of the presidential elections in 2004. In part, the announced referendum dominated the run-up to the election. Since President Chen had merely announced the basic aim of holding a referendum to coincide with the presidential election in 2004, its substantive content was debated later. The debate proved controversial, notoriously evolving around the Cross-Strait conflict. At the same time, Chen also announced his aim to establish a new constitution by popular referendum during his second term, in order for Taiwan to become "a normal and full" state.[312] Contrary, though, to the DPP's declared on-going commitment to a status quo of 'de-facto independence',[313] its coalition partner, the Taiwan Solidarity Union, openly sought to dissociate Taiwan from China as a separate nation, with its 'spiritual father' Lee Teng-hui propagating a new constitution, along with changing the nation's title from 'Republic of China on Taiwan' to simply 'Taiwan'. Any legislation passed after Chen's announcement, however, required that any such referenda on constitutional matters concerning the national status be approved by a three-quarter parliamentary majority.[314] Yet, according to the legislation, the president is permitted to announce a 'defensive referendum' in case of an emergency situation constituting a security threat: "When the country is facing foreign threat which could change the country's sovereignty then the president can put the country's national security issues for referendum after resolution of cabinet".[315]

The administration was quick to capitalize on this passage, with Chen announcing his 'duty' and 'responsibility' to "organize a referendum, to protect our country's sovereignty" around election time in 2004. In addition, other ideas for plebiscites were already in the public domain, such as on WHO or United Nation accession, making any referendum not a "one-time" event.[316] The president elaborated on this, stating that the PRC had "deployed [496] missiles to [get] ready [for] an invasion of Taiwan", with the looming threat calling for a pre-emptive referendum: "If we wait for the old Communists to really attack us, then we won't have time, and holding a referendum would be useless".[317] Chen even went as far as to note a dialectical relationship between a defensive referendum and an emergency: "The main purpose of holding the defensive referendum is to consolidate the psychological defence of the Taiwanese people who lack a sense of crisis".[318] Later, Vice President Annette Lu claimed a "terrorist-style missile threat", with the referendum aimed at "saving Taiwan, China and the entire world from war".[319] Yet the government also insisted that the cited 'defensive referendum' was not meant to contradict the 'five no's policy', nor would it amount to a plebiscite on independence: "Basically we need to set different agenda for referendums depending on the extent of the threat China is imposing on us. If China launches a military invasion against us, we will then hold a referendum on independence", Prime Minister Yu Shyi-kun declared.[320] President Chen similarly stated that the referendum "is aimed at sustaining the status quo and deepening our democratic system".[321] To this effect, the referendum would allow the people to "firmly demand that the People's Republic of China immediately withdraw all the ballistic missiles targeting Taiwan and also openly and publicly announce and promise that they will not use force against Taiwan".[322] In a speech broadcast on 16 January 2004, President Chen formally announced the two questions that would be asked in the 'peace referendum':[323]

1 The People of Taiwan demand that the Taiwan Strait issue be resolved through peaceful means. Should Mainland China refuse to withdraw the missiles it has targeted at Taiwan and to openly renounce the use of force against us, would you agree that the Government should acquire more advanced anti-missile weapons to strengthen Taiwan's self-defence capabilities?
2 Would you agree that our Government should engage in negotiation with Mainland China on the establishment of a "peace and stability" framework for cross-strait interactions in order to build consensus and for the welfare of the peoples on both sides?

Concurrently, the Chen administration reiterated its basic call for dialogue. MAC Council chairwoman Tsai Ing-wen declared it "urgent for both Taiwan and China to resume talks".[324] As with previous pledges, Chen seconded this and undertook to aim for "exchanging representatives, so that we can exchange information and build up mutual-trust [sic!]",[325] to seek peace negotiations under parity,[326] and to start talks on extending direct links.[327] Yet the government made its position on 'parity' particularly clear, rejecting the 1992 consensus that "belittles Taiwan; it marginalizes Taiwan".[328] Accordingly, any 'outside' intimidation on democratic proceedings such as the referendum were unacceptable[329] and considered a threat.

The PRC's deployment of missiles targeting the island was deemed one such move.[330] Expanding on this threat, a DPP report claimed that Taiwan's operational command system could be paralyzed in a "seven minute shock and strike" missile attack.[331] In face of such potential, Chen went on to state that "if China tries to launch any missile – as it did in 1996 to threaten the people of Taiwan to affect the presidential election – I will revoke the 'five no's".[332] Besides vowing to respond to this situation by also upgrading Taiwan's military defense forces,[333] President Chen further embraced the logical conclusion of such a conflict observation and the instrument of a 'defensive referendum', declaring that missile tests in Taiwan's vicinity could lead to a formal sovereignty referendum.[334]

Furthermore, DPP politicians raised the subject of news reports about *Taishang* voting initiatives supported by the Mainland 'influencing' them to elect the 'right' candidate.[335] In a televised presidential election debate, President Chen directly accused Lien Chan and the Kuomintang of collaborating with the CCP and aiming to profit from Chinese Communist interference in the election.[336]

To begin with, Pan-Blue coalition politicians had started out with competing conflict observations. Kuomintang chairman Lien Chan had rejected outright any potential referendum on constitutional matters, declaring that "[i]ssues such as independence are best when left for the future generations to decide, since they now create more problems then [sic!] they solve".[337] Instead, he proposed a 'pragmatic' approach of seeking greater cooperation based on the status quo: "Taiwan and the mainland could very well pursue what I call 'parallel development' for a long time to come without having to make a choice on this unification/independence issue".[338]

As part of their joint ticket for the presidential elections, PFP chairman James Soong announced his 'Five Yeses' policy': "Taiwan's present status quo must be maintained; the two sides of the Taiwan Strait must co-exist peacefully; the people of Taiwan must have the final say on Taiwan's destiny; Taiwan's liberal, democratic lifestyle can never be compromised; and its stability and prosperity must be sustained".[339] Instead of introducing a new constitution, the Pan-Blue coalition proposed amending the existing constitution[340] by referendum in 2005.[341] The Kuomintang and PFP embraced the idea of an amendment out of concern that a completely new constitution might be introduced for a 'Republic of Taiwan' instead of a 'Republic of China'.[342] Yet this proposal also meant accepting the introduction of public referenda, now termed 'a basic right of the people' by Lien.

Nonetheless, Pan-Blue politicians fiercely rejected the idea of holding a defensive referendum on pre-emptive grounds. Presidential candidate Lien urged Chen to refrain from provoking Beijing, while vice-presidential candidate Soong found Chen's proposition "funny and annoying".[343] The opposition further disputed that the legal requirements for a defensive referendum had been satisfied, contesting the existence of a threat to the ROC's sovereignty.[344] Instead, Lien accused the DPP President of embarking on a 'holy war' against China, with his unjustified attacks a risk that could "plunge . . . 23 million Taiwanese people into war".[345] Lien also addressed an appeal to the PRC: "I hope Mainland China will not respond to all these actions and remarks deliberately set down by Mr Chen".[346] Ultimately, the Pan-Blue coalition called for a boycott of the referendum, alleging it was 'illegal'.[347]

Apart from constitutional amendments, the Pan-Blue Coalition proposed its own specific referendum plans. Instead of a defensive referendum, Lien declared that he would hold a referendum on direct links after his election.[348] Lien maintained that President Chen had failed to deliver on his aims to expand direct links.[349] In addition, Lien would embark on a peace trip to the Mainland.[350] Yet this proposition came only after Lien had changed his observation of Cross-Strait relations to 'one country on each side', retreating from his former commitment to joining in a mutual confederation.[351] Lien had also started to make confirmatory statements on the threat posed by PRC missiles[352] and vowed to enhance Taiwan's military capabilities.[353] However, while insisting that Taiwan is a sovereign state,[354] Lien suggested focusing on the expansion of economic exchanges "without touching on the thorny 'one China' principle", but based on the principle of parity.[355]

The results of the presidential election on 20 March 2004 were close, with President Chen being re-elected by a margin of less than 30,000 votes. The DPP incumbent received 50.11 per cent of the vote against the Lien/Soong ticket with 49.89 per cent.[356] The 'peace referendum' however failed to obtain the necessary threshold of votes cast, with a turnout of only around 45 per cent of voters. Of those who came out to vote in the referendum however, more than 90 per cent voted 'yes' to both questions.[357]

The election was immediately preceded by an assassination attempt on President Chen and Vice President Lu on 19 March 2004, while they were campaigning in Tainan. However, neither the president nor the vice president, who were hit by bullets during the shooting incident, were seriously wounded, and they were allowed to leave the hospital after a few hours.[358] They both gave televised statements while still in hospital, telling their audience that "Taiwan's security is assured" and asking voters to go to the polls.[359] In face of its defeat, the Pan-Blue camp instantly demanded the annulment of the election given its 'unfair' circumstances and alleged election irregularities that, according to Lien, raised "clouds of suspicion".[360] Lien demanded a recount and announced his intention to file a lawsuit to annul the election.[361] Although the result was confirmed in a subsequent recount, the Kuomintang continued to take legal recourse during the rest of the year, which was ultimately dismissed.[362]

Summary and analysis

As the above process tracing demonstrates (see Table 5.5), in contrast to previous years, the discursive field on the observation of Cross-Strait relations largely developed into two markedly different positions with less of an overlap than during previous presidential elections. Over the course of the first term of the DPP presidency, the Chen administration's observation evolved from securitizing a PRC threat to a de-facto independent, sovereign Taiwan. The diagnostic framing was

Table 5.5 Taiwan's discursive field on conflict observation, 2004

Political faction	*Pan-Blue coalition*	*Pan-Green coalition*
Diagnostic framing	1992 Consensus	Security threat
Attribution of responsibility	DPP government Independence promoters	PRC
Prognostic framing	Expanding cooperation Military build-up	De-facto independence Military build-up Dialogue
Conflict observation	Interest incompatibility	Identity incompatibility

accordingly characterized by a view of 'state-to-state' Cross-Strait relations, which was overshadowed by a security threat involving missiles that documented the PRC's willingness to eventually resort to the use of military force against Taiwan. Taiwan was furthermore intimidated by PRC coercion of *Taishang* businesses to support pro-China forces (i.e., the Pan-Blue opposition) which was politically implicated in the PRC's coercion attempts. The DPP government's prognostic framing suggested promoting Taiwan's status as a state through constitutional reform and resorting to various popular referenda to assert the DPP government's conflict observation. Although fairly muted, there was a second direction in the DPP government's prognostic framing, however. President Chen indeed reiterated his calls for dialogue, peace negotiations and extending the 'direct links', but only on a 'state-to-state' basis.

The Pan-Blue coalition promoted conflict de-escalation, pointing to interest incompatibilities by advancing an observation of Cross-Strait relations as 'One China, different interpretations' and embracing the '1992 Consensus'. In keeping with this diagnostic framing, the Pan-Blue ticket's prognostic framing was about expanding cooperation and deepening economic ties in order to promote reconciliation. However, this prognostic framing was also bi-directional, with Pan-Blue politicians advocating a build-up of the ROC's military capabilities, despite greatly attributing responsibility for the deterioration in relations to the Chen administration.

In sum, conflict between the PRC and Taiwan consisted of communicated, albeit challenged identity incompatibilities. Given that the discursive field can be clearly divided into two camps, each advancing strongly competing observations of Cross-Strait relations, it is readily apparent that an observation put forward by the Pan-Blue coalition, which would have essentially embraced a '1992 Consensus', would have been more in accordance with the PRC's conflict observation. Similarly, the Pan-Blue prognostic framing was more in line with the conflict de-escalation sought by the PRC in its statements than the prognostic framing of Pan-Green incumbent Chen. In contrast to the preceding waves of negative sanctions, the combined sanctions strategy did not contribute to amplifying identity incompatibilities as strongly and obviously, although threats announced by the PRC and its harassment of Taiwanese businessmen fed into the DPP's stated conflict observation. Moreover, the PRC's missile pile-up was even securitized by the Pan-Blue opposition. Clearly, the election result was not suited to promoting even the slightest converging conflict observations across the Taiwan Strait. In that sense, the combined sanctions strategy failed to sway conflict observation decisively. However, it should be noted that as an intervening factor the shooting incident was too close to polling day to reliably account for its possible influence.

5.2.3 Fruits of positive sanctions: nourishing the possibility of reconciliation

After President Chen Shui-bian's election victory, hardly any changes occurred at first in Taiwanese conflict observation. Chen and his government initially continued with their reconciliatory statements in relation to seeking dialogue, something he had already embarked on during the election campaign.[363] Chen even expressed his wish to visit the Chinese village of his ancestors on the Mainland.[364] To some astonishment on the part of stricter independence advocates, he presented four principles for unification with China.[365] However, the government also continued to emphasize its pragmatic diplomacy, with Chen appointing a prominent independence advocate as foreign minister.[366] Chen further vowed to pursue his pledge to give Taiwan its own proper constitution, but stated that such reform would not touch upon the question of independence.[367] Yet the Chen administration also continued to insist on Taiwan's sovereign status and to reject any notion of 'One China' in their observation of Cross-Strait relations.[368]

After some time, the discursive field on the Cross-Strait conflict in Taiwan once again developed clearly distinct positions. The Pan-Blue opposition camp rejected the promotion of a separate Taiwanese identity by the Chen government and took a reconciliatory position on Cross-Strait relations, in line with the '1992 Consensus' of 'one China, different interpretations'.

In in a four-point statement on Mainland China in July 2005, President Hu re-emphasized the cornerstones of a political re-orientation, asserting that "[t]he one China principle must be maintained. China must not be separated", but also expressing compassion for 'Taiwan compatriots': "We respect them, trust them, rely on them . . . [and we adopt] every means to care for and protect their legitimate rights and benefits under whatever circumstances".[369] Indeed, with this re-orientation occurring at the same time as the transition of the presidency and other top-level positions to Hu Jintao, Jiang's unification deadline was off the table, as were his previous encroachment policies pushing for timely reunification. From 2005 onwards, the military exercises, which had previously been held annually in Taiwan's vicinity, had also stopped (Lin 2008).

Mainland China's conflict observation and sanctions against Taiwan

The People's Republic of China's Cross-Strait policies began to put greater emphasis on positive sanctions in 2005. The measures appeared to support a policy re-orientation which was first apparent in official statements that, on the one hand, began to acknowledge the popular will of Taiwan's citizens and distinguish between the populace and the government and, on the other, stressed the 'bottom line' that secession would not be tolerated, while successively relaxing the timeline for eventual reunification (Wang 2007).

Sanctions in the third case again included economic and political measures, falling broadly into three different categories: a) limited political recognition; b) economic incentives; and c) extended Cross-Strait cultural exchanges. These positive sanctions occurred against the backdrop of the Anti-Secession Law, which, after its introduction in March 2005, remained in force.

Positive incentives were notably introduced to coincide with the start of official cross-party dialogue on Cross-Strait relations with Pan-Blue alliance politicians. From 2005 onwards, the PRC embarked on a targeted, albeit limited political recognition, by entering into dialogue with Taiwan's Kuomintang and PFP parties. The chairmen of both parties met regularly with CCP General Secretary Hu Jintao to discuss Cross-Strait relations at the first official high-level meeting of its kind since the end of civil war hostilities in 1950.[370] Joint communiques published following these meetings promoted a five-point agenda that emphasized cooperation based on equality and the mutual recognition of the '1992 Consensus'.[371] They further vowed to pursue a peace accord and to allow Taiwan's participation in some international organizations. The PRC additionally offered substantive economic benefits.

Following the historic meetings, the PRC offered economic incentives such as lowering restrictions on fishery imports, easing loan restrictions and providing attractive loans exclusively to Taiwanese mainland businesses, extended investment protection, simplifying regulations for Taiwanese citizens and making it easier for them to obtain working permits (for a chronological overview, see Lin 2008). In addition, the PRC offered to eliminate import restrictions on select Taiwanese fruits, leading to a substantial growth in exports (see Table 5.6). However, the PRC insisted on carrying out the required formalities at sub-governmental or extra-governmental level.[372] Most of the fruits covered by the trade expansion are grown in a particular region in southern Taiwan.

Besides economic incentives, the PRC also promoted expanding cultural exchanges. They included the facilitation of student exchanges, offering scholarships to Taiwanese students and permitting Mainland students to enroll at Taiwanese universities. This also enabled Taiwanese citizens to take professional license exams in the PRC. Finally the PRC largely promoted tourism across the Strait by supporting chartered flights and reducing visa requirements (Keng and Schubert 2010). Then, in 2008, the PRC "announced a package of 13 new policies to promote economic, trade, and cultural relations with Taiwan", which greatly facilitated corporate investments into the transport sector (Lin 2008:295).

In sum, the economic and cultural incentives were for the most part targeted specifically at groups deemed supporters of pro-independence policies such as students, academics and farmers in southern Taiwan. The PRC extended limited political recognition on an equally selective basis to Pan-Blue opposition politicians who had a reputation of being pro-unification. In addition to statements by PRC officials expressing compassion for 'Taiwan compatriots' and – besides an

Table 5.6 Selected fruit exports from Taiwan to China, as by Norris (2016)

Fruit	*Export growth, 2004–2005, USD*	*Export growth, 2004 vs.2005*
Carambola	from 69138 to 155214	124%
Custard Apple	from 1399 to 154590	10926%
Guava	from 6088 to 144807	2278%
Mango	from 31068 to 335921	981%
Papaya	from 10937 to 57298	423%
Pineapple	from 1740 to 154263	8784%

institutionalization of the 'bottom line' against separatism – refraining from political encroachment, the introduction of these incentives marked a substantial change compared to previous PRC Cross-Strait policies.

Sanctions conflict observation in Taiwan

Although the ROC government categorically denounced PRC threats to apply force in order to prevent independence,[373] reconciliatory gestures still occurred, along with substantial efforts to pursue dialogue on expanding the 'three direct links'.[374] More remarkably, despite the Chen administration's clear protestation and condemnation of publicly circulating PRC plans, they continued to introduce more explicit negative economic sanctions against suspected pro-independence *Taishang*.[375] For instance, the resignation of Hsu Wen-lung, pro-DPP chairman of Chi Mei Group, was widely considered to have occurred in order to avoid damaging the corporation's Mainland business operations as a result of pressure from Beijing.[376] Reconciliatory statements also prevailed despite ROC military drills and calls for increased defense spending, suggesting heightened tensions and a clear sense of threat.[377] In the end, even these exercises were cancelled in a demonstration of goodwill.[378]

In these first months after President Chen's re-election, the political opposition in Taiwan, consisting mainly of Kuomintang and PFP politicians, remained fairly silent on Cross-Strait relations.[379] However, condemnation of negative PRC sanctions occurred uniformly across the whole discursive field.[380]

Beginning around the time that Hu Jintao more fully assumed formal power, taking up the chair of the CCP Central Military Commission in September 2004, the various positions in Taiwan's discursive field on Cross-Strait relations became more clearly differentiated and subsequently, some fairly profound changes were introduced. Early on, President Chen had already begun to put a different emphasis on observations of Cross-Strait relations. Chen not only clarified that he would "never sacrifice national sovereignty . . . to better cross-strait ties",[381] but further suggested a name change from 'Republic of China' to 'Taiwan' in order to make it clear that it is not part of China.[382] This name change would also affect on-going bids to join the United Nations[383] and would also involve changing the national emblem.[384] These observations were accompanied by the Chen administration increasingly pointing out a continuing and rising military threat from the PRC, arguing a necessity to boost military capabilities.[385] Some government politicians even went as far as to include offensive weapons, requests that had occurred fairly seldom before: "You (China) have the capability to destroy me and Taiwan should have the capability to counter. [. . .] You strike Taipei and Kaohsiung and I shall strike Shanghai", as Prime Minister Yu Shyi-kun put it.[386] Likewise, initiatives to seek dialogue with the PRC began to focus on military trust-building,[387] although other efforts also continued.[388] They thus contributed to the spread of a newly reinforced sense of crisis.

The Pan-Blue opposition rejected the Chen administration's promotion of 'Taiwan identity' in the state's official name.[389] It also claimed a more reconciliatory position on Cross-Strait relations, in line with the '1992 Consensus' of 'one China, different interpretations',[390] again attributing responsibility for the deterioration of relations to the DPP government.[391] After some gains in the parliamentary elections in December 2004, Chairman Lien Chan refuted a 'provocative' Cross-Strait policy and vowed to aim for dialogue and a 'win-win situation'.[392]

This gives an overview of developments concerning the various positions in the discursive field on Cross-Strait relations prior to the introduction by the PRC of its major policy change of the Anti-Secession Law and targeted positive sanctions. Statements on Beijing's planned Anti-Secession Law and its subsequent introduction contributed to a greater distinction between the positions on the Cross-Strait conflict. Once plans for the law became public, DPP administration officials voiced their strong objection, calling it "an extreme and drastic move. We cannot tolerate it".[393] President Chen claimed such a move would "pose the greatest threat to regional stability and world peace".[394] Faced with the law's imminent adoption, DPP officials stressed that the law "exposes China's attempts to annex Taiwan by the use of force", adding that it gave "a blank check to its military".[395] On the passing of the law, new Prime Minister Frank Hsieh observed that the "situation arouses concerns for war".[396] President Chen announced the view of the government that it is "a law of aggression which unilaterally altered the cross-strait status quo".[397]

Pan-Blue politicians rejected the upcoming law, but held 'independence hardliners' (in the words of James Soong) and Chen responsible for its promotion.[398] With the law enacted, Kuomintang politicians expressed their regret at Beijing's lack of goodwill[399] and claimed that it "cast a major uncertainty on bilaterial exchanges", as Mayor of Taipei Ma Ying-jeou stated.[400]

These differences in diagnostic framings between the DPP government and the Pan-Blue opposition likewise extended to prognostic framings. Both camps reacted by calling for Cross-Strait dialogue following the announcement of plans for the Anti-Secession Law. Kuomintang politicians aimed to send a delegation to the Mainland for discussions.[401] Similarly, Prime Minister Hsieh called for dialogue and reconciliation;[402] President Chen similarly reverted to offers of dialogue, stressing his readiness to discuss "any sort of peace agreement – short-term, long-term, midterm", and to patiently wait for China's democratization.[403] However, differences had already become evident before the enactment of the law, when Vice President Lu vowed to "clarify on the fact [of 'two Chinas']".[404] With the law finally introduced, the Chen government declared an end its dialogue efforts and its refusal to engage in any talks with the PRC on Cross-Strait issues: "I think there is going to be no chance for the two sides to go in a positive direction for improvement of cross-strait relations in the short term", MAC chairman Wu stated.[405] Unlike the DPP government, the Pan-Blue camp vowed, however, to continue to seek dialogue despite their disappointment: "We urge China to drop its intention to adopt non-peaceful means to resolve cross-strait issues and to actively promote cross-strait dialogues and negotiations".[406]

Shortly afterwards, the Pan-Blue camp added to its commitment to a distinct conflict observation, when the first Kuomintang delegation in over 50 years embarked on a visit to the Mainland: "Seeing the strained and deteriorating cross-strait ties, the KMT needs to do something to help the 'helpless' government and to provide the people with a different choice", Lien stated referring to the purpose of the visit. Led by Vice Chairman Chiang Pin-kung, the delegation discussed the Anti-Secession Law with CCP officials and also visited Nanjing to pay tribute to ROC founder Sun yat-sen in what was a highly symbolic move.[407] The delegation agreed on a ten-point consensus with the Mainland on expanding exchanges covering, among other things, direct flights, investment protection and, notably, "sales of Taiwanese agricultural products and investment by Taiwanese farmers on the mainland".[408]

In addition, the first Kuomintang delegation arranged with CCP officials for subsequent visits by Pan-Blue politicians. Accordingly, a few weeks later, Kuomintang Chairman Lien embarked on a 'journey of peace' to China for a meeting with CCP General Secretary Hu Jintao. At the beginning of his visit, Lien gave a speech at Peking University, issuing a call to "build a bridge to unite our people" and overcome hostilities: "We can't stay in the past forever".[409] At their subsequent meeting, Lien and Hu emphasized their commitment to reconciliation in their joint public statements.[410] A joint press communique outlined a new five-point agenda which sought to foster cooperation, the main points of which were the mutual recognition of the "Consensus of '92", pursuing a peace accord, enabling mutual participation in 'international activities' such as the WHO and expanding economic exchange, again with an explicit reference to "agricultural and fishery cooperation, resolving the problems of selling Taiwan agricultural products on the mainland".[411] As with the first delegation, Lien paid a visit to the Sun Yat-sen memorial in Nanjing.[412] Lien also paid a visit to Xian, the place of his Mainland roots.[413]

At first DPP politicians criticized any visit to China in the wake of the introduction of the Anti-Secession Law as "not fitting"[414] and condemned the Kuomintang delegation, accusing it of undermining "national sovereignty and public authority of the government".[415] President Chen continued by pointing out the potential legal implications[416], warning that "if the results of the visits have the potential to undermine national security and the wellbeing of the people, then the administration cannot sit idly by, considering its own duty and its mandate from the people".[417] Others considered the visits in themselves to already constitute an attack upon national security, claiming that the PRC was taking advantage of "intense competition between the ruling party and opposition parties" by applying 'united front warfare' tactics.[418] Accordingly, the DPP subsequently alleged that "Lien denied Taiwan's independent sovereignty by accepting the 1992 consensus, depriving the right of the Taiwanese people to choose the future".[419]

Yet, in the end, President Chen endorsed Lien's dialogue effort.[420] Chen insisted, however, that any meaningful negotiation must proceed through official channels, with relations strained as a result of the Anti-Secession Law and the PRC's insistence on its "bogus" 'One Country, Two Systems' formula.[421] The president asked PFP Chairman James Soong to let Chinese leaders know "that Taiwan enjoys sovereignty" and seek their "recognition and respect" on his following trip to China.[422]

Soong's visit followed a similar pattern to those made previously by the Kuomintang. He visited Sun Yat-sen's mausoleum[423] and paid tribute to a monument dedicated to the Yellow Emperor, an important figure in Chinese cultural history. Upon his arrival in China, Soong declared that "[w]e, the PFP, are always of the view that Taiwan independence is not a choice for Taiwan", and emphasized a common heritage as "descendants of the Yellow Emperor".[424] Soong met with CCP General Secretary Hu, followed by the issuance of a joint press release that similarly contained aspirations towards a peace treaty, expanding direct links, and facilitating Taiwanese fruit exports.[425] It also contained a new linguistic variation of the '1992 Consensus' as 'One China, Two Sides'.[426]

In turn, the DPP accused Soong of intending to sell out on Taiwan. DPP General Secretary Lee Yi-yang claimed that "Soong has completely denied the existence of the sovereignty of the Republic of China".[427] President Chen concluded that Soong thereby effectively denied the Taiwanese people a choice.[428] However, Chen observed that Soong's position was but a personal stance[429] and the DPP government consequently rejected an invitation to the Mainland to engage in direct dialogue based on the principle that 'One China, Two Sides' was unacceptable: "I don't see that China has made any concessions on this matter", Chen declared.[430] Instead, he invited President Hu to learn about Taiwanese sovereignty on a visit to the island.[431]

With regard to the agreements on expanding economic exchanges reached by the Pan-Blue camp delegation during its visits to the Mainland, DPP officials voiced suspicions early on regarding PRC concessions on agricultural exports. DPP lawmakers such as Lai Ching-te observed that the PRC is "using farm imports to win the hearts of Taiwanese farmers and further control them".[432] Such interpretations that concessions were being introduced to "help the KMT win support in this region", a traditional stronghold of the DPP, also widely circulated in the media.[433] Consequently, the DPP government aimed to highlight the political stakes for Taiwan of economic offers of this kind: "[China's] motive is 100 per cent political, practically a united front tactic, never in the interest of our Taiwanese farmers, and anyone who has any sense will be able to tell what (China) hopes to gain", President Chen declared, adding that this gain was to promote victory for the opposition in the 2008 presidential election: "This is why China gives the credit to the opposition".[434]

In efforts to limit support for increased exports among farmers, President Chen, pointing to the case of Chi Mei Group's Chairman Hsu, warned against the risks of doing business with the PRC.[435] Chen further pointed to the limited importance of the Chinese market for Taiwanese exports, stating that the Pan-Blue camp "repeatedly exaggerates the possibilities"[436] and proposed diversifying exports to other regions.[437] Yet different views existed within the DPP government on how to handle the 'China fever'. In concrete terms, Prime Minister Hsieh sought to facilitate fruit exports by initiating administrative steps to this end.[438] However, Chen established that any agreement on economic exchange must be negotiated with Taiwan's government, and not with 'lawmakers' or the 'Taiwan Provincial Farmer's Association'.[439] When the PRC finally abolished tariffs, the Chen administration, in line with its reservation against these concessions, reluctantly welcomed the "unilateral announcement made by China to remove trade barriers", only to reiterate that it "exposes China's political motives".[440] Similarly, the DPP sought to contain later PRC overtures to expand exchanges under the 'three mini links'.[441]

Disregarding offers of dialogue based on 'One China', the Chen administration's observation of conflict instead focused on national security, popular sovereignty and protecting the pursued 'New Taiwan Identity' against assimilation by China.[442] A party resolution adopted by the DPP that aimed to turn Taiwan into a sovereign 'normal country' further promoted the 'New Taiwan Identity'.[443] The Chen government sought to promote this identity politically through particular measures, including "abolishing the National Unification Council and GNU [Guidelines for National Unification], applying to rejoin the United Nations under the name of Taiwan and drafting a new constitution and putting it to a referendum".[444] The Council came quickly to an end.[445] Later in 2006, the government filed its first application for 'Taiwan' membership to the UN: "Taiwan and China are two completely different countries", Chen observed.[446] The Chen administration further introduced a popular referendum on joining the UN under the name 'Taiwan' to coincide with the presidential election in 2008, styled by Chen as a vote on unification and a defense against the PRC.[447] Besides adjustments to the polity, constitutional changes were also discussed to cover its territory, limiting it to the island in contrast to referring to the Mainland or even to Mongolia.[448] Yet despite these indications, the focus of constitutional changes discussed was on consolidating democracy.[449] Consequently, President Chen made the elimination of authoritarian rule, along with freedom of speech, press and religion on the Mainland as preconditions for any possible future unification.[450] Chen outright rejected PRC President Hu's offer of a peace accord on the grounds that a "pact within the one-China framework is not a peace pact but is a surrender pact", a move, however, that even independence advocates among the DPP government such as Vice President Annette Lu disagreed with.[451]

In any case, the Chen administration continued to advance an observation of China as "totally different".[452] In the constant absence of the intimidating PRC military exercises of the past, the government nevertheless persistently claimed a 'serious', 'imminent' security threat.[453] Although government officials also referred to some PRC military exercises as training for an invasion,[454] it most frequently referred to the build-up of Chinese missiles targeting the island. In regular statements, President Chen publicly documented the rise in the number of such missiles from 'around 200' in 2000 to 'almost 1000' in 2007.[455] This claim of a threat was further supported by 'invasion simulations', which were held on a frequent basis.[456] In line with this, the administration declared March 14 to be 'Anti-Invasion Day' for Taiwan as "a timely reminder to all Taiwanese about China's anti-secession law".[457] To counter the threat, the DPP government sought to promote Taiwan's own military build-up and to further expand Taiwan's military capabilities.[458] Taiwan even held a military parade on National Day in 2007, presenting advanced weaponry, something not seen in many years.[459] In addition, Chen called for a "collective cooperative mechanism" in East Asia to keep the PRC in check.[460]

For all his statements promoting a "New Taiwan Identity" and his observations of a securitized Cross-Strait conflict, President Chen, who was coming to the end of his second term, with a two-term limit in office, was not the DPP candidate for the presidential election in 2008. Instead, the DPP nominated Frank Hsieh, who advanced a notably more moderate observation of Cross-Strait relations. Although Hsieh claimed Taiwan's identity to be the key issue in the election and endorsed President Chen's referendum pledge – noting that a failure to pass the referendum would damage Taiwan's international standing[461] – he vowed to pursue an approach of 'reconciliation and peaceful co-existence'.[462] Hsieh called for a pragmatic approach which would set differences aside and focus on common interests. To this end, he denied that the question of a '1992 Consensus' should actually matter.[463] Hsieh stated he would seek dialogue with the "talented", "calm and collected" Hu Jintao, a "very good" partner:[464] "I will invite Hu Jintao to visit Taiwan . . . [. . .]. I would like to negotiate with Hu . . . on common economic development. I would like to put controversies aside".[465] In line with that, the DPP nominee vowed to 'ease restrictions' on exchanges across the Taiwan Strait,[466] as well as on investments and flights.[467]

However, despite his commitment to dialogue and expanding exchanges, Hsieh insisted that such engagements would need to take into account national security and sovereignty.[468] Against this, Hsieh was strictly opposed to the creation of a common market with the PRC which would, he believed, more likely lead to a "One-China Market",[469] seconding President Chen's warning that, were this to happen, Taiwan would eventually become a "special economic region" of the PRC.[470] In addition, although generally more diffident in claiming a threat, Hsieh noted that hundreds of Chinese missiles were aimed at Taiwan.[471] DPP nominee Hsieh condemned PLA action on the eve of Taiwan's presidential elections against Tibetan demonstrators, which left several of the demonstrators dead. Opposition Pan-Blue politicians also condemned the incident.[472] Unlike the Pan-Blue opposition, Hsieh afterwards explicitly linked the Chinese response to protests to the threat a possible unification and even a 'One China policy' would pose to the security of Taiwan's citizens: "Today we can elect the president, but if we give up our sovereignty and admit we are not a country, and accept the 'one-China' principle, our future would be very miserable, just like Tibet's".[473]

The Pan-Blue opposition, which had continued its visits to the Mainland and dialogue with the CCP,[474] stuck to a reconciliatory observation of Cross-Strait relations in the months ahead of the presidential election. Based on the 'Five Yeses' formulated in 2006, the Kuomintang vowed to pursue a peace accord under mutual recognition and to expand exchanges.[475] In order to achieve these goals, Kuomintang presidential nominee Ma Ying-jeou[476] sought to advance a concept of 'mutual non-denial' based on the '1992 Consensus' to obtain more diplomatic flexibility.[477] In a white paper, Ma subsequently clarified this "survival model", which would allow Taiwan to expand relations with other countries and international organizations, as long as both the interests of the PRC and the ROC were respected.[478] The Kuomintang nominee stated that even in the face of the PRC's sustained efforts to isolate Taiwan, it must engage with the Mainland economically: "To Taiwan,

Mainland China represents diplomatic and security threats, but economically, it also means opportunity".[479] In order to grasp these opportunities, Ma, and in particular his vice-presidential candidate Vincent Siew, promoted the idea of a 'common market' between the PRC and the ROC,[480] vowing to pursue a step-by-step economic liberalization across the Strait.[481] By way of further emphasizing their different vision of Cross-Strait relations, the Pan-Blue camp advanced its own version of a UN-bid referendum, seeking UN membership under the name 'Republic of China'.[482] Yet, despite this commitment to dialogue, Ma declared that the PRC must remove the missiles it had aimed at the island as a precondition for any negotiations.[483] In addition, Ma declared his commitment to the 'status quo' by adding to his 'Five Yeses' a 'Three No's' principle: "no unification, no independence and no use of force".[484]

The 2008 presidential election produced a clear win for Kuomintang candidate Ma Ying-jeou. Ma received 58.44 per cent of the popular vote, with 41.55 per cent voting for DPP candidate Frank Hsieh. The results show that on the whole the DPP lost votes; however, losses are particularly notable in its traditional strongholds in Taiwan's south-western counties (see Figure 5.2), where people clearly tend to look on themselves as Taiwanese and favor independence (Lay, Yap, and Chen 2008). It is also an area which happens to be the main region for Taiwanese fruit production. Farmers in these counties had already managed to significantly increase their exports to Mainland China between 2004 and 2005, with export values increasing multi-fold, anywhere from double to 110 times their value (Norris 2016).

After the polls, President-elect Ma Ying-jeou vowed to fulfil his promises of reconciliation with the PRC as part of the 'mutual non-denial' approach.[485] Even before the inauguration of the Kuomintang politician as president, restrictions on investment in China had been relaxed.[486] In a similarly quick move, Vice President-elect Vincent Siew met with PRC President Hu only four weeks after the election, a historically unprecedented occurrence.[487] This was followed by setting up permanent exchange offices on both sides of the Strait, formally easing controls on investments both from and into the Mainland and allowing direct flights.[488] In August 2008, the Ma government officially announced a 'diplomatic truce' between the ROC and the PRC.[489] After signing an agreement at a summit in November,[490] 'direct links' were fully opened in December 2008 for the first time since the end of the civil war.[491] It was agreed that "neither the Taiwanese nor the Chinese flags will be flown when a ship enters port", as reported by Agence France Presse.[492]

Summary and analysis

During the years of President Chen's second term and the period leading up to the 2008 presidential election, conflict communication between the PRC and Taiwan's DPP government was characterized by persisting identity incompatibilities. The discursive field on the observation of Cross-Strait relations further evolved along

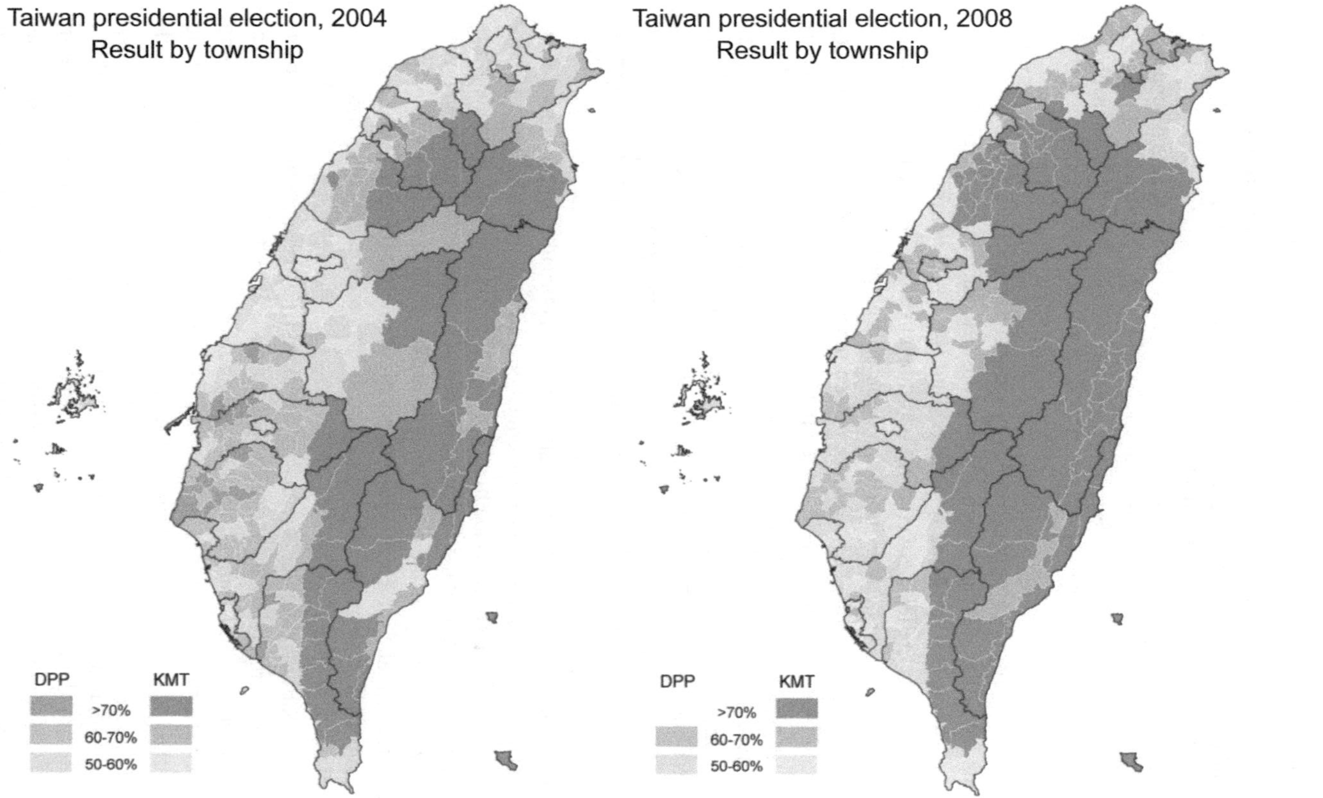

Figure 5.2 Taiwan presidential election results, 2004, 2008

Illustration by Yap Ko-hua, 2011, available at http://nottspolitics.org/2011/11/02/the-geography-of-voting-patterns-in-taiwan; accessed July 23, 2013. Also in Norris (2016:141–142).

Table 5.7 Taiwan's discursive field on conflict observation, 2008

Political faction	*Pan-Blue coalition*	*Pan-Green coalition*
Diagnostic framing	Risk	Security threat
Attribution of responsibility	DPP government Independence promoters	PRC
Prognostic framing	Peace accord Reunification	De-facto independence Dialogue
Conflict observation	Interest incompatibility	Identity incompatibility

the lines of two strongly opposed main positions (see Table 5.7). If anything, competing Pan-Blue and Pan-Green observations became even more distinct, particularly between the Pan-Blue opposition and the Chen administration. In its diagnostic framing, the DPP government continued to posit Taiwan as an independent, sovereign state and, after initial dialogue efforts, persistently securitized a PRC threat. As part of this securitization, Chen repeatedly denounced PRC economic incentives as attempts to infringe upon political sovereignty. More generally, the Chen administration, in the consistent absence of intimidating PRC military exercises, expanded Taiwan's own military drills, not just simulating an invasion from the Mainland but, in a way, 'simulating' a security threat. Effectively, these exercises contributed to the government performing a securitizing act. After the initial pledges to seek dialogue, the Chen administration's most important project became to formalize Taiwan's emancipation from its undemocratic past and to work towards a Taiwanese identity.

Yet again, the DPP's overall prognostic framing is broader and bi-directional. There is a certain tension between President Chen's announced ambitions and DPP presidential candidate Hsieh's statements on Cross-Strait relations. Despite sticking to claims of Taiwanese sovereignty and de-facto independence, Hsieh's vow to put status issues such as the One China controversy aside and to focus on promoting dialogue make for a less confrontational prognostic framing. Accordingly, his warnings against sharing the 'gloomy fate' of Tibet were most of all a commitment to the 'status quo'.

Pan-Blue coalition statements represent a strikingly different, competing observation of Cross-Strait relations. Pan-Blue politicians committed to the 'One China, different interpretations' stance and essentially performed this diagnostic framing during their trips to the Mainland by visiting Sun Yat-sen's mausoleum and, to an even greater extent, the Yellow Emperor monument. Pan-Blue politicians associated their trips explicitly with the failures of the DPP government to whom they attributed responsibility for the lasting crisis. The Kuomintang and the PFP not only aimed for dialogue, but actually engaged in dialogue for the first time in decades. In their prognostic framing they vowed to further proceed with their plans to pursue a peace accord and embark on a path to unification, the first steps of which were supposedly the 'ten point consensus' and the 'five yeses'. A word of caution, however, the 'three no's' may be an indication that there is a long way to go yet. Perhaps the remark by Kuomintang presidential candidate Ma Ying-jeou best sums up the Pan-Blue position in the discursive field on Cross-Strait relations: Mainland China may represent a threat, but it is also an opportunity.

Even more so than during the previous presidential election in 2004, this time round, in 2008, it was all the more apparent that the Pan-Blue coalition's observation on Cross-Strait relations was more in accordance with the PRC's conflict observation. Effectively, the election victory of Kuomintang candidate Ma Ying-jeou largely transformed the conflict from communicated identity incompatibilities to communicated issue incompatibilities. Although identity issues remained, they ceased to dominate conflict observation. The PRC's targeted positive sanctions contributed to evolving positions in Taiwan's discursive field – Pan-Blue politicians promoted their observation of Cross-Strait relations by referring to them, as did the DPP government (yet the latter may have done so by classifying them not exactly as 'positive' sanctions). Positive sanctions, in addition, targeted constituencies that were considered loyal to the DPP. Analyses of voting patterns in the 2008 presidential election uncover a significant switch in voting preferences, precisely in some of the south-western DPP strongholds with large numbers of fruit producers. Insofar as it contributed to the observation of conflict changing to an issue incompatibility, the PRC's positive sanctions strategy was successful. Of course, elections were not solely about Cross-Strait relations. The Taiwanese economy was considered to be in a bad way, and in addition there were corruption charges against several DPP figures, most notably President Chen. However, there is no doubt that the Taiwanese public did not concur with the aggressive pro-independence campaign pursued by Chen's Pan-Green administration. The Pan-Blue coalition articulated a position that amounted to a de-securitization and a changed conflict observation

Notes

1 The controversy around the specific date of the 'National Humiliation Day', newly introduced in 2001, highlights the essence of this shift, as well as its extent: All of the suggested dates referred to exchanges with foreign powers that were considered to be particularly humiliating and the discussion was more about keeping the attribution of responsibility general versus singling out particular foreign powers such as Japan. See People's Daily, April 29, 2001: 'China Fails to Designate National Humiliation Day'.
2 BBC, Summary of World Broadcasts, July 3, 1991, Part 3 The Far East; B. Internal Affairs; 2. China; FE/1114/B2/ 1: 'Jiang Zemin's speech on 70th CCP anniversary'.
3 Xiaoping (2004).
4 Xinhua General News Service, August 31, 1993, Item No. 0831130.
5 BBC, Summary of World Broadcasts, January 31, 1995, Part 3 Asia – Pacific; China; Foreign Relations; FE/2215/G: 'President Jiang's speech on reunification'.
6 Democratization spurred a development that had already begun with the loss of the Chinese UN seat to the PRC, see Callahan (2004).
7 Government report of 1992, quoted by AP, International News, February 10, 1992: 'Taiwanese nationalist leaders blamed for Crackdown on 1947 uprising'.
8 Foreign reports, however, such as that in the *New York Times* mentioned the random killing of people, streets paved with dead bodies and systematic executions (Durdin 1947).

9 UPI, International Section, February 28, 1991: 'Taiwan takes first steps to explain 1947 massacre'.
10 BBC, Summary of World Broadcasts, March 3, 1995, Part 3 Asia – Pacific; Taiwan; FE/2242/F: 'President Li apologizes on "2–28 Incident" anniversary'.
11 Although written in 1964, its lead author was captured before the release of the document, which was published a few years later from exile. See Taipei Times, Editorials, September 19, 2004: 'Learning from Peng's declaration'.
12 Central News Agency, May 21, 1990: 'President Lee's historic inaugural address'.
13 Central News Agency, August 26, 1990: 'Chinese communists urged to implement democratization'.
14 South China Morning Post, April 9, 1995: 'Taipei sets six-point policy on mainland'.
15 After the PRC took over the official representation of China at the UN and, with it, the Security Council seat in the 1970s, accompanied by US recognition of 'One China' and the PRC as its representative, international recognition of the ROC rapidly declined.
16 Central News Agency, November 15, 1991: 'APEC membership milestone in ROC foreign ties'.
17 United Press International, April 12, 1993: 'Taiwan delegation seeks GATT membership'.
18 Central News Agency, May 18, 1994: 'Taiwan hopes to become WTO founding member'.
19 Central News Agency, April 2, 1993: 'ROC to seek WHO membership'.
20 Central News Agency, April 22, 1993: 'ROC to launch UN bid by September 1995'.
21 The full speech is available at www.c-spanvideo.org/program/65610-1; accessed June 10, 2013.
22 Statement issued at 2nd DPP Party Congress in 1988. Cited by Central News Agency, April 20, 1988: 'Lawmakers refute DPP claim of Taiwan's undecided status'.
23 Broadcasting Corporation of China at the 2nd DPP Party Congress; reported by Central News Agency, April 19, 1988.
24 Xinhua, January 28, 2005: 'Jiang Zemin's speech on reunification of motherland'.
25 Xinhua, March 4, 2005: 'Four-point guidelines on cross-strait relations set forth by president Hu'.
26 UPI, International Section, April 5, 1995: 'China protests Taiwan president's trip'. Agence France Presse, May 4, 1995: 'Taiwan pushes for lifting of US ban on Taiwanese presidential visits'.
27 Agence France Presse, May 23, 1995: 'China furious at US approval for visit by Taiwan president'.
28 The statement is cited in Japan Economic Newswire, May 23, 1995: 'China vows strong response to Lee's US visit'.
29 Xinhua News Agency, cited by Japan Economic Newswire, June 7, 1995: 'Chinese press raps Lee Teng-hui over US visit'.
30 BBC Summary of World Broadcasts, June 12, 1995, Part 3 Asia – Pacific; CHINA; FE/2327/G: 'Taiwan; USA "is playing with fire" on Taiwan president's visit'.
31 Chinese media statements reported by AP Worldstream, International Section, August 24, 1995: 'China personalizes attack on Taiwan, targets president Lee'.
32 South China Morning Post, July 7, 1995, p. 10: 'Jiang tells PLA to be prepared'.
33 UPI, July 6, 1995: 'China rattles saber over Taiwan'.
34 Inter Press Service, July 19, 1995: China-Taiwan: Military rumblings from Beijing'.
35 South China Morning Post, July 24, 1995, p. 1: 'China presses for concession'; Central People's Broadcasting Station, July 19, 1995, in BBC Summary of World Broadcasts, July 25, 1995: 'Taiwan: Radio commentary says Taiwan independence will provoke armed invasion'.
36 Lien Ho Pao, July 23, 1995, p. 2, in BBC Summary of World Broadcasts, August 5, 1995, Part 3 Asia – Pacific; Hong Kong and Taiwan; Taiwan; FE/2374/F: 'PRC reportedly preparing for large-scale sea-air exercises'.

37 AP, International News, August 10, 1995: 'China to hold missile test for second time in a month'.

38 Ming Pao news report, cited by The Straits Times, August 17, 1995: 'Beijing exercise "simulates air-and-sea blockade"'.

39 Source: Taiwan Stock Exchange Corporation, Historical Trading Data, available at www.twse.com.tw/en/; accessed May 15, 2013.

40 A first round of exercises was held in the second half of July 1995. See AP Worldstream: 'China launched four missiles'; AP, August 10, 1995: 'China to hold missile test for second time in a month'.

41 The Globe and Mail, July 21, 1995: 'Chinese tests force changes in flight paths'.

42 Agence France Presse, July 21, 1995: 'Opposition parties attack China for missile exercise'; Central News Agency, July 25, 1995, in BBC Summary of World Broadcasts, Part 3 Asia – Pacific; Hong Kong and Taiwan; Taiwna; FE/2366/F: 'Relations with China: Taiwan to upgrade Marine Police; fishermen complain of Chinese harassment'.

43 ROC Ministry of Economic Affairs, cited by The Nikkei Weekly, August 14, 1995, p. 24: 'China's war games scare investors: Taiwanese businesses put mainland projects on hold'.

Agence France Presse, July 26, 1995: 'Taiwanese firms in China hit by worsening cross-strait ties'.

44 See, for example, The Straits Times, November 17, 1995: '"Republic of China on Taiwan" label attacked by Chinese news agency'.

45 Ming Pao, March 7, 1996, in BBC Summary of World Broadcasts, Part 3 Asia-Pacific; Hong Kong and Taiwan; Taiwna; EE/D2555/F: 'Chinese air force reportedly favours "war of high attrition" in event of conflict'; Sing Tao Jih Pao, March 10, 1996, in BBC Summary of World Broadcasts, March 12, 1996, Part 3 Asia-Pacific; Taiwan; Missile Crisis; EE/D2559/F: 'Chinese joint army letter calls for attack against Taiwan'; Ping Kuo Jih Pao, March 13, 1996, in BBC Summary of World Broadcasts, Part 3 Asia-Pacific; Hong Kong and Taiwan; Taiwan; EE/D2560/F: 'Chinese army reportedly formulates plans to attack outlying Taiwan islands'.

46 The Straits Times, January 31, 1996: 'Teng-hui under fire for "lying" about tensions'.

47 Taiwan Stock Exchange Corporation, Historical Trading Data, available at www.twse.com.tw/en/; accessed May 15, 2013.

48 Sing Tao Jih Pao, February 5, 1996, in BBC Summary of World Broadcasts, February 6, 1996, Part 3 Asia-Pacific; Hong Kong and Taiwan; Taiwan; EE/D2529/F: 'Relations with China: Mainland's "military action" exercise imminent'.

49 The Straits Times, February 25, 1996: 'China's war zones "combat-ready"'.

50 The Straits Times, March 16, 1996: 'China to stage fresh round of drills to overlap with Taiwan's polls Lee'; Xinhua News Agency, March 20, 1996, in BBC Summary of World Broadcasts, Part 3 Asia-Pacific; Taiwan and Hong Kong; Taiwan; EE/D2566/F: 'Xinhua announces end of Chinese live-fire military exercises'.

51 Japan Economic Newswire, March 5, 1996: 'China to surround Taiwan with missile exercises'.

52 The Straits Times, March 9, 1996: 'China fires 3 missiles off Taiwan coast'.

53 Japan Economic Newswire, March 9, 1996: 'China hints at Taiwan economic blockade as trade falls'.

54 South China Morning Post, March 10, 1996, p. 1: 'Live-firing tests to seal off sea lanes'; Central News Agency, March 12, 1996, in BBC Summary of World Broadcasts, Part 3 Asia-Pacific; Taiwan; Missile Crisis; EE/D2559/F: 'Flights diverted from Chinese military exercise area'.

55 Ming Pao, July 13, 1999 in BBC Summary of World Broadcasts, July 14, 1999, Part 3 Asia-Pacific; Relations with China; FE/D3586/F: 'China reportedly considers military exercises in response to Taiwan move'.

56 Agence France Presse, July 16, 1999: 'China puts southern regions on military alert amid Taiwan row'; Japan Economic Newswire, July 20, 1999: 'China moves field troops closer to Taiwan'; AP Worldstream, August 2, 1999: 'Report: China puts area near Taiwan on military alert'; Deutsche Presse-Agentur, August 13, 1999: 'China announces plan for major military exercise in August'; Agence France Presse, August 15, 1999: 'Chinese forces in Hong Kong on alert: Report'; August 18, 1999: 'China puts pressure on Taiwan with military exercise upgrade'.
57 Agence France Presse, August 10, 1999: 'China moves PLA elite to Taiwan region: Report'.
58 Agence France Presse, August 6, 1999: 'China gives "strike first" approval against Taiwan: Report'.
59 The Washington Times, August 4, 1999: 'Tension escalates over Taiwan Strait'.
60 Kyodo News Service, September 14, 1999, in BBC Summary of World Broadcasts, September 16, 1999, Part 3 Asia-Pacific; Relations with Mainland; FE/D3641/F: 'Chinese military drills continue in south'.
61 Deutsche Presse-Agentur, July 28, 1999: 'Chinese navy chief warns Taiwan as manoeuvres start'.
62 Xinhua, cited by AP, International News, September 10, 1999: 'Report: China holds massive military exercises near Taiwan'.
63 Japan Economic Newswire, September 4, 1999: 'China to stage war games in isles near Taiwan: Paper'.
64 Agence France Presse, July 15, 1999: 'China's neutron bomb claim comes amid regional tension over Taiwan'; August 2, 1999: 'China test-fires long-range missile'.
65 China Times Express, August 15, 1999, reported by AP Worldstream: 'China orders "total mobilization" to isolate Taiwan.
66 It is, however, inappropriate to attribute this loss solely to PRC announcements, without taking into account the related Taiwanese observations of Cross-Strait relations depicted below. Then again, losses would hardly have occurred on this magnitude without PRC proclamations. Data source: Taiwan Stock Exchange Corporation, Historical Trading Data, available at www.twse.com.tw/en/; accessed May 15, 2013.
67 Agence France Presse, September 2, 1999: 'Chinese army drills near Taiwan force airlines to divert flights'.
68 The New York Times, August 7, 1999, p. 7: 'China Seizes Taiwan ship, accusing crew'.
69 The Washington Times, July 13, 1999, p. A1: 'Taiwan abandons one-Chine doctrine; Beijing says the island is "playing with fire"'; Agence France Presse, July 18, 1999: 'Force "an option" against Taiwan, Jiang tells Clinton'.
70 The Washington Times, November 23, 1999, p. A1: 'China points more missiles at Taiwan'.
71 Singtao Jih Pao, cited by Central News Agency, November 19, 1999: 'Beijing resumes vocal attack and military intimidation toward Taiwan'.
72 Chung Kuo Shih Pao, December 13, 1999, in BBC Summary of World Broadcasts, December 18, 1999, Part 3 Asia-Pacific; Foreign Relations; FE/D3721/F: 'China's US envoy says all presidential candidates acceptable except DPP's Chen'.
73 Japan Economic Newswire, February 21, 2000: 'Beijing issues Taiwan white paper'.
74 AP, International News, February 21, 2000: 'Stepping up pressure on Taiwan, China offers unification or war'.
75 The Straits Times, February 24, 2000: '2007, 2010 . . .? Beijing said to be setting deadline for Taiwan'.
76 Agence France Presse, March 8, 2000: 'Chinese army asked to prepare for Taiwan war, as leaders talk peace'.
77 Xinhua General News Service, March 15, 2000: 'Chinese premier warns against "Taiwan Independence"'.
78 AP, International News, March 15, 2000: 'China's premier warns Taiwanese about independence'.

79 Xinhua General News Service, March 15, 2000: 'Chinese premier warns against "Independence of Taiwan"'.
80 I rely on extensive existing work by other researchers for accounts on sanctions imposed on Taishang.
81 AP, Business News, April 23, 2000: 'Chinese scholar warns business not to support Taiwan independence'; South China Morning Post, June 2, 2000, p. 1: 'Trade threat sparks anger'.
82 Japan Economic Newswire, April 10, 2000: 'China puts pressure on pro-independence Taiwan businesses'; AP, Business News, April 27, 2000: 'Taiwan businessman, rebuffed by Chinese leaders, says plans unchanged'.
83 Agence France Presse, April 19, 2000: 'China to step up pressure on pro-independence Taiwan investors: Report'.
84 AP Worldstream, International Section, August 20, 1995: '20,000 demonstrate to denounce Chinese missile tests'.
85 Agence France Presse, August 13, 1995: 'Thousands demand reunification with China'.
86 DPP Deputy Tsai Ming-hsien, cited in Agence France Presse, July 21, 1995: 'Opposition parties attack China for missile exercise'.
87 BBC Summary of World Broadcasts, July 25, 1995, Part 3 Asia – Pacific; Taiwan; Relations with PRC; FE/2364/F: 'Thousands in Taipei protest missile tests'.
88 Governor James Soong, cited in AP, July 24, 1995: 'Taiwan compares missile tests to Tiananmen square'.
89 BBC Summary of World Broadcasts, July 24, 1995, Part 3 Asia – Pacific; Taiwan; Relations with PRC; FE/2363/F: 'Taiwan figures angry at "international hooliganism" of PRC missile tests'.
90 Agence France Presse, September 14, 1995: 'Taiwan opposition leader presses US on China'.
91 South China Morning Post, July 28, 1995, p. 1: 'Lee urges military buildup'.
92 BBC Summary of World Broadcasts, August 3, 1995, Part 3 Asia – Pacific; Taiwan; FE/2372/F: 'President Li's address to the nation on 27th July'.
93 Japan Economic Newswire, July 27, 1995: 'Taiwan continues to seek international recognition, Lee says'; The Washington Post, September 25, 1995, p. A21: 'Perils of Taiwan Independence'.
94 Central News Agency, July 28, 1995: 'Lee reiterates opposition to secessionism'.
95 AP Worldstream, International Section, July 23, 1995: 'Taiwan: China launched four missiles in tests'.
96 BBC World Broadcasts, 'Taiwan figures angry'.
97 Agence France Presse, July 27, 1995: 'Lee says Taiwan wants recognition with reunification'; Central News Agency: 'Lee reiterates opposition'.
98 Agence France Presse, August 3, 1995, 'Taiwanese president slams China for blocking reunification'.
99 Central News Agency, July 26, 1995: 'Wu reiterates bid to reunify China, urges Beijing to stop menacing Taiwan'.
100 Japan Economic Newswire, September 3, 1995: 'Taiwan's Lee stresses reconciliation with China'.
101 Agence France Presse, September 3, 1995: 'Taiwan president seeks peace with China'.
102 Agence France Presse: 'Thousands demand reunification'.
103 The Straits Times, August 22, 1995: 'Deep split in Taiwan over next president'.
104 South China Morning Post: 'Conservatives form one-nation alliance'.
105 Japan Economic Newswire, August 23, 1995: 'Taiwan president seeks re-election, party set to split'.
106 Japan Economic Newswire, September 1, 1995: 'Re-election of Lee could worsen relations, says rival'.
107 The Washington Post, 'Perils of Taiwan Independence'.

108 Taipei Mayor Chen Shui-bian, cited in Japan Economic Newswire, October 23, 1995: 'Taiwan opposition undeterred by Chinese threats'.
109 AP Worldstream, September 24, 1995: 'Advocate of Taiwan Independence wins presidential election'.
110 The Straits Times, October 13, 1995: 'New Party slams Lee Teng-hui over "ROC on Taiwan" phrase'.
111 The Straits Times, November 13, 1995: 'Two KMT leaders may team up to run in presidential polls'.
112 The Straits Times, November 30, 1995: 'Lin-Hau team "has given New Party edge in polls"'; emphasis added by author.
113 The Straits Times, November 4, 1995: 'Taipei rejects China's "one country, two systems" formula'.
114 The Australian, December 1, 1995: 'Taiwan voters ignore China's war games'.
115 The Washington Post, November 7, 1995, p. A19: 'Taiwan candidates muffle freedom call to calm voters fearful of China backlash'.
116 Agence France Presse, December 2, 1995: 'Taiwan's ruling Kuomintang wins frail majority in parliament'.
117 E.g., The Australian, 'Taiwan voters ignore China's war games'.
118 Japan Economic Newswire, December 2, 1995: 'Ruling KMT keeps majority in Taiwan election'.
119 Wang Chien-shien, New Party presidential candidate, cited in South China Morning Post, December 3, 1995, p. 1: 'Taiwan votes for peace; KMT retains its majority but the breakaway New Party capitalises on rising desire for reconciliation with Beijing'.
120 Reuters News Agency, December 2, 1995: 'Taiwanese party attacks China in vote bid'.
121 The Washington Times, March 23, 1996, p. A6: 'Taiwan's leader vows democracy will win'.
122 BBC Summary of World Broadcasts, February 26, 1996, Part 3 Asia-Pacific; Taiwna; EE/D2545/F: 'President's news conference; Taiwan President Li Teng-hui holds news conference'.
123 The Straits Times, February 4, 1996: 'Lee to extend an olive branch to China if he is re-elected: Report'.
124 Agence France Presse, March 20, 1996: 'Taiwanese premier offers to sign peace agreement with China'.
125 Agence France Presse, January 13, 1996: 'Taiwan to set up air, shipping zones to provide direct links with China'; Agence France Presse, February 16, 1996: 'Taiwan premier calls for peace and understanding from China'.
126 Japan Economic Newswire, February 23, 1996: 'Taiwan's Lee cautious on direct links with China'.
127 AP, International News Section, February 16, 1996: 'President Lee: China must change before reunification'.
128 BBC Summary of World Broadcasts, 'President's news conference'.
129 Japan Economic Newswire, March 20, 1996: 'Taiwan's Lee faces 3 challengers in presidential race'.
130 UPI, March 21, 1996: 'Taiwan presidential campaign winds down'.
131 Agence France Presse, March 20, 1996: 'Taiwan's debate over its future heats up ahead of elections'.
132 Summary by Agence France Presse, March 8, 1996: 'Taipei's opposition mayor condemns China's missile drill'.
133 Agence France Presse, February 8, 1996: 'Taiwan's opposition demand all-party taskforce to tackle China crisis'.
134 Sissy Chen, DPP spokeswoman, cited in Agence France Presse, March 10, 1996: 'Taiwan opposition parties stage protests against Chinese drills'.

135 Peng Ming-min, cited indirectly in Agence France Presse, 'Taiwanese premier offers peace agreement'.
136 Japan Economic Newswire, February 23, 1996: 'Taiwan independence advocate sends letter to Beijing'.
137 Japan Economic Newswire, March 20, 1996: 'Taiwan's Peng says China to back down after election'.
138 The Straits Times: 'Teng-hui under fire'.
139 Japan Economic Newswire: 'Taiwan's Lee faces 3 challengers'.
140 Agence France Presse: 'Taiwan opposition parties stage protests'.
141 UPI: 'Taiwan presidential campaign winds down'.
142 Japan Economic Newswire: 'Taiwan's Lee faces 3 challengers'.
143 Agence France Presse: 'Taiwan's opposition demand all-party task force'.
144 Results published by ROC Central Election Commission, available at http://engweb.cec.gov.tw/ezfiles/30/1030/img/144/1996.htm; accessed June 19, 2013. Independent candidate Chen Li-an, a sceptic of President Lee's foreign policy, came in fourth place.
145 Agence France Presse, March 24, 1996: 'China made Taiwan's president a hero'.
146 The Washington Times, March 23, 1996, p. A6: 'Taiwan's leader vows democracy will win'.
147 UPI, March 23, 1996: 'Taiwan's Lee wins presidential race'.
148 Hsieh, Shih and Peng cited in South China Morning Post, March 24, 1996, p. 3: 'Chairman resigns as losers offer apology'.
149 The Straits Times, March 24, 1996: 'Reactions of the vanquished'.
150 The New York Times, March 24, 1996, p. 16: 'From a defeated ex-leader, a warning'.
151 Japan Economic Newswire, May 19, 1996: 'Full text of president Lee's inauguration speech'.
152 Agence France Presse, August 19, 1996: 'Taiwan needs to beef up defences, diplomacy and reform: Lee'; September 4, 1996: 'Taiwan foreign minister in Indonesia'; Central News Agency, December 15, 1996: 'FM Chang to visit Guatemala'; July 10, 1998: 'Three ROC envoys to visit four Allies before September'.
153 Agence France Presse, August 12, 1996: 'Taiwanese vice president leaves for US, ignoring Beijing protest'; January 7, 1997: 'Taiwan vice president in US for stopover despite Beijing's protests'; Central News Agency, April 2, 1997: 'Gingrich meets Lien for wide-ranging talks'; June 17, 1997: 'John Chang explains ROC's position to L.A. audience'.
154 Japan Economic Newswire, June 10, 1996: 'New Taiwan foreign minister vows to seek U.N. seat'; August 19, 1996: 'Taiwan's Lee vows to pursue bid for U.N. seat'; Agence France Presse, September 2, 1996: 'Taiwan opposition member to lead delegation to regain UN seat'.
155 Agence France Presse, June 25, 1996: 'Taiwan foreign minister says UN membership not a priority'.
156 Agence France Presse, October 10, 1996: 'Taiwanese president calls on China to resume talks'; November 17, 1996: 'Taiwanese president renews offer for Chinese leaders to visit'; October 22, 1997: 'Taiwan ready for new talks with China'; Central News Agency, September 17, 1998: 'MAC chief proposes new three links with Mainland China'.
157 Agence France Presse, May 5, 1996: 'Taiwan aims to sign peace accord with China in 2000'.
158 Agence France Presse, May 26, 1996: 'Taiwan may allow companies with Chinese partners to invest in Taiwan'; June 10, 1996: 'Taiwan prepares for economic talks with China: Premier'; June 25, 1996: 'Taiwan to allow senior Chinese officials to visit here'; AP Worldstream, August 29, 1996: 'China should focus on trade, not politics, Taiwan official says'; April 28, 1998: 'China, Taiwan talk after three-year freeze';

Central News Agency, January 15, 1997: 'Taiwan ready to discuss 'three links' issues with Mainland: Koo'; August 8, 1998: 'KMT official meets top Mainland negotiator with Taiwan'.

159 The Straits Times, July 10, 1996: 'Teng-hui warns of risks in direct links with China'; Agence France Presse, October 21, 1996: 'Taiwan to tighten up mainland policy'; AP Worldstream, May 13, 1997: 'Taiwan's Lee renews call to limit China investment'.

160 Agence France Presse, August 25, 1996: 'Government to restrict Taiwanese investments in China if ties worsen'; AP, January 19, 1997: 'Report: Taiwan to ban major investments in China until ties improve'. Agence France Presse, July 2, 1997: 'Taiwan tightens control over investments in China'.

161 Agence France Presse, March 29, 1997: 'Taiwan's Formosa confirms start of unauthorized China power project'; August 14, 1997: 'Taiwan investment in China rises despite government control'.

162 Central News Agency, April 2, 1997: 'ROC need not declare Independence: Lee'; AP Worldstream, July 22, 1998: 'President spells out terms for reunification, urges more cooperation'.

163 Agence France Presse, October 10, 1996: 'Taiwanese president calls on China to resume talks'; November 17, 1996: 'Taiwanese president renews offer for Chinese leaders to visit'; April 2, 1997: 'Taiwanese president Lee rules out independence'; August 25, 1997: 'Lee pledges to reunify with China at Taiwan's Kuomintang congress'; Central News Agency, July 21, 1997: 'President Lee delivers state-of-nation address'; July 22, 1998: 'President Lee reaffirms no timetable for national unification'.

164 Central News Agency, May 17, 1996: 'China ruled by two political entities, president Lee says'. Agence France Presse, July 2, 1997: 'Taiwanese president Lee rejects "one country, two systems"'; November 8, 1997: 'Taiwan is independent from China, president says: Report'; AP Worldstream, October 18, 1998: 'All niceties aside, Taiwan flatly rejects "one China" position'; Central News Agency, December 18, 1998: '"New Taiwanese" is not precursor to Independence: Premier'; Agence France Presse, February 17, 1999: 'Taiwan is an independent state says Lee'.

165 South China Morning Post, February 24, 1997, p. 8: 'Taiwan policy forecast to increase tensions'; Agence France Presse, March 11, 1997: 'Taiwan Lien vows to boost island's image as sovereign state'.

166 Agence France Presse, July 16, 1996: 'Taiwan's assembly endorses motion to drop claims over Outer Mongolia'; UPI, November 16, 1996: 'Taiwan recognizes Outer Mongolia'; The Straits Times, December 28, 1996: 'KMT and opposition party agree on charter changes'; AP Worldstream, July 19, 1997: 'Taiwan affirms separate identity from China in government overhaul'.

167 Deutsche Presse-Agentur, March 22, 1997: 'Dalai Lama visit to Taiwan causes controversy'.

168 Central News Agency, March 22, 1997: 'Dalai Lama arrives in Taiwan'; Deutsche presse-agentur, March 24, 1997: 'Dalai Lama wants to open representative office in Taipei'; Agence France Presse, March 27, 1997, 'Dalai Lama meets Taiwan president at dawn of new era of ties'.

169 Central News Agency, October 17, 1997: 'DPP willing to hold dialogue with Beijing'; Japan Economic Newswire, December 25, 1998: 'Chen Shui-bian offers to visit China for dialogue'.

170 Agence France Presse, May 13, 1996: 'Taiwan opposition says consensus a must before dialogue with China'; Central News Agency, October 13, 1998: 'DPP calls Koo-Jiang meeting private in nature'.

171 The Straits Times, December 22, 1996: 'Taiwan's status debate likely to provoke China'; 'KMT and opposition party agree'; Agence France Presse: 'Taiwan's assembly endorses motion to drop claims'.

172 Agence France Presse, September 2, 1996: 'Taiwan opposition member to lead delegation to regain UN seat'.
173 Japan Economic Newswire, May 13, 1996: 'Taiwan won't declare independence, says DPP's ex-chief'; AP Worldstream, October 9, 1996: 'Opposition leader rejects unification council seat'; Central News Agency, December 8, 1997: 'DPP not to sell off Taiwan people's interests: Chen'; December 10, 1997: 'DPP head rules out plebiscite on Taiwan Independence'; Deutsche Presse-Agentur, July 1, 1998: 'Taiwan's opposition party demands referendum on Taiwan's future'.
174 Agence France Presse, March 26, 1997: 'Dalai Lama to meet high-ranking Taiwan political leaders'.
175 The Straits Times, June 25, 1996: 'Taiwan may see more radical independence party'; Deutsche Presse-Agentur, August 18, 1996: 'Taiwan's opposition party faces split'.
176 Deutsche Presse-Agentur, September 26, 1996: 'Taiwan's DPP torn by discord as it fetes its founding'.
177 Deutsche Presse-Agentur, October6, 1996: 'Taiwan's opposition party splits'.
178 AP Worldstream, December 27, 1996: 'Taiwanese back Lee in fighting China's diplomatic blockade'; Central News Agency, May 19, 1997: 'Legislators concerned over diplomatic war with Mainland China'; Agence France Presse, October 18, 1998: 'Pro-unification leader asks Taiwan to drop UN bid'.
179 The Straits Times, July 14, 1996: 'Teng-hui calls for rethink of Taiwan's claim to Mongolia'; Agence France Presse: 'Taiwan's assembly endorses motion to drop claims'.
180 The Straits Times: 'Taiwan's status debate'; 'KMT and opposition party agree'.
181 AP Worldstream: 'Taiwan affirms separate identity'.
182 Agence France Presse, March 19, 1997: 'Taiwan cautiously opens arms to Dalai Lama's visit'.
183 Central News Agency, February 22, 1998: 'NP lawmakers air "1 China, 2 Chinese states" formula'.
184 Central News Agency, October 20, 1997: 'ROC legislators urge peaceful resolution to cross-strait tensions'.
185 Central News Agency, February 27, 1998: 'New Party member proposes "unique version" of cross-strait policy', in BBC Summary of World Broadcasts, March 2, 1998, Part 3 Asia-Pacific; Relations with China; FE/D3164/F; The Straits Times, October 7, 1996: 'Teng Hui's call for slower trade leads to uncertainty'.
186 The Straits Times, November 30, 1997: 'Pro-independence opposition grabs majority in Taiwan polls'; AP, August 19, 1998: 'Challenging government ban, Taiwan activists sail to China'; Central News Agency, November 22, 1998: 'Taiwan: Pro-unification new party unveils campaign themes, platform', in BBC Worldwide Monitoring.
187 Agence France Presse, April 26, 1998: 'Taiwan opposition party leader wants to send 'peace corps' to China'; Central News Agency, September 28, 1998: 'Taiwan opposition party official proposes second channel contact with China', in BBC Worldwide Monitoring; AP, December 15, 1998: 'Taiwanese party plans visit to Chinese military sites'.
188 Central News Agency, June 23, 1998: 'New party to establish Beijing office'; AP, February 23, 1999: 'Taiwan group to boost China contacts outside official channels'.
189 Central News Agency, February 8, 1998: 'New party delegation heads for Mainland China'; June, 28, 1998: 'Taiwan: Opposition leader says delay in talks works to Mainland's advantage'.
190 AP, International News, July 10, 1999: 'Taiwan's Lee redefines relations with China as nation-to-nation'.
191 President Lee, interview with Deutsche Welle, July 9, 1999, available at www.taiwandc.org/nws-9926.htm; accessed Monday, July 8, 2013.

192 Central News Agency, March 19, 1999: 'President Lee's new book emphasizes Taiwan's existence'; Agence France Presse, May 16, 1999: 'Taiwanese leader recommends China be broken into seven blocs'.
193 AP, International News, July 20, 1999: 'Taiwan president stands by controversial statehood claim'.
194 Agence France Presse, August 2, 1999: 'China test-fires long-range missile'; Central News Agency, September 2, 1999: 'President Lee reaffirms no change in policy toward Beijing'. AP Worldstream, November 25, 1999: 'Taiwanese leader criticizes Chinese missile deployment'.
195 Agence France Presse, September 30, 1999: 'Taiwan to continue military buildup as China shows off muscle'.
196 BBC Summary of World Broadcasts, September 16, 1999, Part 3 Asia-Pacific; Relations with Mainland; FE/D3641/F: 'Chinese military drills continue south'.
197 Agence France Presse, March 14, 2000: 'Taiwan vows to continue arms buildup after China's war of words'.
198 Japan Economic Newswire, March 6, 2000: 'Taiwan's Lien says "two state" concept national policy'.
199 Agence France Presse, 'Taiwan to continue arms buildup'.
200 Central News Agency, July 16, 1999: 'Vice president says state-to-state clarifys [sic!] ROC stance'.
201 Central News Agency, July 27, 1999: 'Vice president urges Beijing to start from reality'.
202 Central News Agency, August 17, 1999: 'No need to retract "special state-to-state" theory: Premier'.
203 AP, International News, August 12, 1999: 'After stirring fight with China, Taiwan tries again to enter U.N.'.
204 Central News Agency, July 28, 1999: 'VP reiterates "three noes" policy toward Beijing'.
205 BBC Summary of World Broadcasts, October 30, 1999, Part 3 Asia-Pacific; FE/D3679/F: 'Premier stresses "two-state-theory" not aimed at split'; Central News Agency, October 30, 1999: 'President Lee reaffirms commitment to national unification'; Taipei Times, February 26, 2000: 'Lien emphasizes stability and security'.
206 BBC Summary of World Broadcasts, January 28, 2000, Part 3 Asia-Pacific; Taiwan; China Relations; FE/D3749/F2: 'Presidential candidate Lien not to propose confederacy in China policy'.
207 Japan Economic Newswire, August 30, 1999: 'Lien says no need to write statehood into constitution'.
208 Agence France Presse, July 14, 1999: 'Taiwan seeks to defuse China row with reunification pledge'; July 20, 1999: 'Taiwan president denies seeking independence'.
209 Agence France Presse, February 13, 2000: 'Taiwan vice president voices hopes of meeting China's Jiang'.
210 Central News Agency, December 3, 1999: 'Presidential candidate to make "journey of peace" to China if elected'; Agence France Presse, March 16, 2000: 'Taiwan presidential candidate calls for Taipei-Beijing hotline'.
211 Taipei Times, January 20, 2000: 'Lien ready to go faster, less patient'; Central News Agency, February 12, 2000: 'ROC May allow point-to-point direct cross-strait trade: Vice president'.
212 Agence France Presse, February 17, 2000: 'Lien calls for courage from both sides of Taiwan straits'.
213 Central News Agency, December 28, 1999: 'Lien calls for exchanges between Taiwan and Mainland China'; Taipei Times, February 1, 2000: 'Lien urges Taiwan strait "peace zone"'; February 19, 2000: 'Siew boosts "peace zone" plan'.
214 Central News Agency, February 17, 2000: 'KMT candidate unveils campaign platform for cross-strait ties'.

215 Agence France Presse, March 16, 2000: 'Lien Chan: Presidential candidate for the status quo'.
216 The New York Times, January 21, 2000, p. 10: 'Taiwan candidate eases on China policy'.
217 Taipei Times, January 25, 2000: 'Lien Chan tests the waters for "confederacy"'.
218 Japan Economic Newswire, August 29, 1999: 'Lien-Siew presidential ticket endorsed at KMT congress'.
219 Agence France Presse, February 23, 2000: 'Taiwan refuses to bow to China's ultimatum'.
220 Taipei Times, March 1, 2000: 'Lien says he will walk "Lee's path"'; March 17, 2000: 'Lien tries to blunt Beijing's wrath'.
221 Taipei Times, March 16, 2000: 'Candidates hit back at Zhu Rongji'.
222 Agence France Presse, July 16, 1999: 'Former Taiwan governor James Soong to run for presidency'.
223 AP, International News, July 16, 1999: 'Taiwanese politician breaks with ruling party to run for president'.
224 Taipei Times, January 6, 2000: 'Soong eyes 50-year China deal'.
225 Agence France Presse, January 5, 2000: 'Taiwan presidential hopeful appeals for non-aggression for 30 years'.
226 Agence France Presse, January 2, 2000: 'Taipei-Beijing ties "quasi-international": Taiwan presidential hopeful'; Taipei Times, January 5, 2000: 'Editorial: Soong's China policy worrying'; Chung Yang Jih Pao, January 7, 2000: 'Mainland policy body head asks candidate Sung to explain stand', in BBC Summary of World Broadcasts, January 10, 2000, Part 3 Asia-Pacific; Taiwan; Foreign Relations; FE/D3733/F2.
227 Central News Agency, November 19, 1999, in BBC Monitoring: 'Taiwan presidential running mate Chang Chao-hsiung on China ties'.
228 Central News Agency, March 4, 2000, in BBC Monitoring: 'Taiwan independent candidate Soong to invite mainland negotiator if elected'.
229 Agence France Presse, March 15, 2000: 'Urgent – Independent Soong offers to visit China, sign peace treaty'.
230 AP, International News, November 21, 1999: 'Presidential candidate criticizes restrictions on China investment'; Taipei Times, January 12, 2000: 'Soong wants to phase out "go slow, be patient"'; Central News Agency, March 15, 2000: 'Soong promises dialogue with Beijing if elected'.
231 Agence France Presse, February 24, 2000: 'Taiwan presidential candidate Soong offers direct links with China'; Taipei Times, March 12, 2000: 'Soong sells himself on stability and free trade'.
232 The Straits Times, January 6, 2000: 'Soong outlines "firm" stand on cross-strait ties'.
233 AP, International News, January 5, 2000: 'Major presidential candidate discusses Taiwan-China relations'; The Straits Times, 'Soong outlines firm stand'.
234 Central News Agency, November 24, 1999: 'Taiwan people will not bend under Beijing's military threat: Soong'; Central News Agency, December 9, 1999, in BBC Monitoring: Taiwan: 'Top US liaison officer meets presidential candidate Soong'; Central News Agency, February 14, 2000: 'Soong stresses need to reopen cross-strait dialogue channel'; February 27, 2000: 'Taiwan candidates share views with time'; March 15, 2000: 'Soong touts direct "useful" dialogue with Beijing'.
235 Agence France Presse, February 22, 2000: 'Taiwan's presidential candidates urge China to drop bellicose stance'; Central News Agency, February 22, 2000: 'Soong: Taiwan won't bow to Beijing's threat'.
236 Agence France Presse, March 4, 2000: 'Taiwan's presidential hopefuls say won't talk to China under pressure'.
237 Taipei Times, February 23, 2000: 'Soong speaks out against China white paper'.
238 The Straits Times, March 18, 2000: 'The mood in James Soong's camp. . . fighting on'; Taipei Times, March 18, 2000: 'New party caucus convener quits for Soong'.

239 Li Ao, a dissident writer critical of the political establishment but in favor of unification, ran a partially satirical election campaign. See, for example, Taipei Times, March 12, 2000: 'Li Ao backs Soong, but Hsu hangs on'.
240 Taipei Times, February 1, 2000: 'More Soong supporters expelled from KMT'. March 10, 2000: 'Two more join Soong'.
241 Chung Kuo Shih Pao, December 25, 1998, in BBC Summary of World Broadcasts, Part 3 Asia-Pacific; China Relations; FE/D3422/F, January 1, 1999: 'Opposition party platform rethink unlikely, daily says'; The Straits Times, January 18, 1999: 'Taiwan's DPP does some serious soul-searching'.
242 Central News Agency, April 23, 1999: 'DPP presidential hopeful prefers to keep Taiwan's status Quo'; May 5, 1999: 'DPP revises platform to prepare for presidential race'.
243 Central News Agency, May 9, 1999, in BBC Monitoring: 'Taiwan: Democratic progressive party issues declaration on 2000 presidential poll'.
244 Deutsche Presse-Agentur, July 10, 1999: 'DPP candidate calls for new phase of democratic reform'.
245 Japan Economic Newswire, April 20, 1999: 'Chen suggests "peace zone" in Taiwan strait'; Agence France Presse, September 20, 1999: 'Taiwan pro-independence party wants normalised ties with China'; Ming Pao, January 17, 2000, 'Chen Shui-bian: The two sides of the strait are like distant relatives and close neighbours', in BBC Summary of World Broadcasts, January 26, 2000, Part 3 Asia-Pacific; China; Europe; FE/D3747/G: 'Presidential candidate Chen Shui-bian interviewed.'
246 Agence France Presse, January 27, 2000: 'Taiwan's presidential candidate's peace gesture to China'; Ming Pao, 'Chen Shui-bian: The two sides of the Strait'.
247 Agence France Presse, September 20, 1999: 'Taiwan pro-independence party wants normalised ties with China'.
248 Agence France Presse, November 6, 1999: 'Taiwan's pro-independence party wants "common market" with China'.
249 Ming Pao, 'Chen Shui-bian: The two sides of the strait'.
250 Central News Agency, November 2, 1999, in BBC Monitoring, November 3, 1999: 'Taiwan opposition presidential candidate calls for China links'.
251 Deutsche Presse-Agentur, November 7, 1999: 'DPP's Chen urges talks on direct links with Beijing'.
252 Central News Agency, April 22, 1999: 'DPP presidential hopeful stresses importance of national security'.
253 Japan Economic Newswire, March 7, 2000: 'Taiwan's Chen calls Chinese threats "counterproductive"'.
254 AP, International News, January 30, 2000: 'Presidential candidate: Taiwan will only declare independence if attacked'; Central News Agency, January 30, 2000, in BBC Monitoring: 'Taiwan party not to seek independence – presidential candidate Chen'.
255 Deutsche Prese-Agentur, November 28, 1999: 'DPP's Chen calls for "new internationalist" foreign policy'.
256 Central News Agency, March 9, 2000: 'DPP candidate pledges to tap president Lee to be envoy of peace'.
257 AP, International News, November 15, 1999: 'Taiwan's top opposition candidate lays out his china policy'.
258 Ming Pao, 'Chen Shui-bian: The two sides of the strait'.
259 Results published by ROC Central Election Commission, available at http://engweb.cec.gov.tw/ezfiles/30/1030/img/144/2000.htm; accessed July 23, 2013. Some 0.13 per cent of the population voted for New Party candidate Li Ao and 0.63 per cent voted for former DPP chairman and Formosa faction member Hsu Hsin-liang (both pro-reunification candidates).
260 Taipei Times, March 19, 2000: 'President Chen'.

261 Taipei Times, March 19, 2000: 'Chen offers "peace, sovereignty"'; see also Agence France Presse, March 18, 2000: 'New Taiwan president rejects China's reunification overture'.

262 Agence France Presse, March 18, 2000: 'KMT's Lien Chan admits defeat in Taiwan elections'.

263 Agence France Presse, March 18, 2000: 'Urgent – Taiwan independent candidate Soong to form new party'; Taipei Times, March 19, 2000: 'Soong's supporters urge him to form a new party'; Central News Agency, March 29, 2000: 'People first party to officially be established on Friday'.

264 Central News Agency, March 19, 2000, in BBC Monitoring: 'Taiwan: New Party moots cooperation with independent candidate Soong'.

265 See also: Central News Agency, October 21, 2000, in BBC Monitoring: 'Taiwan president says no 1992 consensus reached with Beijing'.

266 Chung-Kuo Shi-Pao, May 23, 2000, in BBC Summary of World Broadcasts, May 25, 2000: 'Taiwan mainland policy chief wants increased cross-strait dialogue'; Central News Agency, July 19, 2000, in BBC Summary of World Broadcasts, July 21, 2000: 'Premier urges Beijing to resume formal talks'; Central News Agency, January 16, 2001, in BBC Summary of World Broadcasts, January 18, 2001: 'President hopes for resumption of cross-strait dialogue soon'; Central News Agency, February 9, 2001, in BBC Summary of World Broadcasts, February 12, 2001: 'President interviewed on relations with Beijing'; AFX, November 1, 2001: 'Taiwan president Chen calls for talks with China without conditions'.

267 Japan Economic Newswire, June 2, 2000: 'Taipei to review ban on direct links with China'; Central News Agency, September 16, 2000, in BBC Monitoring: 'Taiwan president prepared to lift ban on direct links with mainland'; Central News Agency, January 7, 2001, in BBC Monitoring: 'Taiwan cross-strait body says "no haste, be patient" policy to be reviewed'; Agence France Presse, May 25, 2001: 'Taiwan to ease investment restrictions, open direct links with China'; Sydney Morning Herald, August 27, 2001, p. 7: 'Taipei moves to expand direct links with mainland'.

268 For example, see Agence France Presse, September 19, 2000: 'Taiwan asked to recognise "One China" for transport links, talks'; Central News Agency, September 11, 2001, in BBC Monitoring: 'Taiwan president responds to China's Qian on cross-strait relations'.

269 Kyodo News Service, January 30, 2001, in BBC Monitoring: 'Taiwan leader says direct links a done deal if talks resume'; Agence France Presse, July 7, 2002: 'Direct links not domestic affairs, Chen tells Beijng'; Central News Agency, October 31, 2002, in BBC Summary of World Broadcasts: 'Taiwan president says talks on transport links government, not public role'; Japan Economic Newswire, January 1, 2003: 'Chen urges Taiwan-China talks over direct air links'.

270 Agence France Presse, December 13, 2000: 'Taiwan cabinet approves "mini-links" with China'.

271 Agence France Presse, August 27, 2002: 'Taiwan "independence forces" biggest threat to peace: China's Hu'.

272 South China Morning Post, November 19, 2003, p. 1: 'Beijing threatens war on Taiwan'; Agence France Presse, December 2, 2003: 'China attacks "deceitful" Taiwan independence forces'; December 3, 2003: 'Chinese military ready for "necessary" casualties over Taiwan'.

273 E.g., Agence France Presse, August 5, 2002: 'China extends military drills across from Taiwan: Report'.

274 Xinhua News Agency, August 7, 2002, in BBC Summary of World Broadcasts, August 9, 2002: 'Beijing spokesperson claims Chen's "separatist" remarks will threaten peace'; Agence France Presse, August 8, 2002: 'It's war if Taiwan holds referendum, Chinese press warns'.

275 People's Daily, cited by AP, International News, August 7, 2002: 'China: Taiwan could face "use of force"' if independence-minded forces keep pushing'.
276 Statement by State Council Taiwan Affairs Office, Xinhua News Agency, November 17, 2003, in BBC Summary of World Broadcasts: 'Chinese official blasts Taiwan president's "splittist" moves'; see also Xinhua News Agency, August 6, 2003, in BBC Summary of World Broadcasts, August 7, 2003: 'Chinese communist daily blames Taiwan president for deadlock in ties'.
277 Agence France Presse, December 25, 2003: 'Chinese president Hu adopts "good cop" approach with Taiwan delegates'.
278 Xinhua News Agency, January 1, 2004: 'President calls for world peace and prosperity in New Year address'.
279 US Government Printing Office, Public Papers of the Presidents of the United States, George W. Bush, Book II (2003), pp. 1700–1702: 'Remarks following discussions with premier Wen Jiabao of China and an exchange with reporters'.
280 AP, International News, December 11, 2003: 'China lauds Bush statement on Taiwan, amplifies claim to island'.
281 Agence France Presse, January 27, 2004: 'Chirac strengthens criticism of Taiwan's referendum'.
282 AP, International News, January 27, 2004: 'France, China band together against Taiwanese referendum, France wants arms embargo lifted'.
283 Xinhua General News Service, January 14, 2004: 'Referendum threatens peace across Taiwan strait: Official'; AP, February 25, 2004: 'China blasts Taiwanese president's referendum plans as threat to peace and stability'.
284 Xinhua General News Service, March 14, 2004: 'China firmly opposes attempt to separate Taiwan from motherland: Premier'.
285 Agence France Presse, January 8, 2004: 'China demands Taiwan president "stop playing with fire"'.
286 Xinhua News Agency, January 19, 2004, in BBC Summary of World Broadcasts, January 20, 2004: 'Chinese Politburo member Tang Jiaxuan has delivered a speech at a seminar to mark the ninth anniversary of Jiang Zemin's 1995 eight-point proposal for reunification with Taiwan'.
287 Ren Airong, Head of the Taiwan Affairs Office at the Ministry of Agriculture, cited in South China Morning Post, January 15, 2004, p. 6: 'Island's farmers offered incentives to invest'.
288 AP, Financial News, February 5, 2004: 'Taiwanese businesses investing in China become political force'.
289 South China Morning Post, June 16, 2004, p. 7: 'Under-fire tycoon cuts ties with firm'.
290 Deutsche Presse-Agentur, June 3, 2004: 'China war games and economic sanctions trigger Taiwan stock plunge'.
291 South China Morning Post, July 16, 2004, p. 6: 'Jiang Zemin sets 2020 deadline for return of island to mainland'.
292 Xinhua General News Service, March 14, 2005: 'China's parliament adopts Anti-Secession Law'.
293 Xinhua General News Service, March 14, 2005: 'Chinese premier says anti-secession law to advance cross-strait ties'.
294 AP, International News, July 21, 2002: 'Taiwan urges China to talk peace'.
295 Agence France Presse, August 3, 2002: 'President Chen calls for referendum on Taiwan's future'.
296 8, 9, 10.
297 See, for example, Central News Agency, November 23, 2000, in BBC Summary of World Broadcasts, November 25, 2000: 'Taiwan agency reports meeting between KMT vice-chairman, Chinese vice-premier'.
298 Central News Agency, December 2, 2000, in BBC Monitoring: 'Kuomintang to firmly oppose Taiwan independence – party chairman'; Central News Agency, February 23,

2001, in BBC Monitoring: 'Taiwan's ruling, opposition parties disagree over unification guidelines'; Central News Agency, October 10, 2001, in BBC Monitoring: 'Taiwan: Kuomintang chairman says independence "would be disaster"'.

299 Lien Ho Pao, January 6, 2001, in BBC Summary of World Broadcasts: 'Taiwan MP says Beijing can accept confederation as phase of reunification'; Central News Agency, July 7, 2001, in BBC Monitoring: 'Taiwan: Kuomintang unveils position paper on "confederation" with China'.

300 Central News Agency, Jun 29, 2001, in BBC Monitoring: 'Taiwan: "Confederation" idea conducive to reconciliation – Kuomintang official'.

301 Taipei Times, August 4, 2002: 'Chen reckless: Opposition'.

302 Taipei Times, August 5, 2002: '"Pan blue" camp pans Chen's talk'.

303 Central News Agency, August 2, 2002, in BBC Summary of World Broadcasts, August 3, 2002: 'Taiwan opposition PFP party against independence referendum'.

304 Central News Agency, August 7, 2002, in BBC Summary of World Broadcasts: 'Taiwan's opposition parties continue criticism of president's remarks'.

305 AP, International News, May 13, 2002: 'Opposition leader endorses joining with another party to defeat Taiwan's president in next election'.

306 South China Morning Post, September 3, 2001, p. 14: 'Reviving the spirit of '92'; Central News Agency, June 4, 2002: 'Taiwan opposition parties call for direct links with mainland China'.

307 Japan Economic Newswire, July 24, 2001: 'Lee-backed political group unveils name, logo, flag'.

308 Central News Agency, July 24, 2001, in BBC Monitoring: 'Taiwan party announces name, policies'.

309 AP, International News, August 15, 2001: 'Former Taiwanese president supports China policy of rival party'.

310 Japan Economic Newswire, September 21, 2001: 'KMT decides to strip Lee Teng-hui of party membership'.

311 Monty Chang, director of TSU's international affairs department, cited in South China Morning Post, November 27, 2001, p. 16: '"Troublemaker" back on form'.

312 Central News Agency, November 1, 2003, in BBC Summary of World Broadcasts, November 2, 2003: 'Taiwan: "Pan-green camp" represents mainstream values – president Chen'; see also Taipei Times, September 29, 2003: 'President makes DPP birthday pledge'; Deutsche Presse-Agentur, October 7, 2003: 'Taiwan president tries further to turn island into "complete state"'.

313 Central News Agency, February 3, 2004, in BBC Summary of World Broadcasts: 'Taiwan president reiterates 2000 election pledge on mainland policy'.

314 Japan Economic Newswire, November 27, 2003: 'Taiwan adopts historic referendum law despite Beijing threats'.

315 Agence France Presse, November 27, 2003: 'Taiwan passes controversial referendum law'.

316 Tai Wan Jih Pao, December 4, 2003, in BBC Summary of World Broadcasts, December 6, 2003: 'Taiwan official says defensive referendum not a "one-time thing"'.

317 AP, International News, November 30, 2003: 'President says China's missile threat justifies Taiwan independence vote'.

318 Agence France Presse, December 4, 2003: 'Taiwan president Chen defends referendum proposal'.

319 Central News Agency, January 12, 2004, in BBC Summary of World Broadcasts: "Taiwan vice-president to remind world of China's "terrorist-style missile threat"'.

320 Agence France Presse, December 2, 2003: 'Sovereignty referendum unrelated to independence: Taiwan premier'.

321 Central News Agency, December 4, 2003, in BBC Summary of World Broadcasts: 'Taiwan president says "defensive referendum" aimed at keeping status quo'.

322 President Chen Shui-bian, interview with The New York Times, December 6, 2003: 'Running for re-election, Taiwan leader takes on China'.

323 Deutsche Presse-Agentur, January 16, 2004: 'Text of Taiwan president's speech on referendum'.
324 Japan Economic Newswire, November 20, 2003: 'Taiwan tells china to back off'.
325 Deutsche Presse-Agentur, January 10, 2004: 'Taiwan president suggests Taiwan, China exchange representatives'.
326 Central News Agency, February 2, 2004, in BBC Summary of World Broadcasts: 'Taiwan president to unveil plan for peace negotiations with Beijing'; Central News Agency, March 11, 2004, in BBC Summary of World Broadcasts: 'Taiwan president promises ties with Beijing based on parity'.
327 Agence France Presse, January 30, 2004: 'Taiwan offers talks with China on direct air cargo service'.
328 Central News Agency, October 7, 2003: 'Taiwan president says "one-China principle" should not exist'.
329 Central News Ageny, November 26, 2003: 'Spokesman says Taiwan's resolve to pursue full democracy will not be deterred'.
330 Central News Agency, December 11, 2003, in BBC Summary of World Broadcasts, December 12: 'President says China wants to change Taiwan's status'; Deutsche Presse-Agentur, December 16, 2003: 'Taiwanese resolution demands China remove missiles'.
331 Taipei Times, December 20, 2003, in BBC Summary of World Broadcasts, December 21, 2003: 'China could "paralyse" Taiwan command system in seven minutes – report'.
332 Taipei Times, December 23, 2003: 'Chen tells China he may revoke "five noes" pledge'.
333 Taiwan News, March 1, 2004, in BBC Summary of World Broadcasts: 'Taiwan president urges strengthening defence to counter China "threat"'.
334 Taipei Times, December 18, 2003: 'Missile test would trigger sovereignty vote: Chen'.
335 AP, Business News, February 5, 2004: 'Taiwanese businesses investing in China become political force'; AP, International News, February 10, 2004: 'China says it won't get involved in Taiwan elections'; Agence France Presse, March 15, 2004: 'Taiwan expats in China urged to return and vote in presidential election'; South China Morning Post, March 18, 2004, p. 6: 'Businessmen on mainland mobilised to cast ballots'.
336 Chinese Television System (CTS), February 14, 2004, in BBC Summary of World Broadcasts, February 15, 2004: 'Text of second part of Taiwan presidential election debate on 14 February'.
337 Agence France Presse, October 20, 2003: 'Taiwan presidential candidate slams referendum campaign on US visit'.
338 Japan Economic Newswire, October 20, 2003: 'KMT pres. candidate Lien eyes better ties with China'.
339 Central News Agency, September 30, 2003, in BBC Summary of World Broadcasts: 'Taiwan's Soong outlines "five yeses" before leaving for South Korea'.
340 Central News Agency, October 25, 2003, in BBC Summary of World Broadcasts: 'Opposition rallies against creation of new Taiwan constitution'.
341 Agence France Presse, November 15, 2003: 'Taiwan's opposition parties to finish constitutional reform in 2005'.
342 The Straits Times, November 21, 2003: '. . .as Lien Chan does U-turn to back new charter'.
343 Central News Agency, November 30, 2003, in BBC Summary of World Broadcasts: 'Taiwan opposition warns president not to push "defensive referendum"'.
344 Deutsche Presse-Agentur, January 17, 2004: 'Taiwan opposition slams president's referendum plan'; Central News Agency, February 4, 2004, in BBC Summary of World Broadcasts: 'Taiwan: Kuomintang leader says referendum "doubly wrong"'.
345 Agence France Presse, March 4, 2004: 'Taiwan opposition leader accuses Chen of waging "holy war" against China'.

346 Agence France Presse, March 4, 2004: 'Taiwan opposition calls on China to stay quiet over election'.
347 Central News Agency, February 17, 2004, in BBC Summary of World Broadcasts: 'Opposition leader Soong will not vote in Taiwan's referendum'; Central News Agency, February 21, 2004, in BBC Summary of World Broadcasts: 'Taiwan opposition leader not to vote in referendum'.
348 Central News Agency, December 1, 2003, in BBC Summary of World Broadcasts: 'Taiwan: KMT chairman to push for referendum on direct air, shipping links'.
349 AP, International News, February 21, 2004: 'Taiwan's candidates argue about China in final debate before election'.
350 Agence France Presse, February 24, 2004: 'Taiwan presidential hopeful eyes "peace journey" to China'.
351 AP, International News, December 21, 2003: 'Taiwan's opposition presidential candidate flip-flops on China policy'; Agence France Presse, February 25, 2004: 'Taiwan presidential hopeful refuses to commit on reunification format'.
352 South China Morning Post, March 14, 2004, p. 6: 'Lien denounces military threats from Beijing'.
353 Agence France Presse, March 5, 2004: 'Taiwan's opposition plans new military force against China threat'.
354 Deutsche Presse-Agentur, February 24, 2004: 'Taiwan opposition leader proposes putting aside sovereignty dispute'.
355 Central News Agency, March 17, 2004, in BBC Summary of World Broadcasts: 'Presidential candidate Lien hopes to make "journey of peace" to China'; South China Morning Post, March 18, 2004, p. 6: 'Lien plans journey of peace to Beijing'.
356 Results Published by ROC Central Election Commission, available at http://engweb.cec.gov.tw/ezfiles/30/1030/img/144/2004.htm; accessed July 22, 2013.
357 Central News Agency, March 20, 2004, in BBC Summary of World Broadcasts: 'Taiwan referendum questions fail to cross threshold for validity'; Agence France Presse, March 20, 2004: 'Historic Taiwan referendums failed: Electoral commission'.
358 Japan Economic Newswire, March 19, 2004: 'Taiwan president leaves hospital after assassination attempt'.
359 President Chen, cited by Agence France Presse, March 19, 2004: 'Taiwan's president assures nation he's "fine" after shooting'.
360 Agence France Presse, March 20, 2004: 'Taiwan in crisis as Chen wins and opposition demands annulment'.
361 Japan Economic Newswire, March 20, 2004: 'Chen wins 2nd presidential term, Lien to challenge vote'.
362 Japan Economic Newswire, April 12, 2004: 'Taiwan's political parties agree to a full recount: High Court'; South China Morning Post, November 5, 2004, p. 7: 'Challenge to Taiwan poll results rejected'; Agence France Presse, December 30, 2004: 'Taiwan court rejects opposition bid to nullify presidential polls'.
363 Central News Agency, May 6, 2004, in BBC Summary of World Broadcasts: 'Taiwan president speaks of commitment to stable peaceful cross-strait ties'; Agence France Presse, May 20, 2004: 'Taiwan's Chen refuses to rule out reunification with China'; Central News Agency, May 21, 2004, in BBC Summary of World Broadcasts: 'Taiwan official urges pragmatism, flexibility in cross-strait ties'.
364 AP, International News, April 20, 2004: 'Taiwan's leader expresses rare wish to search for his Chinese roots'.
365 Deutsche Presse-Agentur, July 28, 2004: 'Taiwan president outlines principles for unification with China'.
366 Deutsche Presse-Agentur, April 11, 2004: 'Taiwan makes former independence activist new foreign minister'; Central News Agency, in BBC Summary of World Broadcasts: 'New Taiwan foreign affairs minister outlines diplomatic programme'; Agence France

Presse, May 28, 2004: 'Taiwan's VP leaves for Latin American, US amid China's criticism'.

367 Agence France Presse, May 20, 2004: 'Taiwan's Chen pledges to review constitution, excludes independence issue'; Central News Agency, June 9, 2004, in BBC Summary of World Broadcasts: 'President says Taiwan needs "suitable" constitution'; Central News Agency, June 16, 2004, in BBC Summary of World Broadcasts: 'Taiwan's president says new constitution will be ready by 2008'.

368 Central News Agency, May 17, 2004, in BBC Summary of World Broadcasts: 'Taiwan's foreign minister responds to Chinese statement'.

369 Xinhua General News Service, July 13, 2005: 'Hu Jintao meets with new party delegation'.

370 South China Morning Post, April 30, 2005, p. 1: 'Hu and Lien grasp chance for change'.

371 Xinhua News Agency, April 29, 2005, in BBC Monitoring: 'Text of press communique on talks between China's Hu, Taiwan's Lien Chan'; Japan Economic Newswire, May 12, 2005: 'Hu-Soong communique calls for end to cross-strait hostility'.

372 South China Morning Post, July 6, 2005: 'Taiwan opposition parties heading to China for agricultural exports'.

373 Central News Agency, May 24, 2004, in BBC Summary of World Broadcasts: 'Taiwan spokesman says threats from China "unacceptable"'.

374 Japan Economic Newswire, June 30, 2004: 'Taiwan firm on direct links and urges China to open dialogue'; Agence France Presse, August 17, 2004: 'Powerful Taiwan group set for Beijing visit over direct links'.

375 Agence France Presse, June 4, 2004: 'Taiwan warns China against imposing economic sanctions on the island'.

376 Agence France Presse, June 16, 2004: 'Taiwan's Chi Mei mulls new investments in China despite hostility'; South China Morning Post, June 16, 2004: 'Under-fire tycoon cuts ties with firm'.

377 Agence France Presse, June 21, 2004: 'Taiwan military jets to practice freeway landings amid tension with China'; Agence France Presse, July 29, 2004: 'Taiwan's Chen pushes for new submarine deal to protect against China'.

378 Agence France Presse, August 31, 2004: 'Taiwan cancels military exercises in goodwill gesture to China'.

379 Instead, it advanced legal challenges to the narrow DPP election victory and engaged in internal repositioning. See Agence France Presse, April 6, 2004: 'Taiwan opposition seeks referendum on probe into Chen's shooting'; Japan Economic Newswire, April 21, 2004: 'Taiwan election recount to start in early May'; The Straits Times, August 7, 2004: 'Kuomintang in crisis; Taiwanese or Chinese? Identity conflict splits former ruling party, leaving its members disenchanted'.

380 Central News Agency, May 24, 2004, in BBC Summary of World Broadcasts: 'Taiwan opposition party denounces Beijing's threats'.

381 Agence France Presse, September 2, 2004: 'Taiwan will not sacrifice sovereignty to improve ties with China: Chen'.

382 Deutsche Presse-Agentur, September 4, 2004: 'Taiwan president: Taiwan should be called "Taiwan," not "ROC"'.

383 Agence France Presse, November 15, 2004: 'Chen vows to press for UN bid under title of "Taiwan"'; Central News Agency, October 26, 2004, in BBC Summary of World Broadcasts: 'Taiwan president says upgrading defence prerequisite to keeping status quo'.

384 Deutsche Presse-Agentur, November 21, 2004: 'Taiwan president suggests changing Taiwan's national emblem'.

385 Japan Economic Newswire, September 23, 2004: 'Taiwan military defends huge arms budget despite strong opposition'.

386 Agence France Presse, September 27, 2004: 'Taiwan plays down PM's remarks on tit-for-tat for Chinese missile attack'.

387 Agence France Presse, October 7, 2004: 'Taiwan calls for cross-strait military confidence-building to avoid war'; Japan Economic Newswire, October 14, 2004: 'Taiwan extends invitation to China's top negotiator for talks'.
388 Deutsche Presse-Agentur, October 11, 2004: 'Taiwan invites China to discuss direct charter flights'; Japan Economic Newswire, November 16, 2004: 'Taiwan's Chen sees goodwill in Chinese leader's remarks'.
389 Agence France Presse, November 10, 2004: 'Opposition condemns plans to separate Taiwan and Chinese history'.
390 Central News Agency, October 10, 2004, in BBC Summary of World Broadcasts: 'Taiwan opposition leader says nothing new in president's address'.
391 The Straits Times, December 6, 2004: 'Taiwan parties go all out to woo voters; Pan-Green camp pushes independence, while Pan-Blue side pushes reunification'.
392 Agence France Presse, December 11, 2004: 'Taiwan opposition wins parliamentary poll, vows to mend China ties'.
393 MAC Chairman Joseph Wu, cited by Central News Agency, December 23, 2004, in BBC Summary of World Broadcasts: 'Taiwan "cannot tolerate" China's anti-secession law – official'.
394 Agence France Presse, January 1, 2005: 'Taiwan president slams China's "anti-secession" law'.
395 Agence France Presse, March 8, 2005: 'Taiwan says law is attempt at forceful annexation'.
396 Agence France Presse, March 15, 2005: 'Taiwan premier says China's anti-secession law raises war fears'.
397 Agence France Presse, March 16, 2005: 'Taiwan's president condemns China's anti-secession law'.
398 South China Morning Post, February 25, 2005, p. 9: 'Chen and Soong reach consensus; Taiwanese president seeks to ease cross-strait tensions'. Deutsche Presse-Agentur, March 3, 2005: 'Taiwan parliament opposes China's anti-secession law'. Channel NewsAsia, March 4, 2005: 'Taiwan increasingly concerned about China's proposed anti-secession law'.
399 Central News Agency, March 14, 2005, in BBC Monitoring: 'Taiwan opposition parties express anger, regret over China's Anti-Secession Law'.
400 AFX, March 14, 2005: 'Taiwan mayors protest China's anti-secession law, call for cross-strait talks'.
401 February 3, 2005: 'Taiwan speaker offers to visit China over "anti-secession" law: Report'.
402 Agence France Presse, January 25, 2005: 'Taiwan's new premier calls for reconciliation with opposition, China'.
403 Chen, in a Newsweek magazine interview, cited in Central News Agency, February 28, 2005, in BBC Monitoring, March 1, 2005: 'Taiwan president ready to discuss "any kind" of peace agreement'.
404 Agence France Presse, March 5, 2005: 'Taiwan VP Lu urges Beijing to recognise fact of "two Chinas"'.
405 Deutsche Presse-Agentur, March 25, 2005: 'Taiwan says no more talks with rival China in short term'.
406 Central News Agency, 'Taiwan opposition parties express anger'.
407 Agence France Presse, March 27, 2005: 'Taiwan's KMT set for ice-breaking trip to China amid fresh tensions'; AP, International News, March 27, 2005: 'Taiwanese opposition leader travels to China for historic visit'; Japan Economic Newswire, March 30, 2005: 'Taiwan Kuomintang leader calls China trip icebreaking'.
408 South China Morning Post, March 31, 2005, p. 5: 'Road map to better ties agreed amid KMT visit; Chiang Pin-kung's trip ushers in 'new era' of dialogue with Communist Party'.
409 Washington Post, April 29, 2005, A Section, A 20: 'World in Brief'.

410 CCTV-1, April 29, 2005, in BBC Monitoring: 'Future within our grasp – Taiwan's Lien Chan tells Chinese president'; South China Morning Post: 'Hu and Lien grasp chance for change'.
411 Xinhua News Agency: 'Text of press communique'.
412 Japan Economic Newswire, April 28, 2005: 'KMT's Lien arrives in Beijing ahead of meeting with Hu'.
413 Japan Economic Newswire, April 30, 2005: 'KMT's Lien visits hometown on 3rd leg of China trip'.
414 MAC spokesman Chiu Tai-san, cited in AP, International News, April 1, 2005: 'Taiwan government condemns timing of opposition party visit to rival China'.
415 President Chen, cited in Central News Agency, April 9, 2005, in BBC Monitoring: 'Taiwan president willing to support Kuomintang chief's China visit'.
416 The criminal code of the ROC prohibits "reaching an agreement with any foreign governments without authorization", as Chen Chuei, spokesman of the High Court's Public Prosecutor's office declared. Cited in Agence France Presse, April 6, 2005: 'Taiwan government investigates opposition KMT's China visit'.
417 Central News Agency, in BBC Monitoring: 'President willing to support Kuomintang'.
418 MAC Chairman Wu, cited in Japan Economic Newswire, April 18, 2005: 'Taiwan gov't warns against opposition leaders' visits to China'.
419 Agence France Presse, April 29, 2005: 'Taiwan's ruling DPP condemns opposition leader Lien Chan'.
420 Deutsche Presse-Agentur, April 21, 2005: 'Taiwan president allows opposition leader's China visit'.
421 Agence France Presse, April 28, 2005: 'Taiwan president attacks anti-secession law as rival visits China'; Deutsche Presse-Agentur, April 28, 2005: 'Taiwanese president blasts China's "one country, two systems"'.
422 Agence France Presse, May 3, 2005: 'Taiwan party leader will carry message to China: President'.
423 Agence France Presse, May 7, 2005: 'Taiwan opposition politician pays homage to Sun Yat-sen'.
424 South China Morning Post, May 6, 2005, p. 1: 'Independence not a choice for Taiwan: Soong'.
425 Japan Economic Newswire: 'Hu-Soong communique'.
426 South China Morning Post, May 13, 2005, in BBC Monitoring: 'Hong Kong paper notes emerging cross-strait terminology'.
427 Central News Agency, May 6, 2005, in BBC Monitoring: 'Taiwan ruling party criticizes opposition leader Soong's remarks in China'.
428 Chen, cited indirectly in South China Morning Post, May 10, 2006, p. 6: 'Chen riles opposition with rebuke'.
429 Taipei Times, May 12, 2005, in BBC Monitoring: 'Taiwan presidential office: Soong rejecting independence is personal stance'.
430 Japan Economic Newswire, May 12, 2005: 'Taiwan president turns down Beijing offer on cross-strait talks'.
431 South China Morning Post, May 4, 2005, p. 1: 'Lien back with "gifts" but Taipei is wary'.
432 AP, Financial News, April 15, 2005: 'Taiwan, China in tug of war over hearts of farmers'.
433 South China Morning Post, 'Lien back with "gifts"'; see also AP Worldstream, June 15, 2005: Taiwanese farmers hunger for closer trade ties with China, but Taipei warns of sour fruit'.
434 Reported by Deutsche Presse-Agentur, July 25, 2005: 'Taiwanese leader dismisses China's fruit trade offer as gambit'.

435 Central News Agency, August 4, 2005, in BBC Monitoring: 'Taiwan president warns farmers not to walk into China's "trap"'; see also South China Morning Post, July 28, 2005: 'Taipei tries to soothe angry farmers'.
436 AP Worldstream: 'Taiwanese farmers hunger for closer ties'.
437 Central News Agency, in BBC Monitoring: 'Taiwan president warns farmers'.
438 Agence France Presse, June 14, 2005: 'Taiwan calls for negotiations in fresh olive branch to China'.
439 Chen, cited indirectly by Central News Agency, July 16, 2005, in BBC Monitoring: 'Taiwan president insists on government role in cross-strait farm talks'.
440 South China Morning Post, July 29, 2005, p. 8: 'Tariffs lifted on 15 fruits from Taiwan'.
441 South China Morning Post, April 26, 2006, p. 7: 'Taipei opens new route to mainland'; Central News Agency, August 2, 2006, in BBC Monitoring: 'Taiwan premier says no change on 40 per cent limit on China investment'.
442 Central News Agency, May 26, 2005, in BBC Monitoring: 'President advocates "new Taiwan identity"'; Central News Agency, January 1, 2006, in BBC Monitoring: 'Text of Taiwanese president's New Year address'.
443 Central News Agency, August 7, 2007, in BBC Monitoring: '"Normal country" resolution key to ruling party election success – chairman'; Agence France Presse, September 30, 2007: 'Taiwan's ruling party passes sovereignty resolution'.
444 Deutsche Presse-Agentur, January 29, 2006: 'Taiwan president plans to abolish national unification guidelines'.
445 Japan Economic Newswire, February 27, 2006: 'Taiwan's Chen announces end of unification council'.
446 AP, International News, September 28, 2006: 'Taiwanese president calls for applying to UN as "Taiwan"'.
447 Central News Agency, May 22, 2007, in BBC Monitoring: 'Taiwan president hopes UN-bid referendum to be held in tandem with elections'; June 22, 2007, in BBC Monitoring: 'President says Taiwan's UN bid aimed at "protecting the status quo"'; July 8, 2007, in BBC Monitoring: 'Taiwan UN referendum most effective "defence" against China – president'; November 20, 2007, in BBC Monitoring: 'Taiwan leader says referendums to show public stance on unification with China'; January 2, 2008: 'Taiwan president says UN referendum aimed at "rejecting unification"'.
448 Deutsche Presse-Agentur, September 24, 2006: 'Taiwan vows to amend constitution despite China's warning'; Central News Agency, August 13, 2007, in BBC Monitoring: 'Taiwan president reiterates need for "viable" new constitution'.
449 AP, International News, October 16, 2006: 'Taiwan president suggests constitutional change to alter island's status'; Central News Agency, March 17, 2007, in BBC Monitoring: 'Taiwan president says new constitution to consolidate democracy'.
450 Agence France Presse, April 11, 2006, 'Taiwan's president sets condition for reunified China'; Central News Agency, May 17, 2006, in BBC Monitoring: 'President says Taiwan might accept reunification if China makes "five changes"'.
451 Deutsche Presse-Agentur, October 16, 2007: 'Taiwan leaders differ on China's call for peace pact'. See also Central News Agency, March 20, 2008, in BBC Monitoring: 'Taiwan president rejects China's peace overture'.
452 Deutsche Presse-Agentur, March 2, 2007: 'Taiwan, China "totally different," – says Taiwan president'. See also Central News Agency, March 6, 2006, in BBC Monitoring: 'Premier says Taiwan "not part of China", unification "not the only option"'; Central News Agency, March 24, 2007, in BBC Monitoring: 'Vice-president says "dangerous" to see Taiwan as part of China'.
453 Central News Agency, July 21, 2005, in BBC Monitoring: 'Taiwan president says China's military rise poses "serious threat"'; in BBC Monitoring: 'Text of Taiwanese president's New Year address'; August 28, 2007, in BBC Monitoring: 'Taiwan says

China "true saboteur" of cross-strait status quo'; December 17, 2007, in BBC Monitoring: 'Taiwan president says China's "intimidation" won't sway push for referendum'.

454 AP, International News, March 12, 2007: 'Taiwan defence minister: Chinese army steps up training for landing on Taiwan'.

455 Agence France Presse, July 27, 2005: 'Taiwan stages military drill, warns of threat from Beijing'; July 17, 2006: 'China aims 820 missiles at Taiwan, Taiwanese president says'; AP, International News, February 6, 2007: 'Taiwan president sees military balance with China slipping'.

456 Agence France Presse, April 13, 2006: 'Taiwan president joins drill simulating Chinese blitz: Report'; July 20, 2006: 'Taiwan holds live war-game, simulates Chinese invasion'; Deutsche Presse-Agentur, April 10, 2007: 'Taiwan stages two exercises to counter possible attacks from China'; Agence France Presse, May 15, 2007: 'Taiwan jets land on freeway in rare drill'; May 16, 2007: 'Taiwan tests harbour defences'.

457 MAC General Secretary Jan Jyh-homg, cited in The Straits Times, March 9, 2006: 'March 14 is "anti-invasion day" for Taiwan'.

458 Japan Economic Newswire, October 10, 2005: 'Taiwan's Chen presses for arms purchase in National Day speech'; Taipei Times, June 15, 2006: 'Cabinet approves new procurement budget for weapons'; Agence France Presse, August 23, 2006: 'Taiwan to boost 2007 military spending, warns of China hostility'; Taipei Times, August 30, 2006: 'MND confirms plan to buy F-16s'; Central News Agency, July 10, 2007, in BBC Monitoring: 'US Apache helicopter most suited to Taiwan's defence needs – army'; The New York Times, September 29, 2007, p. 7: 'Taiwan plans to produce missiles able to hit China'; Agence France Presse, October 29, 2007: 'Taiwan's Chen promises not to develop nukes'; December 18, 2007: 'Taiwan president pushes for naval build-up'.

459 Agence France Presse, October 10, 2007: 'Taiwan unveils missiles at National Day parade'.

460 Deutsche Presse-Agentur, August 14, 2005: 'Taiwan's leader calls for collective mechanism to check China'.

461 AP, International News, October 12, 2007: 'Taiwan presidential hopefuls split on ties with China'; Agence France Presse, December 18, 2007: 'Presidential hopeful Hsieh says Taiwan identity at heart of race'.

462 South China Morming Post, June 12, 2007, p. 6: 'Taiwan hopefuls outline plans for reconciliation'; Agence France Presse, March 21, 2008: 'Taiwan's Hsieh vows dialogue with China as president'.

463 South China Morning Post, 'Taiwan hopefuls outline plans'.

464 Japan Economic Newswire, December 11, 2007: 'Taiwan's DPP presidential hopeful outlines China, Japan policies'.

465 AP, International News, February 18, 2008: 'Taiwanese presidential candidate says he would invite China's leader'.

466 Taiwan News, November 9, 2007, in BBC Monitoring: 'Taiwan ruling party candidate backs easing curbs on wafer facilities in China'.

467 Agence France Presse, January 21 2008: 'Taiwan may ease China-bound investment restrictions: Reports'; The Straits Times, January 28, 2008: 'Frank Hsieh's policy platform'.

468 Agence France Presse, February 24, 2008: 'Taiwan presidential hopefuls back better China ties'; South China Morning Post, March 15, 2008: 'Presidential candidates explain their stances on key issues'.

469 Taiwan News, February 27, 2008: 'Taiwan candidate reaffirms opposition to cross-strait common market'.

470 AP, International News, July 24, 2007: 'Taiwan's Chen criticizes opposition plans for common market with China.'

471 Agence France Presse, March 9, 2008: 'Taiwan presidential rivals trade barbs in last debate'.

472 Central News Agency, March 15, 2008, in BBC Monitoring: 'Taiwan presidential candidates blast Tibet crackdown'.
473 Agence France Presse, March 19, 2008: 'Taiwan candidate lights "Free Tibet" torch'.
474 See Deutsche Presse-Agentur, April 15, 2006: 'China announces measures to boost agricultural trade with Taiwan'; Associated Press, International News, April 28, 2007: 'Chinese president meets former Taiwan opposition leader'.
475 The Straits Times, March 23, 2006: 'KMT leader proposes five "yes" principles'.
476 Ma was the only presidential candidate from the Pan-Blue camp, endorsed by the PFP and the New Party.
477 Taiwan News, June 13, 2007, in BBC Monitoring: 'Taiwan: Opposition floats mutual non-denial concept in cross-Strait interplay'.
478 Central News Agency, November 20, 2007, in BBC Monitoring: 'Taiwan opposition presidential candidate proposes diplomatic white paper'.
479 South China Morning Post, June 7, 2007, p. 5: 'Chen warns successor Beijing will "not give up"'.
480 The China Post, July 3, 2007, in BBC Monitoring: 'Taiwan presidential candidate seeks closer trade ties with China'.
481 Central News Agency, October 10, 2007, in BBC Monitoring: 'Taiwan KMT candidate says president rash in criticizing "common market" idea'; October 20, in BBC Monitoring: 'Taiwan opposition candidate defends "cross-strait common market" idea'.
482 Associated Press, International News, September 15, 2007: 'Taiwan holds rival rallies to support competing UN bids'; Central News Agency, December 11, 2007, in BBC Monitoring: 'Taiwan foreign minister stresses referendum not aimed at changing status quo'.
483 Taiwan News, June 17, 2007, in BBC Monitoring: 'Taiwan presidential nominee: Chinese missiles must go before talks possible'.
484 South China Morning Post, January 21, 2008, p. 13: 'When it's the right time to say "no"'.
485 South China Morning Post, March 24, 2008, p. 1: 'Ma seeks "middle road" in dealing with Beijing'.
486 Agence France Presse, April 3, 2008: 'Taiwan clears first China bank investment'.
487 Agence France Presse, April 12, 2008: 'Taiwan, China sees progress from historic talks'.
488 Associated Press, June 12, 2008: 'Taiwan, China agree to exchange offices'; South China Morning Post, June 27, 2008: 'Taiwan moves to ease cross-strait investment curbs'; Agence France Presse, July 4, 2008: 'China, Taiwan launch direct flights'; July 17, 2008: 'Taiwan raises ceiling on China-bound investment'; Taipei Times, August 1, 2008, in BBC Monitoring: 'Taiwan cabinet permits Chinese firms to list, invest in stock market'.
489 Central News Agency, August 26, 2008: 'Taiwan vice-president backs "diplomatic truce" with China'.
490 Agence France Presse, November 4, 2008: 'China, Taiwan sign deals on closer economic ties'.
491 Associated Press, Business News, December 15, 2008: 'Taiwan, China launch direct shipping, air links'.
492 Agence France Presse, December 15, 2008: 'Taiwan president hails China transport links'.

Bibliography

Callahan, William A. (2004) National Insecurities: Humiliation, Salvation, and Chinese Nationalism. *Alternatives: Global, Local, Political* 29: 199–218.

Chen, Shui-bian. (2000) Taiwan Stands up: Presidential Inauguration Address. *USC US-China Institute*. Available at: http://china.usc.edu/(S(vp0nss55wvfm1kbu11v2nn45)

A(YGDR9ayczQEkAAAAODkwNGQ0ZWUtOWQ5MS00YjkzLTg4YjctMmYwMT A3MjdlMWM0SEsn9Peui1HQ9TJIJFKZZ8t5bkY1))/ShowArticle.aspx?articleID= 1302. (Accessed February 21, 2013).

Chou, Yangsun, and Andrew J. Nathan. (1987) Democratizing Transition in Taiwan. *Asian Survey* 27: 277–299.

Croizier, Ralph. (1990) World History in the People's Republic of China. *Journal of World History* 1: 151–169.

Crossley, Pamela Kyle. (2004) Nationality and Difference in China: The Post-Imperial Dilemma. In *The Teleology of the Modern Nation-State: Japan and China*, edited by Joshua A. Fogel. Philadelphia: University of Pennsylvania Press.

Durdin, Tillman. (1947) Formosa Killings Are Put at 10,000. *The New York Times* March 29, p. 6.

Gold, Thomas B. (1994) Civil Society and Taiwan's Quest for Identity. In *Cultural Change in Postwar Taiwan*, edited by Stevan Harrell and Chün-chieh Huang. Boulder: Westview Press.

Huang, Shuanfan. (2000) Language, Identity and Conflict: A Taiwanese Study. *International Journal of the Sociology of Language* 143. Available at: www.degruyter.com/view/j/ijsl.2000.issue-143/ijsl.2000.143.139/ijsl.2000.143.139.xml. (Accessed February 20, 2013).

Keng, Shu, and Gunter Schubert. (2010) Agents of Taiwan-China Unification? The Political Roles of Taiwanese Business People in the Process of Cross-Strait Integration. *Asian Survey* 50: 287–310.

Lai, Zehan, Ramon Hawley Myers, and Wei Wou. (1991) *A Tragic Beginning: The Taiwan Uprising of February 28, 1947*. Stanford: Stanford University Press.

Larus, Elizabeth Freund. (2006) Taiwan's Quest for International Recognition. *Issues & Studies* 42: 23–52.

Lay, Jinn-Guey, Ko-Hua Yap, and Yu-Wen Chen. (2008) The Transition of Taiwan's Political Geography. *Asian Survey* 48: 773–793.

Lee, Teng-hui. (1995) Chinese Culture and Political Renewal. *Journal of Democracy* 6: 3–8.

Lee, Teng-hui. (1999) Understanding Taiwan – Bridging the Perception Gap. *Foreign Affairs* 78: 9.

Lin, Chong-Pin. (2008) More Carrot Than Stick: Beijing's Emerging Taiwan Policy. *China Security* 4: 1–27.

Liu, James H., Chris G. Sibley, and Li-Li Huang. (2013) History Matters: Effects of Culture Specific Symbols on Political Attitudes and Intergroup Relations. *Political Psychology*. Available at: http://onlinelibrary.wiley.com/doi/10.1111/pops.12027/abstract. (Accessed May 16, 2013).

Mitter, Rana. (2003) Old Ghosts, New Memories: China's Changing War History in the Era of Post-Mao Politics. *Journal of Contemporary History* 38: 117–131.

Nohlen, Dieter, Florian Grotz, and Christof Hartmann. (2001) *Elections in Asia and the Pacific: A Data Handbook, Volume 2: Southeast Asia, East Asia and the South Pacific*. New York: Oxford University Press.

Norris, William J. (2016) Cross-Strait Economic Statecraft. In *Chinese Economic Statecraft: Commercial Actors, Grand Strategy, and State Control*. Ithaca: Cornell University Press.

Peng Ming-min, Hsieh Tsung-min, and Wei Ting-chao. (1964) Declaration of Formosan Self-Salvation. Available at: www.hi-on.org.tw/ad/peng_0707_z04.html. (Accessed April 29, 2013).

Rigger, Shelley. (2001) *From Opposition to Power: Taiwan's Democratic Progressive Party*. London: Lynne Rienner.

Schubert, Gunter. (2013) Assessing Political Agency across the Taiwan Strait: The Case of the Taishang. *China Information* 27: 51–79.

Tanner, Murray Scot. (2007) *Chinese Economic Coercion against Taiwan: A Tricky Weapon to Use*. Santa Monica: Rand Corporation.

Tung, Chen-yuan. (2002) *China's Economic Leverage and Taiwan's Security Concerns with Respect to Cross-Strait Economic Relations*. John Hopkins University. Available at: http://www3.nccu.edu.tw/~ctung/Dissertation.html.

Wang, Jianwei. (2007) Hu Jintao's "New Thinking" on Cross-Strait Relations. *American Foreign Policy Interests* 29: 23–34.

Wang, Zheng. (2008) National Humiliation, History Education, and the Politics of Historical Memory: Patriotic Education Campaign in China. *International Studies Quarterly* 52: 783–806.

Wang, Zheng. (2012) *Never Forget National Humiliation: Historical Memory in Chinese Politics and Foreign Relations*. New York: Columbia University Press.

Winn, Jane Kaufman, and Tang-chi Yeh. (1995) Advocating Democracy: The Role of Lawyers in Taiwan's Political Transformation. *Law and Social Inquiry* 20: 587.

Wu, Guoguang. (2007) Identity, Sovereignty, and Economic Penetration: Beijing's Responses to Offshore Chinese Democracies. *Journal of Contemporary China* 16: 295–313.

Xiaoping, Deng. (2004) One Country, Two Systems. *China Internet Information Center*. Available at: www.china.org.cn/english/2004/Feb/87813.htm. (Accessed February 21, 2013).

Zhao, Suisheng. (2004) *A Nation-State by Construction: Dynamics of Modern Chinese Nationalism*. Stanford: Stanford University Press.

6 Escalating and de-escalating conflict

Sanctions on Iran's nuclear program

Relations between Iran and the US have exhibited extensive identity incompatibilities since the events of the Islamic Revolution, observed in Iran as a great liberation from the machinations of foreign imperialist powers, most notably the US which, according to that narrative, sought to oppress Iran politically and erode its culture. In that vein, the nuclear program represents a proud achievement of technological progress that re-establishes Iran as an advanced, independent country. The Islamic Republic always insisted that its nuclear program was in line with the Treaty on the Non-Proliferation of Nuclear Weapons (NPT), of which it is a signatory. In the eyes of the US, meanwhile, the Islamic Republic blatantly violates global norms, supports religiously-motivated terrorism and destabilizes the region – plenty of reasons to take issue with the nuclear ambitions of this adversary.

While there were US sanctions against the Islamic Republic before, a distinct conflict communication emerged with regard to its nuclear program, with the opponents involved addressing this issue separately from other communicated incompatibilities. The US clearly emerged as the main opponent in the conflict and, from an Iranian perspective, ultimately exerted decisive clout over other protagonists such as the EU-3 and even the IAEA or the UN. Thus while others played a meaningful role in conflict communication as well, it is not quite accurate to depict the conflict as one of Iran against the world community or even the P5+1, although the latter was of course well implicated in the conflict over the nuclear program.

In the nuclear dispute between the US and Iran, sanctions strategies as observed by opponents varied significantly. In the first case, beginning with the revelation of the nuclear program in 2002 and ending with the breakdown of dialogue in 2005, an incoherent, poorly coordinated combined sanctions strategy failed to resolve the nuclear dispute. Subsequently, the second case saw US efforts to isolate Iran, an increase in negative sanctions and conflict communication that deteriorated towards deadlocked securitized identity incompatibilities. During the third case, sanctions again changed significantly after Barack Obama became US president in 2009. Transformation into an issue conflict and its ultimate solution came in the wake of a strategy that combined positive sanctions, consisting of sustained offers of dialogue and incentives, with extensive negative sanctions.

Subsequently, the next part of the empirical analysis of this conflict system establishes its broader setting and history. Based on this understanding, the second part traces the initiated sanctions and conflict development in three distinct cases, each addressing the research questions on conflict observation, the meaning of sanctions therein and the influence of sanctions on conflict development.

6.1 Delineating the conflict between the US and Iran

The dispute over Iran's nuclear program occurred against a broader, pre-existing conflict setting between the US and Iran. Again, this first part of the analysis establishes the kinds of communicated incompatibilities of which the wider conflict consists, in order to enable us to assess what 'cooperation' and 'non-cooperation' would entail in the conflict over Iran's nuclear program. In Iran, the narrative of the revolution that brought the Islamic Republic is one of liberation from foreign dominance. In that narrative, the US is not only the most recent and vivid of a number of foreign oppressors – effectively, the rise of the Islamic Republic is an emancipation from US imperialism. In turn, to the US Iran represents not just an adversary that challenges its vision of order in a certain region, but one that seeks to undermine some of the constitutive norms that represent the foundations of the US-promoted global order. The US itself even became a victim of this disregard of universal norms during the hostage crisis at the US embassy in the wake of the Islamic revolution, a traumatic experience that contributed to the image of the Islamic Republic as an adversary that would take reckless recourse to illegitimate means in order to achieve its no less questionable ends.

Against this conflict setting, dominated by communicated identity incompatibilities, the US had responded by introducing sanctions earlier and separately from the dispute over Iran's nuclear program. The nuclear issue thus occurred against a conflict setting that greatly decreased the odds of finding a sanctions-based solution to the dispute. This first part of the analysis of the dispute over the nuclear program further traces the persisting incompatibilities in conflict observation against which any evolving communication in sanctions conflicts would occur, focusing first on Iran and then on the US. If we wish to understand the meaning of the incompatibilities that emerged in the conflict over Iran's nuclear program, it is imperative that we examine in more detail the conflict observations and historical narratives that inform this setting. This part will also outline the discursive field in Iran as the addressee of sanctions, identifying political factions, their position and lines of contestation within its theocratic political system.

6.1.1 Iran's struggle for independence and recognition

For decades, Iran and the West seemed to be allies, with Iran under the reign of Shah Mohammad Reza Pahlavi siding with the United States during the Cold War and pursuing a program of economic openness towards international oil companies. Although half of the profits went to Iran, foreign oil companies effectively controlled the Iranian oil sector. Underneath the surface of cooperation between

Iran and the West, however, there simmered a narrative of decline from historical heights and humiliation. The Shah's continuing rule was maintained with the help of the United States, which supported a coup in 1953 against the democratically elected Prime Minister Muhammad Mossadegh, who had sought to nationalize the oil industry and forced the Shah into exile.

The sense of subjugation by foreign powers goes back a long way in Iran. In a country that was once home to great empires, Iranians observe a continuing decline in geopolitical power and influence, culminating in a series of humiliations in the 19th and 20th centuries. Military defeats, loss of territory and even bankruptcy in the 19th century were followed by the country being split up into spheres of influence of foreign powers underneath a coat of formal independence (Rezun 1981; Elm 1994; Yodfat 2011), with Iran's most valuable economic resource, the oil sector, falling into the control of foreign firms (Cottam 1979; Limbert 2009). In the 20th century this trend continued. In an effort to balance its development strategy against colonial pressures by imperial powers, notably Great Britain and the Soviet Union, Iran maintained close ties to Germany. During the Second World War, Shah Reza Pahlavi was replaced by his son, Mohammad Reza Shah Pahlavi, and the country was swiftly occupied by Soviet, British and US forces. The military rationale was to secure support routes between the Allied Powers (Coakley 1990).

However, foreign influence did not vanish with the end of the war. On the contrary, the Soviet Union sought to expand its influence, pressing for oil concessions and installing local puppet regimes in northern Iran (Yodfat 2011). The latter move was conveniently countered by Britain, which already enjoyed an oil concession for the Anglo-Iranian Oil Company (AIOC), reflecting imperial traits. Frustration with foreign intervention and striving for national self-determination continued to simmer, fueled in particular by AIOC's exploitative practices and the exclusion of Iran from its fair share in revenues, in a text book case of the arrogance and bigotry of commercial gun boat imperialism (Ladjevardi 1983; Elm 1994).

Regaining control of domestic resources thus was a prime driver of the nationalist movement led by Dr. Muhammad Mossadegh, author of the influential book "Capitulations and Iran". With AIOC's categorical refusal to consider a 50/50 revenue-sharing arrangement, the popular Mossadegh went ahead with nationalizing the Iranian oil sector (Elm 1994). While Mossadegh's government had the sympathy and tacit support of the Truman administration in the US, geopolitical considerations towards the Middle East evolved with the incoming Eisenhower administration in 1953 (Gasiorowski 1987). In a joint operation by the CIA ("Operation Ajax") and the MI6 ("Operation Boot"), Mossadegh's democratically elected government was first discredited domestically, then toppled and replaced, with the Shah emerging as the new 'strong man' in Iran (Kressin 1991; Byrne 2013) and an international oil consortium of mainly US firms receiving an oil concession (Elm 1994).

Mossadegh's Nationalist government was supported by the nationalist clergy in an informal coalition. However, the relationship between the influential reactionary clergy, which had a tradition of resistance against foreign appropriation (e.g. 1891 Tobacco fatwa) and wanted a state governed by Sharia, and Mossadegh's left-wing liberal nationalists, was an uneasy one. Although its main leader, Ayatollah Kashani had been a key figure in foiling a previous attempt to dismiss Mossadegh, in the end their differences prevailed (Kressin 1991). After Mossadegh's fall, Pahlavi continued to tighten his grip on power (Cottam 1979). The Shah's secret police, SAVAK, quelled political dissent, indirectly supported by the US in an effort to prevent Communist agitation (Goode 1997). The most visible resistance now came from the reactionary nationalist clergy, in mass protests and riots led by Ayatollah Ruhollah Khomeini against the foreign-backed government. In addition to some of the government's reform efforts such as the White Revolution[1] of 1963 and women's suffrage, decried as Westernization, the nationalist clergy denounced the country's sell-out to foreign powers, evident for example in the 'Capitulation Law' that sought to grant diplomatic immunity to the scores of US military personnel in Iran (Takeyh 2009). Khomeini further connected the law to a USD 200m loan from the Americans the government was after (Vakili-Zad 1990).

When the Iranian Revolution took place in 1979, Khomeini's virulent stance against foreign (imperialist) intervention can be condensed in his reference to the US as the "Great Satan", the opponent of what the nationalist clergy wanted to achieve politically and culturally (Beeman 2008). In the ensuing hostage crisis at the US embassy led by Islamist students, Khomeini, who was to become Iran's Supreme Leader, approved and used the situation to reinforce support for the proposed theocratic constitution by further fueling anti-Americanism (Bakhash 1985; Arjomand 1988). Embassy documents reconstructed by the occupiers as they searched for evidence of that the US had plotted a counter-revolution seemed to confirm years of US collaboration with the toppled regime (Houghton 2001). The perspective on the US advanced by the nationalist clergy set the tone in Iran's subsequent approach to relations with the US.

Iran's nuclear program surged to become one of the top concerns of international security when the existence of two previously undeclared Iranian nuclear facilities for uranium enrichment was revealed in 2002, and the IAEA declared in 2003 that "Iran has failed to meet its obligations under its [NPT] Safeguards Agreement with respect to the reporting of nuclear material, the subsequent processing and use of that material and the declaration of facilities where the material was stored and processed" (IAEA 2003a:7). Generally, Iran's quest for nuclear power goes back many years. Earlier efforts, under the Pahlavi regime, were supported by the United States (Burr 2009). While the Shah claimed no interest in nuclear weapons, his insistence on Iran's right to the full cycle of nuclear energy technologies as a matter of principle and of energy security was held up by the Islamic Republic.

Politics in Iran is a multifarious affair, carried out between numerous secular and clerical factions. Politics was not homogeneous before the revolution took place, and it did not become so after it. The political system itself introduces some complexity, adding democratic elements to a theocratic system. Some institutions, such as the parliament and the president, are directly elected by popular vote, although candidates for the presidency and additional institutions are pre-vetted by the Guardian Council. In the end, the constitution ensures that the clerical institutions always have blocking powers at their disposal. The head of state and most powerful position is not the president but the Supreme Leader – flatly put, a deputy prophet by appointment. The dualist structure extends well beyond the 'civilian' political institutions to a 'second military' represented by the Islamic Revolutionary Guard Corps (IRGC), a military organization that extends into politics and the economy (Wehrey et al. 2009).

The strict theocratic arrangements in the Iranian constitution, largely built on Khomenei's designs, were not without their critics, even within the nationalist clergy (Hiro 1987). The fault lines of this rivalry were already visible in the late 1980s, with the selection of Sayyed Ali Khamenei as Khomenei's successor as Supreme Leader instead of the popular reformist Grand Ayatollah Hossein Ali Montazeri, who was publicly demoted after criticizing Khomenei's repressive course (Wehrey et al. 2009). The conservative Khamenei had built and nourished an informal coalition with the IRGC. Put very simply, since the 1990s, the conservative Iranian Principlists on the one hand and Iranian Reformists on the other dominate politics, with Pragmatists composed of moderate clerics and some *Bazaaris* as an important third element in the discursive field. After the pragmatist government of Akbar Hashemi Rafsanjani in the early 1990s, which was formed as a coalition between the conservative right and the modernist right factions, President Mohammad Khatami's government from 1997 onwards represented a clear division between progressives and conservative neo-fundamentalists (Moslem 2002): Khatami's reformist government was supported by the left, modern right, intellectuals and progressive clergymen, with its political opponents the conservative right, reactionary clerics and the IRGC.

Khatami's coalition sought to pursue social and political reform that aimed to strengthen an Islamic version of civil society and democracy, thereby scaling back autocratic elements of Iran's political system. Their efforts were met by fierce opposition from conservative neo-fundamentalists (Takeyh 2009). Clerics and protagonists associated with the IRGC decried these domestic reform efforts as Western concepts representing US influence that would eliminate Islam, blocked the initiatives of Khatami's coalition through the (clerical) judiciary, intimidated public proponents and put liberal newspapers out of existence (Moslem 2002:258ff.). Some prominent figures associated with the reform coalition more or less mysteriously lost their lives (Zoeram and Fee 2010). In terms of foreign relations, Khatami pursued a *détente* policy towards the region and, crucially, also towards the US, which strongly set him apart from his conservative opponents to whom such a move was irreconcilable with the Islamic Revolution (Alam 2000; Hunter 2010).

6.1.2 America's struggle with 'the Ayatollahs'

For the United States, the events surrounding the Iranian revolution had a lasting impact as well. The Islamic revolution profoundly changed the terms of the relationship between the US and Iran specifically, and generally brought a defiance to international relations of the etiquette that was deemed sacred by the US. Particularly the events of the hostage crisis were viewed as a painful national embarrassment, as embassy staff was publicly humiliated to the accompaniment of "death to America" chants and the burning of American flags. In terms of the long-accepted norms of diplomatic conduct, this event, and the fact that Iran allowed the situation to continue for months, was an outrageous disregard of international law (Beeman 2008).

Strategically, the US was confronted with the loss of a close ally that took its political establishment widely by surprise (Karabell 1993). It took place only a few months after President Carter gave a toast in Tehran to a Shah 'admired' and 'loved' by the Iranian people (Hiro 1987:311). The Islamic Republic represented a non-aligned power that pursued its own regional agenda in open defiance of the interests of the superpower, through asymmetric means: In the years following the revolution, there were frequent clashes with Iranian proxies in Lebanon and elsewhere. To the US, Iran's continuous support of extremist groups ultimately made it the biggest state sponsor of terrorism (Beeman 2008).

While the US still sought to establish some basic form of dialogue and coordination – despite Iran actively working against it and its allies, vowing to seek the annihilation of Israel (the "Little Satan", in Khomenei's own words) (Takeyh 2009) – its efforts were time and again frustrated. An early attempt, driven by fears of Soviet advancement, ended in another embarrassment that made up one half of the Iran-Contra affair (Crist 2012). With the failed efforts of numerous administrations, the US perception was that its cautious initiatives were either one-sidedly taken advantage of, or outright rejected.

In contrast to its earlier efforts to promote social and political reform, pressing Pahlavi on the White Revolution (Goode 1997), the United States was now confronted with a reactionary religious opponent. The view that was widely proliferated was that a gang of mad, incompetent clerics building their rule on dubious claims of divine principle pitted Iran against secular rationalist modernity represented by the United States (Beeman 2008). This, together with Iran's pursuance of certain political ends through certain political means, both of which are well outside of internationally acceptable norms, makes readily available repertoires for conflict observation of what is at stake when the Islamic Republic begins to pursue a nuclear program.

Although the Islamic Republic declared that it had no interest in nuclear weapons, the US sought to impede its nuclear program early on. The aims of the US were to prevent the development of nuclear weapons and their proliferation (O'Sullivan 2004), and were reflected in US sanctions legislation such as the Iran-Iraq Arms Non-Proliferation Act of 1992, the Iran-Libya Sanctions Act of 1996 targeting Iran's energy sector and the Iran Non-Proliferation Act (2000). Crucially, the latter two of these acts (and the Iran-Iraq Arms Non-Proliferation Act since its amendment in 1996) also have an 'extraterritorial' component, containing provisions against non-US actors who were pressured not to support Iran in that sense.[2]

6.2 Same but different: twice combined sanctions, and a negative sanctions strategy

This second part of the empirical analysis separates the conflict over Iran's nuclear program into three distinct cases of sanctions. It establishes the sanctions policies pursued and promoted by the US, and it traces the development of Iran's conflict observation in each case, applying framing analysis and process tracing. The different sanctions strategies used in each case are accompanied by significant changes in opponents' conflict observations. During the first case, after the revelation of Iran's nuclear program in 2002 by the MEK (Mojahedin-e Khalq),[3] the US on the one hand increased pressure through securitizing the Islamic Republic as part of an 'axis of evil', and sought to isolate Iran internationally. On the other hand, the US lent (limited) support to allied EU-3 efforts to finding a resolution to the nuclear issue through dialogue and incentives. Whereas negotiations centered on interest incompatibilities, an uneasy mix of incentives and negative sanctions easily contributed to communicating an identity conflict when posited against Iran's rights under the NPT, as statements on the purpose of sanctions ranged from enforcing a negotiated solution to averting an Iranian nuclear program entirely.

After the failure of the Paris Agreement to resolve the nuclear issue, the second case, from 2005 onwards, is marked by negative sanctions in a deteriorating identity conflict. Amid communicated identity incompatibilities, positing the Islamic Republic as potentially seeking nuclear weapons against US efforts to deny Iran's rights and independence, the introduction of negative sanctions, with an increasing extraterritorial component, reinforced the prevailing conflict observations. While the stated aim of the sanctions was at least to enforce full Iranian cooperation with the IAEA and coerce Iran to stop enrichment activities, negative sanctions contributed to the Iranian view of a US threat, with a complicit IAEA.

The third case saw a change in sanctions strategy and ultimately a transformation in conflict observation. After Barack Obama became president in 2009, the US, while continuing to securitize an unchecked Iranian nuclear program as a threat, offered a clear perspective on observing the nuclear dispute in terms of an issue conflict. Confronted with sustained offers of dialogue and incentives, and ever more stringent multilateral negative sanctions, Iranian conflict observations evolved substantially from viewing any move by the US in terms of identity incompatibilities to recognizing legitimate international concerns and resolving the conflict over the nuclear issue. The moment of catharsis brought about by the breakthrough between conflict opponents in 2015 and the subsequent implementation of the Joint Comprehensive Plan of Action (JCPOA) represents one of the most remarkable turning points in a sanctions conflict.

6.2.1 Securitized reformists: the failure of incoherently combined sanctions

The revelation of undeclared nuclear facilities in Iran in 2002 was preceded by statements by the neoconservative US administration that expressed and emphasized an identity conflict with Iran. In his State of the Union Address in January 2002, President George W. Bush depicted Iran as part of an 'axis of evil' and vowed to act against states that were pursuing weapons of mass destruction and supporting terrorism: "I will not wait on events, while dangers gather. I will not stand by, as peril draws closer and closer. The United States of America will not permit the world's most dangerous regimes to threaten us with the world's most destructive weapons".[4] Whereas the Bush administration unmistakably labelled Iran a target in the War on Terror and sought to introduce tougher negative sanctions, the EU-3 as its allied partners sought to resolve the nuclear dispute through dialogue and incentives – without full US support.

Following revelations by the MEK, which accused the Islamic Republic of having an undeclared nuclear program, President Khatami emphasized the exclusively civilian purposes of Iran's nuclear ambitions that would aim to serve its energy needs and reduce the country's technological backwardness. Khatami insisted that it was Iran's legitimate right to pursue a nuclear program. While the reformist government was willing to come to a common solution that would put the nuclear program under the extended supervision of the IAEA, it quickly came under attack from conservative hardliners who securitized US efforts to weaken and ultimately subdue the Islamic Republic.

US conflict observation and sanctions against Iran

The US consistently stuck to its position throughout that Iranian uranium enrichment was unacceptable, in spite of its implied allowance under the NPT. Although its rhetoric remained unchanged, the Bush administration did not immediately introduce tougher negative sanctions following the IAEA revelations but pursued a mixed approach of continuing to enforce existing sanctions, exerting pressure through the IAEA and allowing its European allies to seek a solution through engaging with Iran through the EU-3 (France, Germany and the United Kingdom) format.[5]

The IAEA continuously exerted pressure on Iran to provide evidence that it was not developing nuclear weapons (IAEA 2003a), denounced Iran for secretly pursuing some of its nuclear program for almost two decades (2003b) and declared Iran's continuing failure to fully disclose its program (2004a) and to comply (2004b, 2005) with its safeguards obligations. Crucially though, as long as the diplomatic efforts of the EU-3 continued, the IAEA refrained from declaring Iran to be in noncompliance with the NPT.

Meanwhile, the EU-3 offered incentives in the form of negotiations and technology on condition that Iran suspended its nuclear enrichment program and that Iran signed an Additional Protocol to its NPT Safeguards Agreement. The EU-3 and Iran arrived at several accords on the path to negotiating an issue conflict (Sauer 2007). In an agreement signed in October 2003 in Tehran, Iran agreed to sign the Advanced Protocol and to suspend enrichment in order to pave the way for further negotiations. Despite the US stating its reservations and dissatisfaction with Iran's compliance with the terms of the accord, the EU-3 and Iran took a further step towards limiting the dispute to an issue conflict in signing the Paris Agreement in November 2004, with Iran agreeing to suspend its program in exchange for a) nuclear technology and fuel transfer, b) trade concessions and c) security cooperation.

More broadly, the European Union reinforced its non-proliferation approach by adopting the Strategy against Proliferation and Weapons of Mass Destruction (WMD), a move that, among other issues, was also linked to Iran (Portela 2004; Sauer 2004). The arrangement between the US and the EU was far from perfect, though. A further offer, presented by Iran on 23 March 2005 in Paris, which included voluntary restrictions on enrichment, was rejected by the EU-3. In face of US opposition to any uranium enrichment in Iran whatsoever, recently articulated in President Bush's State of the Union Address,[6] the Europeans could not agree to domestic Iranian enrichment.

Although the US agreed to allow the EU-3 to try out diplomacy, it was ultimately unwilling to offer security guarantees or engage in long-term security cooperation, which was an essential part of the deal between the EU-3 and Iran, though (Harnisch 2007). The limitation of this format thus meant that the US was not a party to these negotiations. Instead, the US kept its sights set on a maximalist solution, as indicated by Condoleezza Rice in her senate confirmation hearing for Secretary of State. Pressed by Senator Biden, she declared that the aim was for Iran to verifiably and irreversibly get rid of its nuclear program.[7]

In a rather imperfect coordination of sticks and carrots, the US continued to extraterritorially enforce the Iran Non-Proliferation Act in 2003 and 2004, targeting Chinese and North Korean firms. The US took advantage of its dominant position in the global financial system granted by, among other things, the US dollar serving as the world's reserve currency. In 2004, it also began to target firms in the financial sector such as UBS, a bank, imposing a $100m fine on the financial institution for engaging in illicit US dollar transactions (Kittrie 2009). In a crucial move of financial statecraft, the US declared that for any transactions involving the US financial system (payments, USD-denominated credit lines, securities trading, etc.), US law would apply (cf. Alexander 2009). Hence, any entity engaging in transactions involving the US financial system would fall under its jurisdiction. The US thus sought to expand the support base of its negative sanctions onto a reluctant EU and other actors (Everts 2004).

In 2005, the US further strengthened its sanctions regime through Executive Order 13382, targeting 'WMD proliferators and their supporters', among them Iranian entities. However, the US was finally ready to provide positive incentives as well, lifting its opposition to WTO membership negotiations and dropping as a condition for consultations that Iran stop its uranium enrichment process. However, with continued US non-commitment to the Paris Agreement, this was too little, too late. Following the election of Mahmoud Ahmadinejad as Iranian president, Iran recommenced its uranium conversion and enrichment. This move was seen as a red line for the EU, marking the end of its initiative, and this first case of a badly coordinated combined sanctions strategy.

Sanctions conflict observations in Iran

In reaction to the revelation of Iran's nuclear program, President Khatami, in a televised speech on 9 February 2003, made a detailed statement outlining his government's position on the program's rationale. Khatami emphasized that all nuclear activities were in line with Iran's international obligations and he welcomed the IAEA's supervision. The program served peaceful purposes only and thus Khatami, and Iran, "renews its call to make the world and specially the region free from weapons of mass destruction".[8]

As president Khatami's latter statement already implied, the security dimension of a nuclear program, and its potential 'dual-use' nature, was not alien to political debate in Iran. Commentators in reformist-leaning Iranian newspapers observed that signing the Additional Protocol should therefore not be an issue, and they questioned the basic military value of nuclear weapons as a deterrent (Chubin and Litwak 2003:105).

Conservative pragmatists had different positions on the effectiveness of a nuclear deterrent, such as former president Rafsanjani who, in a statement in December 2001, said:

> We do not want to fall victim to insecurity and we do not want a confrontation to turn into World War III. [. . .] If a day comes when the world of Islam is duly equipped with the arms that Israel has in its possession, the strategy of colonialism would face a stalemate because the exchange of atomic bombs would leave nothing of Israel, while only damaging the Muslim world.[9]

However, later in 2003 Rafsanjani made it clear that Iran should not acquire nuclear weapons as WMD were irreconcilable with Islam.[10]

Whereas political observers across all factions saw it as Iran's right to be able to pursue a non-military nuclear program, conservative neo-fundamentalists went further: Pursuing a nuclear program was as much a quest for (technological) development as a guarantor of national security. In a TV interview, Deputy for International Affairs of Chief Justice Mohammad Javad Larijani summarized that stance, arguing that the enrichment of uranium as well as the acquisition of nuclear weapons was the right of the Islamic Republic of Iran and said that joining the NPT in the first place had been a mistake.[11] Mohammad Zolqadr, Deputy Commander of the IRGC, warned against recklessly accepting the Additional Protocol, implying that it was a gateway for foreign spies.[12]

Conservative media commentators voiced skepticism on international cooperation, pointing to a lack of support by the IAEA in its obligations under the NPT, and their suspicions of a continuing plot by Western powers to undermine Iran's development and progress.[13] Such reasoning sought to appeal to Iranian sentiments across political divides that unanimously took the nuclear program as a source of national pride and a manifestation of independence from foreign interference (Bahgat 2006).

These differences in the observation of Iran's nuclear program in the discursive field are accompanied by more general differences in conflict observation. President Khatami and the reformist camp broadly refrained from securitizing statements in relation to the West (in particular the EU-3). Instead, they emphasized the importance of building trust, determined to observe the dispute over the nuclear program as an issue conflict on technical and legal aspects, as Foreign Minister Kamal Kharrazi put it.[14] The president's brother, Mohammad-Reza Khatami, Vice Speaker of the Majlis, acknowledged that international concern about Iran's nuclear program was a fact, albeit groundless, and argued that fully cooperating with the IAEA was the best way of addressing this concern.[15] In that sense, reformists considered the Additional Protocol as simply a more accurate specification of inspections under the NPT.[16]

Such views translated into a prognostic framing visible in reformist statements that stressed the gains to be made from collaboration. Mohsen Mirdamadi, Chairman of the Majlis Commission for National Security and Foreign Policy, argued that Iran could gain concessions and expected closer collaboration with the EU on the nuclear program and in other areas.[17] At the same time, reformists essentially downplayed negative sanctions by merely stressing that Iran would "not submit to anything under duress".[18] On the other hand, they expected the EU to be more supportive and to decisively follow through on its commitments towards Iran instead of beating around the bush.[19] Furthermore, reformists left little doubt regarding the potential dangers arising from the machinations of their main opponent. Iran must not act in a way that would support US efforts to isolate the country internationally, argued Mirdamadi: If Iran's nuclear case was referred to the UN Security Council (SC), this would be a greater curse than signing the Turkmanchai Treaty was.[20] Mohammad-Reza Khatami laid out that risk, putting forward three possible scenarios: Iran could either follow the Japanese example, become an isolated, desolate place like North Korea, or – and this he regarded to be the 'most humiliating scenario' – end up as "a country which wraps all its nuclear facilities together with its national honour and credibility and presents it as a package to the White House on a silver tray".[21] To avoid such an outcome, reformists were even willing to grant the IAEA access to Iranian military sites.[22]

While conservative pragmatists raised concerns about the implications of signing the Additional Protocol for national security and sovereignty,[23] they generally voiced cautious optimism about the potential benefits of international collaboration. This position was also uttered by Hassan Rouhani, Secretary of the Supreme National Security Council and chief negotiator on the nuclear issue,[24] and echoed by conservative-leaning media.[25] Nevertheless, moderates were more critical and referred to the danger of Iran being blackmailed over the Additional Protocol.[26] Hashemi Rafsanjani, Chairman of the Expediency Council, further warned against the consequences of an escalating conflict, ending in Iran's withdrawal from the NPT.[27]

Finally, to conservative neo-fundamentalists, the 'humiliating scenario' outlined by Mohammad-Reza Khatami was already a reality, or, at the very least, there was an imminent threat of it becoming so. In September 2003, 100 Majlis deputies signed a letter to UN Secretary General Kofi Annan, denouncing a threat posed to Iran by Western countries and criticizing the IAEA for merely implementing the designs of US imperialists.[28] Consequently, references to a threat dominated statements on the dispute, with the IAEA seen as undermining Iranian sovereignty[29] in ways that were historically comparable to the issue of oil nationalization.[30] Although EU-3 offers of collaboration were met with cautious approval, negative reactions to international pressure were decidedly stronger.[31] To conservative hardliners and the conservative media, any deal directed by the EU-3 was more or less useless as they saw the US as the main opponent and driver of the conflict.[32]

Although the Supreme Leader of the Islamic Republic, Ayatollah Khamenei, refrained from extensively commenting on negotiations on the nuclear dispute, the Iranian government was only able to act on his consent. Despite Khamenei's denouncement of the military encirclement of the Islamic Republic by the US, its threats and its subversion efforts,[33] the government did not only enjoy support in its efforts, but Iran even seemed – unsuccessfully – to have proposed a 'grand bargain' on the entire conflict offer to the US, its exact shape remaining somewhat opaque (Harnisch 2007; Katzman 2007).

Already in early 2004 the fortunes of the Iranian reformists began to fade decidedly, in domestic and international politics. Domestically, in January 2004, when vetting candidates for the upcoming parliamentary election, the Guardian Council disqualified hundreds of reformist candidates, including dozens of sitting members of the parliament. Despite President Mohammad Khatami's public condemnation of the decision as being not impartial,[34] the action from conservative clerics, described by prominent reformists as a 'coup', was hardly revised.[35] The conservative coalition that controlled parliament after the election, the Alliance of Builders of Islamic Iran, refused to ratify the Additional Protocol that Hassan Rouhani had negotiated with the EU-3 and demanded to pull out of the NPT. Internationally, although the reformist government succeeded in striking a deal with the EU-3 through the Paris Agreement in November 2004, which, to the dismay of conservatives, temporarily suspended uranium enrichment activities, the US failed to commit. In a desperate effort to speed up talks ahead of the looming presidential election, the initiative put forward by the reformist government to the EU-3 in early 2005 offered voluntary restrictions on domestic enrichment but insisted that Iran would not resign its right to it.[36] The EU-3's dithering on concessions and its ultimate rejection of the initiative was seen as a breach of European commitments to recognizing Iran's rights under the NPT,[37] fueled by US pressure.[38]

In the run-up to the presidential election in 2005, candidates' positions on the nuclear dispute were in line with the stances previously taken by the respective political groups. Reformist candidates vowed to extend international collaboration, including seeking reconciliation with the US.[39] However, there were clear signs of exasperation[40] and pessimistic claims that the US and Israel were continuing to observe an identity conflict.[41] Hashemi Rafsanjani, who quickly became the most popular candidate, declared he would continue to build on the relationship with the EU-3.[42] Ali Larijani, the leading conservative candidate, compared the nuclear program to oil nationalization and explicitly rejected the American 'sticks and carrots' approach as a mere expression of US double standards,[43] a view shared by conservative media.[44] Larijani stated the view that "Americans are humiliating the Iranian people by saying that they are not capable of managing this industry".[45] The US, Larijani declared in observing an identity conflict, sought to undermine Iran's sovereignty and wanted to replace the Islamic way of life.[46]

Finally, far less restrained than Larijani and a most unlikely candidate, at least in terms of pre-election opinion polls, was Mayor of Tehran Mahmoud Ahmadinejad. Scoring consistently low approval ratings that put him outside the top five frontrunners,[47] Ahmadinejad voiced such contempt for reformist policies and Iranian negotiators 'giving in' to the West that he had been banned from participating in government cabinet meetings, which he would have been entitled to do as Tehran mayor.[48] The 'arrogant' US, he claimed, even if ties were re-established, sought to destroy the Islamic Republic. The US 'system of domination' was based on depriving Iran of its culture, its identity. Similarly, the UN was against the world of Islam. There could be no dispute on the peaceful nuclear program, stated Ahmadinejad, as it was Iran's natural right. The Islamic Republic was not going to accept conditions.[49]

Although Ahmadinejad, after his unlikely victory in the presidential election (Naji 2008:chap. 2), vowed to continue negotiating with the Europeans, he was wary of them meeting their obligations.[50] In the wake of the election, both Hassan Rouhani and Kamal Kharrazi emphasized Iran's continuing commitment to negotiations and declared that Iran was not willing to forego its right to enrichment any further.[51] When the EU-3 proposal in August 2005 insisted on a permanent revocation of enrichment rights, Iran rejected the proposal but recommenced enrichment to a limited extent under its new president,[52] who appointed Ali Larijani as the chief nuclear negotiator, replacing the pragmatist Rouhani.

President Ahmadinejad took an assertive position on the nuclear program. He declared Iran's right to a full nuclear fuel cycle and officials disputed any legal basis for the IAEA to send the Iran file to the UN Security Council.[53] While Larijani distanced Iran from the EU-3, claiming it was treating Iran as a second-class country,[54] Ahmadinejad argued that the US was imposing a 'nuclear apartheid' onto the world.[55] The government widened its dialogue partners and while it proposed an international consortium to head the nuclear program in Iran under shared ownership, it went decidedly further by offering to transfer nuclear technology to other Islamic states.[56] The US and the EU rejected Ahmadinejad's proposal; after the IAEA denounced Iran's continuing noncompliance with the NPT in September 2005, Iran subsequently quit the Paris Agreement.

Summary and analysis

Early attempts at resolving the nuclear dispute were impaired by poorly coordinated, inconsistent sanctions and conflict observations on the part of the US and the EU-3 that promoted conflict communication that was evolving into identity incompatibilities, thus strengthening hardline neo-fundamentalist positions in the discursive field on the nuclear issue in Iran. After the nuclear program of the

Islamic Republic became known, the reformist Khatami government sought to observe the dispute in terms of issue incompatibilities. In its diagnostic framing, the government insisted on Iran's rights under the NPT, while also recognizing international concern. As the program was of a peaceful nature, it was willing to sign the Additional Protocol which, in the government's prognostic framing, was a confidence-building measure and a more detailed specification of NPT obligations. It downplayed sanctions and emphasized the potential gains from collaboration. In order to counter skepticism, it securitized a threat of Iran becoming isolated internationally.

In the Islamic Republic's discursive field on the nuclear issue, the reformist government's conflict observation was increasingly challenged by two major alternative positions, both of which were more skeptical (see Table 6.1). Contrary to the government position, in their diagnostic framing moderate pragmatists were more wary of the Additional Protocol's implications for sovereignty. Their prognostic framing was bi-directional; while pragmatists recognized that gains could be won from collaborating, they feared that the Additional Protocol was a blackmailing tool. The strongest challenge to the government in terms of competing frames, however, came from neo-fundamentalists, who observed the conflict strictly in terms of identity incompatibilities: The nuclear program was unquestionably Iran's right and negotiations represented a threat as they were about impeding these rights. The US threatened Iran's independence and the Islamic Republic's existence. In that diagnostic framing, the IAEA was a US tool and the EU-3 irrelevant as they had no power. The Additional Protocol was a means of spying on Iran and was a security issue. In the context of such a threatening environment, the nuclear program would also represent a security measure. In the view of neo-fundamentalists, suspending enrichment was a humiliating defeat which brought nothing in return as the EU-3 did not speak for the US, Iran's main opponent, and did not even stand by their own commitments.

There was a clear tension between the EU-3 and the Khatami government's conflict observation in terms of interest incompatibilities, on the one hand, and the US securitizing Iran and the nuclear program as a threat, on the other. In consequence of this meandering between observing an issue and identity conflict,

Table 6.1 Iran's discursive field on conflict observation, 2003–2005

Political faction	*Reformists*	*Pragmatists*	*Neo-fundamentalists*
Diagnostic framing	Risk	Bi-directional	Security threat
Attribution of responsibility	Neutral	Neutral	America, Reformist government
Prognostic framing	Collaboration	Bi-directional	Non-cooperation
Conflict observation	Interest incompatibility	Interest incompatibility potential security nexus	Identity incompatibility

neo-fundamentalists were easily able to challenge reformists and more moderate pragmatists on their alleged *naïveté* in confronting the enemy. In their securitized conflict observation, the EU-3 efforts of dialogue were not positive, but had to be considered in the context of (US) challenges to Iran's right and efforts to increase pressure through negative sanctions. Even taking into account Ahmadinejad's victory in the 2005 presidential election, which came as a surprise, there is still no question that the inconsistency in conflict observation and the imposition of combined sanctions by the US and EU-3 contributed to a conflict on Iran's nuclear program that evolved from communicated issue incompatibilities towards identity incompatibilities.

6.2.2 Negative sanctions and a deadlocked, securitized conflict

The years after the breakdown of the Paris Agreement saw an escalation of the conflict on Iran's nuclear program, resulting in it being referred to the UN Security Council which brought a continuous tightening of negative sanctions against Iran. Confronted with an assertive, provocative Iranian government, the Bush administration left 'all options on the table'. With a view to limiting Iranian business opportunities globally, the US substantially strengthened negative sanctions and their extraterritorial extension and enforcement, nudging its European allies to do likewise by taking advantage of its central position in the global financial system.

To the conservative neo-fundamentalist government of Mahmoud Ahmadinejad, US (and, by extension, European) unwillingness to accept Iranian uranium enrichment within the framework of the NPT only proved ulterior motives. In its view, the inability of Europeans to deliver on their commitments and to secure US commitment to their position proved their impotence and subordinate role to the US. The Iranian government no longer took European initiatives seriously. It ended its extended collaboration with the IAEA and vowed to pursue Iran's nuclear program as a testimony to the country's independence and progress and to the fact that it would not bow to any foreign pressure.

US conflict observation and sanctions against Iran

The Bush administration continued to claim a security threat if Iran went nuclear[57] and furthermore positioned this dispute within a wider identity conflict. On 31 May 2006, Secretary of State Condoleezza Rice depicted Iran's activities under its nuclear weapons program and its non-cooperation with the IAEA as "a direct threat" and vowed that the US would increase sanctions if Iran did not change course.[58] The US position in the conflict was thus: if it observes Iran as non-cooperating, (negative) sanctions will follow. However, although Rice also promised reconciliation should Iran decide to collaborate, such statements contrasted with public speculations that the US administration would in fact rather seek regime change (Hersh 2006). Such speculations were fostered by comments by President Bush that "all options are on the table",[59] and the appropriation of funds for 'democracy promotion' (Katzman 2007:35–38). More broadly, throughout his tenure Bush continued to portray Iran as an undemocratic, oppressive regime that supports extremism, terrorism and spreads instability in the region.[60]

In February 2006, the IAEA sent the Iran case to the UN Security Council expressing lingering doubts that Iran's nuclear program was exclusively for peaceful purposes (IAEA 2006). The UN SC refrained at first from directly taking action. However, when its call on Iran to change course and negotiate came to no avail, and an ultimatum to suspend enrichment within a month (SC Resolution 1696) was ignored, the Security Council finally introduced negative sanctions (SC Resolution 1737) under Chapter VII of the UN Charter that were gradually strengthened (SC Resolutions 1747, 1803). UN sanctions imposed a ban on Iranian arms exports, asset freezes, a trade ban on dual-use goods and travel restrictions.

Contrary to the fragmented approach of the preceding sanctions case, in June 2006 the US joined the EU-3 together with China and Russia to form the P5+1, representing the five permanent members of the UN Security Council + Germany.[61] A common multilateral approach to the conflict was enabled by the US proposal to engage in direct multilateral talks with Iran, announced by Rice in her abovementioned statement on 31 May 2006. While the US was stepping up to its international partners, it was also stepping up its negative 'secondary' sanctions (covering non-US persons) against Iran. On the one hand, it continued to list foreign firms as so-called Specially Designated Nationals and Blocked Persons (SDNs), e.g. under the Iran Non-Proliferation Act;[62] in consequence, they were sanctioned within the US and its financial system.

On the other hand, the US further embarked on a comprehensive "weaponization of finance"[63] (Lohmann 2016:7): isolating Iran from the global financial system by leveraging the central position of the US within it. The US took a threefold approach in pursuing this goal. First, it tightened negative sanctions against Iran, targeting in particular its financial sector. By revoking its authorization for so-called "U-turn transactions" (allowing US banks to process payments involving Iran that begin and end with a foreign bank) for Bank Saderat in September 2006,[64] the US Treasury effectively denied it the right to process USD transactions. This represented a severe blow to Iran's economy given its dependence on the oil trade that is carried out in USD. All other major Iranian banks were subsequently targeted (Bank Sepah: January 2007; Bank Melli, Bank Mellat: October 2007; Export Development Bank of Iran: October 2008),[65] with access to the US financial system denied through asset freezes, before the entire U-turn transactions provision for Iran were finally revoked in October 2008.[66] A year earlier, the IRGC was put on the SDN list as well – a move with considerable implications, given the IRGC's broad presence in the Iranian economy (Wehrey et al. 2009).

Second, the US sought to impose an international control regime, executed by financial institutions. To this end, the Treasury embarked on an information campaign, touring the international financial industry and pointing out the regulatory and reputational risks of (involuntarily) becoming involved in Iranian proliferation activities (Lohmann 2016). At the same time, the US pushed foreign governments to strengthen oversight. In October 2007, the Financial Action Task Force (FATF), an OECD institution charged with setting anti-money laundering (AML) standards and those for counterinf the financing of terrorism (CFT) for the global financial system, issued a statement warning of Iran's deficient AML and CFT standards. This meant that engaging with Iran significantly increased the risks and raised due diligence requirements (i.e. costs) for the financial industry.

Third, the US prepared the ground for, and increasingly took, robust enforcement action against foreign financial institutions which violated or evaded sanctions against Iran. In 2005, ABN Amro received a $80m fine. In January 2009 at the end of the Bush administration's second term, Lloyds TSB was handed a $350m fine. The European financial industry responded to these developments across the board by winding up its business activities involving Iran (Loeffler 2009).

The UN supported extending pressure on Iran by targeting its financial sector, e.g. through SC Resolutions 1747 and 1803. Although generally more reluctant, the EU also applied sanctions beyond those mandated by the UN, imposing an asset freeze on Bank Melli in 2008.[67] Although these developments portrayed the notion of the US as the leading driver of sanctions and main opponent in the conflict on Iran's nuclear program, they also testify to the fact that the negative sanctions strategy pursued by the Bush administration did not succeed in forcing Iran back to the negotiation table.

Sanctions conflict observations in Iran

In face of the breakdown of the Paris Agreement in late 2005 and the prospect of the IAEA transferring the Iran file to the UN Security Council, the Ahmadinejad government continued to see Iran's fundamental rights under the NPT as being threatened, thanks to the machinations of its hostile opponent, the US. The Ahmadinejad government continued to pursue its politics of confrontation and defiance towards the West, both generally and specifically towards the US In the same vein, conservatives in Iran continued to observe an identity conflict: The government and Supreme Leader Khamenei consistently generalized the nuclear issue as being part of a "national consensus" on Iran's quest for development and technological progress,[68] which in turn was posed against US attempts at a humiliating denial of the Islamic Republic's goal. Neo-fundamentalists promoted the 'national consensus' through harassment and intimidation, up to the point when the former head of Iran's nuclear negotiation team, Hossein Mousavian, was accused of treason and briefly detained.[69] As Kasra Naji (2008:132f.) observes, "Ahmadinejad had elevated the nuclear programme into an issue of national honour", into a nationalist cause, drawing an analogy to the quest for oil nationalization in the 1940s/50s. Giving up enrichment would mean giving up independence. Indeed, as Adviser to the Head of the Iranian Judiciary Mohammad Javad Larijani claimed, there was a pattern of attempts by the US to subjugate the entire Islamic world: "They want us to be terrified and leave Islam aside. This is what they have obliged many of the Muslim countries to do despite the preference of their nations; they got scared, were deceived and surrendered and today they are humiliated".[70]

With regard to the deadlock with the EU-3, chief nuclear negotiator Ali Larijani continued to insist on Iran's right to uranium enrichment under the NPT: based on the unqualified recognition of this right, Iran would be ready to fully cooperate with Europe.[71] At the same time, Larijani emphasized that Iran would not give in to pressure and bullying.[72] With the IAEA reporting Iran to the UN SC in February 2006, the government's reaction was to revert to the established pattern of conflict observation. Foreign Minister Manuchehr Mottaki announced that Iran would end its cooperation in response to the move and would not give in to the imminent threat of sanctions.[73] The IAEA resolution was not impartial but the result of US pressure,[74] 'the enemy' that was, according to Ahmadinejad, 'elbow-deep' in the blood of other nations and had treated Iran as a second-class nation without civilization and culture.[75] Subsequent to the IAEA referral, Iran indeed terminated its implementation of the Additional Protocol, as President Ahmadinejad had promised.[76]

Conflict observation by conservatives continued to deteriorate along these lines. European proposals and calls from the P5+1 for a diplomatic solution were not viewed as positive incentives and were broadly denounced as 'one-sided' and 'groundless threats'.[77] Upon the adoption of UN SC Resolution 1696, Iran's envoy to the organization denounced the 'injustice' and again compared it to the struggle for oil nationalization.[78] Although the government declared that it would continue with its nuclear program within the framework of the NPT, conservatives condemned the 'illegal securitization' of the program and called Iran's membership of the treaty increasingly into question.[79] Diagnostic and prognostic framings concerning UN SC Resolution 1737 fell into a similar pattern; the government denounced the nuclear issue as a pretext for Western enmity and the UN as irrelevant.[80] Ahmadinejad vowed not to yield to sanctions and threats and to continue unrestrained with the nuclear program.[81] Conservatives stood by these views, also in the context of UN SC Resolution 1747, vowing not to back down in the face of the threats and sanctions of 'the enemy'.[82] Supreme Leader Khamenei at the same time dismissed sanctions as a meaningless expression of US 'global arrogance' that sought to subdue Iran, pointing out that Iran had already acquired nuclear technology under sanctions.[83] Instead, Iran extended its enrichment activities and further reduced its cooperation with the IAEA.[84]

As for the financial sanctions imposed, Iran sought to challenge them legally[85] and find ways to work around them. Banks began converting their USD reserves into € and promoted trade financing in non-USD by issuing letters of credit denominated in €.[86] The governor of Bank Markazi, the Iranian Central Bank, denied the economic impact of financial sanctions.[87] Confronted with allegations against Iranian banks of financing terrorism, he tried to reinsure the heads of other central banks around the world of the clean record of Iran's banks.[88] However, there was increasing public disagreement on the impact of sanctions, despite the state applying stricter media controls and its attempts to restrict reporting.[89] Tehran newspaper Etemaad argued that the banking system and even the entire economy was threatened and published a report signed by dozens of economists, tracing the consequences of failed government policies and sanctions and criticizing the government for their increase.[90] Subsequently, in the wake of FATF actions against Iran, reports emerged of Iranian 'money laundering' through Azerbaijan.[91]

In face of the endless optimism by government officials and their denial of the economic impact of sanctions, the public appeared to be increasingly losing confidence in censored domestic media reports.[92] Public criticism was on the rise of Ahmadinejad's unprecedented populist exuberance and excrescences that embarrassed even those in the Supreme Leader's circles (e.g. the 'International Conference on the Holocaust'), lamenting the power support structures of neo-fundamentalist clerics and the IRGC behind the government.[93]

The opposition, comprising reformists and pragmatists, held the conservative majority in parliament and government responsible for the economic woes of the country, pointing to the damaging impact on and isolation of Iran due to UN sanctions.[94] Reformists urged a return to diplomatic engagement, a proposition also put forward cautiously by conservative pragmatists such as Hassan Rouhani, who criticized Ahmadinejad's divisive approach towards domestic and international affairs.[95] Even though reformists underlined Iran's squarely incompatible strategic interests with the US, they nonetheless advocated the need for comprehensive dialogue.[96] Conservative pragmatists such as Rafsanjani, despite denouncing threats and bullying by the US, similarly advocated re-engaging in negotiations.[97]

In the parliamentary election in 2008, reformists and pragmatists did not make any meaningful gains in a campaign that was criticized for biased reporting, harassment, irregularities and military interference.[98] Ahead of the voting, the Guardian Council excluded hundreds of reformist candidates, a move that provoked harsh public criticism of Kafkaesque disqualification practices.[99] Prominent moderate pragmatist clerics remained notably absent from the race.[100] As a result, neo-fundamentalist conservatives continued to dominate the Majlis. Moreover, among them, a substantial number had an affiliation with the IRGC, testifying to the thorough influence that the military organization had gained in politics and its conversion into a political and ideological force (Alfoneh 2008).

Instead of moderation, the neo-fundamentalists in the government and legislature continued to put forward the notion of an imminent threat due to military encirclement by the US that used the nuclear issue as a pretext for undermining Iran.[101] Based on that reasoning, US efforts to drive a rift in Iranian society were supported by unpatriotic reformists and other subversive groups.[102] Conservative media celebrated the electoral victory as a defeat of foreign and domestic enemies and praised the aggressive course taken by the government.[103] Ahmadinejad continued to scoff at what he deemed ineffective sanctions imposed for the purpose of humiliating and suppressing Iran.[104]

Summary and analysis

The years following the breakdown of the Paris Agreement saw a deterioration in conflict communication between the Islamic Republic and the US, or, more generally, the P5+1. To the Ahmadinejad government, the transfer of the nuclear issue to the UN Security Council and the subsequent introduction of sanctions vindicated its views on a securitized identity conflict. In its diagnostic framing, the nuclear program was a question of national honor and fundamentally an expression of Iran's independence. Iran's nuclear program, including enrichment, was its inalienable right. Consequently, any efforts to limit or constrain it, whether originating internationally or even domestically, were securitized as a threat to the Islamic Republic. The neo-fundamentalist government either marginalized IAEA and UN statements, declaring them an expression of US threats, or denounced them as securitizing the nuclear issue. Although some efforts of dialogue by the EU-3 did in fact continue, they were not taken seriously, largely ignored or even ridiculed by Ahmadinejad. Consequently, in the government's prognostic framing there was little room left for other options than for an uncompromising stance of 'resistance'. US negative sanctions and threats conveniently reinforced and fed into Ahmadinejad's confrontational conflict observation.

Yet, if you look at it from the opposite perspective, were there any viable alternatives to sanctions that would sway the neo-fundamentalist government's conflict observation towards a more reconciliatory stance, apart from abandoning all concerns about the nuclear program? In the prevailing securitizing rhetoric, with its emphasis on identity incompatibilities, even such a radical move would have had little prospect of promoting a de-securitizing conflict vision by the government. Yet the discursive field on the nuclear conflict in Iran far from resembled a 'national consensus' on viewing the nuclear program as a question of national honor that de-legitimized any opponent's concerns and rendered any steps towards a compromise as essentially constituting treason. Significant parts of Iranian society considered Ahmadinejad's views extreme and would have been potentially more receptive to a more concessive approach towards Iran's rights. Indeed, in the wake of the escalating conflict and the resulting economic woes, reformists and pragmatists even directly attributed responsibility for sanctions to the government. Of course, Supreme Leader Khamenei seemed inclined to support Ahmadinejad's stance. However, the US hardline approach that emphasized negative sanctions put reformists and pragmatists clearly on the defensive. It failed as conflict communication that could have supported a solution from an Iranian perspective.

6.2.3 'Heroic flexibility': consistent combined sanctions and conflict transformation

When President Barack Obama took office in early 2009, the US on the one hand kept the pressure on Iran due to its non-cooperation on the nuclear issue through negative sanctions. On the other hand, however, Obama returned to positive engagement: Right from the start, the Obama administration emphasized that it would offer to engage in direct dialogue without preconditions – a significant departure from its predecessor that insisted that Iran first suspend its enrichment program.[105] President Obama also clarified that negotiations would have to be result-oriented and that he was ready to swiftly move to tougher negative sanctions if Iran did not take decisive steps and prove the peaceful nature of its nuclear program.[106]

After years of deteriorating relations towards a protracted identity conflict and increasing negative sanctions, Iranian President Ahmadinejad responded to signs of a change in the US approach under newly-elected President Obama by outlining the views of the neo-fundamentalists on the changes required for reconciliation. In response to Obama's call for dialogue and his offer of direct talks between Iran and the US without preconditions, Ahmadinejad emphasized Iran's readiness for comprehensive dialogue – provided that the change in the US approach was not 'tactics' but was based more fundamentally on US 'identity'.[107] One welcome step in that direction, according to Ahmadinejad in a broadcast speech on the 30th anniversary of the revolution, would be to put former US President George W. Bush and his allies in government to trial for the death of a million of people killed due to military interventions in the Middle East.[108] Iran would further wholeheartedly support global nuclear disarmament, starting from 'the top'.[109]

US conflict observation and sanctions against Iran

Contrary to his predecessor, President Obama exercised restraint in securitizing statements regarding Iran and even raised a vision that would transform the dispute into an issue conflict. Crucially, President Obama held firmly to that approach, addressing the people and the government of Iran directly in a call for dialogue on the Iranian New Year in 2009,[110] as well as in all subsequent years of his presidency. However, when early signs of a constructive Iranian response to the incentives offered in P5+1 negotiations in 2009 (Kerr 2009:6) turned out to be illusive, in 2010 the US and its allies introduced unprecedented negative sanctions, systematically targeting forces perceived as obstructive to a solution, as well as key sectors of the Iranian economy. Notably, among them were the energy, shipping and import-export industry, areas deemed well-penetrated by the IRGC (Najdi and Karim 2012; Rizvi 2012). The UN, in June 2010, enacted a massive expansion of its existing sanctions, aimed at excluding the country from the international financial system (SC Resolution 1929). The EU likewise targeted Iran's energy sector and further strengthened trade restrictions (including arms, dual-use goods, energy sector technology).[111] The US followed suit, targeting Iran's energy sector from 2011[112] onwards and its shipping industry in 2013.[113] In 2012, The EU maximized its restrictive measures towards a full embargo of the oil and gas industry and it froze the assets of the Central Bank of Iran and major Iranian commercial banks.[114] The impact of these measures on Iran's oil exports was significant (see Figure 6.1). In addition, severe constraints were imposed on financial transactions as the EU laid down notification and authorization requirements for funds transfers above certain thresholds[115] and banned Iran from SWIFT, an essential system for worldwide electronic payment.[116]

These multilateral moves were accompanied by a further 'weaponization of finance' by the US. The Obama administration stuck to the threefold approach laid down by its predecessor: First, it further tightened sanctions that targeted Iran's

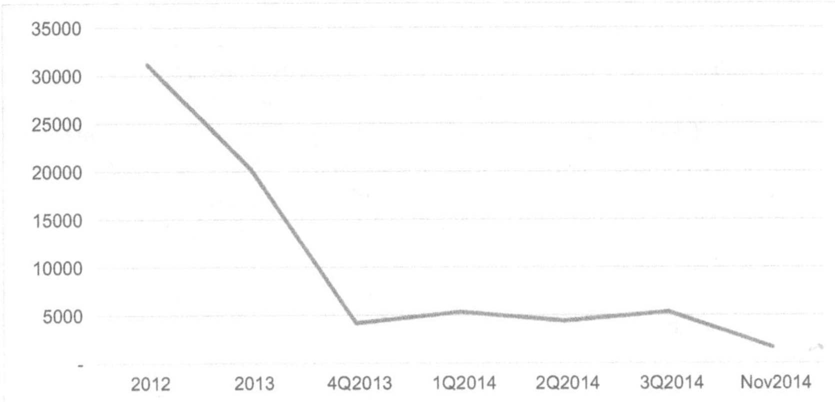

Figure 6.1 Iran oil exports to OECD, in thousand metric tons
Source: OECD Monthly Oil Survey, November 2014

financial sector, especially extraterritorial ones. The Comprehensive Iran Sanctions, Accountability, and Divestment Act (CISADA),[117] introduced in 2010, includes penalties for business relations of any type between Iranian banks and US and international financial institutions. To this end, banks that do business with Iranian partners are barred from maintaining correspondent accounts in the US market. Since such accounts are generally indispensable due to the role of the US dollar in the international financial system, this is an effective means of exclusion. In 2011, the Financial Crimes Enforcement Network (FinCEN) of the US Department of the Treasury designated Iran as a "jurisdiction of primary money laundering concern"[118] under Section 311 of the USA PATRIOT Act, again increasing due diligence requirements, legal and procedural obligations for, and the overall operational risk of, engaging with Iran's financial sector. The designation included the Central Bank of Iran (Bank Markazi).[119] Subsequent Executive Orders targeted sanctions evaders,[120] foreign financial institutions facilitating petroleum sales[121] and vowed to block the assets of banks doing business in rial, Iran's currency.[122]

Second, in its stance against Iran, the US pushed for reinforcing the multilateral control regime that protected the global financial system against money laundering (ML) and the financing of terrorism (FT). Following its depiction from 2008 onwards of Iran as a high risk, non-cooperative country, in 2009 the FATF tightened its stance by calling on all jurisdictions to apply countermeasures against ML and FT risks emanating from Iran, the only country apart from North Korea consistently in that category on the FATF blacklist (the list of so-called "Non-Cooperative Countries or Territories"). Moreover, the FATF tightened the screws on countries with 'continuous strategic AML/CFT deficiencies', among them notably Iran's neighbor Turkey, which was threatened with active countermeasures and membership suspension.[123]

Third, the US extended the enforcement of fines levied on financial institutions in a way that made previous fines appear timidly symbolic. In 2009, Credit Suisse had to pay more than $500m USD for violating sanctions regulations. Three-digit million USD fines were no longer unusual. In 2012, HSBC paid $1.9bn USD. The largest fine thus far for violating US sanctions was levied against BNP Paribas in 2014: $8.9bn USD. To the global financial industry, these fines communicated a zero-tolerance attitude that was difficult to translate into the 'risk-based approach' towards ML and FT risks propagated by regulators and multilateral watchdog-institutions like the FATF (Keatinge 2017). Iran became thoroughly isolated in the global financial system.

At the same time, the US and the P5+1 kept offering positive incentives as part of their vow to engage in dialogue and negotiations. Brief meetings with Iran took place in Istanbul in 2011 and in 2012. The P5+1 continued to offer technical assistance in support of a peaceful nuclear program and trade incentives (Kerr 2009:9f.). In face of persisting deadlock it was, however, at least agreed that technical negotiations be sustained at a lower level. The P5+1 had offered to take a step-by-step approach based on reciprocity.[124] In November 2013, the P5+1 renewed their offer of positive incentives, including a limited de-freezing of assets (4.3bn GBP) and providing a channel for humanitarian goods purchased with frozen oil revenues; suspension of some sanctions on the auto industry, petrochemical exports and gold/precious metals; and a commitment that no additional nuclear-related sanctions would be imposed. In an interim accord that became known as the Joint Plan of Action (JPOA), Iran in return agreed to limit its nuclear program activities and not to engage in plutonium reprocessing activities, accept IAEA safeguards and monitoring.[125] This interim agreement was valid for a limited period of time in order to allow for continuing negotiation on a comprehensive deal. The P5+1 put positive sanctions on the table in form of significant relief in a step-by-step approach.

Sanctions conflict observations in Iran

With Iran's presidential election approaching in mid-2009, Hassan Rouhani pointed out that a possible policy change was unlikely to happen ahead of it.[126] The statement made by the conservative pragmatist reflected the dire disagreements over Iran's foreign policy course among Ahmadinejad and the other contenders and political factions in the presidential election race. Rouhani, who did not run as a candidate in the election but was closely aligned to the reformist foreign policy position, outlined two chronologically consistently opposed views in Iran: One was inclined to seek a solution with the West through dialogue and negotiations and the other one content with confrontation and hostility.[127] Indeed, these two positions became clearly visible between reformists and conservative pragmatists on the one hand and neo-fundamentalist principlists on the other in the election run-up.

Ahmadinejad continued to observe an identity conflict, with Iran defiant of bullying, hegemonic foreign powers that sought to humiliate the country into succumbing and forfeiting its rights.[128] He pointed to the successful resistance of the nation against sanctions.[129] Although the government left the option of dialogue and negotiations on the nuclear issue open,[130] Ahmadinejad's attacks on reformist contenders for being complicit in a 'historic humiliation' that would eventually have brought down the revolution by agreeing to the 'one-sided' and 'oppressive' deal in Paris gave a clear glimpse of their prospect.[131] In his view, the nuclear case was closed anyway.[132] Conservative media supported these lines of reasoning with occasional reports alleging that reformists were colluding with the enemy[133] and observing the US dialogue offer as a plot against Iran.[134]

Apart from Ahmadinejad, Mohsen Rezaei, former commander and 'primary architect' of the IRGC (Wehrey et al. 2009) and now Secretary of the Expediency Council, took part in the presidential election campaign as a moderate conservative alternative to Ahmadinejad. Rezaei's positions on foreign policy and the nuclear issue differed sharply from those of the neo-fundamentalist incumbent. Depicting Ahmadinejad's rhetoric as outlandish and damaging, the system's resilience fortunately kept extremism under control, argued Rezaei. He emphasized a common interest in the security of the region between Iran and the US.[135] Although he sought to continue the nuclear program including uranium enrichment, Rezaei wanted to do so under the auspices of an international consortium and in agreement with the West,[136] supported even by a female foreign minister 'to stand in front of Ms. Clinton'.[137]

On the reformist side, two contenders challenged the observation of the nuclear conflict put forward by Ahmadinejad and proposed a positive response to the 'changed approach' of the US administration. Mehdi Karrubi, former speaker of the parliament, struck a reconciliatory tone, by seeking to de-securitize the nuclear issue and vowing to cooperate with the IAEA and the international community.[138] He denounced the provocative actions of Ahmadinejad, held him responsible for UN sanctions imposed on Iran, the disconcerting state of the economy, and advised the incumbent to "focus on stabilizing the price of tomatoes" rather than fantasizing about being a global leader.[139] Reformist candidate Mir-Hoseyn Mousavi, who was Prime Minister in the 1980s, similarly put forward an observation of the nuclear issue that was more inclined to see it as an issue conflict. In a move to reassure the P5+1, he vowed to engage in dialogue with them in an effort to achieve transparency on the nuclear program and raised the possibility of normalizing the relationship with the US. However, Mousavi was careful to emphasize that there would be no compromise on Iran's rights to nuclear technology and that 'extortion' was unacceptable.[140]

The election ended in an apparent landslide victory for incumbent Ahmadinejad. Although the result was bitterly contested, and protests were held in streets across the country after allegations of voting irregularities,[141] it was ultimately confirmed by the Supreme Leader. Ayatollah Khamenei's reaction leaves little doubt of what conflict observation he subscribed to: The West, Zionists and the British government were responsible for the spread of unrest following the protests that were called upon by 'certain candidates', revealing the enemy's true intentions behind the mask of a 'changed approach' towards Iran.[142] Protests by the reformist 'green movement' were subsequently violently suppressed as agents of the enemy; Mousavi and Karrubi were put under indefinite house arrest.[143]

Despite that fact that Khamenei continued to securitize statements of identity incompatibilities,[144] Iran nevertheless embraced the opportunity that arose in autumn 2009 to engage in dialogue. Amid signs of appreciation (especially among the opposition) that the West was discussing an Iranian proposal and for the US engaging in direct dialogue as recognition of the Islamic Republic's legitimacy,[145] Ahmadinejad boasted of the fruits of his policy that forced the West, which 'ran out of ammunition' in sanctions, into negotiations.[146] Khamenei, who took a more active position in the wake of the 2009 election, suggested familiar 'sinister motives' behind the 'velvet glove' on the outstretched American hand. After the rapid collapse of efforts of dialogue and the stepping up of sanctions against Iran from 2010 onwards, Ahmadinejad condemned 'the colonialist enemy's nuclear pretext' which, he said, was aimed at preventing Iran's cultural rebirth. At the same time, however, he promised that economic/financial sanctions would have no effect: Iran would rely on its own financial resources and award energy sector contracts locally.[147] Head of the Majlis National Security and Foreign Policy Committee Alaeddin Borujerdi denounced the US 'carrot and stick policy' as an 'illegal' effort to cause disunity in Iran.[148]

Negative sanctions targeting Iran's energy and financial sectors provoked defiant public responses from industry representatives and officials. Banking agents claimed that the sanctions had no adverse impact, in part because, as the governor of Bank Markazi stated, Iranian banking assets were pulled out of Europe in anticipation of such moves.[149] When the Central Bank itself became a target, officials dismissed attempts at 'paralyzing' Iran's financial system as ineffective and illegal as Bank Markazi was politically independent.[150] The Islamic Republic sought to counter energy sector sanctions by selling oil in the currency of buyer countries, by replacing international insurance services and by legally challenging the bases of measures against its shipping line.[151] Reports emerged that Iranian businesses sought to circumvent isolation by using close proximity markets such as Turkey and the United Arab Emirates, and resorted to expanding *hawala* structures, informal payment systems (Sadjadpour 2011).[152]

The discursive field around the time of Iran's parliamentary election in 2012 was noteworthy not for a display of disunity between neo-fundamentalists and reformists, but for the absence of the latter. Apparently, many conservatives, too, felt unhappy about the political course the country had taken, domestically and internationally, with conservative principlists continuing to advance a more restrained conflict observation than the neo-fundamentalist government, and criticizing the latter for the country's economic situation.[153] Even the strictly conservative press such as Kayhan, considered close to Khamenei, was critical of the 'extremist' course taken in relation to the nuclear conflict.[154]

In the view of the principlists, sanctions were not just a tool of power advanced against Iran's legitimate nuclear program, but given their tough economic impact, an expression of war against principlists, conspicuously supported by absent reformists.[155] The Kayhan newspaper's portrayal of the Majlis election outcome as a defeat for the Western 'combined strategy' of sanctions represents the conservative principlist and neo-fundamentalist line on the conflict.[156] Ahmadinejad claimed Iran was fighting an economic war against the West that targeted the Iranian people, and not just the IRGC, and that sought to manipulate the 2013 presidential election.[157]

None of the more 'radical' reformist candidates ran in the 2013 presidential election, which instead developed into a contest between moderate pragmatist conservatives, conservative principlists and neo-fundamentalists. Yet almost all candidates agreed that the course of the country in the conflict and the government's economic response had to change, moving away from the provocative, extremist and ignorant positions taken by Ahmadinejad, while insisting on Iran's right to pursue a nuclear program. Mohsen Rezaei, who again ran as a candidate, sought to strike a balance between defiance against 'enemy' sanctions and pledges to change course and engage with the P5+1 in a more constructive way.[158] Beneath the favorable rhetoric, there was still a lack of transparency on the part of the US. Rezaei claimed that instead of openly pursuing regime change, sanctions were 'death by a thousand cuts'. He also wanted to obtain a commitment from the US that a failure in negotiations would not be answered by a military attack. Speaking on the outgoing government, Rezaei commented: "They did not take the economic sanctions seriously. What sort of judgment is this?"[159] This comment underlines his skepticism of passive resistance as a strategy in the conflict.[160] Remarkably, Rezaei also vowed to reverse course, remove the IRGC from the economy[161] and engage in constitutional reform to institutionalize 'freedom'.[162]

To the right of Rezaei were candidates who were critical of the Ahmadinejad government's economic policies and foreign policy style, but less so of the latter's substance. Ali Akbar Velayati, a former foreign minister, emphasized the connection between the economy and foreign policy and vowed to pursue a policy of 'wise resistance': A strong economy requires good foreign policy and successfully tackling the nuclear sanctions issue with the P5+1 in a way that nevertheless preserves Iran's 'dignity'.[163] Mohammad Baqer Ghalibaf, former IRGC air force commander who became mayor of Tehran after Ahmadinejad, perceived the relationship between the economy and foreign policy the other way around: He emphasized religious-national identity and domestic unity as being at the service of 'national interests and security', based on a view of power as exclusively informing foreign policy.[164] Although critical of a confrontational approach, Ghalibaf was pessimistic about finding a quick resolution to the nuclear conflict, which he linked to Iran's 'honour'.[165] Ghalibaf and Velayati were part of the 2+1 conservative candidate coalition along with Gholam Ali Haddad-Adel, who summarized their common position as being against 'the enemy's' machinations of (reformist) sedition and sanctions',[166] to which they had different answers, the most hardline of which being that of the latter. Haddad-Adel called for an 'economy of resistance' against the sanctions imposed by the US given its opposition to Iran's independence.[167] Saeed Jalili, Secretary of the Supreme National Security Council and Iran's chief nuclear negotiator since 2007 and representative of Ahmadinejad's approach, similarly promoted a view of America as being fundamentally opposed to Iran's independence.[168] Jalili vowed resistance and emphasized his opposition to the kind of dialogue pursued under the presidencies of Rafsanjani and Khatami.[169] As an analyst for the newspaper Sharq summarized, Jalili was the man of 'negotiation for the sake of negotiations', taking them as a zero-sum game, who saw 'no place for any kind of compromise with imperialists'.[170]

To the left of principlist and neo-fundamentalist candidates, moderate pragmatist Hassan Rouhani entered the race, his candidacy supported by former presidents Rafsanjani and Khatami, under whom he had served as chief nuclear negotiator. Rouhani pursued a moderate-reformist agenda.[171] Not only was he committed to supporting free speech and opposing censorship, he also emphasized his disagreement with 'extremists'.[172] At campaign events, supporters chanted the names of Mousavi and Karrubi.[173] Dr. Rouhani, Head of the Center for Strategic Research, a think tank, also observed a securitized (nuclear) conflict, but in stark contrast to other candidates, he described the fatal logic of its consequences: "The US and Israel want [Iran's] ties with the world to be governed by security. If we are able to bring the circle of our relations out of the security climate [. . .] it will undoubtedly be in the interests of the people and beneficial to our national interests".[174] Rouhani laid out a path towards de-securitization: He would negotiate with the US, promised to promote greater transparency and trust concerning the nuclear issue, but in return expected the US to recognize the legitimacy of the Islamic Republic and commit to non-interference.[175] Along this reasoning, Rouhani stated that the 'economy of resistance' promoted by Supreme Leader Khamenei means 'economic sustainability', not autarky in isolation.[176]

On 14 June 2013, with an absolute majority, Rouhani was elected president. In his first press conference, he reiterated his agenda to tackle the nuclear issue and his commitment to seeking de-securitization by focusing on common interests and 'overcoming old scars'.[177] Rouhani vowed to fully embrace the continued offers of negotiation made by the P5+1 and in particular offers of dialogue by the US Foreign Minister Javad Zarif described the first meeting between Iran and the P5+1 at the end of September 2013 and the bilateral discussions with the US as 'very constructive' discussions on recognizing Iran's right to 'technology for peaceful purposes including enrichment' and addressing 'concerns at the international level'.[178] The state news agency noted that the US had welcomed the 'change in tone.'[179] Zarif emphasized appreciation for repeated US efforts to initiate dialogue between the US president and his Iranian counterpart that took place on September 29 for the first time since 1979.[180] Rouhani in turn was more reserved, declaring that he had rejected meeting President Obama in person and had emphasized Iran's dissatisfaction with 'unjust sanctions' during the conversation.[181] Presidential advisor Hesamoddin Ashna declared that the Iranian initiative represented the 'last ultimatum' in the nuclear conflict.[182] Endorsed by Supreme Leader Khamenei as 'heroic flexibility', the new approach of the Islamic Republic demonstrated a combination of initiative and engagement with pressure and principle.

The Iranian delegation presented a new proposal that outlined the roadmap for the subsequent resolution of the nuclear conflict: "Within one year of talks between Iran and P5+1, Iran will fully implement two commitments – ensure transparency in its nuclear programme and honour its international commitments. P5+1 will guarantee that all sanctions will be lifted".[183] After further negotiations with the

P5+1, that formula was incorporated as a mutual understanding into the 'Joint Plan of Action' on 24 November 2014. Lauded as a decisive trust-building milestone, it was indeed historic, as it recognized the country's rights, as observed by the Iranian government. Foreign Minister Javad Zarif stated: "The Americans claim that they do not officially recognize Iran's right to enrichment but that they recognize enrichment programmes. This is a stance that a country can have for itself, but what is important for us is what I said: the inalienable right to enrichment has been officially recognized in the NPT. [. . .] [T]he Americans have always had unique interpretations of the international law".[184] From that perspective, the JPOA represented a formal agreement to disagree, and included a clear, binding roadmap that reduced existing sanctions and promised full relief upon resolving an 'unnecessary crisis'.[185] With the interim agreement widely celebrated, by the population because of sanctions relief and by the establishment because of continuing enrichment,[186] the government hence fully embarked on observing an issue conflict, described as a 'win-win game' by Rouhani.[187] Its performative move on the nuclear conflict was cautiously supported by the Supreme Leader.[188]

After several extensions of dialogue under the JPOA, negotiations for a comprehensive deal resulted in a breakthrough in early April 2015.[189] A final agreement on a solution to the conflict over Iran's nuclear program was reached between all parties involved on 14 July 2015 in the Joint Comprehensive Plan of Action (JCPOA).[190] Despite Rouhani praising the nuclear accord as a 'win-win deal',[191] Iranian officials had been careful to keep the issue separate from relations with the US more broadly.[192] Indeed, as Supreme Leader Khamenei noted on the eve of the agreement, Iran's policies would continue to 'differ by 180 degrees' from those of the US, especially towards the region.[193]

Summary and analysis

In the years of President Obama's combined sanctions strategy, conflict observation of the Islamic Republic evolved substantially. The discursive field developed along two clearly opposed poles (see Table 6.2). Neo-fundamentalists, and to a lesser extent principlists referred to the nuclear issue in terms of identity incompatibilities. Following the 2009 election, neo-fundamentalists who supported the Ahmadinejad government continued in their diagnostic framing to posit a defiant

Table 6.2 Iran's discursive field on conflict observation, 2013

Political faction	*Neo-fundamentalists, Principlists*	*Reformists Moderate pragmatists*
Diagnostic framing	Security threat	Risk
Attribution of responsibility	America, Reformist seditionists	Neutral Neo-fundamentalists
Prognostic framing	Resistance	Reconciliation
Conflict observation	Identity incompatibility	Interest incompatibility

Islamic Republic against US oppression and included the reformist 'seditionist' opposition in its securitization. The nuclear issue and sanctions were a means by the US to challenge Iran's independence and hinder its development. Accordingly, they attributed responsibility for the situation to the US and even to 'seditionists'. Based on this reasoning, there was no viable alternative prognostic framing to resistance and confrontation. 'Dialogue' merely seemed to serve the purpose of reiterating fundamental differences.

Reformist and, more cautiously, moderate pragmatist statements represented a markedly different, competing vision as they engaged in observing the nuclear dispute in terms of issue incompatibilities. While in their diagnostic framing they condemned sanctions as unjust and illegitimate, and framed Iran's nuclear ambitions as legitimate, both reformists and pragmatists recognized international concerns and requests for comprehensive checks and transparency. Consequently, in their prognostic framing, reformists and pragmatists emphasized the need for dialogue and negotiations and saw reconciliation on the nuclear issue as the only viable way forward. While maintaining restraint with regard to attributing responsibility, they blasted neo-fundamentalist 'extremists' for the deteriorating crisis. While radical reformists were severely punished for an overly reconciliatory stance that openly challenged conservatives regarding international and domestic affairs, moderate pragmatists led by Rouhani succeeded in artfully walking the tightrope between reconciliation and assertiveness. Rouhani shrewdly pointed to the vicious circle of a securitized conflict and separated the nuclear issue with surgical precision from conflict relations with the US more generally. That way, his government succeeded in de-securitizing the nuclear dispute into an issue conflict while even managing to ensure the support of Supreme Leader Khamenei, who continued to observe relations, with the US (and Israel) in particular, in terms of fundamental identity incompatibilities.

Across the discursive field in Iran, the tightening of negative sanctions was condemned as an unjust response to Iran's legitimate nuclear program. There was less of a consensus about their impact. Neo-fundamentalists disputed that sanctions were an issue economically, feeding into their response to a securitized identity conflict for which they saw reconciliation as pointless. Accordingly, dialogue efforts of the P5+1 and the US proper were not just met with skepticism but viewed as deceptive moves that made compromise a threat. By contrast, moderate pragmatists and reformists clearly viewed offers of dialogue as positive and recognized that there may be legitimate concerns about certain aspects of a nuclear program.

The combined sanctions strategy of the Obama administration clearly succeeded in that it communicated two clear alternatives in conflict development on the nuclear issue. However, the case also demonstrates that sanctions do not simply communicate a definite meaning to a receiver. Their meaning depends on their construction in broader conflict communication and it may vary substantially. Effectively, across the dividing lines of the two main factions, different reference points in observing sanctions became apparent. In disputing any legitimate grounds for the opponent's concerns, neo-fundamentalists blasted sanctions for an infringement of Iran's rights and judged sanctions against *the status quo ante*; to moderate pragmatists and reformists, sanctions relief was a positive reward that was worth the compromise.

Based on sanctions relief and the terms agreed to under the JCPOA, the EU terminated some and suspended other nuclear-related sanctions in the financial, energy and transport sectors; for certain metals and dual-use goods, the EU kept its licensing requirements; proliferation-related activities, war material and ballistic-missile activities remain prohibited under EU law.[194]

The US committed to suspending its secondary sanctions and to offering some limited additional relief through licenses (soft commodities, carpets, aircraft). Primary sanctions, i.e. those applying to US persons and the US financial system, remained in place, with only strict and limited provisions made for the further expansion of trade relations between the US and Iran for non-US entities owned or controlled by US persons. Similarly, any concerns regarding ML and FT risks as administered by the FATF are not part of the JCPOA and have to be addressed separately. The 'weaponization of finance' thus largely remains a contentious issue.

The JCPOA represents a trust-building exercise for the peaceful pursuit by Iran of its nuclear program that goes well beyond the NPT's obligations (Fitzpatrick 2015). It is certainly one of the most sophisticated agreements ever seen in international diplomacy. And it is one of the most remarkable exercises in turning identity conflict communication into an issue conflict on the use of nuclear technology. However, the JCPOA also includes an 'exit' plan for the return to a securitized identity conflict. The agreement contains a so-called 'snapback' provision which essentially means that[195] having exhausted the dispute resolution mechanisms specified in the JCPOA, any of the P5+1 may notify the UN Security Council, which will subsequently vote on the *continuation* of the lifting of sanctions. That is, if the vote is not unanimous, then previously lifted sanctions will automatically be re-imposed. In addition, although the JCPOA states that such action would not have a retroactive effect on contracts signed prior to the date of application, provided that they are consistent with the JCPOA, the US indicated that no grandfathering of existing contracts would be available under US sanctions.[196]

Although the snapback provision seemingly makes it easy to reapply sanctions in the face of an unsatisfactory performance by Iran under the JCPOA, it would in fact amount to a decisive escalation of and deterioration in the conflict, with all its previous downsides and security issues. It is therefore more of a last resort option in an issue conflict with perceived interest incompatibilities. It seems unlikely that minor compliance issues would trigger a snapback. It might become a more likely option if opponents were to revert to observing the nuclear program in terms of a securitized identity conflict.

One of the most sensitive points in terms of conflict observation incorporated into the JCPOA, however, seems to lie in a statement in its preface: "[The parties] anticipate that full implementation of this JCPOA will positively contribute to regional and international peace and security". While the conflict opponents succeeded in meticulously separating the nuclear issue from the broader conflict setting, the JCPOA in its preface re-introduces exactly that connection. If this declaration is not just an expression of hope but observed as a forceful commitment by the parties involved, whether or not the agreement's terms are in fact being honored may turn into a point of contention. The possibility to re-establish a connection between the JCPOA and a broader conflict communication still characterized by profound identity incompatibilities between the US and the Islamic Republic may prove a great liability for the JCPOA's continuing existence.

Notes

1 A major aspect was land reform; significant parts of the clergy were large landowners.
2 E.g. The Washington Post, November 7, 1992, 'US halted nuclear bid by Iran; China, Argentina agreed to cancel technology transfers'.
3 The 'People's Mojahedin Organization of Iran' is a militant resistance organization in exile that is seeking to overthrow the current regime.
4 The White House, President Delivers State of the Union Address, January 29, 2002, available at https://georgewbush-whitehouse.archives.gov/news/releases/2002/01/20020129-11.html
5 For an excellent chronological overview of negative and positive sanctions against Iran from 1990–2009, see Reynolds and Wan (2012) Appendix B.
6 The White House, State of the Union Address, February 2, 2005, available at https://georgewbush-whitehouse.archives.gov/news/releases/2005/02/20050202-11.html
7 US Senate Committee on Foreign Relations, The Nomination of Dr. Condoleezza Rice to be Secretary of State, January 19, 2005, available at www.congress.gov/109/chrg/shrg22847/CHRG-109shrg22847.htm
8 IRNA (Islamic Republic News Agency), February 9, 2003, in BBC: 'Iran entitled to nuclear technology for civilian use – president Khatami'.
9 Akbar Hashemi Rafsanjani, cited in Naji 2008:118f.
10 BBC, August 4, 2003: 'BBC Monitoring Iranian media roundup'.
11 BBC, September 22, 2004: 'Paper analyses stance of key political forces on nuclear crisis'.
12 BBC, August 4, 2003: 'BBC Monitoring Iranian media roundup'.
13 BBC, September 22, 2004: 'Paper analyses stance of key political forces on nuclear crisis'.
14 Parliamentary Q&A, cited in Sharq, August 11, 2004, in BBC, August 18, 2004: 'A fully nuclear session'.
15 Iranian Students News Agency (ISNA), October 12, 2003, in BBC, same date: 'Khatami's brother says Iran responsible for concern over nuclear programme'.
16 ISNA, September 26, 2003, in BBC, same date: 'Prominent reformist says Iran should maintain US-EU rift over nuclear programme'.
17 IRNA, November 30, 2003, in BBC, same date: 'MP calls for expansion of nuclear cooperation with EU'.
18 Kamal Kharrazi, Voice of the Islamic Republic of Iran, September 25, 2003, in BBC, same date: 'Kharrazi, Straw discuss nuclear programme'.
19 Kamal Kharrazi, Voice of the Islamic Republic of Iran, December 5, 2003, in BBC, same date: 'Kharrazi reminds Solana, Patten of time for EU to fulfil commitments'.
20 ISNA, September 26, 2003, in BBC, same date: 'Prominent reformist says Iran should maintain US-EU rift over nuclear programme'; Aftab-e Yazd, November 10, 2004, in BBC, November 12, 2004: 'Iranian reformist warns about nuclear case referral to UN Security Council'.

21 BBC, September 22, 2004: 'Paper analyses stance of key political forces on nuclear crisis'.
22 ISNA, October 17, 2003, in BBC, same date: 'Security committee chairman says Iran willing to open bases to inspectors'.
23 SOUCE R1.
24 Hassan Rouhani on Iranian TV, October 16, 2003, in BBC, October 19, 2003: 'media Roundup'.
25 Entekhab, October 18, 2003, ibid.
26 IRNA, December 19, 2003, in BBC, same date: 'Rafsanjani warns against blackmailing Iran over additional protocol'.
27 Shargh, June 30, 2004, in BBC, July 2, 2004: 'Rafsanjani warns of withdrawing from NPT if pressures continue'.
28 Fars News Agency, October 12, 2003, in BBC, same date: 'One hundred MPs sign letter to Annan to say NPT lacks "credibility"'; Jomhuri-ye Eslami, in BBC, October 19, 2003: 'media roundup'.
29 ISNA, September 29, 2003, in BBC, September 30, 2003: 'Khamenei's representative lambastes EU, rejects NPT'.
30 ISNA, November 21, 2004, in BBC, November 23, 2004: 'Failure to close Iran nuclear file at IAEA risks Paris deal'.
31 Jomhuri-ye Eslami, September 25, 2003, in BBC, same date: 'Leader's advisor says Iran will not be pressured'.
32 Zanjan Ra'fat Bayat, cited in Fars News Agency, November 7, 2004, in BBC media roundup, November 9, 2004; Kayhan, March 16, 2005, in BBC, April 1, 2005: 'Columnist sees "not much reason" to continue nuclear talks'.
33 Ayatollah Sayyid Ali Khamenei, Leader's Address to Education Ministry Officials, July 17, 2002, available at http://english.khamenei.ir/news/159/Leader-s-Address-to-Education-Ministry-Officials; Khamenei: 'Leader's Address to Government Officials', August 6, 2003; accessed March 23, 2017.
34 VIRI (VIRI) Network 1, January 13, 2004, in BBC, January 14, 2004: 'Khatami criticized his opponents for describing reformists as American agents'.
35 E.g. Iranian Labour News Agency (ILNA), January 11, 2004, in BBC, same date: 'Senior reformist says "coup" shaping next Majlis'.
36 New York Times, March 24, 2005: 'Nuclear accord eludes Iran and Europeans'; IRNA, April 20, 2005, in BBC, same date: 'Iran prods Europeans for progress in nuclear talks'; see also Hassan Rouhani, in Kayhan, July 26, 2005, in BBC July 31, 2005: 'Nuclear negotiator says Europeans have not fulfilled commitments'.
37 Etemaad, February 5, 2005, in BBC, same date: 'Iran reacts to president Bush's state of Union address'.
38 Voice of the Islamic Republic of Iran, March 12, 2005, in BBC, same date: 'European "inflexibility" in nuclear talks due to US pressure'; Jomhuri-ye Eslami, Editorial, March 16, 2005: 'Recap of Nuclear Negotiations', in BBC, same date: 'Conservative paper sees US behind European demands at IAEA'.
39 IRNA, May 11, 2005, in BBC, same date: 'Mo'in signs up for Iran's presidential election'; Mardom-Salari, April 30, 2005, in BBC, same date: 'Reviewing presidential candidates' positions on relations with US'.
40 IRNA, May 24, 2005, in BBC, same date: 'Iran says still waiting for Europe's positive move'.
41 Former speaker of the parliament and presidential candidate Mehdi Karrubi, cited in IRNA, June 8, 2005, in BBC, same date: 'Candidate in Iran presidential election says US hostile to Islamic world'.
42 IRNA, May 11, 2005, in BBC, same date: 'Rafsanjani says continuation of Iran-EU3 dialogue "best option"'.
43 IRNA, June 8, 2005, in BBC, same date: 'Presidential candidate Larijani says Iran "hard goal to attain" for US'.

44 Javan, January 25, 2005, in BBC, February 2, 2005: 'Psychological warfare to escape failure'; Etemaad, February 8, 2005, in BBC, same date: 'Etemaad's analysis of America's dual policies towards Iran: America's new game'; Voice of the Islamic Republic of Iran, March 12, 2005, in BBC, same date: 'US offer of economic incentives "mischievous plan".
45 VIRI Network 1, June 2, 2005, in BBC, June 3, 2005: 'Presidential candidate Larijani calls for nuclearization of Iran'.
46 Fars News Agency, June 1, 2005, in BBC, same date: 'Iran presidential candidate stresses indigenization of nuclear technology'.
47 In a poll by IRNA, Ahmadinejad scored 1.2 per cent, March 11, 2005, in BBC, same date: 'Iranian opinion poll puts former president in election lead'. In a comparison of right-wing candidates by Iranian Students Polling Agency, Ahamdinejad came in third place with 8 per cent, behind Rafsanjani (52per cent) and Ahmad Tavakkoli (18per cent), and a poll by Fars put Ahamdinejad in fifth place at 5 per cent, in BBC, May 19, 2005: 'Opinion polls on presidential election move to the Internet'.
48 BBC Monitoring Middle East, May 17, 2005: 'Ahmadinezhad backed by right-wing political group Abadgaran'.
49 IRNA, June 8, 2005, in BBC, same date: 'Presidential candidate Ahmadinezhad says use of nuclear technology Iran's right'; VIRI Network 1, June 7, 2005, in BBC, same date: 'Iranian presidential candidate says ties with USA not a key issue'.
50 Islamic Republic of Iran News Network (IRINN), June 26, 2005, in BBC, same date: 'Iran to consider national interests in nuclear talks'.
51 Sharq, July 14, 2005, in BBC, same date: 'The elections do not influence talks'.
52 IRNA, August 10, 2005, in BBC, same date: 'Iranian statement at IAEA session'.
53 IRNA, September 12, 2005, in BBC, September 13, 2005: 'There is no legal basis for sending Iran's nuclear file to UN'; IRNA, September 16, 2005, in BBC, same date: 'Ahmadinezhad stresses Iran's right to acquire nuclear fuel cycle'.
54 IRINN, September 20, 2005, in BBC, same date: 'Iranian security chief holds news conference on nuclear programme'.
55 Etemaad, in BBC, September 21, 2005: 'Iran press: Paper alleges nuclear apartheid'.
56 IRNA, September 15, 2005, in BBC, same date: 'Iran ready to transfer nuclear technology to Islamic states'.
57 E.g. Reuters, October 17, 2007: 'Bush: Threat of World War III if Iran goes nuclear'.
58 US Department of State Archive, Press Conference on Iran, May 31, 2006, available at https://2001-2009.state.gov/secretary/rm/2006/67103.htm
59 BBC News, April 18, 2006: 'Bush keeps Iran military option'.
60 US President George W. Bush, State of the Union Address 2006, 2007, 2008.
61 Germany not only possesses great political weight in the EU but is Iran's biggest trading partner (Jones 2007).
62 Federal Register, Vol. 70, No. 250, December 30, 2005, Department of State [Public Notice 5257].
63 The term was also coined by Bremmer and Kupchan (2015).
64 US Treasury, Press Center, Treasury Cuts Iran's Bank Saderat Off From US Financial System', September 9, 2006, available at www.treasury.gov/press-center/press-releases/Pages/hp87.aspx
65 US Treasury, Press Center, Iran's Bank Sepah Designated by Treasury, January 9, 2007, available at www.treasury.gov/press-center/press-releases/Pages/hp219.aspx; US Treasury, Press Center, Fact Sheet: Designation of Iranian Entities and Individuals for Proliferation Activities and Support for Terrorism, October 27, 2007, available at www.treasury.gov/press-center/press-releases/Pages/hp644.aspx
66 US Treasury, Press Center, Treasury Revokes Iran's U-Turn License, November 6, 2008, available at www.treasury.gov/press-center/press-releases/Pages/hp1257.aspx
67 EU, June 23, 2008, 'Council decision 2008/475/EC'.

68 Interview with Ali Larijani on Iranian TV News Channel, February 1, 2006, in BBC, February 2, 2006: 'Nuclear negotiator's press conference in Tehran'; Newspaper Iran, February 1, 2006, in BBC, February 3, 2006: 'Conservative activist lauds national consensus on nuclear issue'.
69 Saeed Barzin, BBC, November 13, 2007: 'Disagreement over Iran's "nuclear spy" flares up among senior leaders'.
70 Aftab-e Yazd, January 28, 2006, in BBC, February 1, 2006: 'Judiciary official says West trying to intimidate Iran'.
71 IRNA, February 19, 2006, in BBC, same date: 'Nuclear row can be settled if EU recognizes Iran's right'.
72 IRINN, February 1, 2006, in BBC, same date: 'Larijani says Iran will not back down under pressure'.
73 Interview with Iranian TV Channel Two, January 31, 2006, in BBC, February 1, 2006: 'Iranian minister threatens to end nuclear cooperation if case referred to UN'.
74 IRNA, February 6, 2006, in BBC, same date: 'Iranian envoy says IAEA resolution issued under political pressure'.
75 Speech of President Ahmadinejad, Iranian TV News Channel, February 1, 2006, in BBC, same date: 'Iranian president defiant on nuclear issue, Bush criticism'.
76 Etemaad, February 6, 2006, in BBC, February 12, 2006: 'President "ordered" end to cooperation with IAEA'.
77 Siyasat-e Ruz, July 15, 2006, in BBC, July 18, 2006: 'European incentive package has been opened: Diminutive incentives, repetition of groundless threats'; ISNA, August 5, 2006, in BBC, August 6, 2006: 'Former nuclear chief says five-plus-one group's proposal one-sided'.
78 In IRNA, July 31, 2006, in BBC, same date: 'UN envoy deplores UNSC resolution against nuclear programme'.
79 Aftab-e Yazd , August 1, 2006, in BBC, August 5, 2006: 'Majlis deputy for Tehran: Iran will reconsider its policies'; Aftab-e Yazd, August 6, 2006, in BBC, August 8, 2006: 'Member of majlis national security committee: Securitizing Iran's nuclear dossier wrong, illegal decision'.
80 Mehr News Agency, December 13, 2006, in BBC, same date: 'Nuclear issue excuse for Western countries' enmity towards Iran'; Ahmadinejad speech on Iranian TV News Channel, December 19, 2006, in BBC, December 20, 2006: 'Iran president warns EU against hostility towards Iranian nation'; ISNA, December 21, 2006, in BBC, same date: 'Tehran to give proportionate response to any anti-Iran resolution'; BBC, December 27, 2006: 'Iranians debate and respond to UN sanctions'.
81 VIRI Network 1, in BBC, December 24, 2006: 'Iran president says Tehran not scared of "frowning faces"'.
82 Al-Sharq (Qatar), March 14, 2006, in BBC, March 16, 2006: 'Iran not to give in to pressure, go back on nuclear programme – Larijani'; Ahmadinejad on March 15, 2006 on Yazd Provincial TV, in BBC, March 18, 2006: 'Iranian president rejects "hollow" threats'; IRNA, March 25, 2006, in BBC, same date: 'Iran not to give up demands under any sanction, threat – foreign minister'.
83 Khorasan Provincial TV, March 21, 2006, in BBC, March 22, 2006: 'Iran supreme leader calls for Persian Gulf defence pact, plays down sanctions'.
84 Fars, March 11, 2006, in BBC, same date: 'Iran to start next enrichment phase'. IRNA, March 28, 2006, in BBC, same date: 'Iran's atomic organization told to limit cooperation with UN agency'.
85 IRNA, October 24, 2008, in BBC, same date: 'Iran bank condemns US sanctions, says will lodge complaint'.
86 Voice of the Islamic Republic of Iran, September 16, 2006, in BBC, same date: 'Iran to convert part of its dollar reserves to other currencies'; IRNA, November 29, 2006, in BBC, same date: 'Iranian bank adopts euro to "thwart" US sanctions'.

87 ISNA, March 29, 2007, in BBC, same date: 'Sanctions will not affect Iran's economy – Central Bank governor'.
88 ISNA, April 10, 2007, in BBC, May 12, 2007: 'Central bank chief calls Iran banks proper and legal'.
89 Saeed Barzin, BBC Monitoring, November 5, 2007: 'Disagreement over impact of sanctions on Iran'.
90 Etemaad, June 12, 2007, in BBC, June 14, 2007: 'Economic experts criticise government policies'.
91 Yeni Musavat (Baku), February 14, 2008, in BBC, February 18, 2008: 'Iran launders money through Azerbaijan'.
92 Aftab-e Yazd, March 5, 2008, in BBC, March 6, 2008: 'Top power in reporting news'.
93 Etemaad, March 17, 2007, in BBC, March 31, 2007: 'US, power bloc'.
94 Saeed Barzin, BBC, December 27, 2006: 'Iranians debate and respond to UN sanctions'; Etemaad, January 27, 2007, in BBC, January 28, 2007: 'Ex-ministers criticise government's nuclear, economic policies'; Etemaad, February 20, 2007, in BBC, February 25, 2007: 'Party criticises Iran's nuclear policies, urges return to "detente"'; Advar News Website, April 11, 2007, in BBC, April 12, 2007: 'Two questions for Ayatollah Khamene'I'; Aftab-e Yazd, January 5, 2008, in BBC, January 9, 2008: 'Neither government nor parliament, just the principle-ists!'.
95 ISNA, November 22, 2007, in BBC, November 27, 2007: 'Rowhani: Societies that make up enemies always fail'.
96 Radio Goftegu, January 3, 2008, in BBC, January 7, 2008: 'Radio dialogue broadcasts discussion with strategists on ties with US'.
97 Voice of the Islamic Republic of Iran, September 22, 2006, in BBC, September 24, 2006: 'Iran keen to negotiate, US seeks mischief'; VIRI Network 1, in BBC, December 31, 2006: 'Senior cleric says UN resolution on Iran "dangerous"'; IRINN, in BBC, November 30, 2007: 'West ought to talk to Iran and stop "harassment" and "threats"'.
98 Saeed Barzin, BBC, March 17, 2008: 'Iran 2008 elections: Were they free and fair?'.
99 Etemaad, January 24, 2008, in BBC, January 26, 2006: 'Why object?'.
100 Etemaad, February 7, 2008, in BBC, February 12, 2008: 'The great absentees of election'.
101 Radio Goftegu, January 3, 2008, in BBC, January 7, 2008: 'Radio Dialogue broadcasts discussion with strategists on ties with US'.
102 Kayhan, January 13, 2008, in BBC, January 13, 2008: 'Ebrahim Yazdi: Reformists like us very much'; Iran Newspaper, January 13, 2008, in BBC, January 14, 2008: 'Reasons for America's support for some political groups, and the need for action'; Kayhan, February 20, 2008, in BBC, February 22, 2008: 'Soft assassination; squads and targets'.
103 Resalat, December 17, 2007, in BBC, December 20, 2007: 'A look at the final declaration of the tenth congress of the participation party on the Islamic republic of Iran's foreign policy'; Iran Newspaper, March 15, 2008, in BBC, March 18, 2008: 'Correct resolve'.
104 VIRI Network 1, December 27, 2008, in BBC, December 29, 2008: West disappointed in its anti-Iran sanctions'.
105 The Guardian, January 21, 2009: 'Barack Obama: Administration willing to talk to Iran "without preconditions"'.
106 The White House, Office of the Press Secretary, Remarks by the president on the meeting of the P5 plus 1 regarding Iran, October 1, 2009, available at https://obamawhitehouse.archives.gov/the-press-office/remarks-president-meeting-p5-plus-1-regarding-iran
107 Interview on VIRI Network 1, February 17, 2009, in BBC: 'Change in US approach entails changes in its principles'.
108 VIRI Network 1, February 10, 2009, in BBC: 'President says Iran to become "genuine superpower"'.
109 IRINN, April 9, 2009, in BBC, same date: 'Iran says nuclear disarmament should start from "the top"'.

110 Available at YouTube https://youtu.be/HY_utC-hrjI; accessed March 22, 2016.
111 EU, July 26, 2010: 'Council decision 2010/413/CFSP'; EU, October 25, 2010: 'Council regulation 961/2010'.
112 US Executive Order 13590, November 21, 2011.
113 US Congress, Public Law 112–239, January 1, 2013: 'Iran freedom and counter-proliferation act of 2012'.
114 EU, January 23, 2012: 'Council decision 2012/35/CFSP'; EU, October 15, 2012: 'Council decision 2012/612/CFSP'.
115 EU, March 23, 2012: 'Council regulation 267/2012'.
116 EU, March 15, 2012: 'Council decision 2012/152/CFSP'.
117 US Congress, July 1, 2010: 'Public law 111–195'.
118 US Treasury, Press Center, November 18, 2011: 'Fact sheet: New sanctions on Iran'; Full FinCEN Finding, available at www.treasury.gov/press-center/press-releases/Documents/Iran311Finding.pdf
119 US Congress, December 31, 2011: 'National defense authorization act fiscal year 2012, sec. 1245'.
120 US Executive Order 13608, May 1, 2012.
121 US Executive Order 13622, July 30, 2012.
122 US Executive Order 13645, June 3, 2012.
123 FATF Public Statement, Rome, June 22, 2012; FATF, Paris, October 19, 2012: 'Statement on Turkey'.
124 BBC News, April 15, 2012: 'Iran nuclear talks in Istanbul "constructive".'
125 Joint Plan of Action, Geneva, November 24, 2013, available at www.treasury.gov/resource-center/sanctions/Programs/Documents/jpoa.pdf; accessed March 15, 2017.
126 Press TV, March 5, 2009, in BBC, same date: 'Iranian official expects no change in Iran-USA ties until after polls'.
127 Aftab-e Yazd, February 14, 2009, in BBC, February 18, 2009: 'Rowhani: We do not welcome policy of continued hostility between Iran and America'.
128 IRNA, May 30, 2009, in BBC, same date: 'Iranian nation will never yield to "bullying powers"'; Press TV, May 30, 2009, in BBC, May 31, 2009: 'Iran not to bow to foreign "hegemony"'.
129 Voice of the Islamic Republic of Iran, May 18, 2009, in BBC: 'Iran president plays down possible petrol sanction'; VIRI Network 1, May 25, 2009, in BBC: 'President emphasizes Iran's achievements'.
130 Mehr, April 22, 2009, in BBC, same date: 'Iran officially welcomes nuclear talks with 5+1'.
131 Radio address, Voice of the Islamic Republic of Iran, May 22, 2009, in BBC: 'Iran president slams ex-government nuclear policy'.
132 VIRI Network 1, May 25, 2009, in BBC: 'Iran president says nuclear case closed'.
133 E.g. Kayhan, December 8, 2008, in BBC, March 4, 2009: 'Five eventful years'.
134 Kayhan, February 4, 2009, in BBC, June 23, 2009: 'What is not being seen'; Kayhan, May 24, 2009, in BBC, May 26, 2009: 'Please believe that we do not believe!'.
135 Fars, May 4, 2009, in BBC, May 6, 2009: 'Iran top council secretary explains his decision to contest poll'.
136 IRINN, May 27, 2009, in BBC: 'Iran candidate Reza'i pledges to continue uranium enrichment'.
137 VIRI Network 2, in BBC, June 1, 2009: 'Iran candidate Reza'i says likely to appoint female foreign minister'.
138 Discussion on VIRI Network 1, in BBC, May 26, 2009: 'Iran reformist candidate Karrubi says supports free media'.
139 Press TV, in BBC, May 27, 2009: 'Iranian candidate says Ahmadinezhad "ignorant" of problems'.
140 Press TV website, March 5, 2009, in BBC, same date: 'Ex-premier slams president's economic policies'; Press TV Website, May 29, 2009, in BBC, same date: 'Reformist candidate ready for nuclear talks with major powers'; Qods Website, May 31, 2009,

in BBC, same date: 'Musavi in a press conference with the foreign media: America should estimate our red lines accurately'.

141 Press TV, in BBC, June 17, 2009: 'Musavi urges probe into alleged ballot rigging'; VIRI Network 2, in BBC, June 18, 2009: 'Reza'i urges authorities to respect people, take complaints seriously'.

142 Khamenei, Friday Prayer Sermons, Islamic Republic of Iran News Network, in BBC, June 19, 2009: 'Western intelligence services, Zionists behind post-election disturbances'.

143 The Green Voice of Freedom Website, in BBC, February 28, 2011, available at http://en.irangreenvoice.com.

144 Khamenei, March 21, 2009, available at http://english.khamenei.ir/news/1076/Leader-s-Speech-in-Mashhad; September 10, 2009, available at http://english.khamenei.ir/news/1179/The-Leader-s-View-of-Global-Arrogance; September 20, 2009, available at http://english.khamenei.ir/news/1267/Leader-Rejects-Nuclear-Allegations; accessed November 21, 2016.

145 Etemaad, September 14, 2009, in BBC, September 23, 2009: 'Meeting in the 90th minute: Meeting at the earliest opportunity'; chief nuclear negotiator Said Jalili, IRINN, October 1, 2009, in BBC: 'Iranian nuclear negotiator says 5+1 talks "positive"'; Jomhuri-ye Eslami, October 8, 2009, in BBC, October 13, 2009: 'Negotiations with America, why and how!'; Aftab-e Yazd, October 26, 2009, in BBC, same date: 'Continued uranium enrichment in Russia; Ahmadinezhad government's proposal or Westerners' ploy?'.

146 IRINN, October 29, 2009, in BBC, October 30, 2009: 'Iran president says conditions ripe for nuclear cooperation'; see also Javan, October 28, 2009: 'From humiliation in Sa'dabad to strength in Geneva'. Ahmadinejad interview in VIRI East Azarbayjan Provincial TV, November 20, 2009, in BBC, November 22, 2009: 'Ahmadinezhad says West has "run out of ammo" against Iran'.

147 Jomhuri-ye Eslami, May 30, 2010, in BBC, June 4, 2010: 'Iran to neutralize sanctions: Allocating and allotting of 70bn dollars in oil industry'; IRINN, June 15, 2010, in BBC: 'Iran president hails major contracts to develop South Pars gas field'; IRINN, June 28, 2010, in BBC, July 1, 2010: 'Iran president outlines conditions for nuclear talks'; IRINN, July 3, 2010, in BBC: 'Iran president pledges "bloody nose" to the West'; IRINN, July 5, 2010, in BBC: 'President says sanctions aimed at preventing Iran's cultural rebirth'.

148 VIRI Network 2, June 19, 2010, in BBC: 'West's "carrot, stick policy" against Iran, "rusty ploy"'.

149 Javan, February 4, 2010, in BBC, same date: 'Failure of psychological war on Iranian banks'; Fars, August 27, 2010, in BBC, same date: 'Assets of Iranian banks pulled out of Europe'.

150 IRNA, September 11, 2011, in BBC, same date: 'Official dismisses US sanctions on Iran's Central Bank'; IRNA, November 28, 2011, in BBC, same date: 'Governor says sanctions against Iran's Central Bank "illegal, irrational"'.

151 Jaam-e Jam, August 7, 2010, in BBC, August 10, 2010: 'Iran's three complains against shipping sanctions'; Jaam-e Jam, August 14, 2010, in BBC, same date: 'Possibility of oil deals with the currency of buyer countries'; Fars, December 23, 2012, in BBC, same date: 'Oil Minister: Iran launches international tankers insurance company'.

152 E.g. Today's Zaman (Turkey), October 16, 2011, in BBC, October 17, 2011: 'Iran trying to break sanctions through Turkey'; Today's Zaman, April 25, 2012, in BBC, same date: 'Iranian banks seek licenses in Turkey'.

153 Majlis Speaker Ali Larijani, Press TV, January 12, 2012, in BBC, same date: 'Speaker says Iran ready to resolve nuclear issue if P5+1 changes approach'; Mohsen Rezaei, Tabnak News Website, January 25, 2012, in BBC, January 26, 2012: '"Lack of expertise", "ignorance" led to economic turmoil'; IRNA, January 25, 2012, in BBC, same date: 'Iranian speaker says sanctions "opportunity" for government'; Mehr, February

25, 2012, in BBC, same date: 'Iran Speaker says government's management of economy "weak"'.

154 Analysis in Mardom Salari (Newspaper), January 21, 2012, in BBC, February 2, 2012: 'The silence of the government in the face of the economic chaos'.

155 Hamshari (Newspaper), January 2, 2012, in BBC, January 10, 2012: 'Sanctioning Bank-e Markazi is the start of America's psychological war against the principlists in the elections'; Manuchehr Mottaki, ISNA, January 31, 2012, in BBC, same date: 'USA to use parliamentary polls to increase pressure on Iran'; Parviz Soruri, ISNA, February 3, 2012, in BBC, same date: 'MP warns principle-ists against reformists' move to damage unity'; Siyasat-e Ruz, February 7, 2012, in BBC, February 18, 2012: 'Principlist front's poll list shows division'.

156 Kayhan, March 15, 2012, in BBC, March 27, 2012: 'Who is the year's big loser?'.

157 Ahmadinejad, VIRI Network 1, September 4, 2012, in BBC, September 8, 2012: 'President says Iran fighting full-blown war against West'; ISNA, July 17, 2012, in BBC, same date: 'Western sanctions aimed at manipulating 2013 elections'; Javan, August 12, 2010, in BBC, August 17, 2010: '"Fruitless efforts to weaken the Corps'.

158 VIRI South Khorasan Provincial TV, May 17, 2013, in BBC, May 25, 2013: 'Roundup of South Khorasan Province Friday prayer sermons'; Press TV, May 24, 2013, in BBC, same date: 'Presidential hopeful Reza'i says will continue talks with P5+1 if elected'; Jam-e Jaam, June 3, 2013, in BBC: 'West prolongs nuclear talks to weaken Iran through sanctions'.

159 VIRI Network 1, May 25, 2013, in BBC: 'Iran presidential candidate promises reforms in government, economy'.

160 VIRI Network 1, June 7, 2013, in BBC: 'Candidate slams "economy of resistance" doctrine'.

161 Sharq, June 3, 2013, in BBC, same date: 'I will work together with the leader to remove the guard corps from the economy'.

162 VIRI Network 4, June 11, 2013, in BBC: 'Reza'i says nuclear talks "priority"'.

163 Press TV, May 17, 2013, in BBC, same date: 'Presidential candidate vows to resolve Iran nuclear dispute with West'; Sharq, June 1, 2013, in BBC, June 5, 2013: 'Foreign policy and the presidential candidates'.

164 VIRI Network 4, June 9, 2013, in BBC: 'Candidate stresses role of diplomacy in foreign relations'.

165 Press TV, April 24, 2013, in BBC, same date: 'Fiery rhetoric in foreign policy will do more harm than good'; Jaam-e Jam, June 1, 2013, in BBC, June 2, 2013: 'Iranian presidential candidate on economic, foreign policy, nuclear plans'.

166 Baztab-e Emruz, December 17, 2012, in BBC, January 1, 2013: 'Haddad confirmed the alliance of the three'.

167 VIRI Network 1, June 7, 2013, in BBC: 'Iran election third TV debate on foreign, domestic policy: Haddad-Adel'.

168 IRINN, May 16, 2013, in BBC: 'Iran official speaks about nuclear talks, security in region'.

169 VIRI Network 1, June 7, 2013, in BBC: 'Iran election third TV debate on foreign, domestic policy'.

170 Farangis Bayat, Sharq, June 1, 2013: 'Foreign policy and the presidential candidates'.

171 Interview in Sharq, June 12, 2013, in BBC, June 14, 2013: 'I will certainly change the country's condition'.

172 Press TV, April 22, 2013, in BBC, same date: 'National interests redline for Iran'; VIRI Network 2, May 27, 2013, in BBC: 'Iran's moderate contender vows to resolve nuclear issue'.

173 Mehr News Agency, June 1, 2013, in BBC, June 2, 2013: 'Candidate's supporters chant names of Iran opposition leaders'.

174 Sharq, 'I will certainly change the country's condition'; also in VIRI Network 1, May 28, 2013, in BBC: 'Iran moderate candidate calls for improved foreign relations'.

175 VIRI Network 2: 'Iran's moderate contender vows to resolve nuclear issue'; VIRI Network 1, June 7, 2013, in BBC, June 9, 2013: 'Iran election third TV debate on foreign, domestic policy: Hasan Rowhani'; IRNA, June 8, 2013, in BBC, same date: 'Iran hardliner cleric slams presidential hopefuls open to US ties'; IRINN, June 17, 2013, in BBC: 'Iran to show more transparency on nuclear activities'.
176 IRINN, June 3, 2013, in BBC: 'Iranian presidential candidate vows to ease restrictions on culture'.
177 IRINN, June 17, 2013, in BBC, June 18, 2013: 'President-elect hopes for "constructive cooperation" with world'.
178 Press TV, September 27, 2013, in BBC, same date: 'Iran hopes to resolve nuclear issue in "timely fashion"'.
179 IRNA, September 26, 2013, in BBC, September 27, 2013: 'Foreign minister confirms "brief" talk with US counterpart'.
180 IRNA, September 29, 2013, in BBC, same date: 'US-Iran presidential phone call, "thorn in eye of ill-wishers"'.
181 FARS, October 2, 2013, in BBC, same date: 'Iran president reports to parliament'.
182 VIRI Network 2, September 30, 2013, in BBC, October 1, 2013: 'Iran president advisor says talks with US "last ultimatum"'.
183 Reported by Iranian news website Nuclear Iran, September 27, 2013, in BBC, same date: 'Iran announces new proposal on its nuclear programme'.
184 IRINN, November 24, 2013, in BBC, same date: 'Foreign minister expresses optimism on sanctions relief'; President Rouhani, cited in IRINN, November 24, 2013, in BBC, same date: 'Iran president hails historic nuclear deal'.
185 Zarif, cited by Press TV, November 24, 2013, in BBC, same date: 'Nuclear deal opportunity to end "unnecessary crisis"'; IRINN, 'Foreign minister expresses optimism'.
186 ISNA, November 20, 2013, in BBC, November 21, 2013: 'Poll shows Iranians highly back nuclear negotiating team'; Fars, November 25, 2013, in BBC, same date: 'Nuclear deal "cracked structure of sanctions" – Iran atomic chief'.
187 VIRI Network 1, November 20, 2013, in BBC: 'Iran seeks "win-win game" in nuclear talks'.
188 IRINN, November 20, 2013, in BBC, same date: 'Iran supreme leader backs president's policies'; Fars, November 24, 2013, in BBC, same date: 'Supreme leader terms nuclear agreement "success"'.
189 IRINN, April 2, 2015, in BBC, same date: 'Iran and P5+1 issue joint statement hailing "decisive step" in nuclear talks'.
190 UN SC Resolution 2231, Annex A, July 20, 2015: 'Joint Comprehensive Plan of Action (JCPOA)'.
191 VIRI Network 1, July 14, 2015, in BBC: 'Iran president welcomes "historic" nuclear deal'.
192 E.g. Foreign Minister Zarif, cited in IRINN, April 2, 2015, in BBC, same date: 'Nuclear deal has nothing to do with Iran-US ties'.
193 IRINN, July 18, 2015, in BBC, same date: 'No change in Iran's policy towards USA after nuclear deal – Supreme Leader'; Khamenei's Comments in a Speech on August 17, 2015, available at http://english.khamenei.ir/news/2109/Leader-s-speech-to-members-of-Ahlul-Bayt-World-Assembly-and-Islamic; accessed March 25, 2017.
194 EU, October 18, 2015: 'Council regulations 2015/1861 and 2015/1862'; Council Decision (CFSP) 2015/1863.
195 JCPOA, pp. 19–20.
196 US Treasury, Office of Foreign Assets Control, FAQs relating to the lifting of certain US sanctions under the Joint Comprehensive Plan of Action (JCPOA) on implementation day, January 16, 2016, available at www.treasury.gov/resource-center/sanctions/Programs/Documents/jcpoa_faqs.pdf

Bibliography

Alam, Shah. (2000) The Changing Paradigm of Iranian Foreign Policy under Khatami. *Strategic Analysis* 24: 1629–1653.

Alexander, Kern. (2009) *Economic Sanctions: Law and Public Policy*. London: Palgrave Macmillan.

Alfoneh, Ali. (2008) The Revolutionary Guards' Role in Iranian Politics. *Middle East Quarterly*. Available at: www.meforum.org/1979/the-revolutionary-guards-role-in-iranian-politics.

Arjomand, Said Amir. (1988) *The Turban for the Crown: The Islamic Revolution in Iran*. Oxford: Oxford University Press.

Bahgat, Gawdat. (2006) Nuclear Proliferation: The Islamic Republic of Iran. *Iranian Studies* 39: 307–327.

Bakhash, Shaul. (1985) *The Reign of the Ayatollahs: Iran and the Islamic Revolution*. London: Tauris.

Beeman, William O. (2008) *The Great Satan vs. the Mad Mullahs: How the United States and Iran Demonize Each Other*. Chicago: University of Chicago Press.

Bremmer, Ian, and Cliff Kupchan. (2015) *Top Risks 2015*. Eurasia Group. http://www.eurasiagroup.net/

Burr, William. (2009) A Brief History of U.S.-Iranian Nuclear Negotiations. *Bulletin of the Atomic Scientists* 65: 21–34.

Byrne, Malcolm. (2013) *CIA Confirms Role in 1953 Iran Coup*. Washington, DC: The Natioal Security Archive, George Washington University. Available at: http://nsarchive.gwu.edu/NSAEBB/NSAEBB435/.

Chubin, Shahram, and Robert S. Litwak. (2003) Debating Iran's Nuclear Aspirations. *The Washington Quarterly* 26: 99–114.

Coakley, Robert W. (1990) *The Persian Corridor as a Route for Aid to the USSR*. Center of Military History, Washington, D.C.: US Army.

Cottam, Richard W. (1979) *Nationalism in Iran: Updated through 1978*. Pittsburgh: University of Pittsburgh Press.

Crist, David. (2012) *The Twilight War: The Secret History of America's Thirty-Year Conflict with Iran*. New York: Penguin.

Elm, Mostafa. (1994) *Oil, Power, and Principle: Iran's Oil Nationalization and Its Aftermath*. Syracuse: Syracuse University Press.

Everts, Steven. (2004) The Ultimate Test Case: Can Europe and America Forge a Joint Strategy for the Wider Middle East? *International Affairs* 80: 665–686.

Fitzpatrick, Mark. (2015) Iran: A Good Deal. *Survival (00396338)* 57: 47–52.

Gasiorowski, Mark J. (1987) The 1953 Coup D'Etat in Iran. *International Journal of Middle East Studies* 19: 261–286.

Goode, James F. (1997) *The United States and Iran: In the Shadow of Musaddiq*. London: Palgrave Macmillan.

Harnisch, Sebastian. (2007) Minilateral Cooperation and Transatlantic Coalition-Building: The E3/EU-3 Iran Initiative. *European Security* 16: 1–27.

Hersh, Seymour M. (2006) The Iran Plans. *The New Yorker*. Available at: www.newyorker.com/magazine/2006/04/17/the-iran-plans.

Hiro, Dilip. (1987) *Iran Under the Ayatollahs*. Abingdon: Routledge.

Houghton, David Patrick. (2001) *US Foreign Policy and the Iran Hostage Crisis*. Cambridge: Cambridge University Press.

Hunter, Shireen. (2010) *Iran's Foreign Policy in the Post-Soviet Era: Resisting the New International Order*. Santa Barbara: Praeger.

IAEA. (2003a) *Implementation of the NPT Safeguards Agreement in the Islamic Republic of Iran*. Vienna: International Atomic Energy Agency.
IAEA. (2003b) *Implementation of the NPT Safeguards Agreement in the Islamic Republic of Iran*. Vienna: International Atomic Energy Agency.
IAEA. (2004a) *Implementation of the NPT Safeguards Agreement in the Islamic Republic of Iran*. Vienna: International Atomic Energy Agency.
IAEA. (2004b) *Implementation of the NPT Safeguards Agreement in the Islamic Republic of Iran*. Vienna: International Atomic Energy Agency.
IAEA. (2005) *Implementation of the NPT Safeguards Agreement in the Islamic Republic of Iran*. Vienna: International Atomic Energy Agency.
IAEA. (2006) *Implementation of the NPT Safeguards Agreement in the Islamic Republic of Iran*. Vienna: International Atomic Energy Agency.
Karabell, Zachary. (1993) "Inside the US Espionage Den": The US Embassy and the Fall of the Shah. *Intelligence and National Security* 8: 44–59.
Katzman, Kenneth. (2007) *Iran: U.S. Concerns and Policy Responses*. Washington, DC: Library of Congress.
Keatinge, Tom. (2017) *Transatlantic (Mis)Alignment: Challenges to US-EU Sanctions Design and Implementation*. London: Royal United Services Institute.
Kerr, Paul K. (2009) *Iran's Nuclear Program: Status*. Washington, DC: Library of Congress. Available at: www.dtic.mil/docs/citations/ADA511967.
Kittrie, Orde F. (2009) New Sanctions for a New Century: Treasury's Innovative Use of Financial Sanctions. *University of Pennsylvania Journal of International Economic Law* 30: 789–822.
Kressin, Wolfgang K. (1991) Prime Minister Mossadegh and Ayatullah Kashani. From Unity to Emnity: As Viewed from the American Embassy in Tehran, June 1950–August 1953. University of Texas, Austin.
Ladjevardi, Habib. (1983) The Origins of U.S. Support for an Autocratic Iran. *International Journal of Middle East Studies* 15: 225–239.
Limbert, John W. (2009) *Negotiating with Iran: Wrestling the Ghosts of History*. Washington, DC: US Institute of Peace Press.
Loeffler, Rachel L. (2009) Bank Shots: How the Financial System Can Isolate Rogues. *Foreign Affairs* 88: 101–110.
Lohmann, Sascha. (2016) The Convergence of Transatlantic Sanction Policy against Iran. *Cambridge Review of International Affairs* 29: 930–951.
Moslem, Mehdi. (2002) *Factional Politics in Post-Khomeini Iran*. Syracuse: Syracuse University Press.
Najdi, Youhanna, and Mohd Azhari Bin Abdul Karim. (2012) The Role of the Islamic Revolutionary Guards Corps (IRGC) and the Future of Democracy in Iran: Will Oil Income Influence the Process? *Democracy and Security* 8: 72–89.
Naji, Kasra. (2008) *Ahmadinejad: The Secret History of Iran's Radical Leader*. Berkeley: University of California Press.
O'Sullivan, Meghan L. (2004) *Shrewd Sanctions: Statecraft and State Sponsors of Terrorism*. Washington, DC: Brookings Institution Press.
Portela, Clara. (2004) *The Role of the EU in the Non-Proliferation of Nuclear Weapons: The Way to Thessaloniki and Beyond*. Frankfurt am Main: Peace Research Institute Frankfurt.
Reynolds, Celia L., and Wilfred T. Wan. (2012) Empirical Trends in Sanctions and Positive Inducements in Nonproliferation. In *Sanctions, Statecraft, and Nuclear Proliferation*, edited by Etel Solingen. Cambridge: Cambridge University Press.

Rezun, Miron. (1981) *The Soviet Union and the Iran: Soviet Policy in Iran from the Beginnings of the Pahlavi Dynasty Until the Soviet Invasion in 1941*. Leiden: Sijthoff.

Rizvi, M. Mahtab Alam. (2012) Evaluating the Political and Economic Role of the IRGC. *Strategic Analysis* 36: 584–596.

Sadjadpour, Karim. (2011) *The Battle of Dubai: The United Arab Emirates and the U.S.-Iran Cold War*. Washington, DC: Carnegie Endowment for International Peace.

Sauer, Tom. (2004) The "Americanization" of EU Nuclear Non-Proliferation Policy. *Defense & Security Analysis* 20: 113–131.

Sauer, Tom. (2007) Coercive Diplomacy by the EU: The Iranian Nuclear Weapons Crisis. *Third World Quarterly* 28: 613–633.

Takeyh, Ray. (2009) *Guardians of the Revolution: Iran and the World in the Age of the Ayatollahs*. Oxford: Oxford University Press.

Vakili-Zad, Cyrus. (1990) Organization, Leadership and Revolution: Religiously-Oriented Opposition in the Iranian Revolution of 1978–1979. *Journal of Conflict Studies* 10.

Wehrey, Frederic M., Jerrold D. Green, Brian Nichiporuk, Alireza Nader, Lydia Hansell, Rasool Nafisi, and S. R. Bohandy. (2009) *The Rise of the Pasdaran: Assessing the Domestic Roles of Iran's Islamic Revolutionary Guards Corps*. Santa Monica: Rand Corporation.

Yodfat, Aryeh. (2011) *The Soviet Union and the Arabian Peninsula*. London: Routledge.

Zoeram, Vahid Amani, and Lee Yok Fee. (2010) Criticism in Public Sphere: The Press Development in Iran's Civil Society 1997–2000. *Journal of Politics and Law* 3: 222–238.

7 Evolving sanctions strategies, changing conflict observations

This final part of the empirical analysis, with its two systems, each involving three case studies, draws together the findings of all six cases analyzed. It gives a short summary of how sanctions policies and conflict observation evolved in the six cases. In order to throw some light on the social conditions conducive to cooperation and non-cooperation in sanctions conflicts, the above analysis empirically addressed three specific questions: the meaning attached to sanctions, the construction of conflict and the influence of particular sanctions strategies. The analysis illustrated specific analytical configurations resulting from the triad of conceptual elements. Particular sanctions strategies met different constructions of conflict and contributed distinctly to conflict transformation (see Table 7.1).

Across the six cases, various sanctions strategies encountered a dynamic conflict involving identity incompatibilities. Across the cases, a positive sanctions strategy contributed more successfully to conflict transformation, whereas a negative sanctions strategy contributed differently to conflict observation, escalating securitization and identity incompatibilities. Combined sanctions had a decidedly mixed record. During the two waves of substantial negative sanctions in the first case of the conflict between China and Taiwan, positions in Taiwan's discursive field on observing Cross-Strait relations became more similar and converged towards the unequivocal securitization of an identity conflict (Table 7.1, case I.I). In the second case of the conflict on Iran's nuclear program, negative sanctions met with deteriorating conflict observations, putting de-escalating voices on the defensive (Table 7.1, case II.II).

The situation with cases involving combined sanctions strategies is complex. When the discursive field consisted of strongly competing conflict observations, combined sanctions strategies contributed to the polarization of opposing political factions. In Taiwan, competing views of Cross-Strait conflict led to a close political stand-off. The results of the 2004 presidential election, insofar as it was a close call, ultimately perpetuated an observation of a securitized identity conflict. The impact of the shooting incident on the election remains speculative, as does the question as to whether the PRC refraining from negative sanctions and potentially putting a stronger emphasis on positive incentives could have swayed the vote towards a different conflict observation. The two cases involving combined sanctions against Iran illustrate their ambivalence; and they further demonstrate

Table 7.1 Sanctions strategies and conflict observation across cases

I. China – Taiwan			
	Case I.I	*Case I.II*	*Case I.III*
Sanctions strategy	Negative	Combined	Positive
Conflict transformation	Securitization	Polarization/ Securitization	De-securitization
Conflict Observation	Identity incompatibilities	Identity incompatibilities	Interest incompatibilities
II. United States – Iran			
	Case II.I	*Case II.II*	*Case II.III*
Sanctions strategy	Combined	Negative	Combined
Conflict transformation	Polarization Securitization	Securitization	Polarization De-securitization
Conflict observation	Interest → Identity incompatibilities	Identity incompatibilities	Identity → Interest incompatibilities

that combined sanctions strategies are a politically sensitive affair since the dialectical relationship between sanctions and conflict communication is fully played out in light of their inherent 'openness'. Combined sanctions in the first Iran case (Table 7.1, case II.I) were badly coordinated, involved ambivalent conflict communication that ultimately deteriorated into a securitized identity conflict. The reformist government of President Khatami was under pressure for its reconciliatory stance from conservative hardliners, who securitized the conflict, claiming that Western false promises were ultimately a trap. US non-commitment to the EU-3 position and the latter's limited willingness to stand by their commitments (from an Iranian perspective) weakened moderate conflict observations. By contrast, the consistent combined sanctions observed after president Obama took office thoroughly isolated the neo-fundamentalists led by Ahmadinejad. With tough multilateral negative sanctions, the confrontational, uncompromising approach of his government began to appear to be a dead end. The sustained prospect of unconditional direct dialogue with the US along with positive incentives (sanctions relief, etc.) in turn communicated the clear possibility of a different path, strengthening moderate pragmatist positions to the extent that even Khamenei, otherwise dearly committed to observing rather fundamental identity incompatibilities, was able to engage in 'heroic flexibility'.

The cases involving combined sanctions strategies demonstrated the dialectical relationship between the meaning that sanctions acquire and conflict observation. An eventual transformation of conflict communication is a result of the interplay between the two. One key element with regard to combined sanctions pertains to the 'reference point'. For instance, it never occurred to the Ahmadinejad government to take a reduction of negative sanctions as a positive incentive. This would have been irreconcilable with the neo-fundamentalist observation of an identity conflict that considers the fundamental rights and independence of Iran challenged by an opponent whose position had no legitimacy at all. Consistent combined sanctions that resonate with conflict observations by the addressee in the discursive field may indeed succeed in promoting conflict transformation, but this remains a great challenge in conflict communication.

With positive sanctions in the third China-Taiwan case, positions on conflict observation in the discursive field became ever more distinct: from statements portraying a securitized identity conflict and a contesting position, while strongly reinforcing the latter, to statements de-securitizing the conflict towards issue incompatibilities. For sure, President Ma's concise summary of the conflict . . . observation which prevailed at the time of his election in 2008 referred to 'opportunities' and 'threats'. Yet this in fact confirms the transformation towards an issue conflict. Ma essentially claimed a 'risk', not a 'security threat'. Effectively, China and Taiwan agreed not to agree on concrete reunification prospects; the mutual commitment to 'One China' provided the common ground for the recognition of the legitimacy of different interests.

In the course of the case studies, an additional factor emerged that merits appreciation. Conceptually speaking, Taiwanese engagement with the Cross-Strait conflict varied between a 'security threat' and a 'risk'. However, what is notable is that although conflict was securitized most of the time, the framings of particular positions in the discursive field of conflict observation were to some extent bi-directional: claims of a threat were frequently accompanied by reconciliatory statements (and the other way around). In Iran, similar framings existed, advanced by moderate conservatives like Rafsanjani in the first case and by Mohsen Rezaei in the third case (Table 7.1, cases II.I and II.III). However, in Taiwan, unqualified securitization in terms of a 'binary choice' did in fact seldom dominate conflict observation. Instead, bi-directional framings document statements that move along a range between, at one end, reconciliatory engagement and an emphasis upon commonalities and, at the other end, securitizing discord by restricting Cross-Strait exchange, independence referenda and a military build-up. Apart from perhaps the 1996 presidential election, such bi-directional framings implied that another conflict observation, in terms of issue incompatibilities, was possible – or at the very least, could not be ruled out. In the run-up to the presidential elections in 2000 in Taiwan, candidate James Soong and his New Party supporters advanced a reconciliatory framing, while acknowledging a PRC threat. They thus observed the Cross-Strait conflict more in terms of a 'risk' than as a 'threat'. The Kuomintang made reconciliatory statements as well; however, securitizing claims were stronger and more prominent in its bi-directional framing. Accordingly, the Kuomintang by and large securitized the Cross-Strait conflict. The DPP's framing was even more distinctly a securitizing move, with reconciliatory engagement clearly subordinate to concerns for protecting and emancipating

Taiwan. In the run-up to the presidential elections in 2004, both Pan-Green and Pan-Blue framings were bi-directional, yet with markedly different emphases. While hedging against possible PRC military ambitions, the Pan-Blue coalition's framing already centered on reconciliation, promoting an observation of Cross-Strait conflict as a 'risk'. With the DPP's framing amounting to little more than qualified securitization, overall conflict observation at first remained securitized after Chen's re-election. With a reconciliatory framing finally prevailing in 2008, Cross-Strait conflict became predominantly observed in terms of a risk, centered on issue incompatibilities. Given such basic flexibility in socially constructing conflict as expressed in bi-directional framings, it seems on the one hand that the influence of sanctions on on-going conflict relations became more distinct. With imposed sanctions, framings changed considerably, yet they also indicated that conflict escalation was not inevitable. On the other hand, when bi-directional framings were low during the Chen administration's second term, this in turn had an impact on the meaning of sanctions. Positive incentives were conceived of as a threat. This illustrates how the meaning of on-going conflict indeed affects the meaning that sanctions acquire.

In sum, the empirical analysis illustrates the interrelation between coercive sanctions and conflict communication and it traces the influence of sanctions on international conflict and its transformation. The analysis of the developing Cross-Straits conflict from the 1990s to 2008 and beyond, as well as of the conflict on the Islamic Republic's nuclear program, demonstrates the utility of the distinctions proposed in the conceptual relations of the theoretical elaboration on sanctions conflicts.

Part III

Conclusion

8 Conclusion and implications

What are the social conditions in sanctions conflicts that are conducive to either cooperation or non-cooperation? The study theorized these conditions on the basis of a notion of coercive sanctions as social facts within relationally constructed international conflicts. Its main research interest is how sanctions acquire meaning within conflict and eventually contribute to its transformation. Since they are socially constructed facts, the meaning of sanctions is not pre-given, nor does it unequivocally 'transmit' a cost/benefit logic along a simple sender–receiver model of communication. Instead, sanctions as relational phenomena dialectically acquire meaning in on-going conflict. Moreover, sanctions influence how agents in turn construct the conflict itself.

This chapter first provides a review of the sociological theory developed and offers a critical reflection on its merits and limitations. It reviews the conceptual approach and its empirical illustration; it notes the model's limitations in terms of concept and method. Second, the chapter develops the study's conceptual and practical implications. Conceptually, the study suggests that, when examining sanctions conflicts, we should refocus our attention on the social processes and practices that construct meaning. The study suggests the development of contingent scenarios for possible futures. Practically, there are implications here not just for the potential role of particular sanctions strategies in conflict development, but also for the prevalence of unintended consequences. In conclusion, the chapter points to avenues for future research.

Review

The analytical model focused on the social conditions within sanctions conflicts involved in the emergence and development of meaning in order to understand how cooperation and non-cooperation become possible. It conceptually unfolded a triad of interrelated elements that each addressed a more specific research question: First, what meaning sanctions acquire in conflict; second, how sanctions conflicts are socially constructed; and third, regarding conflict transformation and the influence of particular sanctions strategies.

In the first element of the triad, the study conceptualized coercive sanctions as actions that are socially constructed as decisions in mutual conflict. As relational decisions, sanctions give rise to a distinction between self-attributed (as risk) and externally imposed decisions (as danger) regarding conflict. Depending on the meaning they acquire, sanctions communicate accordingly either a utility rationale, implying a decision on the costs/benefits of a political position, or they communicate a power rationale, implying an externally imposed decision. Particular sanctions strategies emphasize these meaning potentials differently.

As the empirical analysis illustrated, sanctions may acquire a distinct meaning suggesting a power rationale that pushes aside cost/benefit calculations and the utility rationale. In the first case study, which looked at the sanctions conflict between China and Taiwan, the actors constructed negative sanctions in this way during the first wave particularly. The resulting costs of defying the sanctions, although considerable, were eventually held to be irrelevant by the political actors (except for the Soong presidential ticket, which later leaned towards a utility rationale). In the second case study, the meaning of sanctions was much more contested. However, the Chen administration's position, which insisted on conceiving of sanctions along a power rationale and did not consider the costs relevant, again illustrates the logic outlined. This is also true for the Kuomintang opposition's observation of a utility rationale and its inclination to consider costs and benefits, while it at the same time rejecting the idea of an attempted externally-enforced decision, communicated by a power rationale. In the third case, the meaning of the sanctions was on the whole different. The Pan-Blue faction constructed sanctions along a utility rationale. Yet despite positive sanctions, the incumbent Chen administration continued to conceive of the sanctions along a power rationale and was somewhat inclined to deem their possible benefits irrelevant.

In the sanctions conflict over Iran's nuclear program, actors similarly stayed with the proposed logic: neo-fundamentalists and hardline conservative principlists, most prominently of course president Mahmoud Ahmadinejad, saw sanctions negatively along a power rationale throughout all three cases. Offers of dialogue and positive incentives were denied and ridiculed; costs were irrelevant, as they proposed an 'economy of resistance'. Taking costs into consideration meant a change in direction away from observing sanctions along a power rationale, either cautiously as moderate conservatives/pragmatists like Mohsen Rezaei and Akbar Hashemi Rafsanjani did; or decisively as reformists generally did until their political elimination in the wake of the 2009 Green Movement protests. Reformists and, increasingly, moderate pragmatists like Hassan Rouhani fully embraced a utility rationale.

The second element of the triad introduced a sociological conceptualization of international conflict that permits conflict to be conceived of as a dynamic, ongoing process. Coercive sanctions occur within evolving conflict communication. Issue conflicts that exhibit incompatible interests are susceptible to meaning along a utility rationale. In identity conflicts, agents question each other's position, deny it legitimacy and securitize the Other as a threat. Such conflict observation is more susceptible to meaning that reflects a power rationale, and to its prompt rejection. Sanctions as actions in conflict communication influence what meaning conflict acquires and may thus promote conflict transformation.

The empirical analysis illustrated how the meaning of conflict evolves dynamically, and it also illustrated the endogenous relation between the meaning of conflict and the meaning of sanctions. The analysis of the Cross-Strait sanctions conflict depicted the general development of conflict, escalating from détente and an inclination towards issue incompatibilities and ultimately towards an identity conflict. Conflict communication between China and Taiwan then changed towards an issue conflict. The analysis also illustrated the way in which conflict meaning influences the meaning that sanctions acquire. At the height of the identity conflict and when particular actors were strongly constructing identity incompatibilities, sanctions acquired meaning along a power rationale. Actors did this even with positive sanctions, as the Chen administration's statements in the third case study illustrate. Then again, actors also tended to observe negative sanctions to some extent along a utility rationale when they constructed conflict in terms of issue incompatibilities, which was partly what the Soong ticket did during the second wave of negative sanctions. However, sanctions did not just merely acquire meaning as on-going conflict communication suggested, but influenced how agents socially construct conflict, contributing to conflict transformation.

In the dispute over Iran's nuclear program, the conflict gradually deteriorated from being a contained one, to the nuclear program being conceived in terms of issue incompatibilities, as the Khatami reformist government did, and then to the Ahmadinejad government's observing it as part of a fundamental identity conflict. With the escalation of the conflict, sanctions meaning evolved from a utility rationale to a power rationale, and then reverted back to a utility rationale when conflict communication changed towards the observation of the nuclear program as an issue incompatibility. Remarkably, the combined sanctions strategies observed during the first and the third case occurred alongside converse developments in conflict meaning, deteriorating in the first case and de-escalating in the third case, further testifying to the close linkage to conflict communication. A combined sanctions strategy that consistently included positive incentives was able to contribute to conflict de-escalation. However, it depended on whether conflict opponents tended to observe sanctions in terms of a utility rationale.

The third element of the triad conceptualized conflict transformation as a securitization process. Securitization describes a decisive process that dissolves the bases of cooperation. Identity incompatibilities prevail in conflict communication over any common orientation towards a contested issue. Coercive sanctions may promote conflict escalation in that securitization offers the possibility of adopting and rejecting a power rationale and the implied deprivation of agency. Securitization asserts agency and implies non-cooperation. By contrast, the prospects of cooperation hinge on a de-securitized conflict or on conflict transformation to that effect. In sanctions conflicts, securitization represents an agency-centered process of conflict transformation and a causal mechanism for prospects of cooperation and non-cooperation.

In the empirical analysis, securitization first described conflict transformation between communicated issue and identity incompatibilities and, second, represented a causal mechanism within the sanctions conflict. Regarding the first aspect, securitization took conflict escalation away from dialogue on a mutually recognized issue towards securitizing the Other as a threat. Conversely, in a de-escalating conflict, threat claims faded as a re-orientation took place towards a dialogue on a common issue. The analysis of securitization processes also demonstrated how sanctions influence conflict meaning and are able to transform it. Negative sanctions did not promote a conflict meaning centered on issue incompatibilities, but instead contributed to its transformation into the securitization of identity incompatibilities. Negative sanctions reflected a power rationale in the form of an externally imposed decision, reinforcing the particular identity conflict between China and Taiwan as well as between the US and Iran. By contrast, a positive sanctions strategy is more pertinent to promoting conflict de-escalation by advancing an observation of risk and meaning along a utility rationale. In the third case of sanctions in the conflict between China and Taiwan, the role of incentives was significant in supporting the reconciliatory stance of the Pan-Blue opposition and proving their point.

For securitization and combined sanctions, the relationship was not as simple and straightforward, but the same mechanism ultimately applied: Observing sanctions along a power rationale was accompanied by securitization, diminishing any prospects of cooperation. By contrast, when the pragmatist government de-securitized the nuclear dispute and started to observe it as an issue conflict, this prepared the ground for cooperation on the pursuit of a negotiated solution. Rouhani's dissection of the fatal logic of security, describing how it played into the hands of those who either did not want a negotiated solution or who wanted Iran isolated internationally, remains among the most astute observations in the conflict. From the conceptual perspective developed throughout this book, it is no less impressive how opponents on both sides of the conflict, but especially the pragmatist government of President Rouhani, succeeded in separating the nuclear *issue* from the wider *identity* conflict that largely defined the relationship between the United States and the Islamic Republic – a necessary and crucial step for finding (and maintaining) a solution to the conflict over Iran's nuclear program.

Regarding the second aspect, political actors in practice attributed causal responsibility to the consequences that were conceptually proposed. In the China–Taiwan conflict, the Lee administration in the 1990s and later the Chen administration attributed causal responsibility solely to the PRC, resulting in non-cooperation. Complementarily, during the first and second wave of negative sanctions, New Party politicians as well as Soong attributed causality for their securitizing moves towards supposed independence promoters. These actors in turn promoted a meaning of conflict that aimed at enhanced prospects of cooperation. Likewise, Kuomintang politicians attributed responsibility mainly to the DPP in 2004 and 2008. Notably, both the newly-elected Ma administration as well as the PRC broke with the pattern of mutual attribution of responsibility and reciprocal accusations across the Strait, transforming the conflict towards one of issue incompatibilities, opening the way to cooperation.

In the conflict over Iran's nuclear program, attribution of responsibility corresponded in a similar way to sanctions and conflict observations as conceptually proposed: To neo-fundamentalists and hardline conservative principlists, the US was the main culprit. The reformist giver-ins of the Khatami government and seditionists led by Mousavi also bore some responsibility, in their view. By contrast, reformists and pragmatists attributed responsibility for the deteriorating conflict and the tough negative sanctions in large part to the neo-fundamentalist 'extremists'. Although pragmatists and moderate conservatives condemned sanctions as 'unjust', they still refrained from simply blaming the US. Pragmatists and reformists were willing to concede that there might be legitimate international concern over Iran's nuclear ambitions.

In review of the image that the analytical model provides of coercive international sanctions, specifically remarkable is the performance of the combined sanctions strategy. The contribution of negative and positive sanctions strategies (when acquiring a meaning along a power or a utility rationale respectively) to a changing conflict meaning is clearly discernible. Negative sanctions contributed to conflict escalation whereas positive sanctions encouraged conflict de-escalation. However, the influence of a combined sanctions strategy was far more ambiguous. In general, combined sanctions strategies contributed to polarized positions on Cross-Strait relations within Taiwanese politics. Yet while some actors in Taiwan built on the positive incentives in reinforced calls for a reconciliatory conflict observation, the simultaneous negative sanctions to some extent undermined that. Instead, they reinforced observations of an identity conflict among actors from both the Pan-Blue and the Pan-Green political factions in Taiwan. The meaning of the combined sanctions strategy remained ambiguous, and so was its contribution to evolving conflict meaning.

In Iran, combined sanctions also had a polarizing effect on the discursive field on the nuclear issue. While their incoherent invocation in the first case, together with the fact that continuing US threats undercut EU-3 dialogue efforts, ultimately contributed to a deterioration in conflict relations, the consistent combined sanctions strategy observed in the third case, although further polarizing positions on the conflict, helped to firmly isolate extremist positions such as that of the Ahmadinejad government. Hence overall the meaning of combined sanctions strategies is complex and its pursuance a sensitive affair.

To sum up, the individual conceptual elements and the triad together present a sociological theory of international sanctions conflicts that focuses on the meaning that sanctions and conflict acquire in an on-going social process. It takes both coercive sanctions and international conflicts as socially constructed facts, delineates them as relational phenomena and conceptualizes the meaning of conflict and of sanctions as endogenous to each other. The model gives a dynamic account of conflict transformation.

Methodologically, the case studies highlighted the utility of the analytical differences between the ensuing particular configurations that the analytical model proposes. The detailed case studies served to illustrate the processes and practices which were proposed in the theory-generating exercise as being *generally* involved in the transformation of sanctions conflicts. Thus, the conceptualization does not restrict itself to the peculiarities of a particular instance of a sanctions conflict, but formulates its propositions for coercive sanctions in international conflicts in general. It provides an understanding of how non-cooperation ensues and how cooperation in international sanctions conflicts becomes possible – no more, no less. It does not, however, explain cooperation.

The study addressed a number of specific aspects that have been hitherto neglected in other approaches to coercive international sanctions. It questioned the presumed logic of 'economic impact → political pressure'; it rejected the idea that a pre-given meaning of sanctions can unproblematically be 'transmitted' as part of a simple sender–receiver model of communication; crucially, it refuted the notion of conflict meaning as exogenous to sanctions. Finally, the investigation included positive sanctions, and combined sanctions strategies. Accordingly, the study aimed to gain insights into sanctions conflicts that previously did not exist.

However, given the different premises, the study does effectively claim a higher utility for the empirical image that its analytical model provides for understanding how non-cooperation ensues and how cooperation becomes possible. How would an approach centered on economic conditions based on a logic of 'economic impact → political pressure' fare with regard to the conflict between China and Taiwan? Arguably, Taiwanese corporations and economic groups already had significant vested interests in Cross-Strait relations in the 1990s. These interests were hurt by deteriorating conflict relations, and by PRC sanctions. Yet economic factors were not decisive, either in the 1990s or in the 2000s: Particularly in terms of economic policies, differences between the Pan-Blue candidate Ma and the Pan-Green candidate Hsieh were not as great in the 2008 election campaign. By contrast, the PRC's positive sanctions and generally reconciliatory stance helped de-escalate the conflict and tempered emancipatory aspirations. Positive sanctions certainly contributed in terms of their economic impact on fruit producers – as part of transforming conflict and under particular conditions of possibility. The developed conceptualization does not preclude that, but subsumes it to the primacy of meaning in conflict relations.

In the conflict over Iran's nuclear program, economic factors did have a significant impact – even though the prevailing wisdom for years had been that (negative) economic sanctions would not work. The US succeeded in isolating Iran economically and excluding the country from the global financial system to an unprecedented extent. At some point, this was largely recognized in the Iranian political discourse, although political actors also identified numerous other significant reasons for the country's lackluster economic performance. Consequently, the prospect of sanctions relief became a meaningful positive incentive. However, analytical models that simply center on an 'economic impact → political pressure' rationale could neither explain why exactly reconciliation took place at the point in time it did, and not earlier e.g. in 2009 when civil unrest occurred; nor why exactly the sanctions conflict deteriorated in the first place. In Luhmann's terms, the impact of economic factors depends on how they are observed politically. Economic factors contributed to transforming the conflict under particular conditions of possibility, derived from the processing of meaning in conflict communication.

Critical reflection

The study is confined to delineating conflict transformation and to understanding the conditions of possibility for cooperation. While it offers new insights, it also has clear limitations. First of all, the study maintains that straightforward prediction along a simple input/output scheme is an inherently problematic undertaking. The study's focus on meaning as part of an evolving process, its notion of agency as creative engagement with contingency and of 'causation in practice', impair any ambitions to decisively predetermine from an initial 'input' the 'outcome' of an unfolding sanctions conflict. Although this approach effectively limits engagement with contingency to securitization, the possibilities for constructing threats and identity incompatibilities remain unrestricted.

On theoretical matters, the analytical model is highly reductionist. It considers the processes of conflict transformation by an addressee in a fairly broad perspective as securitization but refrains from more formally investigating in detail the domestic political conditions that might structure its discursive field. Different conditions may affect the ability to challenge dominant political positions in the first place. Put simply, democratic environments will differ from autocratic and despotic ones. Yet there is, of course, a trade-off involved in choosing reductionism. The model essentially subsumes a great number of possible domestic conditions and practices neatly under the notion of securitization. If all these components were to be considered, the picture could quickly turn into an excessively complex image composed of many individual elements, although all of them contribute to the overarching process of securitization. Still, a more detailed consideration of the components that could potentially affect the possibilities of conflict transformation would make for a more fine-tuned analytical model.

Another conceptual limitation results from the focus the study places on the addressee of coercive sanctions. Conflicts, and sanctions as part thereof, are relational phenomena, and the meaning they acquire for an initiator may also become contested. In fact, conflict meaning in China evolved over the period covered in the case studies; so did, obviously, US approaches to the Iranian nuclear program. In this particular instance of a one-party state, meaning changed in an evolutionary way with each succeeding party leadership. In other instances, with more openly accessible political discourses, especially democracies, analyzing meaning emergence in terms of various evolving political positions within a discursive field might be able to provide useful insights into the reasons for imposed sanctions and their possible contestation.

Although it is true that, given its analyticist methodological position, the empirical analysis of the study does not engage in 'testing' for any ostensibly external reality, there are also limits to the analysis on the grounds of its own methodology that merit critical reflection. The model proposed by the sociological theory suggests a number of analytical configurations (e.g. different sanctions strategies, stages of conflict communication) but the empirical illustration concentrates heavily on an identity conflict and its transformation. On the one hand, that reflects the intended key contribution of the study. On the other hand, it leaves other possible configurations less thoroughly examined. Among these are notably those involving, and remaining, issue conflicts, i.e. the ones for which possible securitization attempts fail. Considering the extent of the model's ambitions to broadly cover coercive sanctions conflicts, there are thus still grounds for further empirical analyses in order to conclusively illustrate the model's utility for other conflict situations as well.

Implications

The particular image of coercive sanctions in international conflict created by a sociological perspective has a few additional conceptual and practical implications. Conceptually, the difference between this and the many positivist-empiricist notions of coercive sanctions suggests a re-evaluation of the focus of attention in assessing sanctions conflicts. Furthermore, the skepticism towards linear prediction raises the question of finding an alternative way of anticipating possible developments so that conceptual utility may translate into practical insights. Essentially, this does not just have implications for the role of particular sanctions strategies in evolving conflict, and for the prospects for cooperation, but also for any possible unintended consequences of coercive means on the construction of antagonists. In escalating conflicts, responsibility is not always or necessarily attributed to an initiator as the Other. Rather, the domestic opposition may also become part of the antagonistic Other.

The sociological theory outlines a notion of coercive sanctions that significantly differs from the often presumed logic of 'economic impact → political pressure'. Conceptually, it follows that the sociological perspective provides a different answer to what matters in an evolving sanctions conflict. Thus, assessing the way in which agents construct conflict is at least as instructive as an assessment of the economic impact of coercive sanctions. However, although the developed approach gives primacy to meaning in conflict relations, it does not categorically reject the relevance of an economic impact of coercive sanctions.

Not all of the study's premises or the insights gained place it in a competing position to alternative approaches. It does not necessarily preclude attempts to explain cooperation and actual conflict resolution. Nonetheless, it formulates conditions of possibility and raises the stakes for such endeavors. Explanatory accounts need to reflect on them carefully. In some cases, their preconditions (e.g. exogenously given, constant, 'objective' facts) are prohibitively high; in other cases, they might even be justifiable.

However, besides the point that there is no 'direct' translation into political pressure (but only 'mediated' by the processes and practices that construct meaning), the study claims that economic attributes take on a different significance at particular stages in a conflict. When conflict communication centers on issue incompatibilities and agents construct sanctions along a utility rationale, the economic attributes of sanctions are more significant than in securitized identity conflicts. Accordingly, meaning in conflict communication determines in the first place the possibility of an economic impact of sanctions.

As the study amply demonstrates, continuity in conflict communication to the extent that it becomes an exogenous factor simply cannot be presumed *a priori*, though. This means that claims of being able to precisely predict the development or outcomes of sanctions conflicts can no longer be made. Yet it seems that theories which embrace abstraction and develop conceptual images of empirical phenomena are inclined towards generalization. The study's ontological position, however, rejects any law-like generalizations of the kind aspired to by positivism. More generally, the fundamental presence of contingency in the social processing of meaning and in social relations makes any generalizations effectively contingent as well. *Contingent generalization* stems "from the abstracting power of concepts" (Pouliot 2007:379), such as the analytical configurations developed by this study. These configurations are not ahistorical laws. The concepts are "analytical categories, the content of which is necessarily historically and culturally contingent" (Price and Reus-Smit 1998:274). Generalization is possible but remains contingent, since these concepts demand attention to the particular social context, practices and the contingent development of social relations.

Obviously, the developed analytical model and the notion of a (contingent) causal mechanism in sanctions conflicts do not at all imply that 'anything goes' in unfolding sanctions conflicts. Rather, the analytical model allows the possibility to develop plausible scenarios on possible future developments, "narratives with plot lines that map a set of causes and trends in future time" (Bernstein, Lebow, Stein, and Weber 2000:53). Scenarios "differ from classical predictions in that they emphasize contingency and uncertainty" (Jasper 2013:186). Thus, in particular cases, scenarios on possible future developments combine iterative elements with discontinuities; they combine relatively certain factors with uncertain and contingent ones. However, since the future is open and uncertain, there is a need for a multiplicity of scenarios that captures a range of possible developments: "A set of scenarios often contains competing or at least contrasting assumptions" (Bernstein et al. 2000:54). With the notion of contingent causation in practice as part of a dynamically evolving construction of conflict, the developed approach invites the creation of possible scenarios on an essentially unpredictable future.

In addition, scenarios based on a social ontology avoid simple linear extrapolation of past developments into the future. The past is constructed from the present. Among the competing discursive positions on an international conflict there can be competing narratives of the past, with different implications for the present and projections of the future (Neumann and Øverland 2004:268). In its empirical analysis, the study pointed to such competing narratives. These competing positions and the development of the discursive field on sanctions conflicts more broadly are a straightforward starting point for the development of multiple scenarios on possible futures. Of course, any scenarios, however, need to include contingent political developments concerning the meaning of conflict and sanctions on the side of the initiator of sanctions as well. In the end, the sanctions conflict is a relational phenomenon.

Practically, the study's delineation of an endogenous relation between sanctions and conflict meaning within a dynamically evolving process prompts a plea for reflexivity. 'Successful' sanctions policies, successful in the sense that they promote cooperation, require a continuous evaluation of the social practices involved in constructing conflict meaning. Quite generally, the supreme goal of any sanctions policy should be conflict de-securitization or the avoidance of securitization, as the case may be. This is what makes conflict transformation so important: A conflict constructed in terms of issue incompatibilities forms the basis of any substantial further agreement that might resolve the particular conflict entirely. Also, and obviously, de-securitization avoids the other alternative of a conflict further deteriorating towards war. At some point, it will just be another step from coercive sanctions to openly violent coercion.

Sanctions, however, will not always play a decisive role in changing conflict. Conflict meaning may also affect the meaning that sanctions acquire. A changing discursive field, newly emerging positions or evolving existing positions may provide new opportunities for transforming a securitized conflict that may not have existed before. Some political actors on the side of the addressee may construct the conflict differently, de-securitizing it. Their rise to power may not necessarily be related to sanctions. Yet a successful sanctions policy reacts to such developments accordingly.

Based on the premise that the intentions of initiator policies are fairly unambiguous insofar as they consistently aim for enforcing cooperation, the study offers specific insights into each of the sanctions strategies. Such insights pertain in particular to unintended consequences. The study strikes a note of caution against excessively optimistic expectations regarding negative sanctions strategies that are applied in order to coerce, as other authors have done before (Drezner 1999). In the common conflict constellation of constructed identity incompatibilities, negative sanctions may further contribute to conflict deterioration and the continuance of securitization. In addition, negative sanctions strategies may promote the escalation of conflict and the securitization of a threat in the first place. However, other sanctions strategies may bring their own peculiarities and complications. Positive sanctions strategies, which are more disposed to promoting issue incompatibilities and potential de-securitization, suggest a utility rationale and decisions constructed in the form of risk. In the end, though, opponents may construct the Other as being untrue to its commitments. With the implied distinction as being affected by a decision by the defecting Other, the form of risk might collapse and instead the initiator might construct a danger. In short, positive sanctions strategies of course still carry the risk of failure. Combined sanctions strategies have the potential to discriminatively promote fairly divergent views on the conflict constructed by particular domestic political actors within the addressee's discursive field. However, contestation in the discursive field may result in fierce polarization and deadlock.

The case studies in this investigation only hinted at the distinct possibility that domestic political polarization may ensue in the case of an addressee: Political actors may well attribute responsibility to other domestic agents, enacting boundaries between those responsible and those affected not only in terms of a domestic/international border, but primarily between particular domestic groups. Securitizing other domestic actors as a threat may turn into a violent conflict. The

China-Taiwan conflict did not develop seriously in that direction. However, in the case of other sanctions conflicts, with a different domestic context, this might happen eventually. Sanctions are not exogenous to conflict development, and the domestic dimension of the addressee, including securitized polarization, should be taken into account.

Questions for future research

The study established a sociological notion of coercive sanctions conflicts that addressed the basic conceptual parameters of the emerging meaning of sanctions and conflicts, and of conflict transformation. Its elements focused upon relational aspects in constructing sanctions conflicts. In the course of its development, new questions have emerged that merit further research and investigation. Some questions have already been raised implicitly; others bring in new aspects. Some questions concern coercive sanctions; others emerge from the conceptual elements which have been developed.

In critically reflecting on the investigation, a few limitations were noted that would merit more detailed attention. First, it is important to consider the domestic political conditions of the addressee of coercive international sanctions. How do different polities affect the way in which agents construct conflict; how do they affect the prospects of conflict transformation? A number of contributions to the sanctions literature have investigated the effects of democratic and autocratic political systems on the possible responses of addressees. A constructivist analysis may add some insights into this still unsettled question. It may also open the way to further investigation into the social practices and discursive constellations involved in constructing meaning. The contribution of Lee Jones (2015) Gramscian study of the social forces at work takes a decisive step in that direction. The (externalist) literature on securitization offers a starting point for additional steps (Bubandt 2005; Stritzel 2007, 2011). In particular, Juha Vuori's work on securitization politics in non-democratic China offers some fascinating insights. Likewise, the literature inspired by Pierre Bourdieu's work may be able to offer further promising insights into the practices of constructing conflict and foreign policy (Bourdieu 1990; Barnett 1999; Guzzini 2000; Emirbayer and Goldberg 2005). Second, a similar study could investigate in more detail the social practices involved in the formation of sanctions policies and the evolving meaning of conflict for the initiator of sanctions.

As regards new aspects, constructed conflict meanings and the policies involved often heavily reflect or enact particular norms. On the one hand, this applies to contested discursive fields on sanctions conflicts in the case of an addressee. Particular positions are often interrelated in terms of normative agreements and disagreements. On the other hand, this also applies to sanctions, in that initiators relate sanctions to particular norms (e.g., human rights). Sanctions may relate differently to particular normative discursive positions in the case of the addressee. How does such normative convergence contribute to evolving conflict development? Norms may become a means in conflict relations, not only an end. Social constructivist literature on international norms and social change (Klotz 1995; Checkel 1997,

2001; Finnemore and Sikkink 1998; Schimmelfennig, Engert, and Knobel 2006) offers a basis for further investigation into that question.

An additional aspect of sanctions and conflict relations, but one that was not explicitly addressed in this study, concerns targeted sanctions. However, by implication, its analytical model also covers targeted sanctions inasmuch as they relate to how agents construct conflict. In principle, targeted negative sanctions may promote conflict securitization, just as more comprehensive sanctions may. Clearly though, initiators of targeted sanctions aim to avoid this or the often related 'rally-round-the-flag effect' (Jaeger 2016). Thus the question arises: Do targeted sanctions have any significant particularities when it comes to conflict construction?

Finally, in proposing securitization as a theory of agency in conflict communication, an avenue of further research has emerged. The study formulated the fundamentals of such an approach in delineating securitization as agential engagement with contingency. Essentially, the study focused on conflict escalation. Yet it seems that this perspective has much greater potential. Further integrating the pragmatist notion of agency developed by Emirbayer and Mische may offer promising ways of conceptualizing the normalization of securitization as a temporal re-orientation of agency towards iteration. In addition, that would grant a new perspective on de-securitization, again as a temporal re-orientation towards projectivity in engaging contingency. What then remains to be clarified are the precise conceptual characteristics of a de-securitizing agential engagement with contingency.

This study investigated coercive sanctions conflicts in international relations from a sociological perspective. It made a conceptual argument for the primacy of meaning over materialist-instrumentalist accounts of conflict relations. The meaning that sanctions acquire and the meaning that conflict acquires are endogenous to each other. Coercive sanctions are social facts that agents construct in on-going conflict communication. The sociological theory advanced a dynamic notion of conflict, as an evolving social process. It argued that imposed sanctions potentially change the meaning of conflict for opponents. That is, sanctions are not passive in terms of how opponents construct the conflict in which they partake. Particular sanctions strategies bear different meaning potentials. Some sanctions may escalate a conflict. Once opponents securitize each other as a threat, prospects of cooperation diminish. Other sanctions may promote conflict de-escalation, with greater prospects of cooperation. The investigation developed an analytical model that centers upon conflict transformation and the conditions of possibility for cooperation. The bottom line is that the aim of the study was not to make sanctions more 'effective'; the aim was an intervention to prevent conflict escalation and deterioration.

Bibliography

Barnett, Michael. (1999) Culture, Strategy and Foreign Policy Change: Israel's Road to Oslo. *European Journal of International Relations* 5: 5–36.

Bernstein, Steven, Richard Ned Lebow, Janice Gross Stein, and Steven Weber. (2000) God Gave Physics the Easy Problems: Adapting Social Science to an Unpredictable World. *European Journal of International Relations* 6: 43–76.

Bourdieu, Pierre. (1990) *In Other Words: Essays towards a Reflexive Sociology*. Stanford: Stanford University Press.

Bubandt, Nils. (2005) Vernacular Security: The Politics of Feeling Safe in Global, National and Local Worlds. *Security Dialogue* 36: 275–296.

Checkel, Jeffrey T. (1997) International Norms and Domestic Politics: Bridging the Rationalist – Constructivist Divide. *European Journal of International Relations* 3: 473–495.

Checkel, Jeffrey T. (2001) Why Comply? Social Learning and European Identity Change. *International Organization* 55: 553–588.

Drezner, Daniel. (1999) *The Sanctions Paradox: Economic Statecraft and International Relations*. Cambridge: Cambridge University Press.

Emirbayer, Mustafa, and Chad Alan Goldberg. (2005) Pragmatism, Bourdieu, and Collective Emotions in Contentious Politics. *Theory and Society* 34: 469–518.

Finnemore, Martha, and Kathryn Sikkink. (1998) International Norm Dynamics and Political Change. *International Organization* 52: 887–917.

Guzzini, Stefano. (2000) A Reconstruction of Constructivism in International Relations. *European Journal of International Relations* 6: 147–182.

Jaeger, Mark Daniel. (2016) Constructing Sanctions: Rallying around the Target in Zimbabwe. *Cambridge Review of International Affairs* 29: 952–969.

Jasper, Ursula. (2013) *The Politics of Nuclear Non-Proliferation: A Pragmatist Framework for Analysis*. Abingdon: Routledge.

Jones, Lee. (2015) *Societies Under Siege: Exploring How International Economic Sanctions (Do Not) Work*. Oxford: Oxford University Press.

Klotz, Audie. (1995) *Norms in International Relations: The Struggle against Apartheid*. Ithaca: Cornell University Press.

Neumann, Iver B., and Erik F. Øverland. (2004) International Relations and Policy Planning: The Method of Perspectivist Scenario Building. *International Studies Perspectives* 5: 258–277.

Pouliot, Vincent. (2007) "Sobjectivism": Toward a Constructivist Methodology. *International Studies Quarterly* 51: 359–384.

Price, Richard, and Christian Reus-Smit. (1998) Dangerous Liaisons? Critical International Theory and Constructivism. *European Journal of International Relations* 4: 259–294.

Schimmelfennig, Frank, Stefan Engert, and Heiko Knobel. (2006) *International Socialization in Europe: European Organizations, Political Conditionality, and Democratic Change*. Basingstoke: Palgrave Macmillan.

Stritzel, Holger. (2007) Towards a Theory of Securitization: Copenhagen and Beyond. *European Journal of International Relations* 13: 357–383.

Stritzel, Holger. (2011) Security as Translation: Threats, Discourse, and the Politics of Localisation. *Review of International Studies* 37: 2491–2517.

Index

Kolibri 360 GmbH
Ferdinand-Jühlke-Straße 7
99095 Erfurt, Deutschland
produktsicherheit@kolibri360.de